The Bible Speaks Today

Series editors: Alec Motyer (OT)
John Stott (NT)
Derek Tidball (Bible Themes)

The Message of Numbers

The Bible Speaks Today: Old Testament series

The Message of Genesis 1 – 11
The dawn of creation
David Atkinson

The Message of Genesis 12 – 50
From Abraham to Joseph
Joyce G. Baldwin

The Message of Numbers
Journey to the promised land
Raymond Brown

The Message of Deuteronomy
Not by bread alone
Raymond Brown

The Message of Judges
Grace abounding
Michael Wilcock

The Message of Ruth
The wings of refuge
David Atkinson

The Message of Chronicles
One church, one faith, one Lord
Michael Wilcock

The Message of Nehemiah
God's servant in a time of change
Raymond Brown

The Message of Job
Suffering and grace
David Atkinson

The Message of Psalms 1 – 72
Songs for the people of God
Michael Wilcock

The Message of Psalms 73 – 150
Songs for the people of God
Michael Wilcock

The Message of Proverbs
Wisdom for life
David Atkinson

The Message of Ecclesiastes
A time to mourn, and a time to dance
Derek Kidner

The Message of the Song of Songs
The lyrics of love
Tom Gledhill

The Message of Isaiah
On eagles' wings
Barry Webb

The Message of Jeremiah
Against wind and tide
Derek Kidner

The Message of Ezekiel
A new heart and a new spirit
Christopher J. H. Wright

The Message of Daniel
The Lord is King
Ronald S. Wallace

The Message of Hosea
Love to the loveless
Derek Kidner

The Message of Joel, Micah and Habakkuk
Listening to the voice of God
David Prior

The Message of Amos
The day of the lion
Alec Motyer

The Bible Speaks Today New Testament *and* **Bible Themes**
series are listed at the back of this book.

The Message of Numbers

Numbers

Journey to the promised land

Raymond Brown

Inter-Varsity Press

InterVarsity Press
P.O. Box 1400, Downers Grove, IL 60515-1426
World Wide Web: www.ivpress.com
E-mail: mail@ivpress.com

Inter-Varsity Press
38 De Montfort Street, Leicester LE1 7GP, England
World Wide Web: www.ivpbooks.com
E-mail: ivp@uccf.org.uk

InterVarsity Press® *is the book-publishing division of InterVarsity Christian Fellowship/USA*®*, a student movement active on campus at hundreds of universities, colleges and schools of nursing in the United States of America, and a member movement of the International Fellowship of Evangelical Students. For information about local and regional activities, write Public Relations Dept., InterVarsity Christian Fellowship/USA, 6400 Schroeder Rd., P.O. Box 7895, Madison, WI 53707-7895.*

Inter-Varsity Press is the book-publishing division of the Universities and Colleges Christian Fellowship (formerly the Inter-Varsity Fellowship), a student movement linking Christian Unions in universities and colleges throughout the United Kingdom and the Republic of Ireland, and a member movement of the International Fellowship of Evangelical Students. For information about local and national activities write to UCCF, 38 De Montfort Street, Leicester LE1 7GP, England.

USA ISBN 0-8308-2428-6

UK ISBN 0-85111-491-1

Printed in the United States of America ∞

British Library Cataloguing in Publication Data

A catalogue record for this book is available from the British Library.

Library of Congress Cataloging-in-Publication Data has been requested.

P	18	17	16	15	14	13	12	11	10	9	8	7	6	5	4	3	2	1
Y	17	16	15	14	13	12	11	10	09	08	07	06	05	04	03	02		

Contents

General
preface

THE BIBLE SPEAKS TODAY describes three series of expositions, based on the books of the Old and New Testaments, and on Bible themes that run through the whole of Scripture. Each series is characterized by a threefold ideal:

- to expound the biblical text with accuracy
- to relate it to contemporary life, and
- to be readable.

These books are, therefore, not 'commentaries', for the commentary seeks rather to elucidate the text than to apply it, and tends to be a work rather of reference than of literature. Nor, on the other hand, do they contain the kind of 'sermons' which attempt to be contemporary and readable without taking Scripture seriously enough.

The contributors to *The Bible Speaks Today* series are all united in their convictions that God still speaks through what he has spoken, and that nothing is more necessary for the life, health and growth of Christians than that they should hear what the Spirit is saying to them through his ancient – yet ever modern – Word.

ALEC MOTYER
JOHN STOTT
DEREK TIDBALL
Series Editors

Author's preface

As an enforced exile, William Tyndale pursued his ambition to make the whole of Scripture available to the English people. When copies of his newly printed New Testament were being smuggled into his home country, he turned his fine mind to the Old Testament. Mastering biblical Hebrew, a rare skill in the sixteenth century, he gave himself to the translation of the Pentateuch. The prologues to each of its five books reveal his passion to apply the message of Scripture to the issues of his own day. That which introduces Numbers relates its teaching to some of the spiritually harmful distractions of the period and shares his conviction that the book still addresses the needs of everyday people. The wilderness generation stubbornly attempted to run their lives without the 'help of faith in the promises of God'. We are on firmer ground if we 'do nothing whereof we could not give a reason out of God's words'. At the beginning of a new millennium, we too are on pilgrimage, with resources infinitely greater than those available to the Israelite travellers. God gave them miraculous help, but, in Christ, we 'be now in the day-light and … he that was promised should come and bless us is come already and hath shed his blood for us … and in him we have all'.

Later imprisoned, Tyndale continued his work, requesting his captors that, with the approaching winter, he might have access to his warmer clothing and 'a lamp in the evening; it is indeed wearisome sitting alone in the dark'. But, 'most of all', he begs he might have his Hebrew Bible, grammar and dictionary, 'that I may pass the time in that study'. He made excellent progress but, the following year, he was executed. Reading a biblical book in our own language is an immense privilege, obtained for us at great cost; discerning its relevance to the issues of our own times is an enriching responsibility.

As part of my own preparation, I have attempted an exposition of selected passages at weekend study conferences, Bible weeks and conventions. I specially valued the opportunity to do so among my friends at the Portstewart Convention in Northern Ireland, and during a memorable week at the Seoul 'Keswick' Convention, where my wife and I greatly appreciated the renewed kindness of Dr Myung H. Kim and the warm-hearted members of the Korea Evangelical Fellowship committee.

I am also indebted to some special people: Peter Jamieson, for his brilliant computer expertise; Dr Alec Motyer, for many helpful comments; Colin Duriez and his IVP colleagues for their editorial skills; and my wife, Christine, for her loving encouragement in my writing ministry during our 'retirement', and for her practical help with this particular manuscript.

RAYMOND BROWN

Chief abbreviations

ANET	*Ancient Near Eastern Texts*, ed. J. B. Pritchard, 3rd edition (Princeton: Princeton University Press, 1969)
JSOT	*Journal for the Study of the Old Testament*
NBD	*New Bible Dictionary*, ed. I. H. Marshall et al., 3rd edition (Leicester: IVP, 1996)
NEB	The New English Bible (NT, 1961; second edition 1970; OT, 1970)
NIDOTTE	*New International Dictionary of Old Testament Theology and Exegesis*, ed. W. A. VanGemeren, 5 vols. (Carlisle: Paternoster, 1996)
NIV	The New International Version of the Bible (NT, 1961, second edition 1970; OT, 1970)
NKJV	The New King James Version of the Bible (OT 1982; NT 1979)
RSV	The Revised Standard Version of the Bible (NT, 1946; second edition, 1971; OT, 1952)

Select bibliography

Works listed here are referred to in the footnotes by the author's surname, or surname and date.

Commentaries

Allen, R. B., 'Numbers', in *The Expositor's Bible Commentary* 2, ed. F. E. Gaebelein (Grand Rapids: Zondervan, 1990), pp. 657–1008

Ashley, T. R., *The Book of Numbers*, New International Commentary on the Old Testament (Grand Rapids: Eerdmans, 1993)

Budd, P. J., *Numbers*, Word Biblical Commentary 5 (Waco, TX: Word, 1984)

Calvin, J., *Commentaries on the Last Four Books of Moses ... in the Form of a Harmony*, 4 vols. (Edinburgh: Calvin Translation Society, 1852–55)

Carson, T., 'Numbers', in *The International Bible Commentary*, ed. F. F. Bruce, rev. ed. (London: Marshall Pickering, 1986), pp. 214–255

Davies, E. W., *Numbers*, New Century Bible Commentary (London: Marshall Pickering, 1995)

Dozeman, T. B., 'The Book of Numbers', in *The New Interpreter's Bible* 2 (Nashville, TN: Abingdon, 1998), pp. 1–268

Elliott-Binns, L., *The Book of Numbers*, Westminster Bible Commentary (London: Methuen, 1927)

Fretheim, T. E., 'Numbers', in *The Oxford Bible Commentary*, ed. J. Barton and J. Muddiman (Oxford: Oxford University Press, 2001), pp. 110–154

Gray, G. B., *A Critical and Exegetical Commentary on Numbers*, International Critical Commentary (Edinburgh: T. and T. Clark, 1903)

Harrison, R. K., *Numbers: An Exegetical Commentary* (Grand Rapids, MI: Baker, 1992)

Hertz, J. H., *The Pentateuch and Haftorahs: Numbers* (Oxford: Oxford University Press, 1934)

Huey, F. B., Jr, *Numbers*, Bible Study Commentary (Grand Rapids, MI: Zondervan, 1981)

Keddie, G. J., *According to Promise: The Message of the Book of Numbers*, Welwyn Commentary Series (Darlington: Evangelical Press, 1992)

Levine, B. A., *Numbers 1 – 20*, The Anchor Bible (New York: Doubleday, 1993)

L'Heureux, C. E., 'Numbers', in *The New Jerome Biblical Commentary*, ed. R. E. Brown et al. (London: Geoffrey Chapman, 1989), pp. 80–93

Marsh, J., 'The Book of Numbers', in *The Interpreter's Bible* 2 (Nashville, TN: Abingdon, 1953), pp. 137–308

Milgrom, J., *Numbers*, The JPS Torah Commentary (Philadelphia, PA: Jewish Publication Society, 1990)

Moriarty, F. L., 'Numbers', in *The Jerome Biblical Commentary*, ed. R. E. Brown et al. (London: Geoffrey Chapman, 1968), pp. 86–100

Naylor, P. J., 'Numbers', in *New Bible Commentary, 21st Century Edition*, ed. D. A. Carson et al. (Leicester: IVP, 1994), pp. 158–197

Noordtzij, A., *Numbers*, Bible Student's Commentary (Grand Rapids, MI: Zondervan, 1983)

Noth, M., *Numbers: A Commentary*, Old Testament Library (London: SCM, 1968)

Olson, D. T., *Numbers*, Interpretation: A Bible Commentary for Teaching and Preaching (Louisville, KY: John Knox, 1996)

Owens, J. J., 'Numbers', in *The Broadman Bible Commentary* 2 (London: Marshall, Morgan and Scott, 1970), pp. 75–174

Philip, J., *Numbers*, The Communicator's Commentary (Waco, TX: Word, 1987)

Plaut, W. G., *The Torah: A Modern Commentary* (New York: Union of American Hebrew Congregations, 1981)

Riggans, W., *Numbers*, Daily Study Bible (Edinburgh: Saint Andrew Press, 1983)

Sakenfeld, K. D., *Numbers: Journeying with God*, International Theological Commentary (Edinburgh: Handsel, 1994)

Smick, E., 'Numbers', in *The Wycliffe Bible Commentary* (London: Oliphants, 1963), pp. 111–154

Snaith, N. H., 'Numbers', in *Peake's Commentary on the Bible*, ed. M. Black and H. H. Rowley (London: Nelson, 1962), pp. 254–268

————, *Leviticus and Numbers*, New Century Bible (London: Nelson, 1967)

Sturdy, J., *Numbers*, The Cambridge Bible Commentary (Cambridge: Cambridge University Press, 1976)

Thompson, J. A., 'Numbers', in *New Bible Commentary Revised*, ed. D. Guthrie and J. A. Motyer (Leicester: IVP, 1970), pp. 168–200

Wenham, G. J., *Numbers*, Tyndale Old Testament Commentaries (Leicester: IVP, 1981)

Other works

Baker, D. W., and B. T. Arnold (eds.), *The Face of Old Testament Studies: A Survey of Contemporary Approaches* (Leicester: Apollos, 1999)

Clines, D. J. A., *The Theme of the Pentateuch*, JSOT Supplement Series 10 (Sheffield: Sheffield Academic Press, 2nd ed., 1997)

Currid, J. D., *Ancient Egypt and the Old Testament* (Grand Rapids, MI: Baker, 1997)

Douglas, M., *In the Wilderness: The Doctrine of Defilement in the Book of Numbers*, JSOT Supplement Series 158 (Sheffield: Sheffield Academic Press, 1993)

————, *Purity and Danger* (London: Routledge and Kegan Paul, 1966)

Gorman, F. H., *The Ideology of Ritual*, JSOT Supplement Series 91 (Sheffield: Sheffield Academic Press, 1990)

Gregory of Nyssa, *The Life of Moses*, trans., with introduction and notes, A. S. Malherbe and E. Ferguson (New York: Paulist, 1978)

Jensen, I. L., *Numbers: Journey to God's Rest-Land* (Chicago, IL: Moody, 1964)

Jenson, P. P., *Graded Holiness: A Key to the Priestly Conception of the World*, JSOT Supplement Series 106 (Sheffield: Sheffield Academic Press, 1992)

Kidner, D., *Understanding the Old Testament: Leviticus, Numbers, Deuteronomy* (London: Scripture Union, 1971)

Olson, D. T., *The Death of the Old and the Birth of the New: The Framework of the Book of Numbers and the Pentateuch*, Brown Judaic Studies 71 (Chico, CA: Scholars, 1985)

Origen, Homily 27 on Numbers, in *Origen*, trans. R. A. Greer, Classics of Western Spirituality (London: SPCK, 1979)

Wenham, G. J., *Numbers*, Old Testament Guides (Sheffield: Sheffield Academic Press, 1997)

Introduction

Numbers might not score a high rating in a 'favourite book of the Bible' competition. Its unexciting lists, tribal statistics, community archives, legal stipulations, ceremonial formalities, priestly duties and ancient laws are strangely interspersed with discouraging stories about leadership crises, family jealousy, widespread discontent, recurrent unbelief and rebellion and even apostasy. One third-century Christian preacher soon discovered that others rarely shared his enthusiasm for its message: 'if the Book of Numbers is read the hearer will judge that there is nothing ... as a remedy for his weakness or a benefit for the salvation of his soul'. If Origen found that, on hearing such passages, his neighbours 'constantly reject and spit them out', dismissing such 'heavy and burdensome food',[1] how will they fare among our contemporaries?

We live in a vastly different world, with speedy mobility, brilliant technology, accessible facilities and limitless resources. How does the story of an unnecessarily delayed Israelite migration impinge on our lives as Christians at the beginning of a new millennium? We begin by considering the book's importance, title, contents, compilation and authorship, and relevance.

Importance

The book of Numbers is not an isolated literary unit that can be conveniently dismissed or marginalized because of its initially forbidding contents; we ignore one part to the detriment of another. Numbers is intimately connected with those books that surround it,[2] with the events graphically described in Exodus,[3] the sacrificial

---

[1] Origen, p. 246.
[2] For example, the repeated promises made to the patriarchs in Genesis 12:2; 13:14–17; 17:3–8; 22:16–18; 26:3–4, 24; 28:3–4, 13–14; 50:24–25.
[3] Num. 3:5 – 4:49 (Exod. 6:16–25); 7:1 (30:26; 40:17); 8:1–4 (25:31–40); 8:16–18 (22:29); 9:1–5 (12:1–30); 9:15–23 (40:34–38); 12:1 (2:21); 14:11b (3:20; 4:17; 10:1;

and priestly detail of Leviticus[4] and the message of Deuteronomy,[5] to say nothing of the later literature of the Old Testament. Its narratives and legislation are recalled in their early[6] and later[7] history, in temple worship[8] and in prophetic preaching.[9]

The message of Numbers was not only meaningful to Old Testament people; it was important to Jesus. Can Christians afford to ignore a book that mattered to him? Stories and teaching from each of these five opening books of Scripture (the Pentateuch) were frequently in his mind and figured prominently in his message.[10] He directed the attention of his contemporaries to those truths entrusted to Moses,[11] as did Paul[12] and the author of the letter to the Hebrews.[13] When he wanted to illustrate the efficacy of his saving death, the book of Numbers (21:4–9) provided Jesus with an appropriate story,[14] and there are echoes of its teaching in his references to restitution (5:7),[15] tassels on garments (15:38),[16] Sabbath (28:9–10),[17] fasting (29:7)[18] and vows (30:2).[19] His 'good shepherd' message[20] may even recall an 'under-shepherd' narrative in this book (27:15–17).

Additionally, several New Testament writers made direct use of this book to explain, interpret and amplify their message. When Paul wrote to the Corinthian believers, some of whom had been delivered from a life of crime, degrading immorality and licentiousness,[21] he turned to the book of Numbers for appropriate illustration. He maintained that stories from Numbers were strikingly relevant for new converts, assaulted by fierce temptation

---

14:13–30); 14:18 (20:6; 34:6–7); 14:22b (14:11; 17:7; 32:1); 15:32 (20:8–11; 31:12–17; 35:1–3); 18:11 (29:26); 18:13 (23:19); 18:15 (13:2, 13); 20:26 (28:1–4; 40:13); 20:28 (29:29); 28:16 – 29:40 (23:14–17).

[4] Num. 3:4 (Lev. 10:1–3); 5:1–4 (13:2–46; 14:2; 15:2); 18:8–11 (2:2; 6:16–17; 7:6, 31–34); 18:14 (27:21); 18:15b (27:1–13); 28:16–29:40 (23:1–44).

[5] For example, the historical recapitulation of Numbers' events and legislation in Deut. 1:3 – 3:29; 4:3–4, 44–49; 8:2–4, 15–16; 9:22–24; 11:5–7; 19:1–10; 23:3–6; 23:21–23; 24:8–9; 29:5–8; 31:1–8, 9–13; 32:48–52; 34:9.

[6] Josh. 1:12–15; 5:10–12; 12:1–6; 13:1 – 20:34; 22:17; 24:8–10, 17–18; 2 Kgs. 18:4.
[7] Neh. 13:2.   [8] Pss. 78:14–41; 95:7–11; 106:24–33.
[9] Ezek. 20:13–24; Amos 2:12; Hos. 9:10.
[10] Matt. 4:4 (Deut. 8:3); 4:7 (Deut. 6:16); 4:10 (Deut. 6:13); 5:21 (Exod. 20:13); 5:27 (Exod. 20:14); 5:31 (Deut. 24:1); 5:33 (Num. 30:2, Deut. 23:21); 5:38 (Exod. 21:24; Deut. 19:21); 5:43 (Lev. 19:18) 8:4 (Lev. 14:2–31); 15:4 (Exod. 20:12, Deut. 5:16, Exod. 21:17, Lev. 20:9); 18:16 (Deut. 19:15); 19:4 (Gen. 1:27); 19:5 (Gen. 2:24); 19:7–8 (Deut. 24:1–4); 19:19 (Exod. 20:12–16, Deut. 5:16–20, Lev. 19:18); 22:32 (Exod. 3:6); 22:37 (Deut. 6:5); 22:39 (Lev. 19:18); Mark 12:19 (Deut. 25:5); 12:30 (Deut. 6:4–5); John 3:14 (Num. 21:8–9); 6:31 (Exod. 16:4).
[11] Luke 24:44; John 7:19, 22–23.
[12] Rom. 9:15; 10:5, 19; 1 Cor. 9:9; 2 Cor. 3:15.   [13] Heb. 8:5; 9:19; 12:21.
[14] John 3:14.   [15] Luke 19:8.   [16] Matt. 23:5.   [17] Matt. 12:5.
[18] Matt. 6:16.   [19] Matt. 5:33.   [20] John 10:1–18; Matt. 9:36.   [21] 1 Cor. 6:9–11.

in a morally decadent first-century seaport. Narratives from the book of Numbers illustrate his conviction that these stories 'were written down as warnings for us ... So ... be careful that you don't fall.'[22]

Other New Testament letters also make special reference to material in Numbers. Jude, Peter, John and the author of Hebrews[23] each draw on its teaching in their desire to help their fellow Christians exposed to numerous moral hazards in a pagan society.

Title

The book has not been helped by its title, which goes back to the early Christian centuries when the Greek translation of the Old Testament (the Septuagint) entitled the book *Arithmoi*. When Jerome later prepared his influential Latin translation, the Vulgate, he called it *Numeri*, a title passed on to later versions.

In biblical times, the Israelite people provided two better titles, both drawn from the book's opening verse. Some called it 'in the wilderness', the fifth word of 1:1, describing its historical context. Others preferred a title focusing on its theological content, from the book's opening word (1:1), 'and he [the LORD] spoke'. What the Lord said to his people and did for them in the wilderness forms the main substance of the book.

Contents

One of the distinctive characteristics of Numbers is the astonishing variety of literature used in its compilation.[24] It includes a diverse collection of prose and poetry, tribal lists, camping instructions, priestly regulations, worship calendars, detailed travelogues, military records, stories, speeches and songs. Recent study has emphasized that, far from being an Old Testament 'junk room',[25] there are clear links between seemingly disparate genres[26] in the unfolding material. Mary Douglas believes that this 'literary masterpiece' has 'been very carefully constructed' and that an 'unexpectedly complex and elegant rhetorical structure' can be discerned in the final literary presentation of the story.[27]

Before embarking on a more detailed study of these chapters, an

---

[22] 1 Cor. 10:5–12.
[23] Jude 5, 11; 2 Pet. 2:14–16; Rev. 2:14; Heb. 3:1 – 4:11.
[24] A 'literary richness' that 'surpasses that of any other book of the Bible' (Milgrom, p. xiii); see 'The genres of Numbers' in Wenham (1997), pp. 26–67.
[25] Seybold, cited, not approvingly, in Wenham (1997), p. 76.
[26] Frequently suggested in Wenham (1981).   [27] Douglas (1993), pp. 39, 83, 21.

overview of its contents may be helpful. The story can be divided into five unequal sections.

The first, 'Getting ready' (1:1 – 10:10), continues the narrative begun in Exodus describing what the Lord said to the redeemed Israelites during their one-year stay at Sinai. The second section, 'Setting out' (10:11 – 12:16) describes the initial stages of their journey, while the central section, 'Drawing back' (13:1 – 14:45), chronicles the major tragedy of the book. Here the people refuse to enter the country and plan to appoint a substitute leader who will take them back to the land of their former captivity. The fourth section, 'Marking time' (15:1 – 25:18), describes some of the events that took place, and the teaching that was given, during their enforced delay in the wilderness. The closing section, 'Pressing on' (26:1 – 36:13), documents the experiences of the new generation from the time of the second census through to the book's conclusion.

Compilation and authorship

Until the early nineteenth century it was generally accepted (with notable exceptions) that Moses was the author of the five opening books of Scripture. Since then, radically different views have emerged, which, dispensing with Mosaic authorship, conjectured that the Pentateuch was the work of editors who used diverse literary sources, all derived from much later periods of Israelite history. This 'documentary hypothesis' has spawned an astonishing number of variants, but its basic idea is that four distinctive sources, identified as J (tenth-ninth centuries BC), E (eighth century BC), D (mainly Deuteronomy, late seventh century BC) and P (Priestly, sixth–fifth centuries BC), were used to compile an account of Israel's beginnings prior to the conquest of Canaan, and that this literary work possibly took shape in its final form either during or after the Babylonian exile.[28]

Those who favour this diachronic ('through time') source hypothesis generally consider that a good deal of the Pentateuch is historically unreliable and that this conflated account of the nation's origins is 'ideological fiction',[29] religiously informative for

[28] J. Van Seters believes that the 'Yahwist's history … was the work of an ancient Israelite (or, more specifically, Judean) scholar living among the exiles in Babylonia'. *The Life of Moses: The Yahwist as Historian in Exodus–Numbers* (Louisville, KY: Westminster/John Knox, 1994), p. 468. For Pentateuchal source criticism, see G. J. Wenham, 'Pondering the Pentateuch: The search for a new paradigm', in Baker and Arnold, pp. 116–144; Wenham (1981), pp. 18–24; idem (1997), pp. 68–80; Davies, pp. xlvi–li.

[29] E.g. R. N. Whybray, *The Making of the Pentateuch*, *JSOT* Supplement Series 33 (Sheffield: Sheffield Academic Press, 1987), p. 240: 'It is well established that a large proportion of the narratives in the Pentateuch are fiction', and 'the whole

the period during which it was recorded but little more than imaginative reflections on possible events. It is held that their primary purpose was inspirational and didactic – to invigorate and teach the Israelite people as they tried to build a new life in a downtrodden Jerusalem after their enforced stay in Babylon.

More recent work on the Pentateuch suggested that, although some of its written sources belonged to a later period, these depended on old traditions, some dating from the time of Moses or earlier, and several of which may have good historical foundations. Archaeological research and study involving comparisons with contemporary ancient near-eastern texts and social customs have offered some support to the reliability of the Pentateuch, the patriarchal narratives[30] for example.

Even among those scholars who remain persuaded that the JEDP documentary hypothesis, or one of its developments, may account for the literary origins of the Pentateuch, there are those who recognize that a book like Numbers ought to be studied as a finished work. It was assembled by people who were not indifferent to literary structure, and deserves to be read and studied as it now is, and not as a series of randomly selected literary scraps of dubious authenticity.

This synchronic ('at the same time') or holistic reading of the book has become increasingly popular, involving the discipline of studying 'the shape of the text at a particular point in time' and discussing its 'shape, literary form and meaning without reference to its earlier stages'.[31] When a commentator has ventured to trace the possible source of a particular passage in the book, the discussion is not over; crucial questions remain unanswered. This holistic approach is evident in more recent expositions of the book such as those by Wenham, Olson, Ashley, Milgrom and Douglas.

Both Numbers (33:2) and its immediate sequel, Deuteronomy,[32] state that Moses exercised his writing skills in the compilation of these books. If he recorded some of this material, oral tradition also played an important part in the reliable communication of ancient stories. In Semitic culture, their poetry was their 'public register ... by its means genealogies are remembered and glorious deeds handed down to posterity'. One German scholar personally

---

presentation of Moses in the Pentateuch in its present form may be described as the religious fiction of a later time'.

[30] M. J. Selman, 'Comparative customs and the patriarchal age', in A. R. Millard and D. J. Wiseman (eds.), *Essays on the Patriarchal Narratives* (Leicester: IVP, 1980), pp. 93–138.

[31] Wenham, 'Pondering the Pentateuch: The search for a new paradigm', p. 140.

[32] Deut. 31:9, 24.

observed 'the extraordinary powers of two Arab herd-boys, to whom he listened at Kal 'at el-Hsa, as they sang the genealogies and great deeds of their own and other tribes'.[33] Over many centuries, ancient near-eastern people became extraordinarily skilled in the accurate transmission of stories from their past.

Moses may have benefited from the expertise of a significant team of gifted helpers in completing such a massive literary exercise. He appointed responsible assistants to help in the first census (1:16–18), and Harrison maintains that these 'literate administrators ... were the šōṭᵉrîm (to use their later name)' whose function was 'to assist in recording and administering judicial decisions'. These associates 'would commit to writing whatever judicial decisions were made' and also record 'the occurrence of important events during the wilderness period'.[34] Although conjectural, it is an interesting suggestion about the possible means whereby such compelling literary material might have been committed to writing by Moses and his associates.

The New Testament Gospels refer to Christ's words about 'Moses' writings'.[35] Were Jesus and his contemporaries merely employing a literary convention, utilizing a traditional tag? Or was the Son of God, 'the truth',[36] affirming his conviction about the gifted mind and skill behind the compilation of these inspired accounts of his people's origins?

The stance adopted here is that source theories are unproven hypotheses, and that there is no firm reason to doubt that, with the help of literate assistants, the extremely well-educated historical figure known as Moses was capable of composing, collecting and editing most of the Pentateuch as it now stands, doubtless making use of other sources (e.g. 21:14–15, 27–30; 22:1 – 24:25). Other hands may have shared in the later editing of these stories. He did not record the factual details of his own death and burial, of course, nor was he likely to have written such a highly commendatory notice about himself as occurs in 12:3. These were doubtless the work of equally inspired contemporary or later editors.

[33] Alois Musil, *Arabia Petrea*, 1: *Moab* (Vienna: Alfred Holder, 1907), p. 84; C. J. Lyall, *Translations of Ancient Arabian Poetry* (London: Williams and Norgate, 1930), p. xv; G. A. Smith, *The Early Poetry of Israel in its Physical and Social Origins*, The British Academy Sweich Lecture for 1910 (Oxford: Oxford University Press, 1912), p. 35.
[34] Harrison, pp. 15–22; see Deut. 16:18. For history-writing in the Old Testament, see V. Philips Long, 'Historiography in the Old Testament', in Baker and Arnold (eds.), pp. 145–175; idem, *The Art of Biblical History* (Leicester: Apollos, 1994); Sidney Greidanus, *The Modern Preacher and the Ancient Text* (Leicester: IVP, 1988), pp. 80–101.
[35] Mark 10:5; 12:19; Luke 20:28; John 1:45.   [36] John 14:6.

Relevance

Any exposition of Old Testament narrative can easily be deflected from its theocentric purpose. The primary question to put to these stories is, 'What does *God* reveal here about himself?'[37] and we ought now to consider the application and relevance of its message about God for the twenty-first-century reader. Essential to the ideal life of humankind in any context is the need to be loved, free, clean and sure.

The need to be loved

The desire to be wanted is a natural craving in any life, whatever the century. We are social creatures, not designed for total isolation. We belong together. Numbers relates the story of a people who have been repeatedly assured that they are valued by God, their lover and (in the art of caring) their exemplar; because they are loved,[38] they too must love.[39] The tribal list that opens the book recalls the names of the patriarchs, the great-grandsons of Abraham, the father of their race. This historical recollection reminds a privileged people that they matter to God; called into being by a miracle of his undeserved grace, they are the object of his special care.[40]

Numbers might seem preoccupied with law rather than with love, but the two concepts are inseparably united, not mutually alienated. It was because God loved them that he entered into a covenant with them, a dependable agreement by which he placed on indelible record his eternal love for them,[41] contracting to care for them and protect them, meeting all their needs. They, in turn, covenanted to love him exclusively, not switching their allegiance to other gods.[42]

The story related in Numbers historically demonstrates the divine love. Infinitely more than an ethereal doctrinal idea, God's love is practical, rooted in history, demonstrating the reality and quality of its compassion by attending to the care of his people in meticulous detail. It even anticipates some of the dangers that might damage their love for one another, such as tribal rivalry; he tells them precisely where the different tribes are to pitch their tents in the camp, and in which order they are to march in their long caravan. He lovingly provides spiritual leaders to be alongside them in times of stress and anxiety: compassionate priests and their supportive assistants. His promised guidance through difficult

---

[37] Greidanus, op. cit., p. 216.   [38] Exod. 19:4–5.   [39] Deut. 6:5; Lev. 19:18, 34.
[40] Exod. 15:13.   [41] Deut. 7:9, 12–13.   [42] Exod. 20:3.

terrain is further evidence of his caring love. They have no well-trained army to protect them, but, when necessary, God's care becomes manifest in his gift of military success (21:1–3, 21–35; 31:1–24). When foes more sinister than pagan soldiers are ranged against them (22:1–7), evil intention is diverted into divine blessing (23:11–12; Neh. 13:2).

Although his love was not always reciprocated by the generation that left Egypt, he lovingly provided for their children, guiding them to the threshold of the promised land. This theme of the new land, a unique token of his compassionate provision, is naturally prominent in the book as this huge community makes its way towards it.[43] Immediately following the rebellious disobedience of the old generation, their children are assured that, though their parents will be kept out of Canaan, they themselves will enter it (15:1); punishment for that sin, at least, would not pass from the fathers to the children.[44]

Ours is a strangely insular society, seriously lacking those strong and dependable relationships characteristic of earlier generations. Marriage is a disposable item. Divorced, separated or unmarried parents have passed a sad message on to their offspring; their children are not remotely sure about the reliability of human love. Work is no longer the secure social environment it was for many of our parents and grandparents. People's lives are more insular, often indifferent to the needs of others; voluntary societies urgently need helpers. Political parties find it difficult to recruit dedicated supporters. It is estimated that 60% of British people do not belong to anything. In such an individualistic context, firm allegiance to the local church is marginalized; it is easier to drift from one congregation to another, idolizing personal preferences, than to make a commitment in church membership. The message of Numbers is of striking contemporary relevance with its assurance that we are greatly valued and made for community by a God who cares.

The need to be free

God's dealings with his people are redemptive. He knew the sustained anguish of their Egyptian captivity and was determined to release them from slavery. The narrative in Numbers describes the pursuit of freedom. Before the redeemed community left Sinai, they celebrated their first Passover since leaving captivity (9:1–5), but the newly liberated people soon discovered that different

---

[43] The 'land' theme is dominant in the Pentateuch as a whole; see Clines.
[44] Exod. 20:5.

tyrannies were lurking in the desert. God protected them from marauding brigands, but there were more sinister enemies: inward adversaries such as dissatisfaction and discontent (11:1–9), bitterness and jealousy (12:1–2), fear and unbelief (13:31 – 14:4), arrogance and disobedience (14:39–45), rebelliousness and irreverence (16:1–14). Even their devoted leaders were exposed to such temptations (12:1–2, 10–11; 20:1–13). Every member of this redeemed people depended on God's power in his or her life to avoid these damaging allurements and to conquer such self-destructive ambitions.

Some of their temptations would, by contrast, come from external pressures. The way ahead was through territory whose occupants worshipped other gods, where they would be exposed to the perilous enticement of apostasy and idolatry, and spiritual and physical adultery (25:1–16; 33:50–56). Individuals and the community were powerless against such onslaughts; the Lord alone could provide the spiritual and moral strength to transform defeated slaves into resourceful conquerors.

The need to be clean

Holiness is a graphically illustrated theme in Numbers, utilizing the categories of space ('camp around the Tent of Meeting some distance from it', 2:2; cf. 3:38), person (priests and Levites, 1:47–53; 3:1 – 4:49; 8:1–26), ritual (sacrifices and cleansing procedures, 15:1–29; 18:1–32; 5:1–4; 19:1–22) and time (as in the calendar of feasts and festivals, 28:1 – 29:40).[45] In visual form, the four facets depict God's ideal community – reverent, submissive, obedient and grateful. There were times when personal and corporate purity was an unachieved ideal. The best people failed sometimes, the worst often. More than once, with varying degrees of rectitude, the offenders cried, 'We have sinned' (14:40; 12:11), 'We shall die! We are lost, we are all lost!' (17:12–13). But, despite their trangressions, they belonged to a forgiving God who made provision for his children's cleansing and pardon. Priests and Levites would always be available[46] to help and counsel. Appropriate sacrifices were to give visible expression to their penitence and gratitude (15:1–29; 28:1–15).

Spiritual and moral pollution (5:5–31) was just as devastating as physical contamination or ritual defilement (19:1–22). Sinful people need the miracle of atonement, and in this book it is vividly portrayed. Christians rejoice that one better than Moses (12:13;

---

[45] For an illuminating exposition of this theme, see Jenson.
[46] Mal. 2:6–7; Lev. 10:11; Deut. 33:10.

14:17–19) is their mediator and intercessor.[47] A greater than Aaron has 'made atonement for them' and still stands 'between the living and the dead', having offered himself for their unique salvation. (16:41–48).

Unhappily, our generation is increasingly less sensitive to sin; 'guilt' belongs to a redundant vocabulary. One of Umberto Eco's fictional characters gives expression to contemporary scepticism: 'If belief is necessary, let it be in a religion that doesn't make you feel guilty ... Like a novel, not like a theology.'[48]

Yet alongside such restless cynicism we witness an undeniable escalation in human sinfulness, glaringly apparent in the columns of every newspaper. With the brilliant technological achievements of modern society, human sin now has the power to propagate itself globally almost at the speed of light. One journalist describes the internet as 'the perfect vehicle for peddling filth'. Another observes, 'Free from censorship or state control, it is the plaything of the pornographer, the pervert, and the salacious gossip.'[49] The dramatic stories, serious warnings and legal provisions related in Numbers concerning human sin and its remedy continue to be relevant in a society where many of our contemporaries appear unconcerned about the tragic consequences of deviant behaviour.

The need to be sure

In a world without firm spiritual and moral foundations, this book portrays a better life, using its warnings to present attractive alternatives.

The book's unfolding drama explores the story of a forgiven past. Some of its best characters made their mistakes, but were cleansed. Aaron's confession was genuine (12:11–12), Moses' prayer answered (12:13) and Miriam 'brought back' (12:15) to a restored life. What happened within that believing family became a paradigm of pardon, widely available for others. When sinners repent, God forgives their sin (14:17–20).

Numbers also tells the story of a guided present. Throughout the narrative, reference is made to the overshadowing cloud, symbolic of God's unchanging presence with his people (9:15–23; 10:11–12, 33–36; 11:25; 12:5, 10; 14:10, 14; 16:42). Its readers are reminded that God's grace is a demonstration of divine generosity, not a reward for moral perfection. God was with his people on days when they least deserved it. He has promised to stay with us,

[47] Heb. 7:25.
[48] U. Eco, *Foucault's Pendulum* (New York: Ballantine Books, 1989), p. 434.
[49] *The Week*, 23 December 2000, p. 4.

even in our wayward diversions. But the cloud is a reminder of his holiness, not solely a token of his nearness. Because he is with us he has every right to expect us to be different.

Moreover, Numbers reiterates the promise of a secure future. The country ahead is the pilgrims' goal; everything in the book moves, albeit gradually, towards that end. The land has been promised and God never breaks his word; that is their strong anchor on the darkest days. It is ours too. A great deal of contemporary thinking is pessimistic about the future, even derisive about life after death and God's ultimate future. This mentality is captured in a cynical graffito: 'Owing to lack of interest, tomorrow has been cancelled.' Postmodernism's communicators urge us to 'live solely for today. Forget about tomorrow; it may never happen.' But Scripture insists that it will happen, as we move closer to our eternal destiny.[50] Rather than depict life as a journey with a clear destination, it is preferable, we are urged, to view our existence as 'a labyrinth that leads everywhere and nowhere. To die with style ... What if there is no cosmic Plan? What a mockery, to live in exile when no one has sent you there. Exile from a place, moreover, that does not exist. And what if there is a Plan, but it has eluded you – and will elude you for all eternity?'

Better by far, insists the postmodern thinker, to create your own religion. Why not deify yourself? 'You invent the Plan, metaphor of the Unknowable One. Even a human plot can fill the void ... Believe there is a secret and you will feel like an initiate. It costs nothing. To create an immense hope that can never be uprooted, because it has no root. Ancestors who do not exist will never appear and say that you have betrayed. A religion you can keep while betraying it infinitely.'[51]

Numbers offers a better paradigm. This 'piece of extraordinarily skilful writing'[52] describes a people with certainties. For all their mistakes, they know they are loved, and that true freedom is to be found only in obedience to the God who made them. Even when they fail he will restore them, and though there are hardships *en route*, he is leading them on to an indescribably better future. Life is an accompanied pilgrimage, not a meaningless maze. Jesus said that he alone was 'the way', imagery gratefully adopted by the earliest believers to declare their identity and affirm their destiny.[53]

The imagery of life as a journey has a long history, memorably captured in Greek mythology, biblical history and Christian allegory. Homer's *Odyssey,* the books of Exodus to Numbers and

---

[50] Heb. 13:14; 1 Pet. 1:13; 4:13; 5:10.   [51] Eco, *Foucault's Pendulum*, p. 434.
[52] Douglas (1993), p. 119.   [53] John 14:6; Acts 9:2.

The Pilgrim's Progress depict the tale of every human life. How we begin, travel and arrive is Scripture's unique story. Numbers plays a significant part in presenting this drama in a specific historical context. Like Paul's readers at Corinth, we too have much to learn from this story of Israel's past.

A Titian portrait in the National Gallery in London depicts the three faces of humanity in late, middle and young life, reckoned to be the artist, his son and grandson. His *Allegory of Prudence* is headed by an indistinct Latin inscription, which reads, 'To the past the man of today does well to turn so as not to put the future at risk.' It would be hard to find a more appropriate maxim for Numbers.

PART 1. GETTING READY
(1:1 – 10:10)

1:1 – 2:34
1. God's people prepare

Numbers describes some of Israel's hopes and fears during a crucial half-century of its corporate life. We recognize the importance of history for the Israelite people; its very identification of the different tribes in this introduction recalls the patriarchal story of Jacob's sons. Nevertheless, a narrative that describes the enforced head-count of their thirteenth-century successors suggests that we may have opened a book that is certainly antiquated, possibly irrelevant, even boring.

It would be a mistake, however, to hurry beyond these opening chapters in the hope of stumbling across something more interesting. Here are people in community, recalling their roots. All this may not be quite as far from the contemporary scene as it first appears. The fascination with family history and genealogy is fast becoming an obsession. Over 80,000 internet websites are devoted to it and, if the number of hits is anything to go by, the subject is second only to sex in popularity. People are interested in their past. These Israelite registers preserve the convictions and ideals of the world's most significant people; here in narrative form is an exposition of their God-given theology of an ideal spiritual community.

A privileged community

The opening verse encapsulates the central truth that the Lord is a God who speaks and acts. Here are the two massive doctrinal themes of Scripture: revelation and redemption.

God speaks

The Israelite people were privileged because God communicated with them. In stark contrast to the silent gods[1] of their surrounding

---

[1] Is. 44:9–20.

neighbours, *The LORD spoke* (1:1). This initial statement is characteristic of the entire book, where over 150 times and in about
twenty different ways are told that Israel's God said something
special to his people.

God spoke through a chosen servant, *Moses*. Here was a man
designated and equipped for an epoch-making task, to lead God's
people from enslavement to freedom, from the old to the new. He
was given unique authority to receive and communicate this
revelation preserved in Scripture.

God spoke in an appointed place, *the Tent of Meeting*. The
intricate details concerning the measurements, construction and
furnishings of this portable worship-centre are preserved in the
exodus narrative.[2] The early chapters of Numbers deal with its
location (2:2), care (3:5–8, 21–38), protection (3:9–10), transportation (4:33), maintenance (7:1–89) lighting (8:1–4) and uniqueness
(9:15–23). Several key events in later chapters take place at this
Tent of Meeting, where God gave his orders, revealed his will,
vindicated his servants, expressed his displeasure and manifested
his mercy.

God spoke at a crucial time. He conversed with Moses in this
Tent *in the Desert of Sinai* just over a year after the Israelites had
been delivered from Egyptian tyranny. They had waited at Mount
Sinai while Moses communicated God's covenant promises to his
people, an agreement enshrined in the law and commandments.
Their enforced stay had been marred by impatience, idolatry,
disrespect,[3] disloyalty,[4] ingratitude,[5] syncretism,[6] irreverence and
debauchery,[7] but, graciously forgiven, the restored people were now
ready for their long trek across the desert. The wilderness ahead was
fraught with danger, and few among them could have viewed the
prospect with unshadowed delight; but if God was among them
to speak with them and they, in turn, were given the grace of
obedience, all could be well.

This opening verse conveys a salutary reminder to the contemporary reader that God continues to address us, uniquely through
the pages of Scripture. In several narratives, Numbers reminds us
to guard against indifference, flippancy or the arrogant rejection of
this word. The message may not be initially palatable or particularly welcome, but several encounters in this book indicate that
refusal to accept God's word robs the disobedient of happiness,
usefulness and peace.

---

[2] Exod. 25 – 31, 35 – 40.   [3] Exod. 32:1.   [4] Exod. 32:2.   [5] Exod. 32:4.
[6] Exod. 32:5.   [7] Exod. 32:6.

God acts

God spoke clearly to them in *the second year after the Israelites came out of Egypt* (1:1). He did not simply issue his orders; he acted mightily on their behalf. The uniqueness of the revelation is attested by the miracle of their redemption. Only God could have achieved a speedy and complete emancipation from four centuries of despotic oppression. The Lord is more than a majestic voice thundering from the distant heights of Sinai. The God who had miraculously delivered them 'from the hand of the Egyptians' was intent on fulfilling the second half of the promise made at the foot of that same mountain when Moses saw the bush aflame with unquenchable fire. The Lord had not only brought them out of captivity but would bring them into 'a land flowing with milk and honey'.[8] He is a redeeming God, always acting powerfully and mercifully in the lives of those intent on listening to what he says.

So, in the opening words of this record of their momentous journey, the reader is reminded that this privileged community was brought *out of Egypt*. The people would need further deliverances in the course of their travels, occasionally from external perils, more often from inward foes. The dangers of hunger, thirst and menacing armies would be overcome by their mighty God, but there would be times ahead when they would not turn to him for help with more threatening adversaries such as grumbling discontent (11:1–9), pride and insubordination (12:1–3), fear (13:27–29), doubt (13:30–33), despair (14:1–4), unbelief (14:5–10), disobedience (14:39–45), insurrection (16:1–14), persistent complaining (16:41; 17:5), a quarrelsome spirit (20:2–5), idolatry and immorality (25:1–2). The recollection of their redemption *out of Egypt* in this narrative's introductory sentence reminds every reader that, once delivered from the condemnation of sin, every believer needs Christ's ongoing work of salvation. Like those Israelite slaves, we have been gloriously delivered, but we need that continuing deliverance promised and made possible by the indwelling power of the Holy Spirit. Salvation in biblical terms is three-dimensional: we have been saved from sin's judgment and are being saved from sin's tyranny; ultimately, in heaven, we shall be saved from sin's presence.[9]

A vulnerable community

The narrative goes on to describe the event from which the book takes its present name. Moses is commanded to number all the

---

[8] Exod. 3:7–8.   [9] 1 Cor. 1:18; Rom. 8:12–13.

28

Israelite men over twenty years of age: '*Take a census ... listing every man by name ... who are able to serve in the army*' (1:2–3). Given the wealth they had brought out of Egypt[10] they might be attacked by marauding bandits. An army was necessary for their immediate defence, but much more for the forthcoming invasion of Canaan. God's plan was that they should steadily make their way across this vast wilderness and, given suitable travelling conditions, they could be on the threshold of Canaan in a matter of weeks (1:2). Then troops would certainly be necessary if they were to conquer the promised land.

Sadly, these prospective soldiers died in the wilderness; it is the book's second census (26:1–65) that preserves the names of those who entered Canaan. The first list became a tragic catalogue of grumblers, doubters and rebels, people who did not fulfil their potential, a sad reminder of life's lost opportunities. Between the first and second censuses in this book lies the tragic tale of Israel's failure to believe the God who speaks and acts. They would not obey his voice and did not trust his power.

Christian readers of Numbers are confronted with the conflict theme in its first paragraph. To be given a place in the life of God's people is an immense privilege, but Scripture constantly emphasizes that it is also a costly experience.[11] There is no discipleship without discipline. Jesus did not shield his followers from the harsh realities that awaited them. If vicious opponents had harassed Jesus, they were not likely to leave his partners in peace. Trusting in what was uniquely achieved by his cross, they must take up their own.[12] Paul told the early Christian people that they must fight as well-equipped soldiers committed to arduous conflict.

A valued community

The records emphasize the significance of the individual, *listing every man by name, one by one* (1:2, 18, 20, *et passim*). The needs of the wider community did not obscure the value of the distinctive person whose name was listed. It was a remarkable achievement. Although its purpose was to calculate the troops, it made Israel aware of its ancestry. Individuals belonged to families, each family was part of a clan, and numerous clans made up the various tribes. They could trace their story back through history to Jacob's sons,[13] who began their life in the land their successors

---

[10] Exod. 11:2; 12:35–36.   [11] John 15:18–21; 16:33; 2 Tim. 3:12.
[12] Mark 8:34.   [13] Gen. 49:1–28.

were meant to occupy. The pilgrims were on their way home, and every one mattered to God.

We live in a depersonalized society. Brilliantly intricate technology has reduced almost everything to pin numbers and barcodes. Face-to-face meeting is in danger of becoming a social rarity. The internet chat-room has replaced the personal encounter. Business partners engage in conversation across the world without meeting in person; we have computerized contact with people on the other side of the world but remain ignorant of the crying needs of a next-door neighbour. Numbers preserves the story of a vast community, but it also confronts us with the influence of the individual. The *one by one* element is not overlooked.

The striking narratives of Numbers illustrate the influence of consecrated individuals such as those who took the Nazirite vow (6:1–8), compassionate individuals such as Moses (12:13), depressing individuals such as the ten spies (14:31–33), encouraging individuals such as Caleb (13:30), resourceful individuals such as Joshua (27:18–23), disappointing individuals such as Miriam and Aaron (12:1–12), insolent and damaging individuals such as Korah, Dathan and Abiram (16:1) and venturesome individuals such as Zelophehad's daughters (27:1–11). No person lives to himself or herself; others are affected by our thoughts and actions. Jesus taught that, in God's sight, every single person is of infinite value[14] with great potential for good or evil. Moses recognized that immense harm can come to the 'entire assembly when only one man sins' (16:22).

An interdependent community

Although the significance of the individual is frequently heightened in this book, the people are taught from the start that each has a supportive and interdependent role in the community. If they are to complete this hazardous desert crossing successfully, task definition is vital. Many of the mistakes and failures that are recorded later can be traced to individuals who refused to acknowledge this basic fact. Moses and Aaron were to conduct the census with the help of *one man from each tribe, the leaders of their ancestral tribes ... the heads of the clans of Israel* (4–5, 16). Moses could not accomplish this immense task without the help of a loyal team. He valued the supervisory gifts of Ithamar (4:27–28, 33), the practical skills of a traveller familiar with the desert's inhospitable terrain (10:29–32), the wholehearted

---

[14] Matt. 6:25–34; 10:30.

partnership of Caleb (14:24) and the dependable support of Joshua and of Eleazar the priest (27:15–23). Precise tasks are assigned to clan leaders (1:16), the role of the priests must not be arrogantly usurped by others (16:1–35) and Levites are told where they are to live in the camp, what specific duties they can undertake, how they are to travel in convoy and what they are to do in their work for God: 'each was assigned his work and told what to carry' (4:49). Individuals must acknowledge their dependence on others.

This interdependence theme is developed throughout Scripture, reaching its finest expression in the New Testament ideal of the church, where Christians are related to one another as limbs in a body, stones in a building and co-partners in a superb enterprise.[15] We belong together; anything that fractures the relationship is to the detriment of the whole community.

A committed community

The names of those who were to assist Moses in the census (5–16) are worthy of reflection. Many carried the divine name and, across the years, testified to the faith of their parents in hard times. In Egypt, they could not live and act as they wished, but they kept the faith alive in their families, providing their children with names that preserved great truths about the God they loved and honoured. *Elizur* (5) meant 'God is a rock', and *Zurishaddai* (6), 'my rock is Shaddai', their dependable strength and protecting shade in the cruel experiences of life. *Shedeur* (5) meant 'Shaddai is a light', a flame of inextinguishable brightness in the darkness of Egyptian oppression. *Shelumiel* (6), 'God is my salvation', *Gamaliel* (10), 'God is my reward', and *Pedahzur* (10), 'the Rock redeems', expressed confidence in the Lord's promise, and hope for better days. *Nethanel* (8), 'God has given', gave voice to at least one family's awareness of the Lord's generosity. *Eliab* (9), 'my God is Father', spoke of his unfailing care, and *Elishama* (10), 'my God has heard', declared that his ear was always open to his people's cry. If they were true to their names, these chosen men (5) had as much to contribute to the enterprise spiritually as administratively. What we are before God is infinitely more important than what we do.

A worshipping community

The book's opening chapter preserves the detail that the men who belonged to the tribe of Levi were not to serve as Israel's soldiers,

---

[15] Rom. 12:3–9; 1 Cor. 3:6–9; 12:4–31; 1 Pet. 2:5.

since they had specific responsibilities in *the tabernacle of the Testimony*, and, as colleagues and partners of the Aaronic priesthood, they were to care for *all its furnishings and everything belonging to it* (1:47–53). They were to protect, erect, dismantle and carry the Tent of Meeting and were to camp around it as guardians. This portable worship-centre was to be at the heart of the camp and, during their travels, its materials, poles and furnishings were carried in the middle of the convoy. By means of this colourful visual aid, the Israelite people were reminded of the priority of worship; its immediate physical proximity was a constant reminder of some essential truths.

First, their worship asserted God's uniqueness. The Levites acted as a protective buffer, preserving any arrogant or ignorant Israelite from approaching the holy place where God's presence was manifest among his people; there was no place for irreverence or flippancy. Any attempt to marginalize him and give priority to other values was doomed to disaster. The Lord alone is God[16] and there must be no rivals.

Secondly, their worship demonstrated God's nearness. Its central location symbolically declared that he was not far from every one of them.[17] If he was with them and for them, who could possibly overcome them?[18]

Thirdly, their worship emphasized God's holiness. The Israelites were *to camp round the Tent of Meeting* yet they were to keep *some distance from it* (2:2). The Levites were a protective barrier, to maintain that essential sense of God's holy presence. It not only helped to preserve that awareness of reverence without which worship is quickly debased, but it became a moral check on their behaviour. They were not allowed to divorce their relationship with God from their moral conduct in society.[19] In the long years that followed, an awareness of what took place at the Tent of Meeting kept alive that sense of unique sanctity.

This provision for the tabernacle's location, both in the centre of the camp yet at a respectful distance from their tents, preserves in visual form two inseparable dimensions in any balanced doctrine of God: his immanence and trancendence. His immanence maintains the truth of his compassionate closeness, preserving us from the fear that he is a remote and inaccessible deity, totally isolated from our lives. His transcendence guards against casualness and irreverent presumption. David Wells reminds us that, among many contemporary Christians, the message of God's immanence is more

---

[16] Exod. 20:3, 23; 34:14; Deut. 6:14–15; 13:1–18.
[17] Deut. 4:7; Is. 55:6; Acts 17:27.   [18] Rom. 8:31.   [19] Lev. 19:2.

popularly acceptable than the truth of his transcendence,[20] but we are not at liberty to emphasize one divine attribute at the expense of another. If we concentrate solely on his immanence we may drift imperceptibly into casualness, becoming flippant about spiritual realities. If we focus exclusively on his transcendence we may come to feel alone, despondent and neglected.

An obedient community

Throughout this introductory section an important phrase is repeated which, in one form or another, recurs throughout the entire book: *as the LORD commanded* (1:19); *the Israelites did all this just as the LORD commanded Moses* (1:54; cf. 2:33–34; 3:16, 42, 51; 4:37, 41, 45, 49). Whatever he told them to do was done without the slightest hesitation or prevarication. It expressed a depth of commitment not characteristic of the long journey. Many later encounters in the book portray a total breakdown in Israel's submissive relationship; tragically, they no longer acted at his command (9:18).

They were repeatedly defiant, for example, over the divinely appointed leadership of Moses (12:1–16; 14:1–4; 16:1–50; 20:2: 21:5) and were disobedient to God's word by refusing to enter the land he had promised to them (13:31–33; 14:10), treating God with contempt (14:23), as they 'banded together against' him (14:35). When, in judgment, the Lord barred their way into the land, they insisted on invading it. An astonished Moses asked, 'Why are you disobeying the LORD's command?' (14:41; cf. 16:10–11, 14).

It was not only the occasionally intractable individual who was disobedient. Large numbers of the people flouted the commandments, engaging in idolatrous practices by worshipping Baal and committing adultery with Moabite women (25:1–3). As if to underline the insidious nature of the wayward spirit, on one occasion even the great Moses was not fully obedient. One hasty act of ill-tempered disobedience cost him his own entry into the promised land (20:8–12), a warning not only to his fellow pilgrims but to generations that followed.[21]

These opening chapters emphasize that obedience was regarded as obligatory, crucial and total. Its obligatory character is reflected in the repeated language of the opening chapters; the community's response to God's word was to do *just as the LORD commanded* (1:54). Later chapters illustrate its crucial nature, negatively demonstrating the disastrous results that followed Israel's acts of repeated

[20] D. F. Wells, *God in the Wasteland* (Leicester: IVP, 1994), pp. 121–122, 133–151.
[21] Ps. 106:32.

rebellion. Moreover, the obedience must be total, not partial; the wilderness community began by doing *everything the LORD commanded* (2:34). Sadly, it was a commitment not sustained.

Obedience is the validating sign of authentic Christian discipleship. It is impossible to exaggerate its importance in the message of Jesus. He not only taught it but exemplified it.[22] Even Jesus, we are told, 'learned obedience',[23] not simply by accepting the inevitable limitations of an incarnate life[24] but throughout his entire ministry.[25] His followers are not content simply to learn what he says; they do it.

This portrait of a closely knit Israelite community appears in stark contrast to the splintered culture and increasing individualism of the contemporary postmodern scene. Richard Tomkins has commented on the fragmentation of western society 'into millions of individuals who are no longer prepared to accept what they are given but want it their way now. In developed countries the "we" people have become the "me" people ... Reluctant to conform to social pressures or stereotypes, they no longer ... submit themselves to the authority of government, Church or the traditional family structure.' Individual empowerment has come at a severe price. 'The erosion of society's traditional structures has taken some of the stability out of people's lives, contributing to feelings of confusion and uncertainty. Greater individualism means people are more likely to put their own interests above those of the common good, leading to a loss of civic mindedness and community spirit.'[26]

The opening section of Numbers describes a radically different ideal. Here, God is supreme and his word honoured. Worship is a priority, life is structured and families matter. Here are people aware of their distinctive identity, strengthened by their corporate solidarity, rejoicing in their spiritual continuity and confident of their promised security. This portraiture of orderly, interdependent corporate life has much to say to fragmenting cultures in a new millennium. With our modern, individualistic preference for 'believing without belonging', it challenges today's churches and units of Christian organizations to be models of loving, supportive, mutually enriching life and service.

---

[22] John 14:15, 23–24, 31; 15:10, 12, 14, 17.   [23] Heb. 5:7–9.
[24] Heb. 10:5–7.   [25] John 4:34; 5:30; 6:38; Luke 22:42.
[26] *Financial Times*, 16 December 2000; see also Robert D. Putnam, *Bowling Alone: The Collapse and Revival of American Community* (New York: Simon and Schuster, 2000).

3:1 – 4:49
2. Community servants

There are over seventy references to the Levites in Numbers, more than in any other Old Testament book. Their distinctive census emphasized the special part they were to play in the spiritual life of Israel (1:47–54). The next two chapters, 3 – 4, describe their protective and supportive role in the story of God's people.

A divine choice (3:1–3)

The overall responsibilities for Israel's priesthood were assigned to a particular member of the tribe of Levi, Aaron, the brother of Moses.[1] To prevent these holy tasks from being coveted, bought or demanded by others, the responsibilities were exclusively assigned to *Aaron's sons, the anointed priests, who were ordained to serve as priests* (3:3), and to no-one else. God acts sovereignly in choosing whoever he wishes for his work, though his decisions are always for the good of his people. He knew the dangers to which his people could be exposed if priests could be selected by their friends or chosen by those who might profit by their privileges.

An initial warning (3:4)

Aaron's sons were not chosen because they were morally superior to people of other tribes. They were exposed to the same temptations as anyone else, and the reader is deliberately reminded of an appalling event that took place some months earlier, during the waiting period at Mount Sinai.

Entirely on their own initiative, Aaron's eldest son, Nadab, and his brother Abihu made an incense offering to the Lord of *unauthorised fire* (4).[2] Their offence was scarcely accidental, for they

[1] Exod. 28:1; Lev. 8:1 – 9:24.   [2] Lev. 10:1–2.

had been given precise instructions about incense offerings. The fire was to be offered by the high priest, not by his sons, and was to be 'taken from the altar'.[3] Theirs appears to have been unconsecrated, 'unclean' or 'illicit' (NEB) fire obtained from beyond the holy place.

The self-assertive Nadab and Abihu failed to do 'just as the LORD commanded' (1:54; 2:34). Their story emphasizes that those called to high responsibility are not exempt from the perils that stalk everyone else, and that the holiest and best things can be marred by sin. Membership of the tribe of Levi did not guarantee protection from the alluring snares of everyday life (16:1–35). Recalling events from Numbers, Paul warned that those who imagine they are standing firm must take special care that they do not fall.[4]

A practical necessity (3:5–10)

The newly consecrated priests from Aaron's family needed reliable colleagues as their assistants in the work. These divinely appointed helpers were to help Aaron and his remaining sons, Eleazar and Ithamar, and their successors in office. They *were to perform duties for him and for the whole community at the Tent of Meeting by doing the work of the tabernacle* (3:7). These supportive partners were to assist the priests and protect the people. Men between the ages of thirty and fifty in the tribe of Levi were to function as colleagues responsible for the tabernacle's 'furnishings and everything belonging to it' (1:50). These practical roles are defined in later verses.

These men were also to act as guardians for the people. The location of their tents around the Tent of Meeting ensured that the tabernacle would not be defiled by unconsecrated people who might wander into it. Even the Levites could not enter the sanctuary, for anyone other than Aaron and his sons *who approaches the sanctuary must be put to death* (3:10).

Across the years that followed, the priests could pursue their role as God's spiritual representatives, pastoral helpers and moral guardians within the community only if the practical aspects of their work were shouldered by this team of supportive partners.

A visible reminder (3:11–13)

The Levites' presence as God's workers was a permanent visual aid to God's people, signifying two great biblical ideas: surrender and substitution.

[3] Lev. 16:12.   [4] 1 Cor. 10:12.

God's deliberate choice of these men recalled the dramatic events of Israel's deliverance from Egypt. The presence of these Levites reminded the Hebrew people that their firstborn were to be presented to the Lord, 'for all the firstborn are mine' (3:13). Just as the first of their cattle, flocks and produce were to be an offering of their best to the Lord, so, in principle, the firstborn son was to be surrendered to God.[5] Rather than take the firstborn male of every family in all the tribes, Levi's male children were to be given to the Lord in their place. When the number of Israel's firstborn males was counted it was found that they exceeded the number of available Levite males by 273, so it became necessary to collect a sum of money for each one 'for the redemption of the additional Israelites' for the work of the tabernacle and its ministry (3:40–51).

This offering of the firstborn deliberately relates to their miraculous deliverance from slavery: '*When I struck down all the firstborn in Egypt, I set apart for myself every firstborn in Israel, whether man or animal. They are to be mine. I am the LORD*' (3:13).

Parents in Israel, blessed with the gift of their first son, were required to make a payment of redemption money for the work of the tabernacle. It reminded them that those Levites were performing their service in the place of their sons, acting as substitutes for the entire firstborn male population of Israel.

The Levites, then, were a perpetual reminder to Israel of these two great spiritual principles of surrender ('*They are to be mine. I am the LORD*', 13) and substitution (*in place of the first male offspring*, 12). Christians particularly treasure these twin truths, remembering that, at the incarnation, Jesus surrendered himself totally to God's will in coming to this world to effect our salvation[6] and repeatedly renewed that offering of himself until, finally, on the cross he gave himself as a unique, perfect, atoning sacrifice for our sins. He took the judgment and punishment that were rightfully ours as sinners, becoming our substitute through his total surrender.

A unique privilege (3:14–16)

The uniqueness of Levi's tribe was accentuated by the fact that they were counted not only separately (1:47–49; 2:33) but twice, once as infants and again for service (4:34–49). All their male children over the age of one month were to be carefully noted in a

---

[5] Exod. 34:19–20; 23:16, 19.   [6] Heb. 10:5–7, citing Ps. 40:6–8.

specific census. As they grew up, these boys knew that they had been chosen by God for his work; it reminds us of the great truth of election and the importance of children in the purposes of God. These male Levites had been chosen by God from infancy. The dominant note is not of privilege but of responsibility. Election in biblical terms means that God chose his servants, such as Abraham, Jacob, Joseph, Moses and Jeremiah, for the specific work he wanted them to do. He did not select them arbitrarily, wanting to make particular favourites of them, or because they had greater spiritual or moral qualities than others. Far from it; they often made serious mistakes. They were chosen because God wanted to use them as his instruments in the world, a central theme in the Old Testament as well as in the New.[7]

This census of Levi's male children *a month old or more* reminds us of our spiritual responsibility towards children. They are to be treasured as God's gift to us and to the world, taught the transforming truths of God's Word, supported by the consistent example of those who love Christ, regularly prayed for by faithful intercessors and encouraged to become committed Christians, recognizing that they too have a destiny in God's purposes for human lives. Millions of children in my country of the UK alone have no appreciable link with any church or Christian organization; it is a perpetual challenge to contemporary Christians to become their 'spiritual parents', devising imaginative ways of reaching them for the Christ who loved, welcomed and prayed for children.[8]

A coordinated ministry (3:17 – 4:49)

The extended families of Levi's three sons, Gershon, Kohath and Merari, made up three clans that were assigned to different responsibilites. When the tabernacle was erected in its central place in the Israelite camp, the Gershonites (3:21–26) were made responsible for the worship-centre's soft furnishings, *the care of the tabernacle and tent, its coverings, curtains, ropes, and everything related to their use.*

The Kohathites were to take care of its furniture, *the ark, the table, the lampstand, the altars, the articles of the sanctuary used in ministering, the curtain, and everything related to their use* (3:27–32).

The Merarites were *to take care of the frames of the tabernacle,*

---

[7] H. H. Rowley, *The Biblical Doctrine of Election* (Guildford: Lutterworth, 1950).
[8] Deut. 4:9; 6:6–7; 11:18–19; 32:46; Ps. 78:5–6; Eph. 6:4; Matt. 19:13–15; Mark 9:36–37.

*its crossbars, posts, bases, all its equipment ... as well as the posts
of the surrounding courtyard with their bases, tent pegs and ropes*
(3:33–37).

Each of the three clans had specific reponsibilities, and special
arrangements were made for the transportation of these considerable items as the camp was moved from place to place (4:1–33).
The priests were to prepare the various items for transportation
and *when the camp* was *ready to move,* the Kohathites, for
example, were *to do the carrying. But they must not touch the holy
things or they will die* (4:15). The priests were to *assign to each
man his work and what he* was *to carry* (4:19). All three clans were
to work *under the direction* (4:33) of the priests Eleazar (4:16) and
Ithamar (4:28, 33).

The three clans were counted, and the best years of all *the men
from thirty to fifty years of age* were given for service *in the work
at the Tent of Meeting* (4:43). The Lord ensured that every man
was *assigned his work and told what to carry* (4:49). There was no
place for ambitious scheming, a competitive spirit or quarrelsome
rivalry about their duties. All were to work in harmonious
relationships with one another and in dutiful submission to their
colleagues, the priests. It anticipated the interdependent and
mutually supportive relationships that were meant to characterize
the early Christian churches.[9] Sadly, this noble and enriching ideal
was not always evident in the subsequent history of either Israel or
the church.

Reflection

As we reflect on these opening chapters, we look beyond their
numerical records, priestly formalities and ceremonial requirements
to its inspired portraiture of the God who prompted these stipulations. The separate censuses, rules and regulations are an unfamiliar
scenario for us in a different culture, but the teaching about God
that lies behind this introductory material is as crucial in our day as
it was in theirs. Before they commenced their wilderness journey,
they were reminded of the nature and attributes of the God who
was leading them to a new land.

First, God is vocal. 'The LORD spoke' (1:1) in their wilderness
encampment at the foot of Mount Sinai and would continue to
address them through his servant Moses during their travels and
throughout their history. His word (a key theme throughout the
book) must be heard, believed, valued, obeyed and shared.

---

[9] 1 Cor. 12:14–31; Eph. 4:11–16; 1 Pet. 4:10–11.

Secondly, God is powerful. Here he was at Sinai, communicating with them a year after they 'came out of Egypt' (1:1). It is the language of redemption. They were a unique people for whom God had acted as guide,[10] deliverer,[11] warrior[12] and provider.[13] They need not fear the future. An almighty God would generously meet their needs and always be their victor if, on their part, they listened attentively and responsively to his voice.

Thirdly, God is reliable. Counting Israel's male population was a remarkable testimony to God's faithfulness in keeping his promises. When the Israelites entered Egypt in the person of Jacob and his sons, they numbered seventy persons.[14] Newly rescued from Egypt, that number had expanded to colossal proportions. What seemed beyond comprehension to childless Abraham had become gloriously true for Moses. What God said had come to pass; his people were as numberless as the grains of the sand on the desert floor and as the countless stars in a night sky.[15] Surely the Lord would fulfil the other promise made to the patriarch at the same time: 'The whole land of Canaan ... I will give as an everlasting possession.'[16] In that confidence, they were to march on to their promised destiny.

Fourthly, God is sovereign. For this enterprise, he had chosen Moses and Aaron as his servants, and also determined that other male members of the tribe of Levi would be their supportive helpers. Always knowing what is best, God makes gracious plans for his believing people; they must trust that when he deals sovereignly with them he is always acting mercifully for them.

Fifthly, God is present. Because he is sovereign they were not to think of him him as remote and distant, reigning on the throne of a far-off eternity. He was alongside them in their camp, a truth graphically captured in the central place given to the Tent of Meeting, where he manifested his presence among them.[17]

Finally, God is holy. While God was certainly present, they must not presume upon that by casual or irreverent behaviour. The practical details of the camp's layout ensured that every Hebrew man, woman and child was aware of that appropriate distance that lay between their holy God and his morally, physically and spiritually needy people.

---

[10] Exod. 13:20–22.   [11] Exod. 14:13.   [12] Exod. 14:26; 15:3; 17:8–16.
[13] Exod. 15:22 – 17:7.   [14] Gen. 46:26–27; Exod. 1:5.
[15] Gen. 13:14–17; 15:5; 22:17.   [16] Gen. 17:2, 8.   [17] Exod. 25:22; 40:34–38.

5:1–31
3. Keeping the camp clean

Before the pilgrims embarked on their onward journey, they were provided with crucial guidelines regarding their spiritual, moral and social responsibilities. Three distinct issues raised in this chapter concern the physical, ethical and spiritual welfare of this desert community and its successive generations. They relate to physical impurities (1–4), moral offences (5–10) and domestic tensions (11–31).

Physical impurities (5:1–4)

Attention is now devoted to matters which, while theologically motivated, are of physical and social importance in the journey across the desert. Keeping the camp free from disease or infection was a top priority. Similar topics have appeared earlier in both Exodus and Leviticus[1] and will recur in the extended message preached by Moses, preserved for us in Deuteronomy,[2] when this desert journey was at its close.

Israel's God is holy, so everyday behaviour must not contradict that divine attribute;[3] defiling practices must not take place within the camp. Three sources of potential danger are highlighted in this first regulation. A person with an *infectious skin disease* was a threat to a primitive community. Any bodily *discharge* might also be regarded as a potential hazard and, in the oppressive heat of those desert communities, a decaying body was a serious threat. Disease could spread like an uncontrollable fire. Anyone who had been in direct contact with a corpse, lovingly caring for a deceased relative, might inadvertently spread disease. Along with the other two possible infection-carriers, that person had to spend some time

---

[1] Exod. 22:31; Lev. 13:1 – 15:33.   [2] Deut. 24:8; 23:9–14.   [3] Lev. 19:2.

outside the camp to check that it was safe for him or her to return to this highly vulnerable nomadic community.

Behind this initial group of community health regulations lie three great doctrinal themes: God's purity, presence and word.

First, God is holy. These potential transmitters of pollution might *defile their camp*, a place where a pure and holy God had promised to dwell. The temporary removal of potentially harmful people became a theological necessity as well as a community safeguard.

Secondly, God is present. This peripatetic community was the *camp where I dwell among them*. Their sensitivity to God's declared presence was a crucial factor in their understanding of community welfare. They did not want to offend *the eye of* an infinitely pure, all-knowing and ever-present God.

Thirdly, God is vocal. Each of the three potential physical, moral and domestic problems addressed in this chapter is prefaced with an identical introduction, *The* LORD *said* (1, 5, 11). He had spoken clearly to his people about such issues, and total obedience is a divine requirement. In these physical matters (1–4) at least, *They did just as the* LORD *had instructed Moses*. They recognized the wisdom of such protective regulations, however inconvenient it might have been when patterns of community health were stringently applied.

Gordon Wenham points out that, although 'the New Testament upholds the moral side of these uncleanness regulations, it abolished each of the symbolic physical distinctions' mentioned here. Jesus touched the leprosy victim, was himself touched by the distraught haemorrhage sufferer and gave life to the dead through a transforming touch.[4] 'In these ways he declared that those conditions which for centuries had separated even the elect people of God from God no longer mattered.'[5]

Moral offences (5:5–10)

Moral breakdown was a community peril just as disruptive as physical infection. Healthy people can be perilously damaging if they act unethically. The next rule relates to someone who has broken one of the commandments[6] by defrauding another member of the community. This regulation provides for appropriate restitution, even covering the possibility that the offended person and his close relatives may no longer be living. A God who is just to the offender and merciful to the offended anticipates this kind of unethical behaviour, its consequences and remedy. The offender

---

[4] Luke 5:12–13; 8:40–56.   [5] Wenham (1981), p. 78.   [6] Exod. 20:15.

has damaged his neighbour, grieved God and defiled himself: three dimensions of the doctrine of sin that recur throughout this practical book.

Damaging our neighbour

Love for our neighbour is an essential characteristic of the covenant community.[7] As the offender becomes ill at ease about his serious breach of moral conduct, he becomes more concerned about cruelty to his neighbour than about his own material welfare. Numerous breaches of moral, social and ethical conduct are covered by the provision, *When a man or woman wrongs another in any way*; instead of regarding his neighbour as someone who might serve his ends, the transgressor now recognizes him or her as a brother or sister he has wronged.

Grieving the Lord

To offend in these ways is not merely socially harmful; it is an act of blatant spiritual disloyalty. Although the wrong may not be known to others, it has been visible and audible to an omniscient God. In this matter, the wrongdoer has been *unfaithful to the* LORD. All sin is an offence against God.[8] If we treasure our relationship with God, the matter must be put right.

Defiling ourselves

The offender has stained his conscience, been less in society than he might have been and disrupted the harmonious relationships that should characterize the life of a godly community. But there are ways in which the harmful situation might be rectified.

First, sin must be recognized. The wrongdoer must face the fact that, while he may have improved his finances, it has been at enormous cost. Its implications must be honestly faced and the misdeed seen for the damaging thing that it is: *that person is guilty*. Something must be done to restore his relationship with God, his neighbour and those in the community aware of his crime.

The trespass must be acknowledged: he *must confess the sin he has committed*. The transgression must never be hidden, overlooked, minimized, excused or disregarded. No-one but a holy, righteous and just God knew the full extent of the damage, and only God could forgive it.

---

[7] Lev. 19:18.   [8] 2 Sam. 11:1–27; 12:13; Ps. 51:4, 11; Luke 15:21.

43

The wounds must be healed. If the offended person was still alive he must be recompensed in full, plus one fifth of the amount concerned as a practical token of penitence and as some reparation for any loss suffered because of the misdeed.

The family must be compensated. The death of the offended person did not exonerate the guilty person from the responsibility of full monetary restitution. The offender's nearest relations must be paid the appropriate sum so that *restitution can be made for the wrong*.

The priest must be involved. In every case, he must offer the necessary sacrifice on behalf of the offender so that *atonement could be made for him*, and so that the entire community would be aware that full restitution has taken place and the transgression has been forgiven. In some cases, where there was no surviving member of the offended family to whom restitution could be made, the priest was to receive the sum involved. Some restitution must be made if the sinner was to experience the generous, complete, immediate and assured cleansing that God alone can provide.

The theme of restitution is easily overlooked in contemporary interpretations of forgiveness. Convinced as we rightly are that 'the blood of Jesus Christ, God's Son', literally 'keeps on' (present tense) purifying us 'from all sin',[9] we are not absolved from responsibility by a sorrowing heart and a prayerful confession. Can anything be done to make things right with our offended neighbour – a profound apology, a monetary payment, a practical gesture of sorrow? J. John has given addresses throughout the UK on the Ten Commandments. Preaching at Liverpool Cathedral on the eighth commandment, provision was made for the large congregation to return stolen goods, which could be deposited in bins so that the meeting's organizers could, wherever possible, return them to their original owners. 'Our meetings give people the opportunity to make restitution,' said the evangelist. 'Giving up the items is a cathartic thing for people to do.'[10]

Domestic tensions (5:11–31)

We come now to a provision that envisages a situation where a wife may have been secretly unfaithful to her husband. She has committed adultery and is therefore guilty of breaking the seventh commandment. Alternatively, a jealous husband is tormented with the sick thought that his wife has been unfaithful to him, though he cruelly abuses her by making such an ill-founded accusation.

---

[9] 1 John 1:7.   [10] *Baptist Times*, 14 June 2001, p. 3.

In the ancient world, such issues might be decided by what has become known as 'trial by ordeal'.[11] The accused person, whether guilty or not, was required to undertake some given procedure, often extremely dangerous, to decide whether or not the offender was guilty. It was a cruel mechanism and it is probably not appropriate to understand this provision in 5:11–31 in these terms. It has similarities with 'trial by ordeal', but is different in several respects. There is no record in the Old Testament of the implementation of this process; it may even have been a temporary provision 'intended only for the wilderness journey'.[12]

First, the aggrieved man, whether justified or not, must *take his wife to the priest* (15). Such an action is a public testimony to the fact that moral accusations are a spiritual issue. God is deeply involved, and disrupted human relationships must be recognized as a serious spiritual issue. If God has made us and set us within communities, then our behaviour in those societies is of immense concern to him. Belief and behaviour are inseparable in biblical thought.

Next, a sacrifice must be offered. The *barley flour* brought to the priest is *a grain offering for jealousy, a reminder offering to draw attention to guilt*. It must be placed in the hand of the accused woman while the priest prepares a drink for her, *the bitter water that brings a curse*. The water is from the holy place and is mixed with dust from the tabernacle floor. On drinking the water, the woman is required to express her agreement (*Amen*) to the priest's pronouncement that, if guilty of the accusation, *her abdomen will swell and her thigh waste away*, but if she is innocent of the crime, no harm will befall her.

In our highly sophisticated society, such procedures for deciding right from wrong seem not only primitive but cruel. At this stage of their history, however, the Hebrew people could not be expected to act other than according to conventions recognized and acceptable in their culture. In this divine provision we have an 'oath which is dramatized',[13] and there are a number of in-built protective devices that are not present in the 'trials by ordeal' typical of the ancient and medieval world.

First, the ritual was eloquent. It was not meaningless magic. Wenham reminds us that in the ancient world, these rituals were

[11] Wenham (1981), pp. 79–85; M. Weinfeld, 'Ordeal of jealousy', *Encyclopaedia Judaica* XII, pp. 1448–1449, T. S. Frymer, 'Ordeal, judicial', *Interpreter's Dictionary of the Bible* Supplementary Volume (1976), pp. 638–640. The practice of drinking a prepared liquid has parallels in both the eighteenth-century BC Mari texts and in Hittite texts.
[12] Philip, p. 77.   [13] Fretheim, p. 115.

valuable visual demonstrations of divine truth. They were the 'television' presentations of the ancient world, just as prophecy was the 'radio' communication. With some exceptions, the prophet relied mainly on the voice, while the priest engaged in visual presentations of spiritual and moral truth. The required drink was composed of *holy water* and *dust* from the floor of the Tent of Meeting. Its two ingredients came from a holy place. Everything depended on whether the woman was holy (guiltless) or unholy (guilty). If the holy met the unholy, judgment was inevitable. If the holy met the guiltless, harmony prevailed. The loosening of the woman's hair (18) was an outward sign of inward remorse. The scrolls' written curses were brought into contact with the bitter water; the accused person imbibed the curses, which would become active if she was guilty but would prove harmless if she was innocent.

Secondly, the requirement was safe. Drinking this prepared water cannot be compared with ordeal patterns prevalent at the time, in which the accused person was required to immerse a hand in boiling water or grasp a red-hot instrument; physical damage was then inevitable.

Thirdly, the provision was just. The more common 'trial by ordeal' began with the cruel assumption that the accused person was guilty until proved innocent by the unlikely event that that hand submerged in boiling water was not scalded. Among the Israelite people, this drinking provision was non-judgmental. It made no assumptions whatever about the moral status of the accused woman.

Fourthly, the result was delayed. In these other instances, immediate burns were 'undeniable proof of guilt', but the provision described here was not expected to have an immediate effect. There was purpose in the ensuing delay. As both husband and wife waited for any physical response to the drink, there was time for penitence on the part of an offending wife, or an acknowledgment of unfounded jealousy on the part of the aggrieved husband.

Fifthly, the procedure was controlled. The demand that the accused woman be brought before God's representative, the priest, guarded against the danger that the suspicious and jealous husband might take matters into his own hands. It took the accusations beyond the narrow confines of the unhappy home into the presence of an objective judge, where some measure of pastoral care could be exercised by a godly man fully in control of the various cultic requirements.

Sixthly, the message was evident. These public measures underlined the sacredness of the marriage bond. The Hebrew people were not to treat their marriage commitments casually. Adultery was a serious offence; transgressors were breaking their vows of commitment to a covenant-keeping God and their promises to a life partner.

In our own time, marriage is casually dismissed as an outdated social convention. In most western and northern European countries cohabitation has eclipsed marriage as the marker of first partnerships. The estimated number of cohabiting couples in England and Wales in 1996 was 1.56 million, a number projected to rise to nearly three million by 2021. Children who experience parental divorce are hesitant about committing themselves in marriage and more prone to cohabiting partnerships.[14] In the western world, it is undeniable that widespread marriage break-down and the consequent increase in divorce are having serious psychological repercussions in the lives of innocent children.

The element of unfaithfulness figures prominently in both the second (5–10) and third (11–31) regulations. The moral offender is *unfaithful to the* LORD (5), and the accused wife is either *unfaithful* (12) to her husband or, at least, accused of such misconduct. These provisions need to be set in the context of Israel's doctrine of a faithful God, who always remains true to his covenant people. He has made an agreement (like a marriage vow) with Israel but, all too often, his people have gone after other lovers and been *unfaithful* to him. If God is holy, his people must also keep their camp free from defiling influences (1–5). If God is righteous, any form of moral injustice or unethical behaviour is an offence to him. God's people must also be just. If God is faithful, any unfaithfulness on their part, either in the wider community (6–10) or within the intimacies of marriage (11–31), is unacceptable to a God who never breaks his promises.

---

[14] Kathleen Kiernan, 'Cohabitation in Western Europe', *Population Trends*, Summer 1999 (London: The Stationery Office), pp. 25–32; Chris Shaw and John Haskey, 'New estimates and projections of the population cohabiting in England and Wales', *Population Trends*, Spring 1999 (London: The Stationery Office), pp. 7–22.

6:1–21
4. Short-term voluntary service

Priests and Levites were conscripts. It is refreshing now to read a passage that makes room for the volunteer, any *man or woman* (2) who wishes to offer time and service to God for whatever purposes he or she may determine.

Here is an episode in the life of people who wanted to express their love for God and gratitude to him in practical terms. The provisions governing the vow of a *Nazirite* (from *nāzar*, to be separated or consecrated) are found only in this chapter, but this vow came to have special importance in the spiritual life of God's people both within the biblical period and later. The Nazirite was separated to the Lord, from the world and for the work.

Separated to the Lord

Six features emerge in this description concerning the nature of the vow.

First, it was unique. It is described as *a special vow* (2). There was no other provision in Israel quite like it. Some of its individual characteristics feature in different contexts elsewhere in the Old Testament. For example, the prohibition about contact with a dead body applied to everyone in the camp (5:2; 19:11–22). The priests were not to shave their heads and were not allowed to drink wine if they were serving in the tabernacle,[1] but, although forbidden to have contact with a corpse, they were allowed to touch the body of a close relative who had died.[2] The Recabites consistently refused to drink wine,[3] and Jeremiah was not permitted to attend a funeral,[4] yet nowhere else are these stipulations brought together as in the vows of a committed Nazirite.

Secondly, it was voluntary. *If a man or woman wants to make a*

---

[1] Lev. 21:5; 10:9.   [2] Lev. 21:1–4.   [3] Jer. 35:1–7.   [4] Jer. 16:5.

special vow (2), they can, but, by contrast with the earlier regulations concerning priests and Levites, there was no obligation to do so.

Thirdly, the vow was personal. Individuals of either sex (*man or woman*), from any tribe and at any time, could give themselves to the Lord for this ministry, perhaps responding to an inward sense of 'call', possibly as an expression of gratitude for some immense mercy received, or perhaps to express a new-found commitment or a personal desire to live closer to God.

Fourthly, the vow was public. Everybody could see that those who entered into it had deliberately let their hair grow, had adopted new eating and drinking habits, and could not share in the normal ceremonies associated with the death of a family member. This act of personal commitment became a valuable visual aid, reminding people of God's prior claim on human life. These Nazirite provisions say something to contemporary Christians about the consistency of our witness and the unbiblical nature and spiritual dangers of secret discipleship.

Fifthly, the vow was costly. *He must be holy until the period of his separation to the LORD is over* (5). The promises the person made prohibited attendance at festivities or funerals, so that *Even if his own father or mother or brother or sister dies, he must not make himself ceremonially unclean* (7). The decision to become a Nazirite was not taken casually or lightly; its obligations made stringent demands on any man or woman who decided to become *consecrated to the LORD* (8). It reminds us that those who surrender themselves to Christ recognize that there is a price to pay.[5]

In normal circumstances, sixthly, the vow was temporary. Provision is made for the time *when the period of his separation is over* (13). In some cases, the vow was expressed in lifelong devotion, as in the case of Samuel and as was intended in the life of Samson,[6] but normally the vow was for a specific period. The idea is similar to the decision of people today to offer themselves for voluntary service, a 'year out' either at home or overseas. Opportunities exist in today's world, not simply for the young but for more experienced people who have recently retired or accepted redundancy. Many have given voluntary service to missionary societies and to churches at home, using their skills as contemporary Nazirites, and the church throughout the world is grateful for their dedicated ministry.

[5] Luke 14:25–33.   [6] 1 Sam. 1:11; Judg. 13:4–7.

Separated from the world

The three provisions that accompanied the vow are interesting. It is appropriate to reflect on their significance in the Israelite community and to ask how these features may suggest parallels to Christian witness in today's world. The presence of these Nazirites was a frequent reminder to God's people of their nature, purpose and destiny; they were a pilgrim, witnessing and holy people.

Continuous pilgrimage

They *must abstain from wine and other fermented drink* and *not eat anything that comes from the grapevine, not even the seeds or skins* (3–4). It was not just wine that was forbidden but even *grapes or raisins*. It took a full three years or more for the vine to become established and fruit-bearing, so the vineyard symbolized perm-anent settlement in the land. Jeremiah maintained that, contrasted with his people's later apostasy, the wilderness years were marked by devotion, like the love of a bride. The desert was 'a land not sown'.[7] In those years Israel had to rely upon God, but once they settled in the land they inherited vineyards they did not plant,[8] and came to rely on economic assets, mineral resources and material benefits[9] rather than on the God who had generously provided them.

When the Nazirites refused anything from the vineyard, then, they affirmed their commitment to live as people destined for a better land. The vineyard symbolized the settled life, whereas this world was not their home. This pilgrimage theme is as important in the New Testament as in the Old. Christians have a better and imperishable destination, 'the city that is to come'.[10]

Distinctive testimony

The most unusual outward evidence of the Nazirite vow was the prohibition regarding the cutting of hair: *no razor may be used on his head ... he must let the hair of his head grow long* (5).[11] This aspect of the vow provided the Israelite community with visible evidence that there were people among them willing to offer them-selves entirely to the Lord. Allowing the hair to grow long was hardly distinctive for the women who took the vow, but for men it was undeniable evidence that they were *consecrated to the* LORD.

---

[7] Jer. 2:1–3.   [8] Deut. 6:11.   [9] Deut. 8:7–9.
[10] Heb. 13:14; 11:8–10, 13–16; 1 Pet. 1:1; 2:11.   [11] Judg. 16:17–22.

While they wore this 'most visible badge',[12] everybody knew that there was someone in the community who believed that God mattered most. Here is another feature that has resonances in the New Testament picture of the Christian life. Every believer is an evident witness,[13] testifying to the transforming reality of new life in Christ.

Costly holiness

The prohibition, *he must not go near a dead body* (6), specifically mentioning his own family (7), illustrates the price paid by those who voluntarily took this vow. Contact with the dead was, as we have seen (5:1–4), a potential hazard in the camp, and here the same phrase is used as earlier (5:2), describing physical contact with a corpse as *ceremonially unclean*. Here, the concern is Israel's testimony to God's unique nature as 'the living God',[14] the God who creates, imparts, sustains and controls all life. With their long hair, the Nazirites were a conspicuous testimony to God's indwelling life in the community, and so must not be in contact with those who were no longer living. This prohibition was so important that it is underlined in two ways, in regard to both family (7) and sudden (9) death.

To be forbidden direct contact with one's own family in a time of bereavement witnessed to the community that God's word must always be honoured and obeyed, whatever its cost in personal relationships. It reminds the modern Christian of the words of Jesus about putting the kingdom first in matters of relationships.[15]

This outward testimony to the living God was so crucial that if the Nazirite came into contact with a dead body accidentally (9–12), the vow was immediately annulled. The renewal procedure involved the presentation of a costly sacrifice (12), underlining the seriousness of the defilement. The true Nazirite must be an unspoilt witness to the presence of the living God.

Separated for the work

The closing verses concentrate on the correct procedure when the period of separation was terminated (13–21). Once again, the required ceremony testifies to the votary's public witness (*He is to be brought to the entrance to the Tent of Meeting*, 13), costly sacrifice (*There he is to present his offerings to the LORD*, 14) and

---

[12] Ashley, p. 143.   [13] Acts 1:8.   [14] 1 Kgs. 17:1.
[15] Mark 10:29–30; Luke 14:26–27.

total surrender: the Nazirite must shave off *the hair of his dedication* (19). The hair, which had symbolized total dedication, was to be presented as an offering to the Lord. The Nazirite had kept this period of consecration not as an act of self-display or to please the spiritual leaders of the community, but as a personal token of surrender to the Lord. That commitment was symbolized in the offering of the hair, the 'crown' (*nēzer*) of the vow. It was a symbolic way of saying that this whole process of Nazirite dedication, separation and service has been an offering to the Lord.

One naturally asks how these Nazirites functioned within the life of Israel. Did the vow promote any practical or pastoral service within these communities? The vow testified to three spiritual realities as relevant in our own day as when these regulations were first given: honouring God, denying self and serving others.

First, Nazirites took the vow because they desired to honour God. It was a public affirmation of loyalty and devotion to the Lord, who had given them life and enriched them totally beyond their deserving. When he had so generously 'crowned' them with innumerable blessings, they were right to offer themselves to him as their grateful response.

Secondly, the vow was an opportunity for self-denial. It affected their personal preferences, physical appearance, family conventions, social values and religious convictions. During that period of separation, they consciously denied themselves some of the things that would normally characterize their everyday life. Jesus taught that self-denial is the essential badge of authentic discipleship.[16]

We do not know exactly how Nazirites were used because most of the relevant references in Scripture refer to outstanding personalities, such as Manoah's wife, Samson, Samuel, John the Baptist and the apostle Paul.[17] The fact that these people were, in diverse ways, used by God to enrich the lives of others, suggests that Nazirites were not religious freaks, bizarre isolationists or social dropouts, but people whose personal surrender was expressed in practical service to others.

Manoah's wife is a model of exemplary Nazirite parenthood,[18] a reminder that those who bring up families in ways that honour God are of inestimable worth in the life of any nation. Samson was destined for outstanding leadership, but made little attempt to accept the denials clearly expected of a Nazirite; yet in his brokenness and total dependence upon God he was used in the greatest possible act of self-denial.[19]

---

[16] Mark 8:34.
[17] Judg. 13:4, 7, 14; 13:5; 1 Sam. 1:11; Luke 1:15; Acts 18:18.
[18] Judg. 13:2–14.   [19] Judg. 16:21–30.

Samuel is a more striking example of a Nazirite who was a prophet,[20] intercessor[21] and judge,[22] and a commendable example of one who honoured God by building 'an altar ... to the LORD'[23] when others worshipped idols.[24] This 'man of God'[25] was in daily communion with his Lord,[26] a Nazirite who served God's people wholeheartedly during a crucial period of transition.

In New Testament times, John the Baptist was separated to the Lord from infancy and, like a devout Nazirite, would 'never take wine or other fermented drink'.[27] His Spirit-anointed prophetic ministry was used to bring thousands of God's people to repentance, and prepared the way for the coming of Christ.[28] Jesus himself testified that, in God's service across the centuries, nobody could equal this herald of truth.[29] A model of perfect humility,[30] he was a Nazirite whose consecration to the Lord transcended all others.

The apostle Paul appears to have taken a Nazirite vow or something remarkably like it.[31] His life, 'set apart for the gospel of God'[32] is a model of sacrificial service. Paul's offering of his hair at Cenchrea symbolized the offering of himself to God, illustrating the appeal he made to the Romans about the sacrifice of their bodies, 'holy and pleasing to God'.[33]

Before leaving this passage, we notice a serious warning regarding people in Old Testament times who tried to hinder Nazirites. In time of widespread spiritual disloyalty, God gave the eighth-century citizens of the northern kingdom distinctive role-models of total surrender by raising up Nazirites among their young men. Yet some of their ungodly contemporaries maliciously diverted these young people from their devotion and 'made the Nazirites drink wine'.[34] It was an act of sacrilegious rebellion by which they tried to bring godly youths down to the sordid level of their own depravity. Those who in any way obstruct the spiritual development of others[35] endanger themselves, lower the standards of the community and are accountable to a God who loves righteousness and hates wickedness.[36]

---

[20] 1 Sam. 3:10–14, 20.   [21] 1 Sam. 7:8–9.   [22] 1 Sam. 7:15–16.
[23] 1 Sam. 7:3–4, 12, 17.   [24] 1 Sam. 7:3–4.   [25] 1 Sam. 9:6–10.
[26] 1 Sam. 9:15–17, 27.   [27] Luke 1:15.   [28] Luke 1:16–17.   [29] Matt. 11:11.
[30] John 3:27–30.   [31] Acts 18:18.   [32] Rom. 1:1.   [33] Rom. 12:1–2.
[34] Amos 2:11–12.   [35] Mark 9:42; Luke 17:1–3.   [36] Heb. 1:9.

6:22–27
5. Inherited riches

The Aaronic blessing, the book's most familiar passage, has been on the lips of praying people across the centuries as they have sought the best of God's gifts for their families and friends.

The LORD *said to Moses, 'Tell Aaron and his sons, "This is how you are to bless the Israelites. Say to them:*

> ' " *'The* LORD *bless you*
> *and keep you;*
> *the* LORD *make his face shine upon you*
> *and be gracious to you;*
> *the* LORD *turn his face towards you*
> *and give you peace.' "*

So they will put my name on the Israelites, and I will bless them.'

A model of brilliant compression, its familiar words were repeatedly pronounced throughout the biblical period, became prominent in later Jewish worship and passed into the liturgy of the Christian church. The Elizabethan theologian Richard Hooker cited its superb words and the Lord's Prayer as authorities for the use of prepared prayers.[1] We consider its significance, artistry and message.

Its significance

This priestly declaration focuses on the blessing of God's people, a theme that dominates the biblical story from creation to consummation.[2] Some words in the Christian vocabulary tend to

---

[1] Richard Hooker, *Laws of Ecclesiastical Polity* (1594), V.xxvi.2.
[2] Gen. 1:22, 28; Rev. 20:6; 22:14.

be overworked, and 'blessing' is one of them. The term seems vague and ambiguous, defying precise definition. With the familiar 'God bless you', is the contemporary well-wisher saying anything more than, 'Hope everything goes well'? It meant something infinitely more than that to Israelite believers.[3] In their thought, blessing was 'a solemn, deliberate act through which specific and concrete advantages are conveyed'.[4] Wenham suggests that, just as our contemporaries long for success, Old Testament people yearned for blessing.[5] For them, the term was multichrome; what was in mind was explicit, precise, almost tangible.[6]

As these Israelite travellers were about to set out on their adventurous journey, nothing could have been of greater comfort than the guarantee that the unchanging God would bless them just as he had so evidently enriched their forebears.

Its artistry

This tersely expressed prayer is perfectly fashioned. Its three lines are presented within a beautifully phrased framework that introduces it (22–23) and then amplifies and concludes it (27). The three lines, in the Hebrew, contain an increasing number of words: 3, 5 and 7 respectively. There is a natural expansion in the use of syllables – 12, 14 and 16 – conveyed also by the increasing use of consonants – 15, 20 and 25 – building up a heightening awareness of divine generosity. This gradual escalation conveys in literary form the sense of God's multiplying and expanding gifts.

Its message

Cast in a form to be used by *Aaron and his sons*,[7] the words express confident proclamation. Rather than vocalize what they want, they expound what God gives. Giving eloquent voice to the people's longings, they confirm the Lord's benevolence. This divine declaration expounds the facets of divine blessing these people need as they leave for their journey across a vast, inhospitable wilderness. Spectacular dimensions of the divine nature are itemized in this memorable benediction, assuring the travellers of their spiritual wealth.

[3] Ruth 2:4, 20.
[4] Harry Mowvley, 'The concept and content of "blessing" in the Old Testament', *Bible Translator* 16 (1965), p. 75.
[5] G. J. Wenham, *Genesis 1 – 15*, Word Biblical Commentary (Waco, TX: Word, 1987), p. 24.
[6] See the range of divine blessings defined in Lev. 26:3–13; Deut. 28:1–14.
[7] Lev. 9:22; Deut. 21:5; and also Levites, Deut. 10:8.

Life's choicest gifts come only from God

He alone is the generous Giver. '*The* LORD *bless you …*' Though the priests pronounced the blessing, they could not bestow it. They were simply the designated heralds of these spiritual realities. The Lord alone is the donor and benefactor, a truth not only declared by the threefold utterance of the divine name but emphasized by the concluding assertion, '*I will bless them.*'

In a consumerist culture, people no longer look to God as the source of life's best gifts. Our neighbours adore their deified alternatives: pleasure, possessions, popularity, sex, self. One of the world's biggest advertising agencies claims that brands 'are the new religion. People turn to them for meaning.' The most successful brands are those that stand 'not just for quality and reliability but for a set of beliefs that they refuse to compromise'.[8] Scripture asserts that God alone is the source of our lasting satisfaction and fulfilment.[9] Alluring substitutes are flimsy commodities, doomed to disappoint the millions who clutch at them.

Erroneous notions about the source of blessing are contradicted by that triple assertion, '*the* LORD *bless you*', not the idolatrous gods of your pagan neighbours,[10] or the religious antics of the beguiling necromancer, or the pietistic acts of the determined do-gooder, the self-righteous moralist or even the benevolent Israelite priest. It is the Lord who blesses, no-one else.

He enriches the corporate life of his people

The literary framework of the benediction (22–23, 27) is in the plural, providing a community reference for this divine proclamation. It is *the Israelites* (23, 27) who are here given the assurance, '*I will bless them*' (27). As the priests spoke, the desert travellers received this irrevocable guarantee that the Lord would look after them as a people. They had already proved his goodness in blessing them with financial resources, physical protection, spiritual confidence, sufficient water, daily food, military success, pastoral support and divine instruction.[11] This declaration of blessing provided such assurance at the beginning of the journey. As their long travels drew to a close, the Lord's continuing blessing was sovereignly conveyed both to the old generation and to the new through the inspired words of a mercenary, pagan soothsayer (22:12; 23:11, 20; 24:9).

[8] *Financial Times*, 1 March 2001.   [9] Is. 55:1–2.   [10] Ps. 115:4–8, 12–15.
[11] Exod. 12:36; 14:19–31; 15:22–27; 17:1–7; 16:1–36; 17:8–15; 18:13–26; 19:1 – 31:18; 34:1–28.

He meets the specific needs of dependent individuals

Although the framework is in the plural, the words of the benediction itself (24–26) are in the singular. '*The LORD bless you*', that is, every single Israelite. Surrounded by thousands of other pilgrims, individuals might feel lost in the vast crowd. With such a deliberate, repeated emphasis on the personal nature of these blessings, these travellers had no reason to doubt the concern of a loving God for each one of them.

His multichrome gifts are innumerable and assured

'*The LORD bless you.*' To the Hebrew mind 'blessing' was certain and specific, a vast store of priceless gifts money could never buy. It included such treasures as human love, the gift of children, the joys of family life, the delight of home and the security of abundant harvests.[12] They did not merit the immeasurable expansiveness of the divine bounty, but their needs were supplied on the basis of his matchless generosity, not as a reward for their unswerving devotion.

He is our reliable guardian in difficult times

'*The LORD ... keep you.*' He was their omnipotent defender. The way ahead was fraught with danger, but while they waited at Sinai God guaranteed their protection: 'See, I am sending an angel ahead of you to *guard* you along the way',[13] the same word as *keep* in this blessing to a fearful people. It is the word Joshua used, when he urged his contemporaries to remember how the Lord alone had been their unfailing keeper: 'He *protected* us [the same word] on our entire journey and among all the nations through which we travelled.'[14]

He delights in his personal relationship with us

'*... the LORD make his face shine upon you.*' The shining face indicated supreme pleasure. Identical words were frequently found on the lips of Israel's psalmists as they yearned for intimate communion with God.[15]

One Israelite in the camp knew about God's radiant face from personal experience. As Moses communed with God during their stay at Sinai, he frequently emerged from the divine presence with

[12] Gen. 9:1; 17:6; 28:3; 41:52; Exod. 1:7; Lev. 26:9.   [13] Exod. 23:20.
[14] Josh. 24:17.   [15] Ps. 31:16.

the divine glory reflected on his own face. The Israelites 'saw that his face was radiant'.[16] This priestly benediction anticipates the time when not only Moses but all who receive God's blessing will know the 'shining face' of God's approval, experience his presence and reflect his radiance[17] in their everyday lives.

Knowing our frailty, he promises to forgive our sins

'... the LORD ... be gracious to you.' That word gracious recalls the moment when, only months before, a man of prayer had pleaded with God for the forgiveness his people desperately needed. They had offended the Lord in the golden-calf apostasy, but as Moses spent time on the mountaintop, speaking with God 'face to face', 'the LORD came down in the cloud ... and proclaimed his name ... "the compassionate and gracious [same word] God, slow to anger, abounding in love"'.[18] It was at this time that the face of Moses shone as he emerged from the divine presence with this promise of the people's forgiveness.

Moses' own brother was the offending leader at the heart of the idolatrous rebellion. Now, here he is, a forgiven man, proclaiming to others in these majestic words the abundant mercy of a forgiving God who would not hold that enormous wickedness (or any other) against them.

His guaranteed presence challenges our unworthy standards

To discern the precise meaning of the positive turn his face towards, perhaps we need to reflect on its negative, 'to turn the face away', to 'hide' the face or to set the face against someone.[19] In other words, this second mention of God's face may have moral connotations. The image, frequently employed by Israel's later prophets, provokes the serious question: is God's smiling face towards me or have I displeased him? God had turned his face approvingly toward Moses[20] just as he had set his face resolutely against those who disobeyed him. Yet even those who have grieved him can be completely, immediately and irrevocably forgiven if they will turn from their sins. John Donne expressed it perfectly:

> Though thou with clouds of anger do disguise
> Thy face; yet through that maske I know those eyes,

[16] Exod. 34:29–35.   [17] Ps. 34:5.   [18] Exod. 34:5–6.
[19] Ezek. 7:22; 39:23; 25:2; 28:21.   [20] Exod. 33:11.

Which, though they turne away sometimes,
They never will despise.[21]

During his difficult ministry in the wilderness Moses often looked into the changeable faces of his contemporaries, but his priority was to ensure that the Lord's face was turned approvingly towards him. If he was pleasing God, little else mattered.

His innumerable blessings include deep inward fulfilment

'... the LORD ... give you peace.' Just as this priestly affirmation opened with a comprehensive term (bless), so it concludes with another Hebrew word (šālôm) that conveys a wide range of meanings – not only health and prosperity but also well-being and inner tranquillity, the serenity that comes from the assurance that God knows and supplies all that is necessary for life's journey. That Hebrew word is from a root that means 'perfect' or 'whole'; it is used to describe perfect weights.[22] Šālôm meant 'wholeness'; it embraced a wide range of countless gifts and rich provisions. Thousands of our contemporaries have material benefits and financial security, but their unfilled hands reach out for more; they lack contentment, fulfilment and šālôm.

The divine ownership ensures our constant care

The benediction's conclusion guarantees that peace: 'So they will put my name on the Israelites, and I will bless them.' To put one's name upon something was to give it the distinctive stamp or mark of ownership.[23] The Lord had put his name upon the Israelite people as their bountiful giver (24a), strong protector (24b), faithful friend (25a), forgiving lover (25b), reliable partner (26a), generous provider (26b) and unique owner (27). God's people were his treasured possession[24] and he had resolved to meet their every need.

As the Israelite priest proclaimed this blessing to the people, the entire community would be sustained by these truths and individual worshippers encouraged. Through this majestic public declaration, the doubter was challenged, the anxious calmed, the offender reminded of assured forgiveness, and the believer fortified.

---

[21] John Donne (c. 1572–1631), 'A Hymn to Christ, at the author's last going into Germany'.
[22] Deut. 25:15.   [23] Deut. 12:5; Jer. 7:10.
[24] Exod. 19:5; Deut. 7:6; 14:2; Ps. 135:4; Mal. 3:17; Titus 2:14; 1 Pet. 2:9.

7:1–89
6. Giving and receiving the best

Numbers 7, which is the longest chapter in the Bible apart from Psalm 119, describes a unique event in the history of Israel. During a twelve-day festival, gifts were brought to be *used in the work at the Tent of Meeting* (4). Each day a different tribe's gifts were presented by its designated leader; there was no variation whatever either in the gifts they offered or in the literary formula used to describe their offerings. Those who brought such gifts *for the dedication of the altar* (11) were the same men who had been responsible for the census (1:5–16; cf. 2:3–31). A list of all the gifts is provided (7:84–88), and a concluding verse focuses on the place where Moses met with God (89).

Although this extended passage is little more than a record of sacrificial offerings, it is far more than an example of biblical accountancy. As with earlier and later lists in this book, some key biblical themes are presented with unmistakable clarity.

The grace of giving

Giving is a crucial dimension of worship. In worshipping God we literally acknowledge his worth, and we do that not just vocally in words and song, thanksgiving and praise, but also by tangible gifts for his work and witness.

Some Israelites offered gifts they had made. *They brought as their gifts before the LORD six covered carts and twelve oxen – an ox from each leader and a cart from every two* (3). In each case, two tribes joined together in the exercise, offering their skills as designers, carpenters, joiners, wheelwrights and metalworkers to produce well-made waggons to convey the heavy tabernacle materials in their long journey across the desert. These leaders brought other gifts that had been manufactured by tribal craftsmen: *one silver plate ... one silver sprinkling bowl ... one gold dish*

(13–14, *et passim*). Skilled metalworkers shaped these valuable utensils, and perfume-makers prepared incense (14) used to express the adoration and prayers of the Lord's people – a reminder that we can bring our distinctive skills to the Lord by offering the best we possibly can.

Some offered animals that God had created – oxen from each tribe – to pull these carts along the wilderness highway. With the wood and metal that God had provided, skilled craftsmen could make their carts; but nobody could make an ox to pull the cart, or the other animals offered by each tribe in daily succession: *one young bull, one ram and one male lamb ... one male goat ... two oxen, five rams, five male goats and five male lambs a year old* (15–17, *et passim*). Only their Creator could make these creatures, so the people were offering to him that which he had already given to them – an essential dimension in the biblical doctrine of giving.

Some brought cereals that God had given: *fine flour mixed with oil as a grain offering* (13). God provided the ability to grow corn and to grind it into fine flour. He had made the olive trees, but the people prepared the oil. Once again, they were giving part of his creation back to him in grateful recognition of his abundant and undeserved generosity. A recent United Nations report says that, in a time of unprecedented plenty, 800 million of our neighbours do not receive enough to eat.[1] In a global village one child dies of hunger every eight seconds. Our responsibility is to offer regularly to the Lord a proportion of what he has given to us, gifts that can be used by relief agencies to meet basic human needs in other parts of our world.

The privilege of meeting

The presentation of these gifts was to service the work of the tabernacle. The *Tent of Meeting* (4), carrying 'a sense of meeting by appointment',[2] reminded them that communion with God was their highest priority. The gifts were for the *grain ... burnt ... sin ... fellowship* offerings (13–17, *et passim*), God's provision for communion with him. The concluding verse tells us that Moses *entered the Tent of Meeting to speak with the* LORD (89); the purpose of the gifts was infinitely more important than their size. The most expensive sacrifice was of little worth if it did not

---

[1] *The State of Food Insecurity in the World, 2000* (Rome: Food and Agriculture Organization of the United Nations, 2nd ed., 2000).
[2] Riggans, p. 6.

express total devotion to God. At later times in their history, the Lord became wearied by meaningless, repetitive sacrifices.[3]

Reference to the *tabernacle* or *Tent of Meeting* (1, 3, 4, 89) reminds us that meeting with God is more important than working for God. All our dutiful service, like the making of the Israelites' gifts, is valueless if we do not take time to meet with God on a regular basis. In our highly subjective age, the discipline of a daily meeting with God has become unpopular, occasionally dismissed as legalistic baggage that can be discarded without loss. Yet Jesus regarded his daily meeting with God as an essential dimension of his spiritual life. His followers can hardly dismiss as optional that which he considered vital.[4] During the last century's East African revival, Christians living in narrowly confined homes made their way each day to their own small clearing in the surrounding bush, gradually wearing a path to the place where they met with God. If anyone neglected this daily meeting, it would soon become evident; a fellow believer would lovingly say, 'There is grass on your path, my brother.'

Loving takes precedence over giving. Before the risen Christ commissioned Peter for pastoral service, he made sure that his under-shepherd acknowledged the priority of loving.[5] The apostle Paul told the Corinthian believers that even if they gave all their material possesions to the poor and surrendered their bodies in martyrdom, they would 'gain nothing' if they lacked love.[6] Love matters most.

The responsibility of listening

At the close of this account of community giving, interest is focused on a solitary individual. When *Moses entered the Tent of Meeting to speak with the* LORD, *he heard the voice speaking to him ...* (89). It was the direct fulfilment of God's earlier promise to Israel's leader that 'there ... between the two cherubim that are over the ark of the Testimony, I will meet with you and give you all my commands for the Israelites'.[7]

Moses had so much to talk to God about and, as the long journey progressed, each new day brought its fresh load of pastoral concerns, unreasonable complaints, arrogant accusations. Yet, desperate as he was to talk about his problems, Moses was overwhelmed with a priority greater than speaking. The Tent of Meeting became the

---

[3] Is. 1:11–17; Amos 4:4–5; 5:21–25; 8:10; Hos. 6:6; Mic. 6:6–8.
[4] Luke 4:42; 5:16; 6:12; 9:18; 11:1; 21:37; 22:39.   [5] John 21:15–17.
[6] 1 Cor. 13:3; cf. Rev. 2:1–4.
[7] Exod. 25:22.

place of attentive listening. Moses *heard the voice ... And he spoke with him* (89).

The unfolding story of biblical revelation is the majestic saga not simply of a God who speaks but of humanity's response to the divine voice. The whole of Scripture is about people who were deaf to what God said or alert to what he said. Some familiar examples illustrate the primacy of the theme.

Samson, possibly the most famous Nazirite, was persistently deaf to what God was saying to him. If Samson had entered a private 'Tent of Meeting' and spent time with God, it could have been a different story. He would have been regularly taught about matters of spiritual importance, graciously guided in times of uncertainty and lovingly corrected when he failed. He was a promising youth but a doomed adult, gifted but unwise.[8] Other qualities are dwarfed when men and women persistently refuse to listen to what God is saying.

David is an example of someone occasionally deaf to the voice of God. Mighty exploits, inspired achievements and magnificent psalms all testify to occasions in his life when his ear was alert to what the Lord was saying to him. However, the best of people are not immune to the worst of sins.[9] One destructive sin followed hard on the heels of another as this physically strong but morally vulnerable man became deaf to the voice of God. It required a prophet with an effective story to capture his renewed attention and to trap him into acknowledging his sin. David was quick to recognize sin in others,[10] but slow to see it in himself. In earlier days, he had often heard God's voice and transmitted its message faithfully in songs that would enrich the people's worship for centuries, but hearing the voice in the past is no guarantee of victory in the present.

David's son, Solomon, was another gifted man who heard God's voice in his earlier days, but failed to continue that discipline of daily listening. His ear, once alert to the divine voice, became increasingly less attentive to what the Lord was saying. God had plainly said that the Hebrew people were not to enter into marriage alliances with their pagan neighbours.[11] Solomon knew that such a policy was spiritually disastrous, yet he implemented it. Although God had forbidden Solomon to follow other gods, Solomon did not keep the Lord's command.[12]

Perhaps the saddest biblical example of a believer's refusal to listen is the tragic event that closed the life of King Josiah. From his earliest years, the young king had attended carefully to God's

---

[8] Judg. 13:2–7, 24–25.   [9] 2 Sam. 11:1–27.   [10] 2 Sam. 12:5–6.
[11] Deut. 7:3.   [12] 1 Kgs. 11:1–10.

word,[13] yet, despite this rich example of attentive listening, Josiah glorified political strategies, following natural impulses rather than divine instructions, and failed to hear God's voice at the end of his life.[14] Past spirituality is an immense enrichment, but it offers no immunity to present dangers.[15]

In stark contrast to these men who were deaf to what God was saying, other characters in Scripture listened eagerly and responded obediently to the Lord's word. Samuel, Isaiah and Jeremiah[16] were of the calibre of Moses, who, though he *entered the Tent of Meeting to speak with the* LORD, discerned a greater need: he *heard the voice speaking to him* and the Lord *spoke with him* (89).

The necessity of cleansing

The divine voice addressed Moses *from between the two cherubim above the atonement cover on the ark of the Testimony* (89). The voice was heard in the place where sin was cleansed. Sin erodes our spiritual receptivity. Samson would have heard the voice of pardon if he had confessed his sin. It came to David[17] when he acknowledged his sin. The *atonement cover* was where the sacrificial blood was sprinkled on the day of atonement.[18] On that day all the sins of the people were pardoned by a compassionate yet holy God. Persistent iniquity isolated sinners from a holy God. The breach could be healed, the relationship restored and the stain eradicated only as a ransom was paid and the costly blood was shed. With the dramatic visual aid of their sacrificial system, the Israelite people were given objective assurance that their sins were washed away.[19]

Nothing is more important than cleansing. A successful life may be envied by others but is unacceptable to God while sin is unforgiven. When Moses entered the Tent of Meeting, he was aware that God was addressing him from the place where atonement ('making at one', from the Anglo-Saxon) was made for sinners. The shed blood on the *atonement cover* anticipated Christ's perfect, eternal and unique sacrifice which continually 'cleanses us from all sin'.[20]

The guarantee of blessing

As Moses *entered the Tent of Meeting* he was visibly reminded of four realities at the centre of Israel's faith. When Moses looked at the ark, he was encouraged to know that the Lord was something

---

[13] 2 Kgs. 22:13.   [14] 2 Chr. 35:20–24.   [15] 1 Cor. 10:12.
[16] 1 Sam. 3:4–20; Is. 6:8–13; Jer. 1:4–19.   [17] Ps. 51.   [18] Lev. 16:14.
[19] Is. 59:2; Heb. 9:22; Lev. 17:11.   [20] 1 John 1:7, RSV.

more than an arresting voice. That portable visual aid portrayed God as their king, lover, teacher and provider.

First, God was their king. The ark was regarded as God's throne, a truth vividly captured in their later writings. The *two cherubim* (89) formed the decorative furnishings for the place where the Lord 'sits enthroned between the cherubim'.[21] An uncertain future lay ahead of them, but their destiny was in the hands of a sovereign God, who ruled over the nations.

Yet, comforting as the assurance of divine sovereignty undoubtedly was, God's people were to think of him not as a remote ruler but as a present friend. This gold-covered box contained the two stone tablets on which were engraved the Ten Commandments, the loving covenant or agreement between God and his people. He had pledged himself to them with a love that could not be equalled and must not be usurped by other lovers of any kind. 'You shall have no other gods before me.'[22]

Consequently, God was their teacher. The stone tablets in the ark are a further reminder that God had spoken uniquely to them and they must obey his word.

Finally, God was their provider. The ark also contained a 'gold jar of manna',[23] recalling the pilgrims' dependence upon God for the provision of their daily food.[24]

These symbols were visible reminders of a God who rules, loves, trains and feeds his people. His people were safe in such firm, unfailing hands.

[21] Pss. 80:1; 99:1; 1 Sam. 4:4; 2 Sam. 6:2; 2 Kgs. 19:15; 1 Chr. 13:6; Is. 37:16.
[22] Exod. 20:3.   [23] Heb. 9:4; Exod. 16:32–33.
[24] Later in their history (Num. 17:10) the ark also contained 'Aaron's staff that had budded' (Heb. 9:4).

8:1–26
7. Israel's role models

When Moses went into the Tent of Meeting to listen to the voice of God (7:89), the Lord spoke with a specific message about the duties and consecration of those who served there. Uniquely set apart for work at the Tent, the priests and Levites were a permanent visual aid, illustrating the qualities God expects of all his servants.

The attentive communicator

Moses was to *Speak to Aaron* about the lighting arrangements in the holy place (1), responsibilities specifically and exclusively assigned to the priesthood. Even Moses could not undertake their tasks. His role was to hear God's word and then to transmit it accurately and faithfully to this desert community. Christian believers are also entrusted with a message to share eagerly with their contemporaries.[1] Preachers have a distinctive stewardship responsibility as reliable communicators of God's word; they are no more free to change, marginalize or ignore that word than Moses was. The contemporary church needs faithful stewards who will expound and apply Scripture, 'not the New Testament only, but the Old as well ... not just the passages which favour the preacher's particular prejudices, but those which do not'.[2]

The responsive listener

Aaron brought his total obedience to God's commands. *Aaron did so; he set up the lamps so that they faced forward ... just as the* LORD *commanded* (2–3). The obedience theme recurs throughout

---

[1] Acts 1:8; 2 Tim. 2:2.
[2] J. R. W. Stott, *The Preacher's Portrait* (London: Tyndale, 1961), p. 22.

this chapter (3, 4, 20, 22). Details of the lampstand's manufacture are repeated from Exodus,[3] its identical language emphasizing the eager response of God's servants in making everything *exactly like the pattern the* LORD *had shown Moses* (4).

This lampstand, with its branches, flowers and blossoms, was like an illuminated tree. It symbolized the nature of God as the giver of life (blossoming tree) and light (lamp), and its position in the holy place, as well as its manufacture, was a matter of some consequence. Its light shone brightly on the table of shewbread, a further visual aid: God faithfully provides for the needs of his people.

The cleansed instrument

The Lord continued to address Moses (5), moving from the responsiblities of the priests to the consecration of the Levites, their appointed helpers. The male members of Levi's tribe were to be set apart and made *ceremonially clean* (6) by the ritual of sprinkling, shaving and washing their bodies and clothes (7). These provisions symbolize the need for total cleansing for God's work, not simply outward ceremonial purification but inwardly. The sincere Levite recognized that these were times when iniquity marred his life, service and witness; he laid his hands on the *sin offering* and the *burnt offering, to make atonement* (12). The sin offering was for those occasions 'when anyone sins unintentionally and does what is forbidden',[4] while the grain offering[5] was a spontaneous gift, possibly expressing the Levite's gratitude for the cleansing God had promised and the privilege of service. The burnt offering, presented in its entirety, was a symbolic token of complete surrender.

To Christians, the message of these regulations hardly needs amplification. Defiled servants in the Lord's work deceive themselves, inflict irreparable harm on others and dishonour God. Peter confessed his sinfulness before responding to the call to serve.[6]

The living sacrifice

The Levites did not merely witness the offerings; they *were* the offerings, living sacrifices offered to God for his use: '*Aaron is to present the Levites before the* LORD *as a wave offering from the Israelites, so that they may be ready to do the work of the* LORD' (11, cf. 13, 15). When the offering was waved it symbolized its

---

[3] Exod. 25:37–40.   [4] Lev. 4:1.   [5] Lev. 2:1–16.   [6] Luke 5:8–11.

public, visible, total presentation to God, *given wholly* (16) to him. The Hebrew emphasizes their complete dedication by repeating the verb, literally 'given, given', earlier used to describe the Levites' wholehearted ministry to the priests (3:9). They were 'given wholly' to the priests in service (3:9) and to the Lord in surrender (8:16). Offering ourselves as living sacrifices is the highest, best, most acceptable and costliest form of Christian worship.[7]

Across the centuries women and men have given themselves wholly in sacrificial service. Inspired by Christ's example, responsive to his teaching and determined to pursue his will, they have 'died' to self-assertive ambitions. Adoniram Judson preached for five years before he baptized his first convert. During that time, he struggled with the Burmese language and produced a translation of the New Testament. He suffered severe family bereavements, imprisonment in ghastly conditions, torture and recurrent illness, but eventually saw the complete Bible translated into Burmese. Most of his children followed his example, becoming ministers, doctors or teachers; and, at the close of his life, over 7,000 committed believers were serving Christ in sixty-three churches. Burma (Myanmar) now has 4.5 million Christians, in a country hardly noted for religious freedom: 'if [a grain of wheat] dies, it produces many seeds'.[8]

The people's representative

The Levites were offered to God by the people. The whole *Israelite community* (9) were to *lay their hands on them* (10). Publicly, in *front of the Tent of Meeting* (9), they were *set ... apart* (14) by the laying on of hands, and so designated to serve as substitutes on behalf of the other tribes. Whenever they functioned as associates and partners with the priesthood, they were doing their work in the place of others.

They were a permanent visual aid, a daily reminder to God's people of their unique redemption, having been given *in place of the firstborn* (16). Whenever they were seen about the camp, their fellow pilgrims recalled the great event of Israel's deliverance from Egypt (17) when Egypt's firstborn were all slain and God's people alone were redeemed. That imagery of exodus and Passover was vividly recalled by Jesus when he met with his disciples for the last time,[9] and was treasured by New Testament writers, notably Paul, Peter and John.[10]

---

[7] Rom. 12:1–2.   [8] John 12:24.   [9] Luke 22:7, 8, 11, 13, 15.
[10] 1 Cor. 5:7; 1 Pet. 1:19; John 19:36.

The surrendered servant

This distinctive tribe of consecrated workers was the Lord's unique possession: *'the Levites will be mine'* (14), *'given wholly to me'* (16). *'I set them apart for myself'* (17). Every Christian is God's property[11] and those who work for him honour his total ownership of their lives – not a popular concept in a postmodern age when self-empowerment is more acceptable than self-surrender. Local bookshops have ample supplies of new titles on self-fulfilment, self-exploration and self-discovery, but little available on self-sacrifice. Contemporary believers are called to a radically different lifestyle, with Christ as their constant model and mentor.

The supportive partner

The Lord had *given the Levites as gifts to Aaron and his sons to do the work at the Tent of Meeting* (19). The Levite was to come alongside the busy priest and relieve him of some of those time-consuming tasks that could easily be undertaken by others. Every Christian minister and worker thanks God for such people. They are not the gifted, up-front evangelists preaching powerful and persuasive messages; they are the devoted people who personally invite their friends to the meetings. They are not the warmly appreciated pastors; they are the unsung individuals who unob-trusively visit the sick and lonely. They are not the outstanding preachers; they are the people who intercede for them every day.

When the apostle Paul described the various gifts the Lord gives to his church, he included 'those able to help others'.[12] Every church needs its dependable helpers, who, by prayer, example, service and love, strengthen its unity, extend its witness and enrich its ministry. Like the Old Testament Levites, they are not simply content to serve in subsidiary, supportive roles, but feel privileged to do so.

The service of these Levite assistants demanded both maturity and vitality. Levitical service could not begin until the man was twenty-five years of age, and he had to be prepared to retire from active duties at the age of fifty. In our culture such a man might justifiably be regarded as in his prime. The message of this stipula-tion is surely that God deserves the best.

Once the Levites reached fifty years of age, they could *assist their brothers* (26), though they were not permitted to perform the main tasks themselves. Women and men who have accepted early

---

[11] 1 Cor. 6:19–20; Rom. 14:7–8.   [12] 1 Cor. 12:28.

retirement or have reached the normal retirement age may undertake important tasks in the church at home and overseas. Missionary societies are grateful for volunteers willing to undertake short-term assignments to undergird the service of overworked partners who are serving Christ in other countries. In our home countries, the work of Christ could forge ahead if churches could count on teams of retired people undertaking vital tasks in ministry to the local community. Such men and women have a unique opportunity to *assist their brothers* in bringing their best to the work of Christ.

The moral guardian

The role of the Levites was to serve as a protective agent for the local community (1:51–54; 3:10, 38). They were the Tent's silent sentinels, on moral guard-duty, ensuring that God's word about the holiness of the place was not ignored, *so that no plague will strike the Israelites when they go near the sanctuary* (19) and so that 'wrath will not fall on the Israelite community' (1:53).

Every community needs its moral watchdogs, alert to the insidious encroachment of potentially dangerous and destructive influences. We need people who will write to broadcasting and television authorities about damaging programmes, who will not be afraid to contact local authorities and upholders of the law about the infringement of standards of conduct or unacceptable behaviour, pornography, drug abuse, the moral welfare of children and so on. Plagues infinitely more serious than anything that might strike Israel's encampments ravage our cities and towns. Unless the Lord's people act as salt and light in local communities,[13] the rapidly declining standards we see around us will degenerate even further, with chaotic consequences, especially for the innocent young.

Contemporary evil prospers in many places because moral mentors are lacking. The Levite was a protective buffer, standing between the unheeding people and their potential danger. Many unsuspecting Israelites may have been saved from death because a faithful Levite was in the right place at the right time. Our sadly depraved societies are in desperate need of spiritually alert and morally responsible guardians.

[13] Matt. 5:13–16.

9:1 – 10:10
8. Three-dimensional grace

These vivid records now focus on three important features in the life of the pilgrim community: their annual Passover festival (9:1–14), the daily appearance of the guiding cloud (9:15–23) and the occasional use of silver trumpets (10:1–10). The Israelite people were reminded of God's former mercies, his promised provision and their present resources.

Encouragement from the past (9:1–14)

The Israelites' first twelve months of freedom had witnessed the shattering extremes of divine revelation[1] and human rebellion.[2] Graciously forgiven and assured of the divine presence,[3] the moment came for them to recall their miraculous deliverance and keep the Passover for the first time since they left Egypt. The narrative relates some crucial aspects of the Lord's dealings with his people.

God communicated his word

The Lord took the initiative in calling his people to this Passover celebration: *Moses told the Israelites to celebrate the Passover, and they did so ... just as the LORD commanded Moses* (4–5).

This unadorned Passover narrative focuses on the central biblical themes of revelation and redemption. The people are responding to God's voice (*The LORD spoke*) in reminding one another of their unmerited deliverance (*celebrate the Passover*) from the tyranny of their oppressors. God transformed the lives of those enslaved Israelites when he unfolded his mind to Moses by

---

[1] Exod. 19:1 – 31:18.   [2] Exod. 32:1 – 33:6.   [3] Exod. 33:13–14, 19–20.

that flaming bush in the desert.[4] Listening to that divine voice in Scripture is every believer's rich privilege.

God displayed his power

This celebration was an unforgettable visual aid reminding them that, whatever hazards the future might hold, nothing was too hard for the Lord. During that first Passover night a year earlier he had identified their need, answered their prayers, vanquished their enemies and reversed their destiny. The sighs and tears of centuries were exchanged for the freedom and joy of a newfound deliverance. When Jesus shared a Passover meal with his disciples he was reminding them that the unique Passover Lamb would effect for them and for humankind a greater deliverance by far.

Hudson Taylor reminded his missionary colleagues that the Christian's response to daunting situations was best expressed in a terse phrase: 'Impossible? Difficult. Done!' Those words eloquently describe the Israelite people's experience of liberation. Humanly speaking, it was ridiculously impossible. As God began to work on the hardened Egyptian ruler, the situation became unquestionably difficult, but because the Lord was omnipotently at work it was miraculously done. Passover assured these pilgrims that the Lord who brought them out of one country could certainly bring them into another.

God manifested his holiness

During that year in the Sinai desert some important questions had arisen about Passover. What if someone in the camp had been caring for a dying relative, inevitably touching the body when the person died? Ceremonially unclean people could not be present at Passover. Must they forfeit the opportunity of keeping the festival and wait for a full year without its rich inspiration and stimulus to faith (6–7)?

There was no question of participating in a holy festival if they had *become unclean because of a dead body* (7). This reference to the possibility of offending their infinitely pure and righteous God has been anticipated in the previous chapters on several occasions (3:4,[5] 10; 8:19; 4:15, 19, 20; 5:1–4; 6:6–12). By these warnings, the Lord was reminding his people of 'the potential risk of mixing divine holiness and human sin'.[6]

The community's request for enlightenment about ceremonial

---

[4] Exod. 3:7–10.   [5] cf. Lev. 10:1–5.   [6] Olson (1996), p. 59.

uncleanness at Passover time indicates how alert they had become to the sin of disregarding the holiness of God. In an age like ours, where blasphemy is rife, where Christ's name is widely used as an uncouth expletive, and where few things are sacrosanct, Christians need to guard against anything that endangers their perception of God's holiness, Christ's uniqueness and the Holy Spirit's sensitivity. We can grieve the Holy Spirit in a variety of ways, infinitely more serious than ceremonial defilement. Such Old Testament provisions were symbolic of a greater need for inward purity.[7]

God revealed his will

Moses did not have the precise answer to the people's enquiry about ceremonial uncleanness at Passover time, but he knew where to obtain it: '*Wait until I find out what the* LORD *commands concerning you*' (8). This was not the only occasion in the book when Moses sought the mind of God on crucial community issues (15:32–36; 27:1–11; 36:1–12).[8] On five occasions,[9] this exemplary pastor and teacher showed the community that, whenever they were in doubt about life's decisions, they must seek the Lord.

The Lord gave Moses further answers to a number of other questions concerning the Passover. Israelites who had become ceremonially unclean and those who were away from home at Passover time were encouraged to keep the festival a month later. Conversely, the member of the community who was free to celebrate the Passover but deliberately chose not to do so *must be cut off from his people* and *bear the consequences of his sin* (13). We cannot be certain whether this meant exclusion from the community or the threat of death consequent upon the offender's no longer being under the protecting care of God. One thing is certain: by severe regulations such as these the pilgrims and their successors realized that they must not trivialize or marginalize God's word. By that uniquely revealed word men and women would live; to reject it consciously and intentionally was to invite God's wrath, the community's rejection and self-despair.

God demonstrated his love

The severity of the threat of exclusion facing the deliberate absentee, emphasizing God's holiness and wrath, is finely balanced with a provision illustrating the Lord's mercy and compassion.

---

[7] 1 John 1:9.   [8] Lev. 24:12.

[9] Wenham (1997), pp. 42–45, provides a helpful exposition of these examples of Israelite 'case law'.

73

God reminded his people that the *alien* (14) who had found a home within the Israelite community was welcome to join the Passover celebration if that person would do so *in accordance with its rules and regulations*. A year earlier the Lord had clearly told his people that aliens were permitted to share in the festival, enjoying the same privileges as the native-born Jew, but they must fulfil the same covenant demands of circumcision and total identification with the people of God.[10] This repeated provision is a further reminder of the Lord's love and generosity to a minority group.

Assurance for the future (9:15–23)

Necessary and helpful as it was to reflect on the past, the pilgrims must face the prospect of the future. On the very day the priests and Levites assembled their *Tent of the Testimony* (15), the symbolic cloud of God's presence descended, casting its huge shadow over it.

The cloud inspired their confidence in God. Despite their evident failings, he had promised to go with them[11] and here was a visible sign of his reliable presence. There were times when their hearts wilfully or carelessly turned away from him, but he did not remove the cloud: *That is how it continued to be* (16). He had promised in his firm agreement[12] that they could count on his unfailing companionship throughout their days. Day and night it was a continuing reassurance to the travellers and a serious warning to their enemies: God was with them.

At different times in their history, God lovingly provided his people with visible signs to confirm his word: a rainbow in the sky, a flaming bush in the desert of Midian, a gold-covered box for them to carry through the wilderness, and this overshadowing cloud; what Calvin called 'symbols of heavenly glory'.[13] Without their explanation in the Word of God, these symbols would be meaningless.[14] Best of all, God's people rejoice that in the incarnation, death, resurrection and ascension of Christ they have undeniable, visible evidence of God's love, holiness, power and sovereignty.

The cloud tested their dependence on God. The vast wilderness was unfamiliar territory, 'a land of deserts and rifts ... drought and darkness ... where no-one travels and no-one lives',[15] and there were lurking dangers. God knew the right days for them to move on and the best times to stay put. The cloud did not move every

---

[10] Exod. 12:48–49. [11] Exod. 33:14. [12] Exod. 34:5–11.
[13] Calvin, *Institutes* I.xi.3, trans. Henry Beveridge (London: James Clarke, 1955).
[14] Gen. 9:12–17; Exod. 3:1–12. [15] Jer. 2:6.

day; its presence demanded their constant attention: *Whenever the cloud lifted from above the Tent, the Israelites set out; wherever the cloud settled, the Israelites encamped* (17). By this objective revelation, the Israelite people discerned the Lord's directions for their journey. It required a good deal of trust. Sometimes they were permitted only a single night's rest (21), whereas at other times they could stay at their appointed campsite *a few days* (20), *a month or* even *a year* (22).

There were days when they could see that they were making progress, but at other times they may have been puzzled because nothing was happening. Why the tiresome delay? For most of us, at some time or another, life has its bewildering waiting times. The evidence of God's continuing care appears limited, even absent. The Puritans spoke about 'the soul's winter times', when everything appears cold, bleak and barren. We wish God would speak to us more clearly about why we are going through such dark days, when it is hard to hold on. But waiting times are not wasted times. When the guidance we look for is just not there, we must calmly renew our confidence in God; 'such a resolution can never go to hell with thee', said Thomas Goodwin.[16] There is some wise purpose in life's bleak experiences. God is still present. 'Moses approached the thick darkness where God was.'[17] In the desolate years of late-seventeenth-century persecution, John Flavel urged his contemporaries to 'exercise the faith of adherence when you have lost the faith of evidence.'[18]

The cloud demanded their obedience to God. The Lord does his part in providing them with the guiding cloud, but they must do theirs in responding to his directions: *At the LORD's command the Israelites set out, and at his command they encamped* (18). The narrative contains eight references to the Lord's orders and the Israelites' obedient response (18, 20, 23). If only they had maintained their teachable and compliant spirit! The story of Numbers is a perpetual warning against the danger of knowing what God demands but failing to do it.[19]

[16] T. Goodwin, 'A child of light walking in darkness', Direction VI, in *The Works of Thomas Goodwin* 3 (Edinburgh: James Nichol, 1861), p. 324.

[17] Exod. 20:21.

[18] J. Flavel, Sermon XXXIII, 'The fountain of life' (42 Sermons) in *The Works of John Flavel* (1820; London: Banner of Truth, 1968), p. 417.

[19] John 2:5.

Priorities in the present (10:1–10)

Once again, Israel's skilled craftsmen were to use their Spirit-inspired skills[20] with valuable metals, this time to make *two trumpets of hammered silver* (1). The message of the trumpets not only directs attention to practical aspects of their journey but reminds us of timeless truths about our commitment to Christ and his church.

Unite the believers

The trumpets were used *for calling the community together* (1). The clear blast of both trumpets sounding together sent its urgent message to every part of the extended camp; it was time to unify the people, and this brilliantly devised communcation aid was the best means of doing it. Numbers relates, at times, the honest story of the people's disunity. The psalmist recalled with gratitude those 'good and pleasant' times when 'brothers live together in unity', for, at such times, 'the LORD bestows his blessing',[21] while disunity damages the individual, disrupts the community and dishonours the Lord.

The unity of believers is given special prominence in New Testament Scripture. Jesus grieved on those occasions when his disciples were fractious and divided. More than once, unpleasant arguments arose among them regarding prominence in leadership,[22] and Jesus then insisted that humility is the key to harmony. The 'unity' theme became increasingly important in early Christian teaching and was frequently developed by the apostles in their letters.[23] When the unity of believers is threatened, the Lord is dishonoured, and their effectiveness is minimized and their witness discredited.

Mobilize the travellers

The silver trumpets were used *for having the camps set out* (2). With a sharp single blast of the trumpet *the tribes camping on the east* (5) began to move off, and at *the sounding of a second blast, the camps on the south* (6) were to start walking. *The blast* was *the signal for setting out*, and different signals were used for gathering and for mobilizing the travellers.

The New Testament frequently reminds us that we too are on a pilgrimage. Life is both a rich privilege and a priceless opportunity,

---

[20] Exod. 31:1–6.　　[21] Ps. 133:1, 3.　　[22] Luke 9:46; 22:24.
[23] Rom. 15:5–6; 1 Cor. 1:10–13; Eph. 4:3; Phil. 2:1–4; 4:2; Col. 3:13–15; James 4:1–3, 11; 1 Pet. 1:22; 3:8–9; 4:8–9; 1 John 2:9–11; 3:11–20; 2 John 5.

but this world is not our home. We are travellers, passing through our present life with a permanent destination constantly ahead. Scarcely anywhere is the truth put more majestically than in the letter to the Hebrews. Its first-century readers were undergoing trials and persecutions likely to increase in frequency and intensity, but they were encouraged by words of firm assurance: 'we are looking for the city that is to come'.[24] Abraham was their inspiring prototype; he lived 'like a stranger in a foreign country' but 'was looking forward to the city with foundations, whose architect and builder is God'.[25]

Hebrews is not alone in calling its readers to 'irrevocable commitment of life to a supernatural end';[26] other exhortations to a pilgrim lifestyle are found elsewhere in the New Testament.[27] Jesus taught his disciples to be more sure of being 'rich towards God' than of earthly securities, all doomed to perish.[28] James and John warn that living primarily for personal satisfaction or social approbation cannot win God's approval.[29] In the psalmist's inspiring words, believers 'have set their hearts on pilgrimage'.[30] Like the Israelites, they hear the morning trumpet call to another day's march towards an infinitely better home, 'a building from God, an eternal house in heaven'.[31]

The pilgrimage lifestyle is the modern believer's opportunity for unobtrusive witness. It challenges contemporary materialistic values, which offer alluring but perishing securities.

Assemble the leaders

There was an occasion when only one of the trumpets was to be used: when *the leaders – the heads of the clans of Israel* – were to assemble (4). This huge community could travel effectively only if it acknowledged the importance of designated leadership. Certain tasks were specifically allocated to chosen individuals, and that proper sense of order and responsibility must be recognized by everyone. For example, these trumpets were made by chosen craftsmen[32] and used only by the *sons of Aaron, the priests* (8).

Nobody can read this introductory section of the book without appreciating the crucial importance of good leadership (1:4–46; 3:1–4; 3:5 – 4:49; 10:14–27). These orderly plans for the community

---

[24] Heb. 13:14.   [25] Heb. 11:9–10, 13–16.
[26] W. Manson, *The Letter to the Hebrews* (London: Hodder and Stoughton, 1951), p. 85.
[27] 1 Pet. 1:1; 2:11.
[28] Luke 12:21; see 12:13–21, 33–34; 18:24–30; Matt. 6:19–21; cf. 1 Tim. 6:6–10, 17–19.
[29] James 4:4; 1 John 2:15–17.   [30] Ps. 84:5.   [31] 2 Cor. 5:1.   [32] Exod. 31:1–6.

were soon challenged by disgruntled Israelites who rejected the authority of Moses and his colleagues; some significant partners disgraced their calling, becoming envious of God's unique leader (12:1–16; 16:1–3). Dismissing the plea of gifted leaders such as Caleb and Joshua, the grumbling people wanted to choose someone else to take them back to Egypt, even preparing to stone Moses, Aaron, Caleb and Joshua (14:1–10).

In contrast to this, the apostle Paul insisted that local church leaders need to be respected and held 'in the highest regard'.[33] The letter to the Hebrews urged its readers to 'remember' their leaders and, valuing their example, to imitate their faith, stability and heroism.[34]

We live in highly divisive times in which warm-hearted unity is a rare commodity. Political parties are torn apart by discord and rivalry. The failure to work as a supportive team can mar the best of enterprises and, sadly, churches are no exception. No venture for God can expect to prosper if it lacks agreed leadership patterns. Israel's community life was seriously fractured during the early settlement years in Canaan: 'everyone did as he saw fit'.[35] Christians must heed the trumpet call to cooperative participation, following their leaders with loyalty and enthusiasm.

Rally the soldiers

A loud call on both trumpets would bring the troops together: '*When you go into battle in your own land against an enemy who is oppressing you, sound a blast on the trumpets*' (9). This urgent summons was designed not only to mobilize the soldiers but also to galvanize their spirits, inspiring the courageous and reassuring the fearful. All Israel's soldiers were conscripts rather than volunteers, and not every man of military-service age felt equipped for the task. Moses' address in Deuteronomy, delivered as God's people were about to enter the land, laid down precise rules concerning military service.[36]

Whatever the soldiers' frame of mind, valiant or diffident, all needed to be assured of the Lord's promised help; and that *blast on the trumpets* was to remind them that they were *remembered by the* LORD *... and rescued from their enemies* (9). The Lord had given his word that he would be alongside them in every conflict situation, assuring them that they would be *rescued* from their enemies. With the sound of that cheering trumpet blast, reminding

---

[33] 1 Thess. 5:12–13.   [34] Heb. 13:7.
[35] Judg. 21:25.   [36] Deut. 20:1–9.

them of the divine promise, they could go out to face the worst of oppressors.

We too are engaged in a fight. In the New Testament ideal of the Christian life the imagery of conflict is just as prominent as that of pilgrimage. Jesus told his followers that, if they committed their lives to him, there would be a price to pay.[37] The early Christians frequently emphasized that they were engaged in a costly struggle.[38] They were soldiers who had entered 'a career of conflict'.[39]

Gather the worshippers

The silver trumpets were also used at the Israelites' *times of rejoicing … appointed feasts and New Moon festivals* (10). On occasions of national thanksgiving they were to *sound the trumpets over their burnt offerings and fellowship offerings, and they* would *be a memorial for* them *before their God.*

A unified, clearly guided, well-mobilized, cooperative community, ready for conflict, was essential. But this was no ordinary crowd of travellers. They were God's people, and their regular *feasts* and *festivals* reminded them that they were special. There must be no rivals for their spiritual allegiance; their annual festivals would bring to their remembrance their sense of immense debt.

By their annual Passover festival (9:1–14) the Lord sought to ensure that Israel would never forget his unique act in delivering them from the cruel tyranny of their Egyptian aggressors. When they came out of Egypt (9:1) they were exuberantly grateful, singing their song of victorious celebration. But, before long, they were in danger of forgetting the miraculous thing God had done for them. Forgetfulness is a common peril. Obsessed by what we want, we devalue what we have. Moses later issued a salutary warning that, while revelling in the prosperity of Canaan, they should not forget the deprivations of Egypt.[40]

God regularly jolted their short memories by providing his people with three annual festivals, described[41] in the later part of the book (28:16 – 29:40). With vivid pictorial artistry, these feasts frequently reminded them of the innumerable blessings they had received at the hand of their generous God. Today's needs quickly

---

[37] Luke 9:23–26, 62; 12:49–53; 14:25–35; John 15:18–21; 16:1–4, 33.
[38] Acts 9:16; 14:22; 20:22–24, 28–31; Rom. 8:35–39; 2 Cor. 1:3–11; 11:23–33.
[39] C. K. Barrett, *A Commentary on the Epistle to the Romans* (London: A. and C. Black, 1957), p. 254. See Eph. 6:10–18; Phil. 2:25–30; 1 Tim. 1:18; 2 Tim. 2:1–4; 4:7.
[40] Deut. 6:12.
[41] Lev. 23:4–8, 15–21, 33–43; and later in Deut. 16:1–8, 9–12, 13–17.

obliterate the memory of yesterday's blessings. Thanksgiving is a vital element in the development of a Christian's communion with God, and quiet recollection is an essential dimension of development. Amid the pressures of an extraordinarily demanding life, the apostle Paul took time to do this, and made special mention of these moments of recollected mercy in his inspiring letters.[42] These blessings were too great to be hurriedly overlooked because of some pressing immediate need. Joseph Alleine, a minister imprisoned during the seventeenth century, reminded his Taunton congregation that, even in persecution, 'Your condition is never such but your mercies are infinitely greater.'[43]

The divine declaration that closes the book's first main section inspired the travellers' confidence: *I am the* LORD *your God* (10). Its familiar words had introduced their covenant obligations[44] and had been repeated throughout Leviticus.[45] This unique assertion recalled his power,[46] described his uniqueness,[47] and reiterated his promise.[48] As they left Sinai, this reassuring affirmation was a call to remember his faithfulness, reflect his character and trust his word.

---

[42] Rom. 1:8; 1 Cor. 1:4–5; 2 Cor. 1:11 (cf. Phil. 1:19); 2 Cor. 7:6–7; 8:16–24; Phil. 2:19–22, 25–30; Col. 1:7; Eph. 1:15–16; Col. 1:3–5; Phil. 1:3–5; 1 Thess. 1:7–8; 2 Thess. 1:3–7.

[43] Charles Stanford, *The Life of Joseph Alleine* (London: Jackson, Walford and Hodder, 1861), p. 317.

[44] Exod. 20:2.

[45] Lev. 11:44; 18:2, 4; 19:2, 3, 4, 10, 25; 19:31, 34, 36; 20:7–8, 24; 23:22, 43; 24:22; 25:17, 38, 55; 26:13, 44–45.

[46] Lev. 26:13.   [47] Lev. 11:44–45; 18:1–4, 30; 19:2.   [48] Lev. 20:24; 25:38.

PART 2. SETTING OUT
(10:11 – 12:16)

10:11–36
9. Sharing good things

The Israelite pilgrims are about to move off on their momentous pilgrimage. This part of the narrative emphasizes three important aspects of every believer's experience: doing what God says (11–28), recognizing that he uses other people to help us (29–32), and acknowledging our indebtedness to him (33–36).

Obeying orders (10:11–28)

The cloud that hovered over their camp gradually lifted and began to move in the direction of new territory. It must have been an exciting moment; their experience is an educative exercise for the Israelites and for us.

It tells us something about divine planning. With such a vast array of pilgrims, nothing had been left to mere human organization, tribal preferences or conflicting opinions. *They set out, this first time, at the LORD's command through Moses* (13). In Israel's marching orders, each tribe's exact placement in the column was spelt out with unmistakable precision. The Levite assistants were also told where they should be in the long caravan, carrying the portable tabernacle and its furnishings.

Meticulous organization was necessary if this massive crowd was to make its way across such inhospitable terrain. It was a hazardous enterprise in itself, without making it more difficult by tribal squabbles about preeminence, petty rivalries about advantageous positions in the column or innate jealousies about traditions and rights, preferences and privileges. People at the front were naturally vulnerable, fearing what might lie ahead. Those at the rear felt equally exposed, dreading the sudden attack of marauding bandits, quick to plunder their possessions. God had told them who must be first in the column, and which tribes should follow and in what sequence. They were to do what he said.

The story also says something about human responsibility. Although God gave the orders, the appointed people must see that his word was obeyed. The tribal leaders, named earlier in Numbers (1:4–16; 2:1–32; 7:10–83), now appear again. For the fourth time, the same names are mentioned. The identical data emphasize afresh the crucial importance of reliable leadership, the need for the people to respect, support and follow their leaders, and the dependence of the leaders themselves on the guidance of God. They were not 'heads of the clans' (1:16) by their own appointment. The Lord had assigned these specific responsibilities to them and they in turn must submit themselves totally to his authority.

By repeating the marching details in correct order, the artless narrative becomes an educative instrument: God has his own way of doing things and our part is to discern precisely what that is. They were responding to *the LORD's command through Moses* (13). As a model leader, he went out to tell the people what the Lord had shared with him (7:89).[1]

If we wish to know what God wants us to do in our lives, we too must listen for our orders as he speaks to us uniquely through Scripture. In contemporary life the popular emphasis is on subjective experience, not objective truth. In this context even some believers have marginalized the disciplinary aspects of the Christian life and dismissed any notion of a daily appointment with God as antiquated legalism. Such a view has been fashioned by the world around us. People in our postmodern culture reject any notion of external authority. Pleasing the self is all that matters. One popular American psychologist advises people experiencing a mid-life crisis not to concern themselves with moral standards, social conventions or cultural traditions, but to be motivated by their feelings.

> Let it happen to you ... You are moving away. Away from external valuations and accreditations in search of an inner validation. You are moving out of roles and into the self ... The inner custodian must be unseated from the controls. It is for each of us to find a course that is valid for our own reckoning ... to emerge reborn, authentically unique, with an enlarged capacity to love ourselves and embrace others.[2]

---

[1] Exod. 19:7–8.
[2] Gail Sheehy, *Passages: Predictable Crises of Adult Life* (New York: E. P. Dutton, 1974), p. 296.

In contrast to this, the apostle Paul knew that the 'self' is not uniformly good.[3] To exalt 'self' is to abandon God's standards, to marginalize Christ's example and to reject the Spirit's power; it opens the door to 'worldliness', moral chaos and spiritual degeneracy. 'Sin is self-deification.'[4] The Lord has given us so much to enjoy,[5] but we need his help to distinguish what is genuinely good from what is ultimately bad. Much that appears attractive is ultimately destructive. We can never find lasting satisfaction and fulfilment unless we listen to the divine voice in Scripture, and, in the power of God's Spirit, obey what he says.

Valuing partners (10:29–32)

Scripture is gloriously balanced. In the preceding verses, the strong emphasis on total obedience to God's commands might create the impression that all we need to do is to wait on him and to pursue his course for us, independent of other people's help, advice and support. The narrative's next item contradicts such insularity. Although Moses had the assurance of the guiding cloud (9:15–23) and the commanding voice (10:13), he still hoped for the support of human companions. His Midianite brother-in-law, Hobab, was now eager to return to his own people. During the preceding months Moses had often been impressed by Hobab's innate skills. He was well acquainted with the vagaries of the desert's weather patterns, the sudden force of contrary winds and the best places to pitch their tents for maximum protection. Hobab knew everything there was to know about the wilderness, and Moses longed to have alongside him a colleague with native skill and ability.

The Midianite rejected Moses' initial invitation, having no desire to move to a totally different country. Moses urged him to come, and Hobab eventually consented.[6] Although Moses was a towering and effective leader figure, he was also a mere man, with all the natural hesitancy and fears anyone would feel on the verge of such a massive enterprise. This story reveals 'his humanity in its weakness (needing help) and in its strength (seeking help)'.[7] He was eager for all the help he could get. The story relates Moses' persuasive testimony as he shared with Hobab what God had said and done.

First, it testifies to God's compassion. Moses was not scolded because he looked for human support as well as divine protection.

---

[3] Rom 7:14–20.
[4] J. R. W. Stott, in J. I. Packer and L. Wilkinson (eds.), *Alive to God: Studies in Spirituality presented to James Houston* (Downers Grove, IL: IVP, 1992), p. 111.
[5] 1 Tim. 6:17.   [6] Judg. 1:16; 4:11.   [7] Riggans, p. 79.

The Lord knows how much we need one another and fully understood when this spiritual giant of a man valued the assistance of a
partner. One needs to guard against a false dichotomy between
reliance on God and an appreciation of others. Each of us is the
Lord's gift to someone else.

Secondly, it testifies to God's providence. In the divine purposes,
Hobab was destined to be Moses' eyes in the unfamiliar terrain
that lay ahead. Many of Christianity's great leaders have been
unspeakably grateful for self-effacing people who have assisted
them in ministry to others.

Every student of the modern missionary movement knows of
the creative contribution of William Carey, who arrived in India in
1793 to begin a distinguished career in evangelism, Bible translation, literature enterprises and education. While he worked
tirelessly abroad, however, his invalid sister played a vital part
back at home. She was paralysed, apart from her right arm, and
bedridden for fifty years, yet from her bedroom she exercised a
ministry of compassionate partnership. She could not preach, travel
or translate, but she exercised her gift in the two ways open to her:
writing to him and praying for him. Propped up in bed, Mary
wrote informative and encouraging letters, interceding for her
brother's ministry thousands of miles away, and did so faithfully
and consistently for almost half a century.[8] Is there a Christian
worker, missionary, evangelist, pastor, Bible-class leader or children's worker somewhere we are meant to support, encourage and
pray for regularly?

Thirdly, it testifies to God's reliability. When Moses sought
Hobab's help, he began not by describing what the leader wanted
but by declaring what the Lord had promised: 'We are setting out
for the place about which the LORD said, "I will give it to you"'
(29). Moses wanted Hobab to recognize that God's word is
trustworthy; if he had made a promise, it would certainly be
fulfilled. Hobab recognized that the way ahead was littered with
hazards and that his skills would be tested to the limit. Moses'
words about God's promise assured the Midianite expert that the
project did not depend on his natural expertise and limited
resources. Israel's God had initiated it, and he would see it
through.

Fourthly, it testifies to God's generosity. Moses told Hobab
that, if he accompanied them, he would be well treated, 'for the
LORD has promised good things to Israel' (29). Moses assured the
Midianite that Israel's God was lavish in his deeds[9] as well as

---

[8] S. P. Carey, *William Carey* (London: Hodder and Stoughton, 1923), pp. 40–41.
[9] Pss. 34:10; 84:11.

dependable in his words, and that his abundant gifts were to be generously shared: *'we will share with you whatever good things the LORD gives us'* (32).

Finally, it testifies to God's mercy. In Egypt, the Israelite community was encouraged to make room for the alien or foreigner in its ranks. Such people were free to join the Israelite pilgrims on their journey as long as they committed themselves to the covenant obligations.[10] The Midianites had been good to Moses when he fled from Egypt forty years earlier as a refugee,[11] and now the well-equipped 'outsider' found a place within Israel's ranks. This invitation, encouragement and promise anticipated later times when Gentiles would be welcomed into the believing community and, most especially, the gospel's generous invitation that 'whoever believes in him', whatever his or her nationality or ethnic background, may enjoy eternal life.[12]

Trusting God (10:33–36)

However reassured they were by Hobab's skills, Israel looked to the Lord for the help no human guide can possibly give: *The ark of the covenant of the LORD went before them* (33) and the *cloud of the LORD was over them … when they set out from the camp* (34). With these visible signs of God's presence, the pilgrims expressed their confidence in God and their indebtedness to him in two exultant psalms, which heartened the people at the beginning and ending of each stage of the momentous journey. As *the ark set out* (35), the pilgrims' songs exalted their powerful and faithful God.[13]

> *'Rise up, O LORD!*
> *May your enemies be scattered;*
> *may your foes flee before you.'*

Everything possible had been done to ensure the safety and well-being of this massive travelling community. Gifted leaders were appointed, potential soldiers counted and trumpet calls agreed for rallying them to action. A great cloud protected them from the scorching rays of the sun, and at night a huge column of fire was a luminous warning to their enemies. This opening psalm assured them that the Lord had the power to overcome their enemies. God's people still need that guarantee. A vulnerable first-century prisoner expressed the same confidence: 'I can do everything through him who gives me strength.'[14]

[10] Exod. 12:48–49.   [11] Exod. 2:15–22.   [12] Ruth 1:16–17; 2:12; John 3:16.
[13] There are echoes of these two brief psalms in Pss. 68:1; 132:8.   [14] Phil. 4:13.

Whenever the ark *came to rest,* Moses gave voice to the community's profound confidence in their faithful God:

> *'Return, O LORD,*
> *to the countless thousands of Israel'* (36).

As they pitched their tents at the close of the day, these simple words recalled the miraculous things God had done for them. The *countless thousands* were undeniable testimony to the total reliability of God's word. He had promised they would become a huge nation, and the promise had come true. At the same time, he had told the patriarch that he would bring his people to the land of promise.[15] As the Israelites looked around, the vastness of their community eloquently assured them that the Lord would not break his word. The God who had created the multitude would certainly provide their home.

---

[15] Gen. 13:14–17.

11:1–35
10. Leadership issues

The next two chapters of the book present an arresting interpretation of leadership issues, their precarious context, inevitable frustrations, promised resources, undeniable encouragements and painful disappointments. They are as relevant for us in a new millennium as when Israel's leader began that long trek across the desert with his mercurial congregation. We begin with the community the leader serves. Here, Moses experienced the frustrations of leadership.

The disappointing people (11:1–9)

The closing words of the previous chapter portrayed the Israelite travellers sharing in the confident and serene prayers of their leader, words that now stand in painful contrast to the ungrateful complaints of the people. Their God was omnipotent, scattering their foes (10:35); omnipresent, sheltering Israel's 'countless thousands' (10:36) with his assured presence; and omniscient, planning their best route (10:34). He also knew everything about their bitter complaints as they murmured day after day *in the hearing of the* LORD (1). Moses might well have prayed as the travellers moved off, but as the pilgrims journeyed, the Lord listened to their sour conversation, and *his anger was aroused* (1). A blazing fire at *the outskirts of the camp* consumed some of those who had spoken bitingly and ungratefully. This was not an occasional grumble but 'an open rebellion'.[1]

Their complaints assumed two forms, as prominent in contemporary life as in the time of Moses. They moaned first about what life had done to them, and then about what had been denied to

---

[1] George Coats, *Rebellion in the Wilderness* (Nashville, TN: Abingdon, 1968), p. 249.

them. Their initial grievance (1–3) was about what they had (hardships); the next (4–9) focused on what they did not have – attractive and appetising food.

Grumbling about life's adversities (11:1–3)

They whined first about the everyday hardships of their desert journey. It was exactly the same when they left Egypt a year earlier.[2] They had been on the desert highway for only three days when they began moaning about their troubles. All of them had suffered immense hardships in Egypt, and a few days' discomfort in the blazing sun could hardly be compared with the 400 years of agony they and their people had suffered under cruel oppressors. Surely they did not imagine that the journey would be effortless! Everything in life that is worth anything demands training, discipline, struggle and sacrifice. Little of value is achieved without pain.

Believers, of all people, must expect some element of costliness in the Christian life. All the main characters of the Bible had to cope with adversities of one kind or another. Jesus himself had to endure jealous enemies who opposed him, mercurial people who insulted him, discontented followers who left him and unreliable colleagues who disappointed him; and in the end he cried out in pain on a lonely hilltop. That was the worst of agonies; as he bore our sin, even God had forsaken him.[3]

From the beginning of Christian history there have been valiant men and women who have not succumbed to this temptation to grumble. They have adamantly refused to complain about their hardships. The apostle Paul testified to the enormous help he had received when things were at their worst. The more intense the suffering, the more he became aware of his own need of the Lord's strength, sufficiency and peace.[4]

If only those Israelites could have seen that those tough days in the bleak desert were God's training days, encouraging them to believe that, having delivered them from their Egyptian captors, he would go on to deliver them from their malevolent moods, ungrateful attitudes and churlish dissatisfaction!

---

[2] Exod. 15:22–24. Cf. Currid, p. 145: 'The groaning began already in Egypt (Exod. 5:21) ... whenever the Hebrews complained, they mentioned Egypt'; Num. 11:5; 14:2–4; 16:13; 20:5; Exod. 14:11–12; 16:3; 17:3.

[3] Mark 15:34.

[4] 2 Cor. 1:8–10. The verb Paul uses indicates the discontinuance of an existing condition; that is, 'all this hardship came about so that we might *no longer* rely on ourselves, but on the God of resurrection' (my translation).

The pilgrims never forgot the place where they whined about their difficulties. The scene of complaint became the arena of judgment. Unchecked fire (perhaps the result of lightning) was a terrifying prospect for a camping community. Reflecting on the event later, they called the place *Taberah* ('burning'), *because fire from the LORD had burned among them* (3). But they did not learn from the grim lessons of experience.

Grumbling about life's deficiencies (11:4–10, 31–35)

Catering for such vast hordes of people was a uniquely miraculous exercise, but before long they were thinking wistfully about the appetising meals that had been freely available during their long captivity: *'If only we had meat to eat! We remember the fish we ate in Egypt at no cost – also the cucumbers, melons, leeks, onions and garlic. But now we have lost our appetite; we never see anything but this manna!'*[5] A number of features in this narrative are worthy of reflection.

First, example is important. The trouble started with unworthy people who were a bad example to their fellow travellers. That word *rabble* (4) is not found elsewhere in the Old Testament; it may describe those non-Israelites who had left Egypt with them.[6] The sick complaints should have died on their lips, but how quickly other people took up their resentments and made them their own!

Secondly, sin is contagious. Before long, this complaining spirit spread throughout the camp: *Moses heard the people of every family wailing, each at the entrance to his tent* (10).

Thirdly, memory is selective. Their minds went back to those delicious meals provided by their ruthless masters in distant Egypt, but how rapidly they forgot the intense hardship, the long nights of sorrow, the merciless killing of innocent children, the vicious whipping by heartless rulers! It is the easiest thing to look back on a distant scene with pleasure, forgetting that earlier days had difficult moments too.

Fourthly, diet is preoccupying. God had provided generously for them ever since that vast crowd had left their Egyptian captivity. Not for one single day had they lacked anything they

---

[5] The accuracy of their memory is fully attested in Egyptian records for this period. Describing the new capital at Rameses, Papyrus Anastasi III says, 'Onions and leeks are for food ... pomegranates, apples, olives, figs of the orchard ... red wedj-fish ... bedin fish', and numerous other kinds of fish. *ANET*, p. 471; Currid, pp. 145–146. Herodotus (II.93) describes the abundance of fish in Egypt.

[6] Exod. 12:38.

needed – food, drink, clothing, shelter, protection, security and hope – and yet here they were, wistfully recalling the superior meals of days gone by.

The Lord has generously provided a wide variety of attractive food for us to enjoy, but there are things in life of greater importance than the next meal. What is the use of a lavishly arrayed table if we are not fit enough to enjoy it? Good health is infinitely more important than an attractive menu. What if we are weighed down with life's greatest sorrows? Who imagines that serious worries can be banished by a full plate? Jesus has taught us that there are higher priorities than the next meal. At the end of a long period of persistent assault by the devil in the wilderness, Jesus was naturally hungry. He had fasted so that he could give his unrivalled attention to spiritual realities, Now he needed a good meal and, knowing it, the enemy invited Jesus to turn one of those desert stones into an appetising loaf to demonstrate that he really was the unique Son of God. Jesus knew how sinister that temptation was: to give an immediate craving a higher priority than an ultimate destiny and to doubt God's earlier word at his baptism ('This is my Son'), which needed no other authentication. Jesus' reply was to go back to these desert experiences: 'Man does not live on bread alone but on every word that comes from the mouth of God.'[7] Jesus knew that there was infinitely more to life than eating.

In oppulent parts of the contemporary world, the preoccupation with food has become idolatrous. Instead of eating to live, millions live to eat. It has become the epidemic of the western world. More than 34 million British adults are overweight, amounting to 58% of the current population. The gross obesity of thousands contrasts cruelly with the gaunt malnutrition of their global neighbours. Huge sums of money are devoted to extravagant delicacies; elsewhere millions die of starvation. Every day, enormous quantities of wholesome food are wasted while others plead for a piece of bread and cold water from a clean well. The Israelites' lust for better food mirrors the inordinate craving of modern times; both come under the judgment of a God who gives generously but grieves over those who squander his bounty. 'Let nothing be wasted.'[8]

Finally, contentment is attractive. If only these disgruntled travellers had expressed their gratitude for the daily manna instead of dwelling unprofitably on their Egyptian banquets! Confined to a Roman dungeon, the apostle Paul told his friends at Philippi that 'whatever the circumstances', he had learnt the lesson of contentment: 'whether well fed or hungry, whether living in plenty or in

[7] Matt. 3:17; 4:1–4; John 4:31–34; Deut. 8:2–4. [8] John 6:12.

want'.[9] Hunger was part of life's everyday coinage; he had 'often gone without food'.[10] Towards the close of his life he told a young colleague that 'godliness with contentment' was of inestimable worth: 'But if we have food and clothing, we will be content with that.'[11] The apostle's experience is captured in the song of Bunyan's shepherd boy:

> I am content with what I have,
> Little be it or much:
> And, Lord, contentment still I crave
> Because thou savest such.
>
> Fulness to such a burden is
> That go on Pilgrimage:
> Here little, and hereafter Bliss,
> Is best from Age to Age.[12]

The vulnerable leader (11:10–15, 18–23)

Moses became seriously *troubled*. The peevish whispers of a minority soon spread throughout the entire camp and there was no escape from their ridiculous sobbing. The minor problem of their monotonous diet had grown out of all proportion. The people wept, Moses grieved, God was angry. In acute distress, the leader took the problem upon his own shoulders; a community grievance became a personal injury. He was not remotely troubled about his food but was totally exasperated by his work. He too became a victim of serious discontent. Agonized by self-doubt, a torrent of fretful questions tumbled from his lips.

> *'Why have you brought this trouble on your servant? What have I done to displease you that you put the burden of all these people on me? ... Did I give them birth? Why do you tell me to carry them in my arms ...? Where can I get meat for all these people? ... I cannot carry all these people by myself; the burden is too heavy for me'* (11–14).

Moses' deep depression finds a sad echo in the lives of many of our contemporaries. People under pressure struggle helplessly with dark thoughts. Britain's Royal College of Psychiatrists has reported that more working days are lost to depressive illness each year than

---

[9] Phil. 4:11–12. [10] 2 Cor. 11:27; cf. 6:5; 1 Cor. 4:11–12. [11] 1 Tim. 6:6–8.
[12] *The Pilgrim's Progress*, Part II (1684), ed. J. B. Wharey, rev. R. Sharrock (Oxford: Clarendon, 2nd ed., 1960), p. 238.

91

to conditions such as heart disease, high blood pressure or diabetes. Many face increasing tensions at work, and some return home to a less than restful scene. A senior university lecturer in psychiatry claims that, at any time, one person in twenty at work is experiencing depression, while one woman in five and one man in ten is likely to have similar problems at some stage. Typical symptoms include loss of self-esteem and guilt. A Royal College representative said, 'If you have a workplace putting stresses and strains on people you are going to get more mental health problems.'[13] Moses' work caused him to cry out to God in anguish.

Scripture is gloriously honest. It inspires us with the heroism and fortitude of its finest characters, but refuses to exaggerate their virtues and does nothing to minimize their failings. Abraham was deceitful.[14] Sarah doubted.[15] Isaac lied.[16] Jacob cheated.[17] The self-confident disciple, close friend of Jesus for three years, denied all knowledge of him when personal testimony became risky.[18] The Bible tells the story as it is. Moses was a gifted leader, not a flawless saint. The narrative describes not only the people's failings but those of their leader as well. Moses' response to the loud weeping of his discontented congregation has much to say to leaders of every generation.

Moses recognized the submissiveness of leadership

What Moses said in the Lord's presence was a recital of grievances, a catalogue of dissatisfaction. But he was right in one thing: he went to God with his troubles. Leaders recognize the importance of their own submission to God, expressed in dependent, honest and attentive prayer.

Submission is an unacceptable concept in our postmodern culture. Don Cupitt expresses the contemporary preference for uninhibited self-expression and the rejection of religious authority, with its 'imagery of domination and submission. God is described as King, Lord, Judge and Father, and the believer appears before him as subject, servant, defender and obedient child ... In him is all power and perfection, in us is all weakness and baseness ... Even the eucharistic liturgy has resounded with cries for mercy and professions of unworthiness.' Reacting negatively to such teaching, Cupitt insists that in our world, 'a man feels he ought, so far as possible, to be his own master'.[19] But, as Murray Harris observes,

---

[13] *Daily Telegraph*, 10 September 1999, p. 6.   [14] Gen. 12:10–20.
[15] Gen. 18:10–15.   [16] Gen. 26:1–11.   [17] Gen. 27:1–39.   [18] Luke 22:54–62.
[19] Don Cupitt, *The Crisis of Moral Authority: The Dethronement of Christianity* (Guildford: Lutterworth, 1972), pp. 106, 120, 140.

while the New Testament certainly exhorts the believer to submission, it has no place for domination, if by that we mean 'the
imposition of one person's will on another who is either unwilling
or reluctant to accept that imposition'. Christians serve their Lord
'voluntarily and enthusiastically, motivated by love, and sensing
their high privilege in belonging to and representing him.'[20]

Moses was supported, not dominated, by God. He was a committed servant, though at this time he was pained by this abrasive
congregation. As he hurled his petulant questions into the divine
presence, he wished they could be his final words on earth: *'If this
is how you are going to treat me, put me to death right now'* (15).
What began as a bitter complaint ended with a supportive solution.
The discovery was made in the place of prayer.

Moses disregarded the cost of leadership

He had known from the beginning that it was not going to be
easy; that is why he had baulked at the prospect.[21] Overwhelmed
by the immediate distress, he forgot the wider canvas. The heroism
of those who had gone before him slipped from his mind. From his
earliest days he had known about their immense courage, and was
to preserve their stories in writing for millions of readers yet
unborn. What about the loneliness of Noah, 'blameless among the
people of his time', when 'the earth was corrupt in God's sight'?[22]
Moses may have forgotten about Joseph, a potential leader who
had to suffer cruel experiences before he was brought to the place
of usefulness.[23] Burdened by trouble, Moses may have overlooked
the courage of his own father and mother, who put their lives at
risk by treasuring their 'fine child'.[24] It was not God's purpose to
meet his servant's request for death simply because an ungrateful
community had become depressed about their diet.

Leadership is tough and it is foolish to deny it. When things go
wrong, it is natural to ask, like Moses, 'Why?' Part of the answer
was in his unwitting confession: *'Why have you brought this
trouble on your servant?'* (11). If he was God's slave, it was inappropriate to grumble simply because the Lord had trusted him
with a difficult assignment. Leaders recognize that there is a price
to pay for faithfulness, integrity and effectiveness.

[20] Murray J. Harris, *Slave of Christ* (Leicester: Apollos, 1999), pp. 151–153.
[21] Exod. 3:11; 4:10, 13; 5:22–23; 6:12, 30.   [22] Gen. 6:9–11.
[23] Gen. 37:1–36; 39:1 – 41:57.   [24] Exod. 2:1–10.

Moses exaggerated the problems of leadership

When we are depressed, our understanding of the key issues is scarcely objective. Moses' vocabulary of complaint must not be submitted to minute scrutiny; angry thoughts easily become explosive verbal missiles.

He jumped to the conclusion that all this was happening because God was displeased with him. Nothing could have been further from the truth. The Lord was angry with the grumblers, not disappointed with the leader. Moses was too wrapped up in his troubles to see that, and spurted out his bitter anguish: *'What have I done to displease you that you put the burden of all these people on me?'* His words reflect a common reaction to trouble: 'What have I done to deserve this?'

He not only blamed himself unnecessarily but exaggerated his role as Israel's leader. He had been entrusted with a mammoth community assignment, but at no point had God told him that it was his personal responsibility to *carry them in his arms, as a nurse carries an infant.* Moses protested, *'I cannot carry all these people by myself'* (14), but the Lord had never suggested that he should. Of course the burden was too heavy. It was impossible, let alone heavy. How could anyone think for a moment that the Lord had made him personally responsible for the safe conveyance of thousands of Israelite pilgrims? But that is the trouble with depression; it maximizes the problems and minimizes the resources.

Part of the secret of effective leadership is to recognize the limitations of human responsibility. There are certain things we must do and the Lord expects us to get on with them. There are other things that only he can do, and all our strenuous exertion will never achieve them. The community had to be 'carried' through the desert. In other words, they would not make it to Canaan if they relied solely on their own energy, but neither would they reach it if they relied solely on Moses' strength. He had told them at the beginning of their journey that the Lord would carry them as an eagle carries her young chicks on her wide pinions, teaching them to fly.[25] At the end of the journey, the next generation were told that the Lord had carried them as a father proudly bears a young child on his shoulders.[26] When things are hard in leadership we must ask ourselves whether we have been trying to shoulder God's responsibilities instead of fulfilling our own.

---

[25] Exod. 19:4.   [26] Deut. 1:31.

Moses anticipated the failure of leadership

One of the worst aspects of a despondent spirit is that everything is portrayed in lurid colours. Moses wants to die, and pleads with God, *'do not let me face my own ruin'* (15). Failure is demoralizing and Moses could not bear the thought of it. They had left Egypt a year earlier with such radiant promise. Now, everyone in Israel was sobbing with disappointment and the peace of every home was marred by sickening discontent. Once again, Moses was mistaken; he was not a potential failure. Pride fears the dereliction of incompetence and, whatever his failings, Moses was not proud.

The humble (12:3) Moses contemplated the horror of his *own ruin* because, crippled by despondency, he could imagine only the worst. Like Elijah and Jonah, he wished he could die.[27] A merciful Lord turned Moses' face to a better horizon. There was a day appointed when he would die, but not for another forty years. Mercifully, the Lord lovingly turns a deaf ear to some of our most urgent requests. Knowing the things that are hidden,[28] he desires only the best for us. Thank God he does not always give us what we want.

Moses forgot the privilege of leadership

In Hebrew thought, to be the Lord's *servant* (11) was an undeserved privilege, not a menial obligation. God had raised Moses up for this very purpose, guided his steps, overruled his mistakes, shaped his destiny and guaranteed his support. Thousands of weeping malcontents were enough to daunt the strongest of men; the loneliness must have been unbearable. It was natural to be dejected, but, in Calvin's view, Moses carried his complaint to excess. He 'ought rather to have been ravished with astonishment, that God had condescended to choose him to be the redeemer of his people and the minister of his wondrous power'.[29]

Moses overlooked the resources of leadership

The Lord responded to his lament with two sentences that expound every leader's theology of sufficiency. His dejected spirit was reminded, first, of the Lord's complete adequacy, and then of his total reliability. Longing for death, Moses felt utterly broken. But God's word invaded his frail mind like infused steel. He had hurled his ill-tempered questions at God; now the Lord put a

[27] 1 Kgs. 19:4; Jonah 4:3.   [28] Deut. 29:29.   [29] Calvin, IV, p. 22.

gentle question to him: *'Is the* LORD*'s arm too short?'* (23). Those words about *the* LORD*'s arm* stirred memories of the invincible power of a mighty God. It was the language of the exodus, used to describe his people's deliverance, a miracle achieved by 'a mighty hand and an outstretched arm'.[30] The imagery was deliberately chosen. The Egyptians exalted Pharaoh as the 'possessor of a strong arm'.[31] The Israelites had witnessed the incompetence of Pharaoh when challenged by the Lord. Overwhelmed by his own frailty, Moses was reminded of God's incomparable strength.

Heartened by God's works, he was reminded of God's words. Among Moses' complaints was the grumble that he could not be Israel's caterer: *'Where can I get meat for all these people?'* (13). The Lord said that his outstretched arm could and would provide abundant meat for the vast multitude, but Moses could not believe what he was hearing: *'Now the* LORD *will give you meat, and you will eat it'* (18). The Lord who, a year earlier, ordered his winds to hold back the waves could use them again in a further manifestation of sovereignty. Moses' response betrayed an unbelieving spirit: would the people *'have enough if flocks and herds were slaughtered for them* and *if all the fish in the sea were caught for them?'* Moses envisaged a menu of meat and fish and considered it impossible. God had planned to give them poultry and had worked out how it could easily be done.

God told Moses that divine words are never wasted. What he says is always done: *'You will now see whether or not what I say will come true for you'* (23). It was a matchless message for a broken spirit. Surrounded by thousands of complaining travellers, Moses was not on the threshold of ruin. He was about to be staggered at the omnipotence of God and the reliability of his promises.

Moses shared the responsibilities of leadership

The Lord knew that Moses' problems had been heightened by a sense of loneliness and isolation. He needed reliable colleagues in each tribe, and God responded not in condemnation but by supporting him in a demanding assignment. Others were to share some of the burdens he imagined he was carrying alone.

---

[30] Deut. 4:34; cf. 7:19; Exod. 3:19–20; 6:1; 7:4; 15:16.
[31] Currid, pp. 154–155; J. K. Hoffmeier, 'The arm of God versus the arm of Pharaoh in the Exodus narratives', *Biblica* 67 (1986), pp. 378–387.

The supportive team (11:16–17, 24–25)

Those who serve Christ are often overwhelmed by the immensity of the task and the slenderness of the resources. Some key issues emerge in this narrative.

Partnership is crucial

No leader can serve effectively without the practical support of dedicated colleagues who are happy with subsidiary roles and willingly offer enabling ministries. Baruch may not have had the eloquence of Jeremiah but he could write down the memorable things his mentor had spoken.[32] Appreciative readers of Paul's magnificent epistle to the Romans should salute the memory of Tertius, the man who used his skills as a devoted amanuensis, as did Silas for Peter.[33] John Wesley's strenuous itinerant evangelism was possible only because hundreds of unnamed Methodists gave him loving hospitality. They could not preach, but they could prepare a nutritious meal and offer a comfortable bed. William Wilberforce was successful in his long and vigorous campaign against the slave trade because Thomas Clarkson worked tirelessly behind the scenes, supplying him with up-to-date information and reliable statistics.

There is an inevitable loneliness in leadership. Most of the heart-aches cannot easily be shared, but the Lord generously provides his servants with good colleagues who can relieve some of the pressures. Moses' lament was a cry for help, and God rallied the support of the community's elders, widely respected as dependable leaders and officials (16).

Gifts are multichrome

We should like to know more about these *elders*. The Israelites had such leaders even during their Egyptian captivity, and, after their deliverance, Moses' father-in-law advised him to make use of dependable colleagues.[34] Such a huge congregation needed a wide variety of gifted people, and the Lord intended the overwrought Moses to delegate some of his responsibilities to others.

The word describing these *officials* is also used of people with writing skills.[35] In addition to pastoral responsibilities, such men may have assisted Moses in preserving the lists, regulations, narratives and other sources that provide the basic material for Numbers

---

[32] Jer. 32:12–16; 36:1–32; 45:1–5. [33] Rom. 16:22; 1 Pet. 5:12.
[34] Exod. 3:16; 4:29; 18:13–26. [35] Harrison, pp. 15–22.

and its adjoining books. Whatever their particular responsibilities, they enabled him to concentrate on tasks he could not easily entrust to others. The New Testament testifies to the wide variety of gifts that the Lord distributes and uses among his people.[36] It is sad when believers waste time coveting or criticizing other people's gifts rather than discerning their own.

Recognition is necessary

These *leaders and officials* were publicly designated for this new ministry so that Moses was helped to *carry the burden of the people* and was relieved of his desolate sense of isolation: *'so that you will not have to carry it alone'* (16–17). This feature about gathering the team at the Tent entrance is no mere locational detail; it indicates that in the work of God the Lord's servants must have the community's acceptance, recognition and support. If these elders were to be of any use to Moses at all, the Israelites must acknowledge that they had been needed by Moses and appointed by God; so they would be welcomed by the people. Their spiritual status and pastoral role are indicated by this public meeting at the Tent door. God's work is teamwork, and the community itself must be respected and informed, and their wholehearted cooperation encouraged, in this new appointment of Moses' colleagues.

Surrender is crucial

Although the people recognized the new partners in leadership, the community did not own them. They belonged to God. These prospective colleagues must *stand there* with Moses at the Tent entrance; it portrayed the total surrender of the persons involved. Servants stood in the presence of their master. Subjects stood in the throne room of the king, ready to respond with speed to the slightest wishes of their lord. Elijah stood in the presence of God while the time-servers in Ahab's court merely stood in the presence of a godless king.[37] For Jeremiah, standing in the presence of God as a submissive servant was a test of the true prophet, distingishing him from false messengers who gave the people a message that pleased.[38] Gabriel stood in God's presence before he visited the old man Zechariah with the momentous news that God had answered his prayer.[39] Now, these elders were to stand submissively with Moses in the Lord's presence to hear what

---

[36] Rom. 12:6–8; 1 Cor. 12:4–11; Eph. 4:7–13; 1 Pet. 4:10–11.
[37] 1 Kgs. 17:1, RSV ('before whom I stand').   [38] Jer. 23:18, 22.   [39] Luke 1:19.

he would say, to receive what he would give and to do what he would command.

Surrendered servants never forget that, however warmly they cooperate with their leaders and serve the people, their primary commands come from the one who appointed them. The tension between doing what the Lord says and what the people want has agonized thousands of God's servants across the centuries.

Resources are promised

God told Moses, '*I will take of the Spirit that is on you and put the Spirit on them*' (17). The Holy Spirit, who had energized Moses' body, enriched his mind, fortified his will and encouraged his heart, would not fail the least of these new partners. Before Christ's followers were sent into a hostile world, he told them to seek God for promised help. The verb Luke uses is present active: they must 'keep on waiting' for the gift the Father had promised. Sending them out, he first assured them of essential strength.[40] Those who obey God's voice, pursue his will and enter his service will never be denied the unfailing supply of the Holy Spirit's resources: wisdom, guidance, grace, love, patience and strength will be generously and continually given. God did exactly what he promised. *He took of the Spirit that was on Moses and put the Spirit on the seventy elders* (25). Each man was equipped with the same sufficient dynamic that had sustained Moses.

Truth is paramount

Although these seventy men may have exercised different gifts in leadership – pastoral, secretarial, administrative – one dominant feature characterizes them all. They were servants of the word. As the Spirit's presence and power rested on the seventy elders, they all *prophesied*. As undeniable evidence of their necessary equipment, these seventy men gave a Spirit-inspired utterance that the community could hear and to which they could respond. Their prophetic utterances were an isolated event to confirm the divine gift, for, although they certainly prophesied on the day of their divine enduement, *they did not do so again* (25).

Although their tasks were not in the direct public communication of God's truth, in those moments they expressed a servant's priority; their function was not to exercise their personal skills or to parade their own ideas but to be subservient to God's word

[40] Acts 1:4–5, 8.

conveyed to them by Moses. The detail that they prophesied on that single occasion may underline the subservient nature of their role. They were partners, not preachers; supporters, not rivals.

God's work has been seriously damaged throughout history when people have become discontented with the jobs assigned to them and wasted their time lusting after work sovereignly assigned to others. Uzziah of Judah was astonishingly successful in his regal responsibilities but coveted the priestly office, insisting on doing things expressly forbidden to Israel's laymen.[41] People who covet the gifts of others may permanently lose their own.

Jeremiah issued a special warning to his discouraged colleague, Baruch: 'Should you then seek great things for yourself? Seek them not.'[42] Possibly the gifted scribe had hoped to become a senior administrator in the royal court. Instead, he would end up in Egypt as a homeless refugee.[43] Yet, although he was denied the career prospects he had dreamt about, such 'great things' would be dwarfed by greater things: doing God's will, recording and preserving God's word and supporting God's servant, Jeremiah. Had his vocational dreams been fulfilled, he would have become a totally forgotten civil servant; instead, his name has gone down in history as a communicator of the unique word. His was a minor role but a lasting one.

The additional helpers (11:26–30)

Once the seventy elders had been equipped by the Spirit and their gift authenticated by that single experience of prophetic utterance, a further novel occurrence caused an uncomfortable stir in the camp. Two of Israel's leaders and officials (16), clearly intended for this new supportive ministry, had not gathered with Moses and their colleagues at the Tent entrance: *Eldad and Medad had remained in the camp.* Despite their absence, they too were equipped by the Spirit for this fresh assignment and, like the others, began *prophesying in the camp.* This intriguing narrative offers further perspectives about the Lord's work.

The sovereignty of the Spirit

The majority of these new workers had been endowed with the Spirit's gift at the appointed place, but the two absentees had not been denied their essential resources. We are not provided with an explanation of their non-attendance with the others. Their absence

---

[41] 2 Chr. 26:1–21.   [42] Jer. 45:5.   [43] Jer. 43:6–7.

could not have been due to disobedience or truculence, or they would not have received the Spirit's equipment.

The story is a persuasive reminder that the Holy Spirit is totally sovereign and acts in any way he determines. He will not be stereotyped and his actions cannot be precisely predicted to conform to purely human conventions. In Christian history, some parts of the world have known extraordinary manifestations of his power, while others have witnessed nothing like the same degree of such activity. It is a mistake to imagine that those who have been denied such privileges have been bereft of blessings because of inadequate prayer or insufficient faith or defective holiness. Prayer, faith and holiness are necessary ingredients in the Christian life, but we must not therefore assume that they guarantee a coveted gift. It is arrogant to suppose that the Lord can be manipulated or manoeuvred by actions we may plan. We must pray, have faith in God and live holy lives, acknowledging the intrinsic value of these things, but not 'using' them to secure what we want from God. After all, we do not always know what is best for us.

The perils of adulation

When an unnamed young man in the community saw that these two elders were *prophesying in the camp* (27), he ran to Moses, reporting the irregular behaviour. The leader's devoted assistant, Joshua, was incensed, urging Moses to stop them immediately. He jumped to the conclusion that Eldad and Medad were acting out of blatant disregard for their leader.

Moses did not support Joshua's criticism. Joshua had been *Moses' assistant since youth*, and doubtless admired the old man intensely, but there was no reason to think that these new colleagues were being disrespectful. We must guard against turning commendable people into perilous idols. Jesus is the only flawless role model for the Christian believer.

Moses' reply to his young assistant, *'Are you jealous for my sake?'* (29), suggests that Joshua was annoyed at the two absentees because he thought they were insulting Moses by their unusual behaviour. He was overprotective, his sensitivity bordering on unhelpful hero-worship. It is wrong to put anybody, however good, on an exalted pedestal.

The danger of monopolies

Without discovering why Eldad and Medad had not been present, Joshua thought there was something improper about their manifestation of the Spirit's enduement. Because God had acted in a particular (and appropriate) way for 'the seventy', he could not tolerate any deviation from that norm. How easy it is to institutionalize the Spirit's work or to endeavour to anticipate, organize or monopolize his ministry! Treasured events quickly become rigid patterns and inflexible traditions. The Holy Spirit will not be shackled by ecclesiastical customs, however good they may be. He will act with total freedom to accomplish whatever purposes he knows are best for his people at that particular time.

This story of Joshua's misplaced criticism of Eldad and Medad has a remarkable parallel in the Gospels, when the disciples tried to stop 'a man driving out demons' in Christ's name. Christ had a larger canvas by far: 'whoever is not against you is for you'.[44] When Walter Cradock, the Puritan minister of Llanvaches, was away in England, he rejoiced to hear how the work at home had prospered in his absence. But there were critics:

> And let us not think so hardly in these days of those men that God hath raised to preach the Gospel ... since I have been from you of late, the Gospel is run over the mountains between Brecknockshire and Monmouthshire, as the fire in the thatch. They have no ministers; but ... there are about eight hundred godly people, and they go from one to another ... And shall we rail at such, and say they are tub-preachers, and they were never at the University? ... what if God will honour himself that way? They are filled with good news, and they tell it to others; and therefore vex not at them.[45]

The story of Eldad and Medad and its companion in the Gospels gently rebuke any who, because of partisan insularity or out of a passion for rigid uniformity, want to restrict the Lord's work to their own prescribed channels.

The comprehensiveness of witness

It is pointless to speculate about the reasons for Eldad and Medad's absence, but there was an evident advantage in their prophetic ministry. Other people in distant parts of the camp had the opportunity to see that, despite the community's sinful grumbling, the Holy Spirit was still at work among them.

In most periods of history, there have been unusual spiritual

---

[44] Luke 9:49–50.
[45] *Glad Tydings* (1648), pp. 49–50, reprinted in *The Works of Walter Cradock*, ed. T. Charles and P. Oliver (Chester: W. C. Jones, 1800), pp. 380–381.

movements which have challenged the *status quo* of established Christianity, and their initial activities have seldom been appreciated. In the Middle Ages, the early Franciscans did a magnificent work, ministering in Christ's name to thousands of deprived people such as homeless beggars and those who suffered from diseases such as leprosy. They spent hours in the service of needy people who sheltered in the grim hovels that clung to the walls of every medieval city. Their humanitarian ministry and simple lifestyle rebuked many of their affluent contemporaries, and they soon became the focus of criticism.

George Fox and his Quaker partners challenged the nominalism of many contemporaries, and their message and activities were not welcomed. The early Friends had a poor press in seventeenth-century England and were constantly subjected to aggression and abuse. In the following century, many of the Methodist people were viciously treated. As he rode through Darlaston, Charles Wesley said it was always easy to identify 'our people's houses' because, following earlier attacks, their 'windows were all stopped up'.[46]

Minorities frequently have a bad time of it, but they are also exposed to potential decadence. Everything needs to be challenged by higher standards. Early idealism is easily corrupted; the best of movements can become fossilized. There is some truth in the cynical comment that organizations exist for the painless extinction of the ideas that gave them birth. Within two centuries, many Franciscans became notorious for greed, and their renewal movement stood in urgent need of regeneration. The passionate evangelism of the early Methodists became tempered by institutionalism in some nineteenth-century contexts, so much so that one of their devoted ministers, William Booth, was disciplined for evangelizing beyond his circuit. His departure from their ranks led to the formation of the Salvation Army. But nothing is sacrosanct; the best of Salvationists will freely admit that good movements need constant reformation.

The magnanimity of grace

Moses' reply to Joshua's criticism illustrated his generosity of spirit. Far from silencing the two, he longed for their blessing to be extended to everyone: '*I wish that all the LORD's people were prophets and that the LORD would put his Spirit on them*' (29). It is a powerful example of Moses' large-hearted leadership qualities.

[46] *The Journal of the Rev. Charles Wesley*, ed. T. Jackson (1849), entry for 5 February 1747.

What a transformed community it would be if every Israelite had a passionate desire to be equipped by the Spirit for spreading his word!

Good leaders are happy when anything is done that honours God, whether they are personally involved or not. The apostle Paul rejoiced that the message was preached by some of his contemporaries even though their motives were suspect; at least the gospel was being proclaimed by someone while he was in prison, and that delighted his heart.[47]

The condemned offenders (11:16–23, 31–35)

It is sad when committed believers quarrel over relatively minor issues when their witness is set in a context of widespread decadence. Life in the Israelite encampment was on the verge of spiritual anarchy, and at such times leaders ought to be thinking about more crucial issues than differing experiences of the Spirit's power. Joshua was worrying about the charismatic authenticity of a couple of elders while the rest of the camp were wishing they had never been involved in God's mighty act of redemption: *'We were better off in Egypt! … Why did we ever leave Egypt?'* (18, 20).

A graphic contrast-picture in this narrative ought not to be overlooked. The words 'Spirit' and 'wind' translate a single Hebrew word, *rûaḥ*. The wind of the Spirit came down upon the appointed leaders and, within minutes, another *wind went out from the* LORD (31), which brought droves of *quail in from the sea.* The boisterous wind was so strong that the birds could scarcely rise more than a metre above the ground, bringing them within easy reach of the Israelite campers. For about two days vast quantities were caught, prepared and laid out to dry in the hot sun.[48] They started to eat this newly collected food but, *while the meat was still between their teeth and before it could be consumed, the anger of the* LORD *burned against the people* (33). A severe plague broke out in the camp and a huge number who *had craved other food* became stricken with disease, died and were buried before the people moved on. They looked back on the place with deep remorse, calling it *Kibroth Hattaavah* ('graves of craving'), *because there they buried the people who had craved other food* (34).

The Spirit who visited the elders with good things judged the offenders with unwelcome things. God's anger or wrath is a serious biblical theme and is in danger of becoming marginalized in contemporary Christian preaching and thinking. God is 'personal',

[47] Phil 1:15–18.   [48] Herodotus II, 77.

compassionate and kind, and cares for his people; but he is also holy, sensitive and capable of being grieved and hurt. Discontented with what God had generously provided in the daily manna, those ungrateful epicures broke the commandments and idolized food. Wistfully recalling those well-laden Egyptian tables, they coveted better meals. In his wrath God satisfied their craving, and they had so much of it that it made them ill.

A number of biblical commentators have claimed that God's wrath is not personal, but 'an inevitable process of cause and effect in a moral universe'.[49] This observation does not do justice to the biblical doctrine of the wrath of God. We have no more right to deny that God's wrath is personal than to deny that his love is. Divine wrath is 'the action of a personal God who hates sin'.[50] Emil Brunner rightly pointed out that men and women are 'always under the power of God, either of his grace or his wrath. God's wrath is the "adverse wind" of the divine will, which he comes to feel who runs into it.'[51] Brunner insists that there is no neutrality; we are either 'in Christ' or 'in sin', 'under grace' or 'under wrath'. Obviously, God's wrath is 'his holy hostility to evil, his refusal to condone it or come to terms with it'. It is 'his just judgment upon it'.[52]

In his wrath, God gave the greedy Israelites exactly what they had craved for, and they suffered the consequences.[53] Many of our materialistic contemporaries soon discover that a lustful appetite can never be satisfied. Over the past few years, several winners of big prizes in the UK's national lottery have confessed that their huge winnings have brought them considerable unhappiness: the loss of friends, serious breaches in family relationships and the gradual disappearance of a sense of purpose in life. To have everything is to value nothing.

The passionate quest for material things is like thirsting for a drink that, far from quenching the thirst, only intensifies the desire for more. At Kibroth Hattaavah, the place of inordinate craving became a scene of intense grieving. What began as a luxurious banquet ended up as a distressing funeral.

[49] C. H. Dodd, *The Epistle of Paul to the Romans*, Moffatt New Testament Commentary (London: Hodder and Stoughton, 1932), p. 23.

[50] D. E. H. Whiteley, *The Theology of St Paul* (Oxford: Blackwell, 1974), p. 69.

[51] Emil Brunner, *The Letter to the Romans: A Commentary* (Guildford: Lutterworth, 1959), p. 17.

[52] J. R. W. Stott, *The Message of Romans*, The Bible Speaks Today (Leicester: IVP, 1994), p. 72.

[53] Ps. 106:14-15.

12:1–16
11. Disloyal colleagues

The sad story of human defiance lingers on, casting up yet another example of distressing rebellion, one even more hurtful in that it came from the older members of Moses' own family. *Miriam and Aaron began to talk against Moses* (1). It must have grieved Israel's leader that two people bound to him by natural blood ties were seriously objecting to his leadership.

The story provides important insights into the theme of handling disagreements. Christians are not always good at it. We sometimes find it difficult to live harmoniously with people who think differently from ourselves; peripheral differences lead to major disruptions. Paul urged the believers in Rome to learn how to deal with variant opinions in a compassionate, constructive, even creative manner.[1] When handling disagreement, several things need to be done.

Identify its source

When people are at loggerheads, differences may not always be confined to the immediate controversy; there are often multiple grounds for the complaint. Hidden resentments frequently underlie fierce objections.[2] Three issues may lurk behind the subversive conversations of Moses' sister and brother.

First, they raised an ethnic objection to his leadership. He had *married a Cushite wife*. Such issues are tragically evident in our own times. Huge numbers of people cannot live happily together because of their clashing racial backgrounds or discordant cultures. Antagonism between disparate racial backgrounds can often be traced to historical factors, tribal conflicts or fierce quarrels over

---

[1] Rom. 14:1–23.
[2] For several examples of the personal element in early Christian controversies, see S. L. Greenslade, *Schism in the Early Church* (London: SCM, 1953), pp. 35–57.

land rights and privileges, issuing in bitterness, mutual hostility and violence. Millions of homeless refugees in our world are heart-rending evidence of this widespread tragic disharmony.

Cushite is a variant term for Midianite, the people with whom Moses had found shelter when he fled from Egypt forty years earlier.[3] Now, two of the people closest to Moses were raising serious objections to the woman he had married, simply because she came from a different ethnic background.

Secondly, they raised a vocational objection to his leadership. Why was Moses regarded among the people as someone special? *'Has the* LORD *spoken only through Moses?'* they asked. *'Hasn't he also spoken through us?'* (2). Envy is showing its ugly face, and not for the last time in the desert journey (16:1 – 17:13). The sin was no less ugly than that of the greedy multitudes; indeed, it was more reprehensible in that it arose among Moses' closest relatives.

Thirdly, behind this grievance, there may be a hint of domestic rivalry. Aaron was senior, and, within the Hebrew tradition, the firstborn son was given precedence within the family. Yet here was the younger brother telling his elders what God wanted them to do. Family rivalries are common, sometimes leading to bitter disputes and acrimonious relationships. It is sad when those who have grown up as contented children cannot live together as mature adults.

Acknowledge its danger

Christians cannot be expected to think exactly alike on every issue in life. There is nothing wrong with holding different opinions; it is how we manage them that matters. Estranged brothers and sisters in the faith are undermining, if not denying, their God-given unity. The bitter complaint expressed by Aaron and Miriam was hurtful to Moses, offensive to God, damaging to the grumblers and a warning to the people.

First, it was hurtful to Moses. The inspired editor of this narrative informs us that *Moses was … more humble than anyone else on the face of the earth* (3). The word *humble* is from a root meaning 'bowed down'; in leadership he was genuinely 'subordinating his personal interests to those of God and his cause'.[4] His sensitive spirit must have been profoundly disturbed when members of his own family questioned his divinely appointed role and, particularly, his responsibility as the Lord's mouthpiece (2). His brother and sister, of all people, knew how diffidently he had undertaken

---

[3] Exod. 2:15–22; cf. 18:1–27; Num. 10:29–32.   [4] Kidner, p. 41.

the demanding tasks God had entrusted to him. God had provided Aaron as his supportive colleague, and the two brothers became devoted partners in confronting Pharoah with God's commands.[5] Yet, little more than a year later, the cooperative partnership was fractured. A genuinely *humble* man who steadily pursued the will of God for the glory of God found the conflict specially distressing.

Secondly, and more seriously, the disagreement was offensive to God. He had appointed Moses to this exacting task, and the community had indisputable proof that he was their divinely chosen leader. Aaron had been given other work to do. His responsibilities were priestly; he and his sons were to officiate at the sacrifices and act as pastoral counsellors within the community.[6] When this damaging relationship problem arose, the Lord responded in a way that identified the sin and exposed, judged and pardoned the sinner.

The Lord acted swiftly. Moses was not the only one who heard Aaron's and Miriam's bitter criticism: *And the Lord heard this* (2). God knew that this family grievance must be dealt with immediately before the poison infiltrated the entire community: *At once the Lord said ...* (4). In acrimonious disagreements additional harm can be done by procrastinating. Nobody ought to rush in without careful thought and dependent prayer, but the longer the problem is left the more likely it is that more harmful things will be said and done. The worst feature of sin is its power to reproduce itself. Iniquity multiplies unless firm and loving action is taken to halt its destructive mission.

The Lord appeared decisively. *Then the Lord came down in a pillar of cloud; he stood at the entrance to the Tent* (5), requiring these two discontented leaders to step forward so that he could expose the seriousness of their rebellion for, there, the *anger of the Lord burned against them* (9).

The Lord spoke authoritatively. He required the three members of this divided family to come to the Tent of Meeting, identifying Moses as someone infinitely more important than merely *a prophet of the Lord* (6–8a).

The Lord acted justly; his anger *burned against them*. The elder brother and sister had asserted that the Lord had *spoken through* them (2) as well as through Moses. They had talked insensitively about the Lord's voice; now they heard that divine voice and were terrified. There they were, at the entrance to the Tent of Meeting,

---

[5] Exod. 4:13–16, 27–31; 5:1; 6:13; 7:1–2, 8–13, 19–20; 8:5–9, 12, 15, 16–17, 25; 9:8, 12, 27; 10:3, 8, 11, 16; 11:10; 12:31, 43, 50.
[6] Exod. 28:1; Mal. 2:4–7; Heb. 5:1–5.

abandoned by God. The Lord *left them* (9) in their sins, isolated in their guilt, silenced by their transgression and subdued by deep remorse. The pillar of cloud, a perpetual reminder of God's presence and holiness, was lifted way above the Tent. God had spoken his word of condemnation and walked out on them, leaving them in their solitariness to feel the enormity of their sin.

The disagreement, thirdly, was damaging to the grumblers. Embarrassed and afraid, these two unhappy people looked into each other's faces, making a shattering discovery. Miriam had been stricken with a frightening skin disease.[7] One wonders why, when both had offended, Miriam alone was afflicted and Aaron spared. Possibly, in this instance, she may have been the ringleader, initiating the complaint, leaving Aaron to be the spokesman. One thing is certain; with mental anguish, he felt equally guilty and did nothing to hide his deep remorse, calling out to Moses, *'Please, my lord, do not hold against us the sin we have so foolishly committed'* (11).

Aaron admitted that they had acted not only unkindly and irresponsibly, but also *foolishly*. Aaron pleaded with Moses (*'Please, my lord'*) and Moses pleaded with God: *'O God, please heal her!'* The man who had objected to Moses' role as leader now called him *lord*, and was glad to do so.

Aaron knew they must repent if the offence was to be pardoned. Saying 'sorry' is a rapidly disappearing courtesy in contemporary society. Ellen Goodman wrote in *The Boston Globe* recently about why saying sorry is un-American. The problem is not remotely confined to the USA. Doctors, hospitals and manufacturers are reluctant to apologize in today's world; they are likely to be sued. An American and a Japanese vessel were involved in a collision at sea. The Japanese looked for an apology, but there was a clash of cultures. In Japan 'it is said that apologies prevent lawsuits', whereas in America an apology is viewed as 'an admission of legal guilt rather than an expression of emotional regret'. But 'the asking and receiving of forgiveness is an important part of civilised coexistence'.[8] It is a vital dimension in our relationship with God, and Moses' family knew it.

Finally, this incident was a warning to the people. Responding to his intercession, God told Moses that, had his sister been disgraced publicly by an earthly father, she would have been required to live outside the camp to mourn for her sin seven days. Now that she had been publicly rebuked by her heavenly Father

[7] Wenham (1981), p. 113, suggests that, as this event pre-dates the arrival of leprosy in that region, the disease may have been severe eczema or psoriasis.
[8] *The Week*, 17 March 2001, p. 11.

she must do the same. The desert community would bring their journey to a temporary halt, giving them a full week in camp to reflect on the seriousness of sin (1–2), the inevitability of judgment (10), the necessity of repentance (11–12), the urgency of prayer (13) and the miracle of forgiveness (14).

Attempt its healing

In this narrative of bitterness, antagonism and disruption, we may trace some therapeutic dimensions of helpful pastoral care.

First, we should value God's servants. Earlier, Miriam and Aaron had been greatly used by God. The sister's young voice had played a crucial role in the deliverance of her baby brother and, later, her prophetic gift had inspired Israel's travellers as they acknowledged God's power. Aaron's strong arms had been used as he shared with Moses in the ministry of prayer.[9] They had both been used in the past, and would be so in the future if they used their own gifts rather than coveting those of other people. The offenders were told two important things about Moses, so that they might value his ministry rather than criticize it.

They were told that Moses was divinely equipped. He had been raised up as God's *servant* (7–8) to perform a specific task for this desert community. Whereas God communicated his message to others by means of visions and dreams, Moses was ushered personally into the audience chamber of God: *'he sees the form of the LORD'*. God was surprised that these two complainers, having witnessed Moses' shining face,[10] had been envious of his special function rather than inspired by God's visible endorsement of his servant.

They were also told that Moses was utterly dependable: *'he is faithful in all my house'* (7). Listening (7:89) and speaking were solemn responsibilities, not coveted benefits. Twice identified in this passage as the Lord's *servant*, he was humble (3), faithful (7), prayerful and merciful (13). When people become embroiled in bitter rivalry, only believers of the spiritual calibre of Moses are likely to exercise an effective ministry of healing.

Secondly, we should enter God's presence. The Lord told the disunited family to come to the Tent of Meeting, where he met with them in the overshadowing cloud. Serious divisions and bitter rivalries will never be rectified away from the mercy seat. It is only when we pray and expose ourselves to the searchlight of God's presence that all parties see their need of him. Unless we do that,

[9] Exod. 2:7–8; 15:20–21; 17:12.   [10] Exod. 34:29–30.

the contestants will struggle to put the opposing party in the dock while they assume the role of the unbiased judge. God often reverses the roles when we spend time with him, helping the aggrieved person to see that he or she may even have played some part, albeit unwittingly, in creating the rift, or at least in making it possible by an unloving spirit.

Thirdly, we should hear God's Word. *'Listen to my words,'* the Lord said (6). He had things to say about himself (that he speaks and appoints), about Moses (as a faithful servant) and about the offenders: *'Why then were you not afraid?'* (8). In times of serious division, all parties need to gather dependently around an open Bible, not to sling texts at one another in self-righteous anger, but to listen attentively to what God may be saying to everyone concerned about the events that have led to such sad disruption.

Finally, we should love God's people. Aaron cried out to Moses because he was heartbroken about Miriam (*'Do not let her be like a stillborn infant'*, 12). Moses cried out to God because he was lovingly concerned for both the offenders. The grumblers' lovelessness had been transformed by Moses' compassion; their anger was met by his mercy.

Learn its lessons

Everyone had something to learn from this episode about handling disagreement.

Moses learnt the importance of silence. Aaron and Miriam complained, but Moses said nothing. When things go wrong in relationships, additional harm is inflicted by unhelpful speech and especially by attempts at self-justification. When people say cruel things about us or about others, why do we find it necessary to answer? It would be better by far to say nothing, letting the offending remark hang in the air, embarrassing the heedless or cruel speaker. Moses kept a still tongue and let the Lord do the talking.

Aaron learnt the value of prayer. The high priest had unique access into the presence of God, but that day he too was glad of a compassionate intercessor. As he heard Moses pray he realized afresh how crucial it is to pray for others as well as for ourselves, and to do so intelligently, lovingly and dependently.

Miriam learnt the generosity of grace. She had offended but was mercifully forgiven. During that week of enforced confinement she reflected on the infinite compassion of God. Once resentful of her younger brother's role, now she treasured healthier priorities. Pardoned, cleansed and healed, there was nothing greater she desired.

The people learnt the seriousness of sin. Eager to press on with their desert journey, they were compelled to wait until everybody had recognized that sin not only grieves God and destroys us; it damages others as well. Whenever we sin, others are always affected in one way or another. Even if we sin 'secretly', we have affected other people by our iniquity, although they may be ignorant of it. Offenders emerge from the sordid transgression as less than they might have been. Their holiness has been defiled, their testimony marred, their resistance weakened. Others are poorer because the offenders' sin was not conquered.

The offence of Aaron and Miriam had held them up in their desert travels, but it would be a week well spent if it taught them to honour God and to shun sin. Sadly, they were not good learners; the Lord's patience was to be tried even more. On the immediate horizon was an act not of family rivalry but of community rebellion. In the desert of Paran, they did not merely denigrate Moses; they defied God, as we shall see next.

PART 3. DRAWING BACK
(13:1 – 14:45)

13:1–33
12. Giants or grapes?

This dramatic narrative, describing the sending of the spies and its consequent events, became engraved on the corporate memory of God's people. Later writers referred back to these incidents with a sense of painful disappointment.[1] It records a time of decision-making, when the desert pilgrims made a catastrophic mistake. It is tragically easy to be influenced by unworthy attitudes, corrupted by impure motives or manipulated by unsuitable people. Walt Whitman's verse expresses what has become the typically post-modern insistence on total freedom of choice, indifferent to moral consequences or social conventions:

> Afoot and light hearted I take to the open road,
> Healthy, free, the world before me,
> The long brown path before me leading wherever I choose.[2]

Believers acknowledge a higher priority. They recognize the importance of waiting upon God. Our dominant thought is not 'What suits me best?' but 'What honours God most?' Like Israel at this crucial time in her history, we too face an unknown future. We like to think we have things reasonably mapped out, but the months and years ahead are not revealed to us.

Millions of our contemporaries long for some comforting assurance about life's imminent events, turning, either seriously or playfully, to the horoscope pages of their daily paper or favourite magazine. Many search for assurance through more sinister occult activity, consulting clairvoyants or using tarot cards, ouija boards and the like. Christians take seriously the clear commands of Scripture that forbid the use of such practices, which 'defile' us and,

---

[1] Deut.1:26–46; 2:14–15; Pss. 95:10–11; 106:24–27.
[2] 'Song of the Open Road', *Walt Whitman: Complete Poetry and Collected Prose*, ed. Justin Kaplan (New York: The Library of America, 1982), p. 297.

more seriously, are 'detestable' to God.[3] Others in the contemporary scene pursue the quest for a secure or prosperous future through eastern mythologies and old and and new religions. In recent years the ancient Chinese preoccupation with Feng Shui has become increasingly popular in the UK, determining for many of its adherents the choice and placing of furniture, the colour of their paintwork, their window preferences – all said to affect the home's energy and to guarantee a prosperous future. In our global village the religious novelties of one continent are speedily transposed to suit the nervous demands of another.

Christians recognize that God alone knows the future and holds their destiny in his strong and reliable hands. Life is more than a series of disconnected accidents, and believers are not to fret about the unknown. Their part is to live each day to his glory, discern his will in times of decision and trust him for the guidance he has promised to provide.[4]

Out of that vast crowd, only four people acknowledged the importance of seeking God's mind and trusting his word. The rest, tortured by uncertainty, plagued with inadequacy and paralysed by fear, refused to press on with their journey. Christian readers will learn from their mistakes and trace their path into the future with the landmarks clearly portrayed in this graphic narrative. There may be times when, like them, we are genuinely fearful about the way ahead. Some have discovered they are seriously unwell or have heard that someone they love has a terminal illness. Security at work is threatened; redundancy and unemployment become a grim probability. Church relationships may have become soured by the damaging example of an admired leader or the defection of valued friends. Family stability has been jeopardized by a partner's unfaithfulness, or parents may be deeply troubled about tensions in the lives of their married children. What seemed a reasonably tranquil and secure life is suddenly tossed into agonizing turmoil. How does the believer react to such a dramatic and unwelcome change of circumstances?

The story before us has been 'written to teach us', so that through God-given endurance and 'the encouragement of the Scriptures we might have hope.'[5] Caleb and Joshua feature in this narrative as the confident encouragers of God's people. Their heartening ministry was rejected by the Israelite community. It must not be lost on us. We must listen again to the buoyant plea of these two returning spies as they urge their incredulous contemporaries to trust in God – what he said in promise (1–16),

[3] Lev. 19:31; Deut. 18:9–13; Is. 8:19–20; 47:8–15.
[4] Ps. 32:8–10; Prov. 3:5–6; Is. 30:19–21.   [5] Rom. 15:4–6.

accomplished in history (17–22), achieves in experience (23–27) and provides in abundance (28–33).

Accept God's promises (13:1–16)

Moses was told to send twelve men *to explore the land of Canaan*, which, God said, *'I am giving to the Israelites'* (2). It is a recognized military maxim that 'time spent on reconnaissance is never wasted'. Before this particular reconnoitre began, God reminded Moses of the promise made to Abraham; here was a land he was determined to give to them. Out of the vast numbers of Israel's people, these twelve men were sent as representative scouts on a venture that 'was more a test of faith than a military expedition'.[6]

The fact that these twelve individuals belonged to such a huge community ought to have been their first encouragement to trust God's word. Those very words, *'the land of Canaan, which I am giving to the Israelites'* (2), recalled the twofold promise of both people and land made centuries earlier to Abraham, the father of their race: 'I will make your offspring like the dust of the earth … Go, walk through the length and breadth of the land, for I am giving it to you.'[7]

When the 'spies' were appointed from those twelve tribes, did they not recall that their huge numbers undeniably testified to God's reliable word? The first part of the divine promise had been gloriously fulfilled. As this vast company of travellers stood on the threshold of the promised land, they were indeed 'like the dust of the earth'. God had assured the patriarch that his descendants would 'take possession of the cities of their enemies'.[8] They had witnessed the first part of God's promise in the massive increase in their numbers; surely they could trust the second part about the guaranteed conquest.

Yet, overcome by fear and terrorized by the possibility that their vast numbers would be decimated by the physically massive people who lived in Canaan, the pilgrims refused to accept God's promise. Their unbelief in what God had plainly said is a sombre warning. As we face the unknown future, we do so with a reliable Bible in our hands. God 'has given us his very great and precious promises',[9] assuring us that, as we encounter the unknown, everything we need will be unfailingly provided.

---

[6] Milgrom, p. 100.   [7] Gen. 13:16–17.   [8] Gen. 22:17.   [9] 2 Pet. 1:4.

Remember God's faithfulness (13:17–22)

As the spies set out, they were clearly told where to go (17) and what to look for (18–20). They were to walk in the footsteps of the patriarchs. *'Go up through the Negev and on into the hill country'* ... *So they went up and explored the land ... They went up through the Negev and came to Hebron* (17, 21–22).

Abraham had 'set out ... towards the Negev'.[10] Assured that his offspring would be like the dust of the earth, he had been told to do exactly what, centuries later, these spies were ordered to do: "'Go, walk through the length and breadth of the land, for I am giving it to you." So Abram moved his tents and went to live near the great trees of Mamre at Hebron, where he built an altar to the LORD.'[11]

In the course of their six-week journey, the spies reached Hebron, the highest town in the entire region, around 1,000 metres above sea level. Centuries earlier, Abraham had bought some land from the local Hittites so that he and his family might be buried there.[12] In that very place, his body and those of his wife Sarah, his son Isaac with his wife Rebekah, and his grandson Jacob with his wife Leah, had all been laid to rest. All Jacob's sons, with the exception of Joseph, were buried there too.

Those twelve spies were on ground hallowed by memories of God's faithfulness. Here the patriarchs had lived and loved, walked and worshipped, believed and obeyed. They too had faced difficult and demanding experiences. Life had been far from easy for any of them, but God had seen them through. At one time or another, they had made huge mistakes and had let God down, but the Lord had not failed them. This very countryside offered its own rich testimony to the Lord's unchanging faithfulness. Surely, in such honoured territory, the spies would be encouraged that the Lord who had helped their forebears would not fail them.[13]

Sadly, although the spies saw the very places where the patriarchs had proved God's goodness, they remained daunted at the prospect of entering the land. We must learn from their sad mistake and, like the patriarchs and millions of others, believe and prove that when we face an uncertain future the Lord unfailingly helps us.

Recall God's generosity (13:23–27)

Not only were they told the route for their journey; they were asked to bring back, if possible (*'Do your best'*, 20), some visible

[10] Gen. 12:9.   [11] Gen. 13:14–18.   [12] Gen. 23:1–20.   [13] 1 Sam. 7:12.

proof that the land was rich and prosperous. Forty years earlier, Moses had been told that their new home would be spacious and abundantly fruitful.[14] It was summertime and, as they stood on the threshold of this new territory, Moses wanted to encourage the people with undeniable evidence of Canaan's abundant provision: *'bring back some of the fruit of the land.' (It was the season for the first ripe grapes.)* (20).

As the spies drew to the close of their precarious exercise they looked for the best grapes they could find. The search ended in 'Cluster Valley', so called because of the huge bunches of grapes that covered its prosperous vineyards: *When they reached the Valley of Eshcol, they cut off a branch bearing a single cluster of grapes. Two of them carried it on a pole between them, along with some pomegranates and figs* (23). When the reconnaissance party returned to base camp they showed the waiting people the fruit of the land.

What God had said to Moses as he had stood by that blazing bush in the desert of Midian was absolutely true: *'it does flow with milk and honey!'* The spies repeated God's words and produced visible evidence that it was exactly as the Lord had said. They were not simply reflecting on the divine message in days gone by. They produced contemporary confirmation of the reliability of God's word.

Here is another important dimension as we face an uncertain future. We must look not only back for assurance but around us for evidence in our lives of his sovereign guidance, unchanging presence and providential care. Abundant clusters of fruit in our everyday lives encourage us to believe that the Lord who has brought us so far will not disappoint us in the days to come, however difficult they may be. When threatened by imminent change we feel hesitant, insecure, vulnerable and even bewildered, but we must look carefully around at our present scene and itemize the 'clusters' from our contemporary experience. If we take a trip to our own Cluster Valley, we are likely to find abundant evidence of God's unfailing generosity. These present tokens of his providential care need to be gratefully transposed into items for thanksgiving and praise. The God who is meeting our present needs will not deny us his future provision.

Receive God's resources (13:28–33)

That cluster of grapes, the present logo of the Israeli Tourist Board, symbolizes the prosperity of the land and the generosity of the

[14] Exod. 3:8.

God who gives abundantly to all his people. Yet, although two of the spies displayed the grapes, the rest described the giants. The description of abundant fruitfulness was dwarfed by lurid details of colossal human monsters and their massive strongholds: *'But the people who live there are powerful, and the cities are fortified and very large'* (28).

In every challenging situation, there is always someone with an apprehensive *But*. The passage starkly portrays the dramatic contrasts between the radiant optimism of the trusting two (*'We can certainly do it'*, 30) and the despairing pessimism of the terrified ten: *'We can't'* (31). The despondent spies magnified the problems and minimized the resources.

They magnified the problems

Undoubtedly, there were tall and strong people but, although daunting to the pilgrims, they were not superior to God. The despondent ten viewed the scene entirely from their limited human perspective, leaving God totally out of the equation.

They had forgotten the God of the patriarchs. Had they the spiritual sensitivity to discern it, the very exercise of walking through the land over the past six weeks was, in God's sight, a symbolic gesture indicating assured future possession. They had been instructed to go *up through the Negev and on into the hill country* (17). As we have seen, that was precisely what Abraham had been told to do centuries earlier when the land was guaranteed to him and his promised progeny. Abraham did just that, settling eventually at Hebron, where the twelve spies had just been. God had done astonishing things for Abraham. If God could work miracles in Abraham's life, he could do it in theirs.

They had forgotten the God of the exodus. They reported on the physical prowess and secure strongholds of the land's inhabitants, but it was a huge mistake to forget about God. The *powerful* people were no worry to the Lord. He was not intimidated by giants and knew how to deal with *fortified* towns. Such communities may have been *very large* to the Israelites but they were ridiculously small to an omnipotent God. Their description of the land's mixed races ought to have heartened them rather than daunted them, for with those words Moses was first assured of conquest. The sighting of the *Amalekites ... in the Negev; the Hittites, Jebusites and Amorites ... in the hill country; and the Canaanites ... near the sea and along the Jordan* recalled the message about possession that God gave Moses. That is precisely how their victories were described: 'I have promised to bring you up out of your misery in Egypt into the land of the Canaanites, Hittites, Amorites, Perizzites, Hivites and Jebusites.'[15]

Nobody in that crowd of frightened pilgrims could doubt what God had done for them in the past. Egypt's superior strength, military resources and impressive chariots were nothing to God. He put them all under the water of the Red Sea. At the exodus they felt equally powerless, but they had trusted his word and witnessed his power: 'Do not be afraid ... The LORD will fight for you.'[16] The God who had vanquished the tyrants of the old land would overcome their enemies in a new one.

They minimized the resources

Paralysed by fears and plagued by inadequacy, they were totally deficient in self-worth: *'We seemed like grasshoppers in our own eyes, and we looked the same to them'* (33). Self-doubt is a cruel and crippling emotion. It robs its victims of security, dignity, composure and resourcefulness. If we are to be used by him, we must certainly begin with a realistic assessment of our limitations. Great things are achieved by God's servants when they are brought to an end of their own slender resources and realize that they have no alternative but to rely totally on his limitless provision. To operate in brash self-confidence is to court disaster; to remain in cowering self-doubt is to distrust God.

Forty years after those unbelieving people refused to enter the land, a series of events took place which they could have witnessed for themselves had they trusted in God. The God of the exodus did at the Jordan what he had accomplished at the Red Sea. Within a matter of weeks, the impregnable walls of one of those dreaded *fortified and very large* cities (28) toppled at the blast of trumpets.[17] Later in their history, a fearful doubter overcame his innate 'grasshopper' mentality and led a totally outnumbered band of troops against a huge army; the battle was won not by swords but by trumpets, jars and torches.[18] Years later a giant, such as those feared by the spies, was conquered by a young boy who merely hurled a stone from his shepherd's sling – but all the power of God was behind it.[19]

Demoralized by self-doubt, those frightened spies in the Paran desert needed a lesson in divinely manoeuvred exploits. Those who are convinced of God's omnipotence never minimize the divine resources. Empowered by God, the smallest of grasshoppers can give giants a rough time.

[15] Exod. 3:17.   [16] Exod. 14:13–14.   [17] Josh. 3:1–17; 6:1–20.
[18] Judg. 6:11–22; 7:19–22.   [19] 1 Sam. 17:1–50.

14:1–45
13. Israel's sleepless night

Caleb and Joshua's optimistic votes counted for little while their ten companions spread 'a bad report about the land they had explored' (13:32). The terrified ten looked like winning the day, but the trusting two were determined not to give up easily. Despite ominous signs of potential failure, they still hoped it might be possible to turn it all around. The ensuing narrative introduces us to five graphically portrayed character studies, worthy of close attention. These people are still with us, and their grim or noble example lingers on.

The hostile multitude (14:1–4)

Gloom spreads like wildfire among an unbelieving community. Pierre Teilhard de Chardin maintained that in the Lord's work pessimism has done infinitely more harm than atheism. Bad reports (13:32) have excess numbers of willing communicators while good news lies waiting to be shared. With the adverse reporting of the ten still ringing in their ears, the distraught multitude started to cry, and their incessant wailing continued through a long night (1). 'Abandoning their hopes for better things, they reviled Moses and God himself',[1] tragic evidence of a threadbare faith. These defiant people rebelled first against their leaders (1–2) and then against their Lord (3–4).

Rebelling against their leaders (14:1–2)

Leadership is a costly privilege. If they were to save the situation, Moses and Aaron had a difficult task ahead. The narrative focuses on three characteristics of the mutinous multitude.

[1] Gregory of Nyssa, *The Life of Moses*, I.66.

First, they were united in their opposition. The narrative underlines the grim pervasiveness of the rebellion. Three times these verses emphasize the widespread consensus and grim solidarity; *all the people of the community* were involved. *All the Israelites grumbled ... the whole assembly.*

Secondly, they were distraught in their opposition. Their raised voices and incessant weeping went on throughout the entire night. Sin reverses their destiny, turning this potentially brilliant new beginning into a tragically bitter ending.

Thirdly, they were defiant in their opposition. The community had become used to complaining (11:1–6; 12:1),[2] but now, terrified of the future, they disowned the past and debased the present. They wished they could reverse the exodus: *'If only we had died in Egypt! Or in this desert!'*

It is their most rebellious language so far. They wished to eradicate from their memory everything that had happened since that first Passover. It was a hideous desire, totally inconsistent for people with even the slightest notion of God's abundant and undeserved generosity. It mattered nothing that he had pledged himself to them in dependable covenant love. They were indifferent to his ideals for society, embodied in the Ten Commandments. What tragic defiance this was, to turn their backs on a God of such incomparable grace and goodness!

The greatest tragedy is that the Israelite defection merely anticipates the disobedience of millions across the centuries. They, and we, have been equally incredulous and rebellious. Those wilderness travellers adopted a course of action remarkably similar to the one Paul described in Romans. 'For although they knew God, they neither glorified him as God nor gave thanks to him, but their thinking became futile and their foolish hearts were darkened ... Therefore God gave them over ...'[3]

Rebelling against their Lord (14:3–4)

As they continued to murmur, they turned imperceptibly from moaning about their leaders to complaining about God. 'Why?' is the most searching question of all,[4] but these rebels had no cause to question God's wisdom or to doubt his sufficiency after all he had done for them.

They despised his generous provision: *'Why is the LORD bringing us to this land ...?'* It was because he loved them, and it was one of

---

[2] Exod. 5:19–23; 14:10–12; 16:1–11; 17:2–3.   [3] Rom. 1:21, 24.
[4] Mark 15:34.

the most lavish things he could have done for them, yet they hurled the choice gift back in his face.

They questioned his promised protection. Did they really imagine that he would bring them so far only to let them fall by the sword? The God who had routed the Amalekites at the beginning of their journey[5] would surely defeat the Canaanites at its close.

They doubted his unfailing love. *'Our wives and children will be taken as plunder.'* It is unthinkable that a God who provided for the communication of the faith through families[6] would allow vast numbers of women and children to be *taken as plunder* by the Canaanite hordes. He was fully able to care for their children, and later told them so (31).

They disowned his unique redemption. *'Wouldn't it be better for us to go back to Egypt?'* All he had done in liberating them from their brutal oppressors was dismissed in a heartless, blasphemous sentence.

They spurned his appointed leader. *'We should choose a leader and go back to Egypt.'* It was one thing to dread the future and make a torture of the present. It was quite another to reject the past as a total embarrassment to them. They were looking for someone who would take them back to a 'pre-Moses' lifestyle – a life without freedom, guidance, security, provision, protection, forgiveness, worship or hope.

The disastrous defection anticipates and illustrates the tragedy later described by Peter when the once-committed Christian jettisons values that were once supreme.[7] This account of Israel's infamous rebellion is a perpetually relevant warning.

The importunate messengers (14:5–9)

Though the rebels rejected Moses, his friends Caleb and Joshua begged them to think again. It was the last chance to convert these resolute rebels into submissive servants. At this moment they were Israel's evangelists, like Pilgrim's guide, 'one of a thousand'; the world was behind their backs and they stood as if they pleaded with their hearers.[8]

Moses and Aaron *fell face down in front of the whole Israelite assembly* (5). They were overcome with remorse that such awful things had been said by this blasphemous, ungrateful multitude.

---

[5] Exod. 17:8–16.   [6] Exod. 10:2; 12:26–27; Deut. 6:6–7, 20–25.
[7] 2 Pet. 2:20–22.
[8] John Bunyan, *The Pilgrim's Progress*, ed. J. B. Wharey, rev. R. Sharrock (Oxford: Clarendon, 2nd ed., 1960), p. 29.

They pleaded with God. Joshua and Caleb *tore their clothes* (6). It symbolized intense grief; mourners did this when suddenly bereaved. These four men felt an acute sense of grievous loss; the people who had journeyed with them as privileged pilgrims were about to return to Egypt as arrogant mutineers. Has sin brought them to this critical parting of the ways? Would this defiant mob actually turn round and march back in the direction of renewed slavery?

Every Christian evangelist stands between a merciful God and an obdurate people. However eloquent and well-informed, the contemporary evangelist is as powerless as Caleb and Joshua on the day they pleaded with that heedless multitude. We can only do what they did: present a portrait of a unique God who has done so much for rebels, and pray that he will melt their hard and stubborn hearts. In their moving, final appeal, Caleb and Joshua presented their hearers with a majestic portrait of God. The truths they shared are as relevant today as when they were first spoken to that hostile yet needy congregation.

God is generous. Their contemporaries may have feared the future, but these two men had seen for themselves Canaan's spacious fields, rich orchards and prosperous vineyards. They had drawn water from its deep wells and nobody, not even the terrified mob before them, could rob them of what they had actually seen with their own eyes: *'The land we passed through and explored is exceedingly good'* (7). They were talking to people who had never known such lavish generosity. Until they entered the land, the spies had lived with limited horizons. They knew only the grim slavery conditions of Egypt or the wild wastes of an inhospitable desert, and they were horrified to think that, in a moment of crowd hysteria, their new life might be thrown away.

Christian evangelists face a similar scenario. They plead with indifferent or hostile listeners from a similar perspective. Yet such messengers are unlikely to have a better response than Caleb and Joshua unless someone infinitely more persuasive invades the minds of their unbelieving hearers, convincing them that they too can experience what the heralds have seen. Only the Holy Spirit can turn obdurate or apathetic hearers into people who respond penitently and gratefully.

God is sensitive. He was not a detached and distant deity, imperiously removed from the realities of the Israelite distress. As their intensely personal God, he was capable of being loved or hurt, delighted or grieved. They could please him (8) or oppose (9) him. Over the past year, these people had adopted a totally damaging value-system. They had come to believe that what

123

mattered most was pleasing themselves, when in reality life's greatest satisfaction comes only by pleasing God: *'If the LORD is pleased with us, he will lead us into that land'* (8). The Lord Jesus had this as his persuasive testimony, that he pleased God.[9] Sharing our humanity, he knew that the only way he could do that was by deliberately deciding not to please himself.[10] Mature Christians identify with Christ in that resolute determination; pleasing the Father is life's greatest priority.[11]

God is holy. People are reluctant to learn that there is no neutrality in such matters; those who will not please him, grieve him. Caleb begged his hostile hearers not to take up arms against God: *'Only do not rebel against the LORD'* (9). To utter an implacable 'No' to his loving purposes was an affront to his holiness. In providing the land he was giving his best; in their hostile disobedience they were offering their worst.

God is powerful. Caleb repeatedly urged the congregation to relinquish their fears: *'And do not be afraid of the people ... Do not be afraid of them'* (9). Canaan's giant fighters and their 'indestructible' defences were no threat to an omnipotent God. If God is around, strong bulwarks are useless; their best *protection is gone.* The useless idols in which the Canaanites trusted were non-existent figments of debased human imagination, helpless defenders indeed.

God is present. Lonely and isolated in their fear, they longed for someone alongside them as a caring, supportive companion. On many a dark day, that assurance of God's presence had sustained the patriarchs.[12] If he had done that for them, how could he possibly abandon their successors? The previous year, as newly released Israelite slaves, they had counted on the firm promise of their omnipresent Lord[13] and he had not let them down.

The two messengers had made an impassioned plea for the people's repentance, a radical change of mind. But it was totally unavailing. Far from responding to their appeal, *the whole assembly talked about stoning them* (10). The congregation incensed, the message spurned, the messengers endangered, the Lord angry – it was a grim scene. *Then the glory of the LORD appeared*, confirming the divine presence and holiness (10; cf. 16:42).

---

[9] Matt. 3:17; 17:5.   [10] John 5:30; Rom. 15:1–3.
[11] Rom. 12:1; Eph. 5:10; Heb. 13:21.
[12] Gen. 21:22; 26:28; 28:15; 31:3, 5, 42; 39:2–3, 20–21, 23.
[13] Exod. 13:21; Deut. 4:37; Is. 63:9.

The compassionate intercessor (14:10–19)

These intractable people were treating the Lord *with contempt*. Although he provided them with incontrovertible evidence of his presence and power, they still refused *to believe* in him (11). He would not tolerate their persistent rejection, and thought it best to start afresh: *'I will strike them down with a plague and destroy them, but I will make you into a nation greater and stronger than they'* (12). God had issued exactly the same threat after the golden-calf defection.[14]

'Striking with a plague' was reminiscent of his judgment upon the obdurate Egyptians. The Lord was proposing to start his plan of salvation history all over again with a fresh line and a new people. Caleb and Joshua had not succeeded with the people. Moses hoped that he might plead effectively with God. Three issues were uppermost in the mind of this compassionate intercessor. He was jealous for God's glory (13–16), committed to God's word (17) and mindful of God's love (18–19).

The intercessor is jealous for God's glory

God's reputation was at stake. *The Egyptians* would *hear about it*, and how they would gloat over the defeat of the Israelite people! 'Egypt's soldiers had not slain them at the Red Sea, but Israel's God has done so on the borders of Canaan!' The exultant Egyptians would pass the news on to the Canaanite nations, rejoicing with them that their potential opponents were vanquished – and killed by their own God at that. If the surrounding nations heard that this vast company had perished just as they were about to enter new territory, they would attribute the failure to God's impotence rather than to his people's iniquity. They would relish the idea that Israel's LORD *was not able to bring these people into the land he promised them on oath; so he slaughtered them in the desert*. 'God's incompetence' – what a theme for pagan rejoicing!

Every intercessor needs to be reminded of the priorities of prayer. It is possible to corrupt this rich privilege and to turn it into a self-exalting and self-seeking exercise.[15] Intercessors long for the blessing of those for whom they pray, but most of all they yearn for God to be glorified through the manner in which he answers their prayers. They do not want the needs of their friends to be met at the expense of God's honour. They would rather their prayers be ignored if his name would in any way be defamed by the answer they desire.

[14] Exod. 32:10.   [15] Luke 18:9–14.

The intercessor is committed to God's word

When Moses entered the audience chamber of God, he reflected on some great truths he had received both at the initial giving of the law and at its renewal after the tragic golden-calf episode. As he came to talk with God, the intercessor rejoiced that God had already talked to him. *'Now may the LORD's strength be displayed, just as you have declared'* (17).

Moses asked that God's strength might be manifest. He pleaded that the Lord's restraining power might be seen and experienced by the rebellious Israelites. The same word, here translated *strength*, appears with a similar nuance in Nahum 1:3, 'The LORD is slow to anger and great in power'; he is great in forbearance. What they deserved was precisely what the Lord had threatened (12), but the intercessor pleaded that God's astonishing patience might be demonstrated.

Moses pleaded that God's word might be remembered. This fervent intercessor had the spiritual audacity to remind God of what he had already said about himself: *'as you have declared'* (17). After the scandalous incident of their wilful idolatry in making and adoring a calf of gold, he had said he would be merciful to those whom he wished to receive his mercy.[16] In making such a bold appeal on behalf of people who least deserved it, Moses cast himself on the divinely affirmed and unchanging compassion of God.

The intercessor is mindful of God's love

Moses repeated in the Lord's presence (18–19) what he had heard from God when he stood at Sinai with Israel's sick idolatry fresh in his memory. Then God had revealed his nature as 'the compassionate and gracious God, slow to anger, abounding in love and faithfulness'.[17] With conflicting emotions, Moses both rejoiced and grieved as he recalled that incident, for on the day the Lord declared his love he also revealed his promise: 'Obey what I command you today. I will drive out before you the Amorites, Canaanites, Hittites, Perizzites, Hivites and Jebusites.'[18] Now, here was Israel's intercessor pleading for God's mercy toward this obdurate people when they had neither obeyed his command to enter the land nor trusted his power to vanquish their enemies. Yet, despite Israel's stubborn unbelief, the intercessor cast himself on all he knew of the multichrome dimensions of the Lord's love for his people.

---

[16] Exod. 34:6; 33:19.   [17] Exod. 34:6.   [18] Exod. 34:11.

It is persistent love. He is *slow to anger* (18). They had repeatedly tried his patience (22), but he kept on loving them, even at a time of widespread defection at Canaan's border.

It is generous love. Overflowing with compassion and *abounding in love* (18), God refused to put limits on his love simply because, at times, they did not appear to love him.

It is reliable love. The word used for *love* here (*ḥeseḏ*) is the great term, variously translated and found about 250 times in the Old Testament, for God's covenant or steadfast love, his unfailing faithfulness to his loving agreement with his people, his pledge of total dependability.[19]

It is pardoning love, *forgiving sin and rebellion*. On the grounds of God's *great love*, the intercessor begged him to *'forgive the sin of these people, just as you have pardoned them from the time they left Egypt until now'* (19). That verb 'to forgive' means 'to carry away', like lifting a crippling load from our shoulders for ever.

It is righteous love. *'Yet he does not leave the guilty unpunished; he punishes the children for the sins of the fathers to the third and fourth generation'* (18). Moses again quotes God's word, this time from the Decalogue[20] with its reminder that sin has a tragic reproductive effect, even within the narrow limits of a family circle. In ancient near-eastern society as many as four generations might shelter under one roof, and, like an unchecked missile, sin pursued its lethal course until every family member became an unhappy sufferer. In the contemporary scene, marriage breakdown is a painful experience not only for the couple concerned but for their parents and grandparents, to say nothing of the psychological damage to the divorcees' children. Of the couples divorcing in England and Wales over the past ten years, over half have children under the age of sixteen.[21] Naturally affected by emotional stress, such children frequently witness the later failure of their own marriages.

The saying can hardly mean that God vindictively penalizes innocent people for their parents' or grandparents' wrongdoing; but, in the moral universe he has designed, sin cannot but have an adverse effect on people other than those who transgressed initially.

The determined Lord (14:20–35)

Israel's intercessor must have been intensely relieved when the Lord answered his prayer for his people's pardon: *The LORD*

---

[19] Jer. 31:3.   [20] Exod. 20:5–6.
[21] 'Annual Update: Marriage and Divorce 1998', *Population Trends*, Autumn 2000 (London: The Stationery Office), p. 72.

replied, 'I have forgiven them, as you asked.' Nevertheless they must live with its tragic effects. Two basic themes are focused in God's response to this rebellious situation: what Israel saw and what they said.

What Israel saw (14:22–23)

'Seeing' or perceiving is a spiritual responsibility. Since leaving Egypt they had repeatedly seen God's glory, which *fills the whole earth* (21). He had manifested that glory in the overshadowing cloud and, briefly, in the radiant face of Moses. They had been privileged to see *the miraculous signs* he *performed in Egypt and in the desert* (22) since their release from captivity.

God said, 'If they can have a vision of all that and yet rebel, I will hide from their vision the sight of the land they have refused to enter.' They and, most importantly, future generations must learn that resolute sinning has bitter consequences: *'not one of them will ever see the land I promised on oath to their forefathers. No-one who has treated me with contempt will ever see it'* (23). God said, 'I will give them precisely what they wanted', and who among them would be able to complain?

What Israel said (14:28–31)

The Lord had listened to the bitter complaints of *these grumbling Israelites* (27). They had said that they wished they had died in the desert (14:2). *'As surely as I live, declares the* LORD, *I will do to you the very things I heard you say: In this desert your bodies will fall – every one of you twenty years old or more who was counted in the census and who has grumbled against me'* (28–29).

They had also *said* that their children would be *taken as plunder* (31), but God refuted their disbelieving grievances. Far from being plundered, their protected children would conquer the land their sceptical parents had refused to enter.

Among Israel's mature population, only two adult males were excluded from this pervasive condemnation. People would see in Caleb and Joshua believers of *a different spirit*, who followed the Lord *wholeheartedly* (24). These loyal servants would possess the land they explored as spies.

Everyone under the age of twenty would become a visible testimony to the immutability of God's word. Over those forty years, the community would see these young people, *suffering for* Israel's *unfaithfulness* (33), working as nomadic shepherds when they might have been permanent residents in a new land. That would go on until the final wilderness funeral of Israel's rebellious people, *'until the last of your bodies lies in the desert'* (33).

Yet, although God judged his people (34), he still acted in compassion. It is not just the blameless children and youths who were in his care; the rebels were still his people and he was determined to provide for them. In his righteous judgment, he could not let them off; in his unique love, he would not let them go.

The condemned rebels (14:36–45)

Two groups of people fall into the hands of God, the righteous Judge.

The seditious spies (14:36–38)

Although all the people of mature age had *banded together against* the Lord (35) and must face the consequences of their rebellion, ten men were specially blameworthy, because they had *made the whole community grumble against* God *by spreading a bad report about* the land. People in leadership bear a special responsibility; much is expected of them and much will be required. The ten spies were influential tribal leaders (13:3), and had betrayed the trust that the Lord and his people had placed in them. They were not even allowed to go into the future wilderness scene. Had they been sent off with the others, their corrupting influence might have caused further damage, infecting the thinking of innocent young people destined to be the first Israelites to enter the land of promise.

The presumptuous soldiers (14:39–45)

Earlier, in their rebellious frame of mind, the people had said that they would not go up; now they said, *'We will go up to the place the LORD promised'* (40). They were repeating their previous rebellious action by not conforming to what the Lord required of them. Moses urged them not to go, *'because the LORD is not with you'* (42). The Lord had told them not to journey into that territory (25), but though he had forbidden it, they resolved to do so, and with disastrous consequences. 'It is catastrophic to treat God with reckless insistence or insolent presumption.'[22]

The sad episode of Israel's persistent rebellion moved to a tragic conclusion. Their defeated soldiers were buried in the desert and

---

[22] Owens, p. 123.

the dejected Israelites began a tediously delayed journey, which lingered in Israel's corporate memory. Through a repeated psalm, it was to teach the generations to come that disobedience to God is the gateway to despair: 'Today, if you hear his voice, do not harden your hearts.'[23]

Only those who pursue his will can enjoy his gifts. It was a theme the New Testament church also learnt from this grim story in Numbers.[24] Those who begin with God must go on with him. Continuance is 'the test of reality'.[25]

---

[23] Ps. 95:7–11.   [24] Heb. 3:6 – 4:11.
[25] F. F. Bruce, *The Epistle to the Hebrews*, New London Commentary (London: Marshall, Morgan and Scott), p. 59.

PART 4. MARKING TIME
(15:1 – 25:18)

15:1–41
14. When God speaks again

The central message of this new chapter is that, despite their disobedience and rebellion, a patient and merciful God was speaking again to his people. He kept the lines of communication open as he talked to them about undeserved grace (1–2), sacrificial worship (3–21), promised forgiveness (22–29) and necessary obedience (30–40).

Undeserved grace (15:1–2)

In his first word to the community after the desert revolt, their gracious God gave them three guarantees: concerning the continuity of the word, the security of the land and the preservation of the people.

The continuity of the word

As they began to travel back 'towards the desert along the route to the Red Sea' (14:25), they recalled God's last words to them. 'For forty years ... you will suffer for your sins ... I, the LORD, have spoken, and I will surely do these things' (14:34–35). Although they would have to pay the penalty for their transgression, God wanted them to know that he was still their God, and would commune with them through Moses, revealing truths and insights not only for their benefit but for all who were to follow them in the pilgrimage of faith.

This 'God still speaks' theme is evident throughout this chapter, and these guilty people desperately need its comfort, repeatedly confirmed in identical words: *The LORD said to Moses, 'Speak to the Israelites and say to them ...'* (1, 17, 37). The message is about keeping *these commands the LORD gave Moses* (22–23, cf. 35, 40). When, so soon after their grim defection, the Lord addressed these people so clearly, they could hardly doubt that he was still among them to direct their steps.

The security of the land

Although his people had frequently treated him 'with contempt' (14:11, 23), God spoke to them in grace, repeating the truth that the new generation would enter the land. His laws about the offering of their sacrifices are prefaced with the word of continuing promise: *'After you enter the land I am giving you as a home ...'* (2), and this assurance is followed by a similar declaration later in the chapter, as if to confirm the reliability of that pledge: *'When you enter the land to which I am taking you'* (18). At his appointed time, the young generation would certainly possess it and enjoy its abundant produce.

The preservation of the people

Every wilderness burial was another reminder of the irrefutable truth of God's judgment, and only the promise of God kept the young from despair. It was a grim prospect, this tedious trudge from one campsite to the next. And how could they be sure that God had choice purposes for their generation and, through them, for his unique people? That firm assurance echoes throughout this chapter with reiterated comfort: *For the generations to come ...* (14, 15, 21, 23, 38). The word he communicated would be obeyed and shared not only with their children and grandchildren but *throughout the generations to come* (21). Despite innumerable hazards, this redeemed community would treasure this truth until his own Son became incarnate in one of those generations, revealing his unique nature, undertaking his sacrificial work and fulfilling the divine purpose.

Sacrificial worship (15:3–21)

The particular laws he now communicated through Moses again confirmed his intention to bring Israel into Canaan. The provisions about their offerings itemized here anticipate the time when they would *enter the land* (2) God would give them. The additional gifts, which were to accompany their animal sacrifices, grain, oil and wine, were the gifts of resident farmers, not of nomadic shepherds. In the barren desert they could not sow seed, gather olives and plant vineyards. God said that the day would come when they would be able to *present to the LORD a grain offering of a tenth of an ephah of fine flour mixed with a quarter of a hin of oil* (4) and *a quarter of a hin of wine as a drink offering* (5).

The gifts they would offer would testify to the generosity of the divine Giver; by these offerings they would be pleasing the Lord, bringing their best, loving his people and supporting his servants.

Pleasing the Lord

Another characteristic note that echoes throughout this chapter is the recurrent phrase, *an aroma pleasing to the* LORD (3, 7, 10, 13, 14, 24). It pleased him because the offering indicated personal obedience (doing what he had commanded), declared their renewed loyalty and confessed their personal faith. The Lord was grieved that, far from pleasing him (14:8), the rebels had treated him 'with contempt' (14:11, 23), refused to believe in him (14: 11), disobeyed him (14:22), repeatedly tested him (14:22), grumbled (14:27) and 'banded together against' him (14:35). One day, on entering the land, the new generation would, through their obedient and grateful response to his generosity, offer gifts *pleasing to the* LORD.

Bringing their best

The offering of cereal products, oil and wine alongside their animals is highly suggestive of the 'sacred meal' aspect in Old Testament sacrifice. Such ingredients would feature in celebratory functions in their homes, and the presentation of sacrifices was meant to include this idea of a participatory meal. On most occasions, part of the animal sacrifice was for the priest, and sometimes part was shared among those who brought the offering.

The injunction about offering wine might even convey a gentle rebuke to a generation that had minimized the visual evidence of Canaan's abundance in that huge cluster of grapes gathered in Eshcol Valley. When God told them to present wine he was promising that it would be theirs to offer in abundance.

The detail about the offering of flour should not be overlooked. The first references are to the presentation of *fine flour* (4, 6, 9), highly refined, of rich quality and used for special occasions[1] or in royal households.[2] It symbolized the offering of their best to the Lord. A later reference to flour is equally important; Israelites were to present *a cake from the first of your ground meal and present it as an offering* as soon as it is available *from the threshing-floor*

---

[1] Gen. 18:6; Ezek.16:13.   [2] 1 Kgs. 4:22.

(20). There was no time to refine it into the best-quality flour, but the initial use of this more coarse grain was making a similar point as it symbolized putting the Lord *first*. They were to do it repeatedly each year they harvested the grain: '*Throughout the generations to come you are to give this offering to the LORD from the first of your ground meal*' (21).

Loving his people

These sacrificial regulations were not restricted to the *native-born* (13), those privileged Israelites brought up from infancy in the covenant community. Provision is also made for strangers, refugees or foreigners, *anyone else living among you* who wished to confess faith in Israel's God (13–16). The *alien* who desired to identify with God's people had to be protected from xenophobic enthusiasts who might use these sacrificial occasions to exclude people from other nations. Of equal importance, the faith itself had to be protected from foreigners who imagined they could simply hold Israel's faith alongside any other religious allegiances they may have liked to have. To become a worshipper of Israel's Lord was to enter the covenant community, to accept its laws and to meet its demands,[3] as well as to enjoy its privileges. This *lasting ordinance for the generations to come*, that the Israelite and the alien *shall be the same before the LORD*, not only reminded non-Israelites of the exclusive nature of their commitment to the Lord; it guarded them from social isolation and clannish embargoes.

The inclusion of the 'stranger' is all the more important in this context, given that Caleb, the hero of the preceding narrative, belonged to their company. In a later passage where, once again, he was praised for his undivided loyalty (32:12), he was deliberately identified as a 'Kenizzite'.[4] Both Joshua, *a native-born* (13) believer, and Caleb, *an alien living among* them (15), followed the Lord wholeheartedly. In contemporary society, where ethnic tensions and racial conflicts sadly characterize life on every populated continent, these two men stand before us as model believers. They insisted that people who put God first will never devalue others. Those who acknowledge God's prior claim on their lives know that to confess him means to live like him; he is lovingly concerned for everyone, whether *a native-born Israelite or an alien* (29).

---

[3] Exod. 20:3, 'no other gods'.   [4] Milgrom, pp. 391–392.

Supporting his servants

The sacrifices they were to offer at their first harvest after entering Canaan were to be special (17–21). They were told to *Present a cake from the first of your ground meal and present it as an offering from the threshing-floor … you are to give this offering to the LORD from the first of your ground meal* (20–21). This gift of the firstfruits was presented for the maintenance of the priests and their families (18:12–13), and provided for God's servants by making their fellow Israelites do so; the offering of the material asserted the primacy of the spiritual.

Promised forgiveness (15:22–29)

This discussion about animal sacrifices and cereal offerings is followed by a further duty allotted to the priesthood: the pastoral care of those who *unintentionally fail to keep any of these commands the LORD gave Moses.* These stipulations provide for offerings in such circumstances for the community (22–26) before dealing with those necessary for the unintended sins of an individual (27–29).

When the community sins unintentionally (15:22–26)

A careful distinction was made in Israel's law between deliberate sinning and inadvertent offences. A group of believers or an individual might grieve the Lord by their failure to do something God required of them (a sin of omission), or sin in ignorance by engaging in some action (a sin of commission) which, though they did not realize it, was expressly forbidden. Sinning in ignorance was to be differentiated from sinning 'defiantly' (30), although, in God's mercy, even intentional sins could be pardoned (5:5–8) because they could be atoned for (Lev. 6:7). Neither David nor Manasseh sinned unintentionally, but they were forgiven.[5] A holy God wanted his people to understand the seriousness of sin, and to do all within their power to keep clear of it; but here were some regulations about what is to be done when they realized that they had unwittingly sinned. The passage helps us to focus on the believer's understanding of the gravity of sin and how it impairs our relationship with God.

First, sin must be identified. God is holy and deeply sensitive to the damaging effects of sin; he has given us his *commands* so that

[5] Ps. 51; 2 Chr. 33:10–19.

his people will know what pleases or grieves him. God's Word plays a crucial role in identifying and exposing human sin; it is like a mirror that shows us what we are like in God's sight.[6] The regular reading and application of Scripture prevent us from accommodating to the increasingly immoral behaviour patterns of the contemporary world. Without Scripture's exposure of the seriousness of sin, we might easily become casual about it, indifferent to it, untroubled by it, even unafraid of it.

Once identified, sin must be shunned. This passage shows us how seriously God views sin, and God's Word not only alerts us to its perils but shows us how to flee from it. The early Christian preacher John Chrysostom emphasized that the Bible serves more than a negative function in exposing our errors. Scripture is 'far more excellent' than a mirror that starkly reveals what we are but is powerless to make us better. God's Word 'not only shows our own deformity, but transforms it too, if we be willing, into surpassing beauty'.[7]

Therefore, sin must be confessed. Concerned about their unintended sinfulness, the community sent representatives to the local priest so that they could acknowledge that they had made this inadvertent error. They knew how easily and speedily sin can contaminate a community, so they were eager to put it right before it spread like an infectious disease. One unconfessed sin quickly propagates another.

Further, sin must be removed. The members of the community wanted to be assured that their sin was pardoned. Only the priest could *make atonement* by means of an appropriate sacrifice *for the whole Israelite community* so that they might be *forgiven*. This term *to make atonement* means 'to wipe off', so that the offence is completely removed. The offence was decisively wiped away from the mind of God, and the offenders were assured of cleansing: *they will be forgiven*.

The sin was forgiven not because the offenders had paid the price of a sacrificial animal, but because God is merciful. The sacrifice confirmed the offenders' penitence and expressed the believers' gratitude. The New Testament takes up this rich sacrificial context in its confirmation that Christ alone is the believer's Priest, who mediates between the sinful offender and a pure and holy God. Our unique Priest became the sacrificial victim as he took upon himself the judgment due for our sins, and bore those sins in his physical body as he died for us upon the cross. By virtue of that

[6] Jas. 1:23–25.
[7] John Chrysostom, *Homilies on Matthew*, IV.16, Library of Nicene and Post-Nicene Fathers X, p. 27.

one utterly sufficient and completely effective sacrifice, we can know that we are totally forgiven.[8]

When an individual sins unintentionally (15:27–29)

It was generous of the Lord to be concerned about the problem of unintended sin when the community had just been so defiantly sinful. He knew the damage that could be done by even one person's corrupting influence in the community, so he turned from the needs of all the people to those of the individual. The Lord is concerned for every one, so that *if just one person sins unintentionally* (27), that single offender should not be distressed, fearful of having caused irreparable damage to his or her relationship with God. This offender too could visit the priest so that he could *make atonement before the LORD for the one who erred* (28).

The individual was not required to bring for sacrifice the same animals that the community had to offer. The presentation of a young *female goat* (27) would be sufficient, but the principle was the same. Sin had to be confessed at the presentation of the sacrifice; by this means atonement would be made before the Lord, and the offence would be forgiven. The guarantee of generous mercy would apply *to everyone who sins unintentionally*, whatever their status, *whether he is a native-born Israelite or an alien* (29).

Necessary obedience (15:30–41)

The Lord addressed the rebellious pilgrims on the highly relevant theme of wilful disobedience. He was not speaking now of inadvertent sinning but of defiant transgression, recently characteristic of the wilderness rebels and soon to be evident in some leaders (16:1 – 17:12). The theme is developed by means of a serious warning (30–31), a contemporary example (32–36) and a visual reminder (37–41).

A serious warning (15:30–31)

Individuals and community must recognize the seriousness of sin. Since their deliverance from Egypt, the Israelites had become casual about it, disregarding God's mercies, rejecting his promises, abandoning his plans, spurning his leaders and discarding his commands. None of these things could be described as unintentional sins; they were calculated acts of contemptuous (14:11, 23)

[8] Heb. 2:17; 7:25–28; 9:12–14, 24–28; 1 Pet. 2:24; 3:18.

insolence – words and deeds that despised what God had done in the past (14:4), what he expected from them in the present (13:30–32) and what he had planned for their future (14:7–8). They needed to be warned that repeating such defiant behaviour would have serious repercussions in their personal and corporate life.

They were first given a vocal warning to remind them of the dire consequences of deliberate disobedience. At Sinai, they entered into a covenant relationship with the Lord, promising to obey him and keep his covenant.[9] Tragically, they grieved him by repeated disobedience. God warned them yet again that, whenever they adopted a rebellious stance, it would be to their serious detriment. A righteous and holy God cannot be indifferent to defiant sinfulness, whoever its perpetrator might be.

The Lord began the warning by addressing the nature of the offence; sinning *defiantly* (30) employs a graphic Hebrew word meaning 'to sin with a high hand' that is 'poised to strike',[10] 'as though the transgressor was about to attack God'.[11] A term describing the confident assertiveness of the Israelites as they marched out *boldly*,[12] 'in full view of all the Egyptians' (33:3) is now employed to describe not their dependence on God but their opposition to him.

Moreover, the Lord emphasizes the implications of the injury. They have not merely *despised the* LORD's *word* (31); they have affronted his person. The wilful lawbreaker *blasphemes the* LORD (30), or reviles him, a word Ezekiel uses to describe the people's idolatrous worship.[13]

The warning also focuses on the universality of the judgment. His word applies to *anyone* who sins in this offensive, insubordinate manner, whatever his racial or ethnic background, whether *native-born or alien* (30). There are no favoured exceptions; nobody can plead religious experience, moral achievements or social status.

The warning further addresses the seriousness of the consequences. The offender must be *cut off from his people* (30), either by execution[14] or by excommunication. To blaspheme is to revile the name of the only one by whom we may be forgiven. The punishment warns the community's younger generation not to follow the sinister example of their parents.

The rebellion described here is coloured by its immediate context of the serious desert apostasy at Canaan's border, and equally influenced by the rebellion narrated in the following chapter. It portrays one who adamantly insists on maintaining a

---

[9] Exod. 15:26; 19:5; Deut. 6:3.   [10] Milgrom, p. 125.
[11] Harrison, p. 227.   [12] Exod. 14:8.   [13] Ezek. 20:27.
[14] For blasphemy, Lev. 24:10–16.

defiant attitude to the Lord. There were wanton sins in Old Testament times that, despite their seriousness, could be forgiven by Israel's gracious God. However, in these cases the offender was required to confess the sin, to make necessary restitution and to offer a guilt offering to the Lord. By these means the priest could 'make atonement for him' so that the sinner might be 'forgiven for any of these things he did that made him guilty'.[15] The difference between this merciful provision for deliberate offences and the implacable rule in Numbers 15 appears to relate to an attitude of penitence in the one and continuing defiance in the other. If the offender insists on displaying an angry clenched fist in the presence of a holy God, he nullifies the only means whereby forgiveness is possible.

A contemporary example (15:32-36)

As a stark example of defiant sinning, a story is introduced that illustrates sin 'with a high hand'. *While the Israelites were in the desert* (32), a man violated the covenant agreement by breaking the fourth commandment about keeping the Sabbath. Knowing full well that work of that kind was prohibited, he persisted in collecting fuel. The Lord had issued clear instructions about the penalty if this prohibition was rejected or ignored,[16] so the man was deliberately flouting the law, especially as it specifically prohibited the lighting of fires on the Sabbath day.[17] He was despising God's word, damaging the harmony of the redeemed community, setting a bad example to the younger generation and inflicting harm on himself.

Ezekiel later insisted that this wilderness generation repeatedly transgressed the Sabbath law,[18] disregarding the day that is different; but this is the only example of such punishment mentioned in the Old Testament. An outward witness to their pagan neighbours, the Sabbath marked them out as a distinctive people who did not work on that day because God had forbidden it. The day provided a precise opportunity for obedient living. 'High-handed' sinning of that kind could be neither ignored nor minimized.

A visual reminder (15:37-41)

The grim story of this defiant wood-gatherer would linger in the community's corporate memory. But something else was necessary

---

[15] Lev. 6:1-7. [16] Exod. 20:8-10; Exod. 31:14-17. [17] Exod. 35:2-3.
[18] Ezek. 20:12; 13-24.

139

to emphasize the priority of obedience. What better than a permanent visual reminder, part of their everyday clothing? They were to attach *blue cord* tassels to their robes, something *to look at* in daily life (38–39). Sewn to the edges of their garments, they encouraged them to *remember all the commands of the LORD* (not just the Sabbath prohibitions) so that they might *obey them.* This colourful visual aid was accompanied by a verbal statement that expressed a negative warning, a positive ambition and an inspiring affirmation.

The negative warning was that, if they did not learn 'the lesson of the blue tassels', they might *prostitute* themselves by *going after the lusts of* their *own hearts and eyes.* Underlining the seriousness of disobedience, the term *prostitute* indicates unacceptable sexual conduct;[19] it also appears in contexts about going after other gods, a form of spiritual adultery when Israel was loved by God.[20]

The word that exposed the danger of *going after* their own *lusts* is used frequently in the preceeding narrative about 'spying out' the land (13:2, 16–17, 21, 25, 32; 14:7, 34, 36, 38). Instead of looking to God's commands, the travellers had fixed their gaze on temporary desert hardships (11:1), Egypt's luscious food (11:4–5), Israel's restricted diet (11:6–9), Canaan's threatening residents (13:27–29) or their own possible slaughter and their families' eventual captivity (14:3). In their search for satisfaction and security they were looking in the wrong places.

The Lord also encouraged them with a positive ambition: *Then you will remember to obey all my commands and will be consecrated to your God.* God's ideal for his people was that by their obedience to his word they would be expressing their commitment to his person. They would be holy (the same word as that translated *consecrated* here), a people separated to him for his work, and therefore separated from anything that might inhibit their communion with God, spoil their lives and damage their witness. God faithfully kept his word to them; they too must be loyally reliable. He was holy, so they must be as well.[21]

Finally, the Lord encouraged the tassel-wearers with an inspiring affirmation: *I am the LORD your God, who brought you out of Egypt to be your God. I am the LORD your God* (41).

This magnificent declaration of God's unique nature (cf. 10:10) and invincible power forms a superb conclusion to this section of the book's teaching, particularly as it follows closely on the wilderness people's disobedient rejection of the promised conquest of

---

[19] Lev. 21:14; Deut. 23:18.   [20] Deut. 31:16; Hos. 2:4–7.
[21] Lev. 11:44; 19:2.

Canaan. It reminded them of the God of revelation. I AM was the name by which the Lord revealed himself to Moses in the Midianite desert. It reappears in the encounters of Moses and Aaron with the Egyptian Pharaoh and at the giving of the law.[22] 'I am' must be obeyed. If Moses had not obeyed (despite his human reluctance), the people would not have witnessed the Lord's mercy and power. The statement also reminded them of the God of redemption. A God who can accomplish the impossible had brought them out of their cruel Egyptian captivity. The people had had to obey his word about Passover or their eldest sons would have perished with Egypt's firstborn. Obedience was the clue and the key. Moreover, he was their God, who would never disappoint or fail them. Obedient people rejoiced in the unchanging affirmation, 'your God', repeated in this closing word of heartwarming reassurance.

[22] Exod. 3:14–15; 6:2, 6; 10:2; 20:1.

16:1–50
15. More leadership tensions

In this book's unfolding story we again switch suddenly from one literary genre to another. Yet the abrupt transition is more apparent than real. Obedience is a central theme in chapter 15 and is followed by a story relating the tragic consequences of disobedience (16:1–50).

Like the earlier spy story, the stark narrative about the rebellions instigated by Korah, Dathan, Abiram and On is a further tragic example of the power of sin to multiply itself. The bad report of the ten spies (13:32) spread rapidly throughout the whole camp like a ravaging disease of discontent, unbelief and fear. What began here as a solitary complaint, voiced by four individuals (16:1), soon became more extensive, gaining the allegiance of 250 well-known *community leaders*, highly responsible people who had been trusted as *appointed members of the council* (2). When God expressed his displeasure in an act of judgment, the entire community united in fierce opposition to Moses and Aaron (41–43).[1] Leadership issues dominate this section of the book as we see God's appointed leadership challenged (1–14), tested (15–22) and vindicated (23–50).

God's appointed leadership challenged (16:1–14)

The serious offences described in this story powerfully illustrate the sinister effects of sin. The four dimensions of this offence continue to be relevant in our not-so-different world: disobedience, discontent, disloyalty and disruption.

---

[1] On the skilful shaping of the material and the subtle interplay of themes in this section of the book, see Thomas W. Mann, 'Holiness and death in the redaction of Numbers 16:1 – 20:13', in J. H. Marks and R. M. Good (eds.), *Love and Death in the Ancient Near East* (Guilford, CN: Four Quarters, 1987), pp. 181–190.

Disobedience is the basic fault. The four offenders and their 250 supporters knew that both Moses and Aaron had been appointed by God to their leadership roles. Neither was a self-appointed executive. Moses shrank from the role, and from the beginning made strenuous attempts to be relieved of the office.[2] If these two men were so clearly designated by God for their specific tasks, it was defiant sinfulness in their opponents not to comply with the Lord's declared word and sovereign will. Many spiritually destructive acts begin with a stubborn refusal to submit to God.

The tribe of Levi, to which Korah belonged, had specific responsibilities; it was tragic that Korah was not content to do the precise work that had been assigned to him and his colleagues. The other three leading grumblers belonged to the tribe of Reuben, which had provided one of the rebellious spies. Here was a chance for them to show they were now intent on better things, genuinely regretting the earlier mistake of their clan leader (13:4).

Disloyalty is the further sadness. Those four grumblers and their supporters were utterly disloyal to Moses and Aaron. Living in that vast wilderness until all the old generation had died was hardly an inviting prospect; their work would be far from easy. As a prophet,[3] Moses might often be commissioned with difficult things to say to the people. As priests, Aaron and his sons would frequently be required to act as mediators between transgressors and their Lord. Such men were worthy of all the best support imaginable. Sin can damage a community of God's people when grumblers and gossipers aim to demolish their leaders, and criticize rather than pray for them. Levites were meant to be supporters, not opponents.

Disruption is the inevitable consequence. There is no such thing as a solitary sin. Once released, sin is like an irretrievable missile; it speeds on its destructive journey, creating havoc wherever it appears. The sin that began in Korah's insensitive heart quickly multiplied as people throughout the camp heard what he and the others were saying about Moses and Aaron. The sin of the four found a ready ear among the 250 leaders before it multiplied throughout the entire camp. What started out in one man's mind as an envious thought reproduced itself until it became a massive human disaster.

We need to develop the difficult art of letting sin die within us instead of sending it forward on its destructive mission. We cannot possibly do that in our own strength; the indwelling Holy Spirit is given so that we can put to death[4] potentially lethal thoughts.

[2] Exod. 3:11; 4:1, 10–17; 17:4; Num. 11:10–15.   [3] Deut. 18:15, 18.
[4] Rom. 6:11–14; 8:12–13.

Without his slaying power, sick thoughts can develop into dominating ambitions and malicious deeds, ruining others.

After introducing the ringleaders, this narrative confronts us with two major complaints: that of Korah, primarily directed at Aaron, the high priest (11), and another (led by Dathan, Abiram and On), seemingly addressed to Moses, the prophetic leader (12–14). The narrative encourages us to consider each story separately to discern its distinctive message.

Grumbling against Aaron

The opening narrative focuses on the rivalry expressed by Korah, and in the course of the story Moses defends the high priest: '*Who is Aaron that you should grumble against him?*' (11). A number of features in this complaint-story are important for us, especially if we encounter leadership tensions.

First, here is an example of misapplied Scripture. The grumblers told Moses that *the whole community is holy, every one of them, and the LORD is with them* (3). Moses would have agreed with his accusers. One of the purposes of the blue tassels on the people's garments was to encourage holiness of life. If, reminded by the tassels, they obeyed the Lord's commands, they would be 'consecrated' or holy (15:40) to the Lord: the same word as that used by the grumblers here. All the Lord's people were meant to be *holy* (3),[5] 'separated' *to* the Lord, with its inevitable corollary that they were 'separated' *from* the things that grieved their God, spoilt their lives, corrupted their neighbours and damaged their witness.

One wonders how seriously one should view the protest of these Levites, given that they were disregarding God's revealed word about their particular duties (8–9), coveting the work assigned to the priests (10), acting against the Lord (11a) and denigrating his servants (11b). They appear to have been interested in 'holiness' more as a verbal tag than as a distinctive lifestyle.

A good many troubles within Christian contexts find people on opposing sides blandly quoting whichever scriptures most support their particular viewpoint rather than giving themselves to an impartial study of the biblical message as a whole. Almost anything can be proved by using a carefully selected verse, robbed of its context. When the Lord described the priests as 'holy', the word was being used with a slightly different inference. All Israel was holy in the sense that the people were the Lord's possession and had been 'set apart' as his instrument of service in the world. The priests had also been 'set apart', but for specific duties and

---

[5] Lev. 19:2.

responsibilities that were not to be undertaken by others – certainly not by Levites, who also had been 'set apart' as the priests' supportive assistants.

Next, here we have an expression of unjust criticism. These grumbling Levites asked why, if everyone in Israel is holy, Moses and Aaron considered themselves superior to the rest. '*Why then do you set yourselves above the* LORD'*s assembly?*' (3). It was an unkind and untrue allegation: these two men had not set themselves over anybody. God had chosen them for their particular ministries. When things go wrong in human relationships, unkind or untrue remarks often fuel the trouble. The unsanctified tongue, a deadly weapon,[6] has destroyed the harmony of many a Christian congregation.

Here is an example also of an envious spirit. Not content with the important subsidiary roles the Lord had assigned to them, these Levites were *trying to get the priesthood too* (10). The fourth-century bishop Gregory of Nyssa described envy as 'that congenital malady in the nature of man'. 'Envy banished us from Paradise, turned Cain into a ruthless murderer and made young Joseph a slave. Envy ... sends the dart against Moses, but it does not reach the height where Moses was'.[7]

In this encounter, Moses also discerns a serious accusation. Although the vicious complaint is addressed to Moses and Aaron, in reality it is directed against God: '*It is against the* LORD *that you and all your followers have banded together*' (11). Moses and Aaron are in God's work because he has put them there; those who assail them revile him.

Grumbling against Moses

After addressing Korah and his cohorts, Moses then summoned Dathan and Abiram to come and speak to these charges made against them. The two men refused to attend the meeting, and proceeded to hurl further insults at the leadership, accusations more directly addressed to Moses as prophet rather than to Aaron as priest. This brief narrative focuses on a number of issues that expose their wrongdoing.

First, they resisted any attempt to discuss their differences. Moses sent for them to come to him so that the issues could be properly talked through. It was 'not only because he was unwilling to pass sentence without hearing the cause, but also because he endeavoured to bring them to repentance, that they might not

---

[6] Jas. 3:2–12.   [7] Gregory of Nyssa, *The Life of Moses* I.61; II.256–260.

wilfully destroy themselves'.[8] They totally resisted any suggestion that there might be a meaningful conversation or reconciliation: 'We will not come!' (12).

They looked back wistfully to times when they were under different leadership. Egypt's cruel tyranny now appeared better than the present regime under the leadership of the humblest of men (12:3). The words used to describe the future delights of Canaan were deliberately transferred to the former pleasures of Egypt: 'Isn't it enough that you have brought us up out of a land flowing with milk and honey ...?' (13).[9] They blamed their leader for everything that had gone wrong. Moses was far from perfect, and Numbers makes that abundantly clear (11:10–15; 20:6–12), but he was not remotely responsible for Israel's present hardships. They were due entirely to the people's disobedience, not to the leader's failures. The people accused Moses of bringing them out of Egypt's bountiful land, whereas in fact the omnipotent Lord had done this by his 'mighty hand and an outstretched arm'.[10]

Wrong motives were attributed to God's servant. The people insisted that Moses was intent on killing them (13), controlling them ('you also want to lord it over us', 13b) and physically assaulting them: 'Will you gouge out the eyes of these men?' (14). The accusation about gouging out eyes, a known punishment for rebels,[11] may be metaphorical, meaning 'to mislead'[12] or 'to deceive', by 'beguiling the people with false promises',[13] but Moses had no intention whatever of duping ('hoodwink', NEB), bullying or hurting them. They were misrepresenting his role; their unjust accusations offended the God who continued to use his maligned servant.

These malcontents diverted attention from their own mistakes by pointing the accusing finger at others. Not content to blame Moses for the past, they saddled him with responsibility for the present: 'you haven't brought us into a land flowing with milk and honey or given us an inheritance of fields and vineyards' (14). Everybody in Israel knew that Moses, Aaron and the two spies had begged the people to trust in God and enter the land. The leader could not be blamed if the fearful community had not responded to God's will. The fruitful vineyards they longed for were all there

---

[8] Calvin, IV, p. 106.

[9] Currid, p. 146, says that Egypt was well known in antiquity for both milk and honey, but an ironic twist is intended in mentioning them here.

[10] Deut. 4:34; 5:15.   [11] Judg. 16:21; 2 Kgs. 24:20; 25:5–7; Jer. 39:4–7; 52:7–11.

[12] Ashley, p. 311.

[13] Davies, p. 171, using Hebrew idiom, 'to throw dust in the eyes'; Thompson, p. 186.

in Canaan. They had seen the evidence in the huge cluster of grapes the spies had carried back to the camp, but had resisted every plea by the believing messengers (13:31; 14:10).

God's appointed leadership tested (16:15-22)

On hearing these allegations, Moses *became very angry* (15). Here was a repetition of what had happened when the spies returned from their expedition. Moses and his colleagues had pleaded with the people, but it was that specific ministry of prophetic communication that irritated them.

The earlier complaint of Miriam had been against Moses' ministry as prophet: 'Has the LORD spoken only through Moses?' (12:2). The resentment now expressed by Dathan, Abiram, On and their confederates also focused on Moses' role in conveying God's commands to the people, vividly and repeatedly expressed in the previous chapter: 'The LORD said to Moses' (15:1, 17, 22–23, 35, 37). Moses did only what God required of him, and insisted that he had not harmed any of them or gained any material advantage from his leadership (15).

Some means had to be found whereby the ministry of Aaron and Moses could be publicly authenticated. With dramatic irony, these discontented Levites who were 'trying to get the priesthood too' (10) were to act out their covetous dreams by an exclusively priestly function. Korah and his partners were to appear at the Tent of Meeting, each bearing a censer with *fire and incense in it* (18). Once again, a biblical narrative serves a theological purpose; the means by which the recognized priests were authenticated presents some rich aspects of the doctrine of God.

First, God is patient. The 250 malcontents were told on one day what was to happen on the next. They were *to appear before the LORD tomorrow* (16). Here was an opportunity for them to reflect on the seriousness of their offence, their opposition to God's revealed will, the hurt they were causing to their leaders and the damage they were inflicting on the community. There was time to repent.

Secondly, God is holy. At such a sick display of human arrogance, *the glory of the LORD appeared* (19). This rebellious demonstration of human sinfulness was made all the more heinous when contrasted with and exposed by God's holiness. The bright light of his shekinah presence was seen by everyone gathered there, and its radiant outshining made these rebellious malcontents all the more sinful. Sin is seen for the ugly thing it is when God reveals his glory. Isaiah experienced that revelation in the Jerusalem temple;

acknowledging God's holiness, he realized he had offended the Lord by his 'unclean lips'.[14]

Thirdly, God is powerful. These 250 disgruntled men with censers in their hands set themselves in fierce *opposition* to Moses and Aaron. The two leaders were totally outnumbered, but the protecting *glory of the LORD appeared to the entire assembly* (19). God's shekinah glory had appeared earlier when Moses and his colleagues were in grave danger (14:10), and here God's presence was manifest again at a time of evident need. It was also visible the following day, when the whole community rose up in further opposition to Moses and Aaron (42). The cloud that had shielded the Lord's people (9:15–23) now came to defend the Lord's servants.

Fourthly, God is righteous. The overshadowing cloud of God's glory was seen by the *entire assembly*. God told his servants to stand aside from the crowd so that he might reveal himself in judgment and *put an end to them at once* (21). Such a serious sin demanded drastic action if it was not to spread and lead to outright anarchy throughout the Israelite camp. When people are determined to treat *the LORD with contempt* (30), it cannot be passed unnoticed.

Sixthly, God is merciful. Moses and Aaron pleaded that innocent people might not suffer alongside the discontented offenders. They appealed to God as the Lord of unlimited compassion. He was the *God of the spirits of all mankind* (22), not just the God of Moses and Aaron. He had declared his covenant love for all the Israelite community and, although they were in danger of being infected by Korah's rebellion, why should the *entire assembly* suffer because one man had sinned in this way?

God's appointed leadership vindicated (16:23–50)

The judgment of God was expressed by three dramatic means: earthquake (31–33), fire (35) and plague (46), visiting the three different types of offenders: the ringleaders and their families (27), their immediate supporters in the 250 associates (35) and the wider company of people who joined in the general discontent (41). Several features in this vivid narrative deserve our attention.

First, people are changeable. The people who stood there witnessing the earthquake and fire had seen for themselves that God was grieved at this self-assertive rebellion by these discontented Levites. Once again, the God of Sinai was making his

---

[14] Is. 6:1–5.

presence known; earthquake and fire were the outward evidences of his incomparable might when God's word was given to them.[15]

On that day at Sinai the people had promised to 'do everything the LORD has said',[16] but here they were, engaged in a discontented feud with the God who had done so much for them. The people who one day ran away in terror (34) had returned on the *next day* (41) to complain, once again blaming Moses and Aaron for everything that had happened. They made them personally responsible for the death of the offenders (*"You have killed the LORD's people," they said'*, 41) when it was evident to all that God alone had intervened in judgment. How could the two leaders organize an earthquake or provide a consuming fire? People are fickle. One moment they are fearful of what might happen to them, and the next they are heedless about grieving God.

Secondly, reminders are important. The censers used by the Levite malcontents were retrieved from the smouldering remains of the judgment fire and hammered into bronze sheets as a new altar-covering. This *sign to the Israelites* (38) reminded them of the penalty that followed the blatant rejection of God's word. Each of the Levite rebels knew that *no-one except a descendant of Aaron should … burn incense before the LORD* (40). The new altar-covering was a visual aid; if anyone in the future took up a similar defiant stance, they too *would become like Korah and his followers* (40).

God graciously provided his people with visible symbols of what he had said and done, and this section of teaching presents us with several of them – blue tassels on their garments (15:39), this new bronze altar-covering and Aaron's staff that blossomed (17:10). The rainbow was an earlier sign of his covenant faithfulness,[17] and circumcision was another.[18] The annual celebration of Passover was a further inspiring 'sign' of God's power and mercy.[19] The memorial stones at the Jordan were a later 'sign' of the Lord's enabling presence,[20] as was the 'stone of help' erected by Samuel as a testimony to the Lord's goodness at a time of trouble.[21]

The Lord's Day is one such 'sign' for Christians, just as the Sabbath was a 'sign' to the Israelite people, reminding them of spiritual priorities and the need for obedience to the covenant commandments.[22] The value of signs is given its best expression in baptism and the Lord's Supper, vividly portraying in visible form Christ's saving death and victorious resurrection.[23]

Thirdly, atonement is crucial. God's anger was forcefully

[15] Exod. 19:18.　[16] Exod. 19:8.　[17] Gen. 9:12.　[18] Gen. 17:11.
[19] Exod. 13:9.　[20] Josh. 4:7.　[21] 1 Sam. 7:12.
[22] Exod. 20:10; 31:12–13; Ezek. 20:12.　[23] Rom. 6:4; 1 Cor. 11:23–26.

expressed when the assembled people *gathered in opposition to Moses and Aaron* (42). The Lord told the leaders he wanted to *put an end to* the rebels, and the two men *fell face down* (45), pleading with God for his merciful intervention. Acting swiftly, Moses urged Aaron to take up a censer and go into the presence of the recalcitrant assembly. It was a matter of extreme urgency; every passing minute, people were collapsing with plague that spread ferociously among the people. Aaron ran into their midst *to make atonement for them* (46).

Israel's high priest *stood between the living and the dead* until *the plague stopped* (48), an arresting picture of an infinitely greater Mediator. God's Son entered a rebellious world where people were indifferent to the power and consequences of sin, and its effects infinitely worse than the deadliest plague, but he *made atonement for them* (47). By his sacrificial death upon the cross, he stands between the living and the dead; our response to his saving work determines whether we shall live with him for ever or pass to a lost eternity.[24]

Fourthly, sin is devastating. What started as a rebellious thought in the mind of Korah and his companions moved on its ugly journey throughout the entire camp. A grumble expressed by over 250 people infected thousands. When, at the end of that grim day, they buried those who had died in the plague, they dug thousands of graves. The Levites were meant to protect the community from plague (8:19), and here some of them had caused it. Inside the tabernacle, the new altar-covering was a tragic reminder of human disobedience; outside the tent, exposed to more public view, were those unnecessary graves, further symbols of disastrous insurrection.

Finally, God is merciful. By the close of these appalling days, huge numbers of heedless people had come under the wrath of God. Ironically, many of the offenders had died in the wilderness – a fate that, in their earlier complaint, they had earnestly desired (14:2). Yet more Israelites were alive than dead. Prayer had been offered as Moses and Aaron interceded, falling *face down* before the Lord (45). Atonement had been made and, for the vast majority, judgment had been averted. Once again, Israel realized that sinning 'with a high hand' has ruinous consequences. It would have been better for those ambitious Levites, Reubenites and their followers to have learnt the lesson of the tassels than to have offended the Lord's holiness.

[24] 2 Cor. 5:14–15, 17–21; John 3:18, 36; 5:24.

17:1 – 18:32
16. Kept as a sign

The distinctive ministry of both Moses and Aaron had been ruthlessly challenged by recent events. The two men were in need of the Lord's encouragement, and it was not denied. In this section God's appointed leadership is confirmed (17:1–18:7) and supported (18:8–32).

God's appointed leadership confirmed (17:1 – 18:7)

Moses' authority had been questioned just as much as Aaron's. Opponents had accused him of abject failure (bringing them from Egypt to die in the desert, 16:13a), rigid authoritarianism ('you also want to lord it over us', 16:13b), broken promises ('you haven't brought us into a land flowing with milk and honey', 16:14a), and deceitful methods (throwing dust in the eyes, 16:14b). Aaron's divinely authenticated priesthood had been attested (16:47–48), and Moses was assured he was God's appointed prophet: *The Lord said to Moses, 'Speak ...'* (17:1–2). Despite the traumatic events of the past few hours, the Lord continued to address his people; they had changed, but he had not. He had devised a way of settling this dispute about the priests' exclusive responsibilities so that those who were not persuaded by his intervention in judgment might be won by his revelation of mercy.

The effective way in which Aaron had stood 'between the living and the dead' (16:48) was convincing proof of the validity of his ministry. Through the sign of a blossoming rod, God was about to give the people further evidence of his divinely appointed work. Before that, Moses himself may have needed affirming. Self-doubt is a debilitating experience, and Moses, undermined by what he had heard from Dathan and Abiram, may have wondered if their complaints had died with them. Were those graves any evidence that all objections to his leadership had gone for ever?

The Lord confirmed to Moses that his ministry was just as divinely attested as that of Aaron. They had different roles; sinful people desperately needed a compassionate intercessor, and ignorant people needed a persuasive prophet. When God said, *'Speak to the Israelites'*, the word must have come to Moses with encouraging confirmation as well as with renewed power. God was still speaking, even to rebels who had not wanted to hear his voice; and he was speaking through Moses, an instrument they had despised.

God's mind concerning the uniqueness of the Aaronic priesthood was expressed in two ways: visibly by means of a blossoming staff (17:1–13), and verbally through precise instructions regarding the distinctive roles of priests and Levites (18:1–7).

Visible confirmation (17:1–13)

In the startling events at the Tent of Meeting, the people had just been given undeniable proof of the divine authenticity of the priesthood, but the Lord knew that not everyone would be convinced. He knew all about 'that disease of obstinacy' which still maintained 'its secret hold upon their hearts'.[1] So, to the existing 'sign' of the bronze altar-covering (16:36–38), he added another. Some who could be overwhelmed by an expression of instant wrath might be persuaded by a manifestation of continuing mercy. Therefore, the Lord added to the daunting testimony of death (the bronze altar-covering), a persuasive testimony of life. A further sign, a fruit-bearing staff, was *to be kept as a sign to the rebellious* (10).

This memorable sign that the Aaronic priesthood was God's revealed will for his people was important for several reasons.

A necessary sign
Its purpose was to establish beyond doubt the legitimate authority of the Aaronic line, a matter of particular significance in view of Aaron's increasing age (20:22–29). The priest had two remaining sons, and these men and their male children would one day take up his responsibilities. There had already been fierce objections to Aaron's distinctive ministry (16:8–11) and, unless the matter was convincingly settled, the death of Aaron might become an occasion for renewed contention and division. God told Aaron that by the miraculous transformation of his rod during its overnight stay in the tabernacle, he would rid himself *of this constant grumbling against* Aaron *by the Israelites* (5).

[1] Calvin, IV, p. 123.

The Lord knew that the murmuring was not simply about Aaron but against him: *'This will put an end to their grumbling against me'* (10). It is a poignant feature of this and similar narratives in Numbers that grumbling about the leaders is complaining against God. When they are going through hard times in leadership crises, their pains are his own.

God's love is such that he cannot possibly be detached from his people's troubles. That was evident way back in the days of Israel's enslavement in Egypt. He told Moses at the burning bush that he had 'seen' and 'heard' and was 'concerned' about their sufferings,[2] the same word as in the Servant Song in Isaiah that says that he 'carried our sorrows'.[3] He not only knows about our griefs but bears them, feeling them intensely in his own divine nature. Even when his people had deserved their sufferings because of their offensive idolatry, he came to help them because 'he could bear Israel's misery no longer'.[4] The glorified Christ, grieved about the intense sufferings of the early Christians, asked their ruthless persecutor, 'Why do you persecute *me*?'[5] When Saul assaulted the believers he was wounding their Lord.

An educative sign

The story demonstrated how God's people were to discern God's will. The leaders of the *ancestral tribes* were to write their names on the individual staffs (2) and Aaron's name was to be put on the staff of Levi's tribe (3). They were to be placed overnight in front of the ark, which symbolized God's throne, and, significantly at this time, the Lord identified the sanctuary as the place where he met with his people. Two things were clearly important; in matters of dispute they were to seek the Lord's presence (*'where I meet with you'*, 4) and submit to the Lord's authority (*'Place them ... in front of the Testimony'*, 4). It is a call to enter the place of prayer in order to discern God's will, not to gain support for our own ideas. The sanctuary was the place where the priests met with God and kept his word, lovingly preserved in the ark's tablets.[6]

A continuing sign

Aaron's priestly ministry had recently been authenticated by his daring and compassionate intercession. 'He stood between the living and the dead' (16:48), yet the memory of such a sensational event might be short-lived. People soon forget. A sign was needed to provide God's people with incontrovertible, visible evidence of

[2] Exod. 3:7–8.   [3] Is. 53:4.   [4] Judg. 10:16; cf. Is. 63:9.
[5] Acts 9:4, my emphasis; Exod. 25:16, 21–22; Deut. 10:1–5.   [6] Heb. 9:4.

the Lord's mind on this crucial issue, and it was given in the form of a once-dead staff that overnight miraculously burst into life.

The Lord gave orders to Moses that this staff was to be preserved *in front of the Testimony, to be kept as a sign to the rebellious*. Characteristically, *Moses did just as the* LORD *commanded him* (11). The rod was made a permanent part of the tabernacle furnishings, preserved with the ark's other visible signs of the Lord's unique authority ('the stone tablets of the covenant'), and unfailing providence ('the gold jar of manna').[7] The blossoming and fruit-bearing staff was a striking tangible reminder of God's incomparable power that caused a lifeless walking-stick to sprout, bud, burst forth into beautiful white blossoms and produce almonds, all in a single night. What normally demanded months had been accomplished in hours. Only the Lord could do that, and such a God was to be reverenced and honoured, not ignored or disobeyed as the rebels had done.

A graphic sign
The fruitful staff was a living branch of an almond tree, and its precise description must be significant. The Hebrew people called the almond tree 'the watcher' or 'the awake one', the first to be roused to life after the sleep of winter. Its attractive blossom figured on the lampstand bowls in the tabernacle (8:4).[8] Jeremiah saw 'the branch of an almond tree' (*šāqēḏ*), for the Lord was watching (*šōqēḏ*) over his word to perform it, even through the bleak winter of Judah's apostasy.[9]

This supernatural event of the fruitful staff spoke eloquently about the uniqueness, faithfulness, holiness and fruitfulness of the divinely appointed order of priests. Their unique authority had been confirmed by this miraculous staff, which sprouted 'through the power which was placed in it by God'.[10] Their close connection with God's word was captured in the name of the tree; the priests were 'watching over the people by instructing them' in God's word.[11] The necessary moral purity of the office was portrayed in its attractive white flowers, and their spiritual fruitfulness in the greatly valued[12] almonds.

The sign was intended to put an end to their *constant grumbling* against his servants (5) and against God himself (10). The Lord knew that, though it might convince the miracle's immediate witnesses, it would hardly silence the complaining multitude as a

---

[7] Heb. 9:4.   [8] Exod. 25:33.   [9] Jer. 1:11–12.
[10] Gregory of Nyssa, *The Life of Moses*, II.284.
[11] Wenham (1981), p. 140.   [12] Gen. 43:11.

whole. Sadly, Numbers returns to the murmuring theme again (20:2–5; 21:4–5).

God was patient with them, and his compassion is revealed in another feature of this story. At the time of the people's obstinate refusal to enter the land, Moses had recalled that the Lord 'punishes the children for the sin of the fathers to the third and fourth generation' (14:18), and the children of the rebels proved its truth by having to wait before they could enter Canaan. Yet Korah's rebellion demonstrated not only God's judgment but also his mercy. His children did not all die as their father did (16:27, 32). Some of them may have responded to the warning to move away from the offenders' tents, even though it meant leaving their parents (16:25–27). Later generations did not suffer, for his line 'did not die out' (26:11);[13] distant members of that family lived to inspire others, through majestic psalms,[14] to put their hope[15] and trust[16] in God, and not to doubt or rebel against him as their truculent ancestor had done.

God had demonstrated his will by this almond-rod sign, but the people were still terrified by what had happened. Sudden fire had consumed the opponents (16:35), and God's judgment had sent a huge number of rebellious people to their graves (16:49). The remaining multitude were panic-stricken that they too might suddenly meet their end. The Tent of Meeting, which for over a year had symbolized their security, now seemed to threaten their peace. The distraught Israelites cried to Moses for help: 'We shall die! We are lost, we are all lost! Anyone who even comes near the tabernacle of the LORD will die. Are we all going to die?' (12).

The Lord who provided an authentic sign to silence their complaints spoke a comforting word to banish their fears. Word and sign belong together. Signs alone are unlikely to remove the doubts of unbelieving people. The New Testament testifies to the inadequacy of signs as 'solvents of scepticism'.[17] Jesus made that abundantly clear to his contemporaries[18] and Paul was similarly unconvinced by their power to clinch an argument.[19] So the God who had revealed his will to Moses now spoke through Aaron (18:1), the priest authenticated by the miraculous sign. Although normally he addressed the people through Moses, he used Aaron as his spokesman as further evidence that the priest was the Lord's appointed servant.

---

[13] 1 Chr. 6:22–24.   [14] See the titles of Pss. 42 and 84.   [15] Ps. 42:5, 11.
[16] Ps. 84:12.   [17] Kidner, p. 45.   [18] Matt. 12:38–42; 16:1–4; John 2:18; 4:48.
[19] 1 Cor. 1:22.

Verbal confirmation (18:1–7)

The sudden transition from lengthy narrative (16:1 – 17:12) to priestly regulations is closely related to what has just gone before. The main point at issue in the disruptive conduct of Korah and his colleagues was the distinction between priests and the Levites. So, following the visible sign, this passage consists of God's authenticating word, repeating the distinction between priests and Levites so that there could be no possible misunderstanding concerning their respective and well-defined roles.

As long as the people acted in accordance with God's word, they were not in the slightest danger of death (17:12–13). Aaron's sons and family were *to bear the responsibility for offences*, so that if there were mistakes about trespassing into the Tabernacle, the innocent Israelite would not be to blame. It was the explicit responsibility of priests and Levites to guard the sanctuary. They would be failing in their responsibilities as 'spiritual lightning conductors'[20] if a thoughtless person strayed in that way and, in such a case, the priests and their Levite assistants would bear the consequences. First the Levites' responsibilities are outlined (2–4), and then those of the priests themselves (5–7).

It was the Levites' subservient and supportive role, to *assist* Aaron and his sons (2), that Korah and his friends found objectionable; yet the willingness to submit to others is an essential component of spiritual leadership.[21] It minimizes the possibility of domineering dictatorship.

Theirs was an accountable role: *They are to be responsible to* the priests (3) for their work in connection with *the Tent of the Testimony* (2). They were meant to be not adventurous initiators but compliant servants of the will of God. Submissiveness in service can be realized only if we take Jesus as our primary role model. As the surrendered Son he was totally submissive in his obedience to the Father,[22] and as the exemplary Servant he was voluntarily submissive in love for his disciples.[23]

It was also a restricted role. The restraint operated on two levels. It was restricted in that they must not assume the priests' responsibilities; they *must not go near the furnishings of the sanctuary or the altar*. If they inadvertently undertook a task intended exclusively for the priesthood, *both they* and the priest would die (3). It was restricted too in the sense that neither could non-Levites undertake the Levites' duties. Their work was to protect the Tent from careless or indifferent intruders.

---

[20] Wenham (1981), p. 143.   [21] 1 Cor. 16:15–16; Heb. 13:17; 1 Pet. 5:5.
[22] Luke 22:42; John 6:38; Heb. 10:5–7, 9.   [23] Luke 22:24–27; John 13:3–17.

It was, furthermore, a privileged role, for they were the Lord's choice gift to the priests: *'I have selected your fellow Levites from among the Israelites as a gift to you, dedicated to the LORD to do the work at the Tent of Meeting'* (6). The Lord knew that the priests would need reliable helpers able to undertake some of the exacting physical jobs, particularly when the Tent of Meeting had to be moved on from one place to another. It demanded people strong enough to dismantle the Tent and its portable courtyard, and to arrange for its careful transportation and erection at the next site.

Ministry in any form is a subservient activity. It is not an opportunity for arrogant self-display. The servant is God's gift to his people, a strong shoulder to lean on, not a rod for their backs. Paul took this idea, of the church's servants as God's loving gift, as the concept of ministry he outlined to the first-century churches. Grace 'has been given' to us all in the wide range of variously gifted and uniquely equipped servants with whom he enriches the life of his people.[24]

The priests were also reminded of their exclusive obligations. Aaron knew only too well that, earlier, two of his sons had grieved God by offering 'unauthorised fire ... contrary to his command'.[25] Moreover, at a later stage in their history, other priests were to fail him by their inconsistent lifestyle[26] or their rejection of his word,[27] so these repeated regulations were necessary. Like the supportive order of Levites, the priesthood also was a gift. They had a clearly defined responsibility in defending the Tent from wilful, irreverent rebels who, like Korah, Dathan and Abiram, might be indifferent to God's Word. King Uzziah of Judah arrogantly grasped a censer as Korah had done before him, and he too came under the stern hand of God's judgment.[28]

God's appointed leadership supported (18:8–32)

The priests and Levites would not be able to serve with the single-minded devotion the work demanded if they were troubled about life's material necessities. The initial set of rules describes how the priests were to be maintained (8–20), before outlining the prescribed support for the Levites (21–32). The passage suggests some important guidelines regarding our own financial responsibilities towards God's servants. It focuses on nine dimensions of their support.

[24] Eph. 4:7–13.   [25] Lev. 10:1–5, cf. Num. 26:60–61.
[26] 1 Sam. 2:12–17; Hos. 4:7–8; 5:1; Mal. 2:1–9.
[27] Jer. 1:18; 26:7–16; Ezek. 8:1–18; Amos 7:10–17.   [28] 2 Chr. 26:15–23.

Its uniqueness

They were to have a personal share in the gifts people made to the Lord himself: *'all the holy offerings the Israelites give me I give to you and your sons as your portion and regular share'* (8). When we provide for the maintenance of the Lord's servants we are giving directly to him, and, conversely, if we withhold that support we are keeping our gifts back from God. To be ungenerous in our giving is tantamount to robbing God, as courageous Malachi told his materialistic contemporaries.[29]

Its variety

They were to receive portions of the regular sacrifices (9–11), the firstfruits of the cereal offerings (12–13), a share of the items specially 'devoted' to the Lord after the capture of an enemy city (14), the firstborn animals (15) and the redemption money paid in lieu of the firstborn male child in every household (15–16). Not all the gifts were identical – a reminder that in our support of the Lord's servants we can offer different gifts. In addition to financial provision, we can bring the gifts of our prayerful remembrance, warm encouragement and practical help, or perhaps a supportive letter to a missionary, or a magazine or book that a Christian worker might find particularly helpful. Just as Israel's gifts differed, so do ours.

Its anticipation

Some of these gifts could not possibly be brought until Israel had become a settled agricultural community. Cereal offerings demanded residence in a land with good soil, not a barren desert. These rules were *a lasting ordinance for the generations to come* (23). The assurance that there would be future generations to offer such gifts cheered the heart of many a disconsolate pilgrim, assuring them that one day they would reach the land.

Its conditions

What was presented to the Lord was to be regarded as *holy* (8, 32) and *most holy* (9, 10); those who ate such food must regard it as *something most holy* and be *ceremonially clean* (10, 13) as they ate it. What was given for the support of these priests and Levites had been deliberately 'set apart' for this godly purpose; those who

[29] Mal. 3:8–9.

received it had to endeavour to live in a manner worthy of the holy gifts which had been presented. It put greater demands on the recipients of the gifts than on their givers. Holy gifts need to be matched by holy recipients.

Its quality

The people were required to present the best. It was the *finest olive oil and all the finest new wine and grain* (12) that they were to give to the Lord for the maintenance of his servants. Moreover, these servants would not only receive the best; they would give the best also.

The Levites were to be supported by the people's tithes (24) and they in turn would give to the Lord a tenth of all that they received. For example, if they received a tithe of a farmer's olives, they must then select from those olives *the best and holiest part of everything given* to them (29), and present them as their own tithe. If any produce had deteriorated since they received it, they must absorb that loss and not pass it on as their 'offering'. In the fifth century, Malachi was grieved that people were presenting to God sub-standard animals they would not dream of giving to an earthly superior.[30] The Lord may sometimes be disappointed with our giving, especially when we spend infinitely more on possessions and pleasures than we would dream of giving to his work.

Its necessity

There was a specific day on God's agenda for his people when, without any doubt, they would enter the promised land. Once they did, the land would be allocated among the tribes, but the tribe of Levi was not to receive any land as their inheritance (20, 23–24). They had been 'set apart' as holy people to undertake specific spiritual responsibilities, and they must not be deflected from those duties by concerns about ploughing land, sowing seed, cultivating fields and gathering harvests. The Lord, not the land, was to be their inheritance.[31] The support system demanded the obedience of the people (who should trust God's word about giving generously) and the dependence of

[30] Mal. 1:8.
[31] Deut. 10:9; 14:27. It 'was a bold stroke that consigned Israel's priestly tribe to landlessness'. They were not meant to be 'a nation in which a clerical hierarchy could wield economic power ... as an exploitive, land-owning elite'; as in Egypt, for example, where 'the temples and priests were major landowners'. (Christopher J. H. Wright, *Deuteronomy*, New International Biblical Commentary (Peabody, MA: Hendrikson, 1996), p. 215.

the servants (who should trust God's provision rather than the ownership of land).

Its organization

To avoid endless debates about how much might be considered worthy as a gift to the Lord, he gave them a basic principle for the allocation of their money and possessions: the idea of giving one tenth as a general guide. The priests and their families would be supported by their share of the sacrificial food, oil, grain and wine that would be offered at the sanctuary, and by the monetary payments of five shekels of silver (about six months' wages) that would come to them every time they received redemption money (16) on the birth of each firstborn male child.

Initially, the Levites would be in greater numbers and would have no part in these sanctuary gifts. Their support would come through the tithing system (21, 24)[32] by which every Israelite offered back to God a tenth of what the Lord had given to him. Without being legalistic about it, huge numbers of Christians throughout the world prove that tithing is still a useful guide to giving and testify that God has ensured that their remaining nine-tenths always go far enough to meet their needs.

Its continuity

These regulations were to be like *a covenant of salt before the LORD for both you and your offspring* (19), a description recognizing the preservative value of salt; the agreement was a lasting provision for the maintainance of God's servants. The rules were something more than temporary regulations; they enshrined biblical principles as relevant in our day as in theirs.

Its purpose

The primary intention was not to provide meals for the priesthood but to please the Lord. Once again we meet the phrase we have come across earlier, about gifts offered as *an aroma pleasing to the LORD* (17). With the exception of the burnt offering,[33] the greater part of those sacrificial animals and all the cereal offerings were to meet the physical needs of the priests and their families. The Lord wanted his people to know that he derived immense pleasure from the assurance that his servants were provided with life's necessities. The primary purpose of Christian giving is not to support the workers but to glorify the Lord.

[32] Neh. 10:37–39.   [33] Lev. 1:1–17.

19:1–22
17. The perils of pollution

God continued to speak, on this occasion to both Moses and Aaron (19:1) about an important issue in the Israelite community – human defilement and its cure. The slaughter and incineration of a red heifer were to guarantee the cleansing of anyone who had been in contact with a dead human body. Although we live in a different thought-world, the truths portrayed here are as relevant as on the day God first spoke to this wilderness community about the dangers of pollution. Discussion of some relevant issues may help in the interpretation and application of this intriguing passage.

Its context

Pollution by death was a matter of extreme concern in the Israelite world (5:2; 6:6; 9:6; 31:19). Such deep apprehension is puzzling to the modern reader, but four important considerations need to be remembered: its historical context, theological dimension, social aspect and pagan associations.

First, there is a historical context to these stipulations. This cleansing ritual was promulgated at a time when the Israelite pilgrims frequently encountered death in the community. It was not only that over the next few decades an entire generation would die in the wilderness; since leaving Sinai they had often been confronted with sudden death, unpredictable, frightening, mysterious.

Actual or potential death is a tragically recurrent theme (11:33–34; 14:2, 10, 15–16, 29, 33, 35, 37, 43). Disobedient individuals (15:36), rebellious groups (16:31–35) and vast numbers of grumblers (16:49) all died in the desert. Witnessing the evidence of God's power in the blossoming rod, the people cried out in terror, 'We shall die! ... Are we all going to die?' (17:12–13). Even the spiritual leaders of the community were not free from this threat of extermination (18:32), and the story of death continues after these red-heifer regulations (20:1, 22–29). With such a recurrent emphasis on death it is natural that, at this point in the story, some instruction should be given to the Israelite people about how they should react to the presence of a dead body.

There was also a theological dimension to death in the community. It challenged their understanding of God as both living and holy. They worshipped the living God,[1] and the presence of a dead human body was alien to all they knew of God, the giver and custodian of life.[2] The departure of life was a sinister phenomenon; it seemed as though God had forsaken the body he had created. They also worshipped a holy God, but their experience of death was that the lifeless corpse would rapidly deteriorate and decompose. Its presence was 'incompatible with the holiness of God',[3] who demanded purity in the life of the community. A dead body exposed them to spiritual defilement as well as to physical contamination. The presence of death affronted the divine holiness; they must keep away from it.

There may have been an innate social aspect to this fear of a lifeless human body. The unburied corpse was a serious health hazard.[4] In oppressive climates, rapid decomposition might lead to widespread infection, and regulations such as these encouraged them to keep their distance from places where a person had recently died.[5] The camp must be kept clean at all costs (5:1–4).

Dangerous pagan associations may also lie behind this healthy concern about death in the community. Israel's neighbours entertained harmful notions about the power of the dead over the living. Pagan rituals associated with 'the cult of the dead' were part of the religious culture of the ancient Near East, and God's people were always in danger of adopting pagan customs involving practices such as 'consulting the dead'.[6] Grief rituals were a common feature in pagan life;[7] the Israelites were warned not to mutilate themselves or to shave their hair on behalf of the dead[8] or to make food

---

[1] 1 Kgs. 17:1.   [2] Gen. 2:7.

[3] Dozeman, p. 152. For death in the ancient Near East, see E. Feldman, *Biblical and Post-Biblical Defilement and Mourning: Law as Theology* (New York: Yeshiva University Press, 1977), pp. 8–11.

[4] For death taboos in the ancient world, see S. Hornblower and A. Spawforth (eds.), *The Oxford Classical Dictionary* (Oxford: Oxford University Press, 1996), pp. 433, 1208.

[5] G. J. Wenham, *Leviticus*, New International Commentary (London: Hodder and Stoughton, 1979), pp. 167–168, criticizes these hygenic explanations, maintaining that they impose modern rational and pragmatic concerns on to a complex cultural symbolism with quite different concerns.

[6] Deut. 18:11–12; Is. 8:19.   [7] Is. 57:9; 65:3–5.

[8] Lev. 19:27–28; Deut. 14:1; Is. 15:2; Jer. 16:6; 41:4–5.

offerings 'to the dead',[9] illustrating the high incidence of occultism. Some of these dangers may well lie behind these regulations regarding contact with a dead body.

Its distinctiveness

Several features distinguish this ritual from the offerings described elsewhere in the Pentateuch.

First, contrary to sacrificial practice, it was a cow, not a bull, that was to be slaughtered. The priest was not a key figure throughout. He was present when the cow was killed, and sprinkled a little of its blood on his finger, *towards the front of the Tent of Meeting* (4); his main function was as a witness of what was happening rather than the leading officiant. The slaughter was to take place not at the Tent of Meeting but at the outskirts of the camp. There is no specific moment when the individual presenting the cow was to identify himself with the offering by laying his hand on the animal, as was customary with animal sacrifices.[10] Most unusual of all, at the incineration even the blood of the animal was to be burnt, which distinguishes it from other Old Testament offerings where the blood was drained away and the hide and offal used for other purposes.

A further unusual feature is that all involved in this cleansing procedure became defiled simply because they had participated. The rabbis noted that these purificatory waters 'purify the defiled and defile the pure'.[11] We are presented here with an ordinance that appears to function in a variant manner and to serve a purpose different from that of the priestly rituals described elsewhere in the Old Testament.

Its most distinctive feature lies in the preservation of these ashes for use at a later event. Other sacrifices in the Old Testament have a sense of immediacy about them; the red-heifer ritual is designed to meet inevitable requirements in the future rather than needs in the present.

Its stipulations

An unblemished red heifer that had never been used was to be brought to the priest Eleazar, Aaron's son, to a place outside the camp, where it was to be killed. Eleazar was to sprinkle some of its blood seven times *towards the front of the Tent of Meeting* (4). The

---

[9] Deut. 26:14.
[10] Lev. 1:4; 3:2, 8, 13; 4:4.   [11] Milgrom, p. 438.

complete animal would then be burnt, *hide, flesh, blood and offal* (5), while the priest would add to the flames *some cedar wood, hyssop and scarlet wool* (6). Both the priest and the one responsible for the incineration must carefully wash their bodies and clothes. They would remain ceremonially unclean until nightfall, and only after these lustrations could they re-enter the camp.

A man uninvolved in these earlier procedures was then to gather the heifer's ashes, preserving them for later use, *in a ceremonially clean place outside the camp* (9). This person would likewise be defiled by his contact with the ashes and must also wash his clothes, remaining *unclean till evening* (10).

Any member of the community, either Israelite or alien (10), who touched a corpse was regarded as unclean for a full week. The polluted person must wash thoroughly on the third and the seventh day after contact with the dead body. Anyone failing to do this was ceremonially *unclean*; he or she *defiles the LORD's tabernacle* and would be *cut off from Israel* (13), a reference to the threat of sudden death at the hand of God, or to execution, or to excommunication from the community.

Stringent regulations are also prescribed governing the occurrence of death. A woman or man entering an Israelite tent after a person's death would also be unclean for a week, and any open container within that tent was similarly polluted. Anyone coming into direct contact with a corpse outdoors, or even touching a human bone in the desert, or a grave, was also ceremonially unclean for a full week.

Anybody so polluted could be purified by a small amount of the preserved ashes of the burnt heifer mixed with fresh water. An uncontaminated person was to dip a branch of hyssop in this water and sprinkle it on the community member defiled by death, in any tent or on furnishings where death has occurred, and on anyone who has touched a human bone or grave. This same person must sprinkle the cleansing waters on the defiled man or woman on the third and the seventh day after their physical contact with death. The person sprinkling the purifying water also became defiled by the procedure and must wash his clothes. Anyone *who touches the water of cleansing will be unclean until evening* (21). Pollution was regarded as a highly contagious danger; *Anything that an unclean person touches becomes unclean, and anyone who touches it becomes unclean till evening* (22).

Its symbolism

The importance of these rituals lies in their visual presentation of essential truths. The prophets expressed God's message vocally, although they were skilled in the use of graphic imagery, arresting word-pictures and symbolic actions that illustrated their message.[12] The priests relied almost entirely on the visual communication of God's word. They were virtually silent as the word was conveyed through eloquent signs of greater realities.

Our difficulty is that, usually, these signs are neither explained nor interpreted; in their culture, the meaning was apparent to all. If we let our imagination run away with us, we can endow these various aspects of ritual with alien meanings. Calvin regretted that some of his contemporaries deduced many 'questionable matters' in their intepretations of this passage. When he came across anything obscure, he felt more comfortable confessing his ignorance than 'advancing anything doubtful',[13] and so avoided the excessive allegorization of every minute detail.

A good guide in explaining symbolism is to allow one passage of Scripture to interpret another. If a symbol is meant to signify a particular truth in one setting, it may well convey a similar message in another. With this in mind, we turn to examine the symbolism employed in these regulations.

The substances used

Three familiar components play a significant part: blood (4), fire (5) and water (17), agents of cleansing in the biblical tradition.[14] The heifer was *red* (2; the only place in the Old Testament where the colour of a sacrificial animal is prescribed), and to the fire the priest added cedar wood, hyssop and *scarlet* wool (6); the colour of the animal and of the wool is the same as that of blood, an essential component in the cleansing process. These three 'ritual detergents'[15] that were added to the flames also figured in the purification of someone suffering from an infectious skin disease,[16] another ritual of cleansing from pollution.

The symbolism of cedar wood illustrates the problem of precise interpretation. Its recognized strength and characteristic durability may suggest permanence and illustrate the continuing effectiveness

[12] Is. 20:1–6; Jer. 13:1–11; 19:1–15; 35:1–19; Ezek. 4:1–17.
[13] Calvin, II, pp. 38–39.
[14] Blood: Heb. 9:22; Lev. 16:15–16; 17:11; Ezek. 43:20–21; fire: Num. 31:22–23; Zech. 13:9; Mal. 3:2; water: Num. 8:6–7, 31:23.
[15] Ashley, p. 366.   [16] Lev. 14:4.

of this cleansing process, or it may simply have been used for its known aromatic qualities, enhancing the 'aroma pleasing to the LORD', a phrase found in other rituals (15:3, 7, 10, 14, 24). Hyssop had Passover associations[17] and may have symbolized deliverance from death, as at the exodus. Its pragmatic use (18)[18] was eclipsed by its spiritual message. As at Passover, it was 'the instrument of the application' and retained the 'symbolism of applied efficacy'.[19] The recipient could gratefully say, 'That sacrifice was for me.'

The locations described

The drama of the ritual focused on two specified places intentionally separated by a considerable distance: the Tent of Meeting at the camp's centre and the farthest point of removal from it, beyond the outskirts. The only mention of the central sanctuary is when Eleazar sprinkled the blood of the red heifer *seven times towards the front of the Tent of Meeting* (4). By this means the sacrificial blood was acknowledged as effective and consecrated for use. Its visual image conveyed the idea that God had accepted the life surrendered for the cleansing of his people. The Lord who, by his word (1–2), initiated this means of purification thus confirmed its efficacy.

The element of distance from the Tent of Meeting deliberately underlined the essential gap between holiness and defilement, purity and uncleanness. Everything that polluted the community had to be removed from it, so the action deliberately took place away from the holy place. The animal was slaughtered beyond the confines of the camp, in the very place where defiled people must remain until they were thoroughly cleansed.

The participants involved

Four individuals took part in the ceremonial from the time of the heifer's death to the moment of the offender's cleansing: the priest who witnessed the death (3–5), the man who burnt the animal (8), the person who stored the ashes (9) and the individual applying the purifying water (18). Although none of these four had encountered a dead human body, their participation in the purifying event contaminated them.

---

[17] Exod. 12:22.
[18] Because 'its hairy surface retains liquid and, hence, is ideal for sprinkling'. Milgrom, p. 159.
[19] J. A. Motyer, *Look to the Rock* (Leicester: IVP, 1966), p. 177.

The offenders portrayed

Although other forms of defilement are described earlier in the book (5:1–3), the pollution here is restricted to contacts with death, which, in turn, is deliberately associated with sin: The *water of cleansing ... is for purification from sin* (9). Sin and death are inseparably linked in biblical teaching. Sin is the cause of death and death is the consequence of sin, teaching that takes us back to the beginning of humanity's story.[20] Those who are defiled can no longer dwell in the sphere where God lives and reigns; they must remain outside its borders until they are decontaminated by the means provided.

The numbers employed

The recurrence of *three* and *seven* is significant. Three leading elements (blood, fire and water) are supported by the three subsidiary components of cedar wood, hyssop and scarlet thread. Defiled people must wash themselves *on the third day* (12) and have the purifying water applied (19). The priest sprinkled the heifer's blood *seven times* (4), defiled people remained unclean *for seven days* (11) and the decontaminating process was not complete until that seven-day period had expired (19). The repetition of the ritual on both the third and the seventh day may emphasize both the seriousness of the pollution and the efficacy of the cleansing; the numbers three and seven both indicate completeness, wholeness and thoroughness in Scripture.[21]

Its message

We must ask what this striking visual aid may be saying to us about ourselves, about life and, most importantly, about the God in whose gracious mind it originated. The picture graphically conveys some crucial aspects of the biblical message.

The seriousness of defilement

Crucial spiritual values and high moral standards were preserved in this basic command about contamination by a corpse.

The defilement polluted the individual. The offence could not be ignored or marginalized. It is a visual reminder of the

---

[20] Gen. 2:17; 3:3–4, 19.
[21] Cf. Eccles. 4:12 (in contrast to two); Hos. 6:2; 1 Cor. 15:4; Josh. 6:4; Lev. 4:6, 17; cf. *NIDOTTE* 4, pp. 144–146, 34–37; Gen. 2:2.

contaminating effects of sin in human life. Men and women are seriously damaged by it, and become less than the people they would, in their better moments, like to be.

Moreover, personal defilement affects others. If it was not dealt with in the manner the Lord prescribed, the contamination would spread from the defiled person to others. An offender who had not been cleansed *must be cut off from the community* (20). Such a person was a moral and spiritual hazard in the camp. That is the really destructive thing about human sin; it speedily transmits itself from one victim to the next. Even when we sin secretly (as in sins of thought), we emerge morally and spiritually less than we might have been.

The pollution problem cannot be dismissed as an unenlightened preoccupation of the ancient world. Our culture has its own defilement dangers, creating increasing havoc in personal, family and community life. Victims of child abuse suffer from defiled memories. The paedophile is only one of the new millennium's pollution agents. Society is globally contaminated by the drug trafficker, leading not only to serious misuse of the body but to the escalation of crime to secure money for the next 'fix'. Sexual promiscuity increases the already alarming Aids crisis, described as 'the most fatal epidemic in history'. In Africa, deaths from Aids are expected to peak around the year 2050, when 1.25 million people will die in Nigeria alone. Minds are befouled through the instant availability of internet pornography, with its chat-room opportunities for damaging contact. A decade or two ago, responsible Christians in the UK endeavoured to protect our children by insisting that pornographic magazines should be placed beyond their reach on newsagents' top shelves. Now, far more degrading and destructive material is at their fingertips via their own computer screens. Recently published research shows that of the 290,000 children who clicked on to pornographic websites, about 8% were aged ten and under. About one child in five under seventeen claimed to have visited these sites at least once a month, remaining on line for an average of 28 minutes.[22]

Defilement grieves God. The Israelite who *fails to purify himself defiles the LORD's tabernacle* (13), and the person who has *defiled the sanctuary of the LORD* (20) by failing to seek cleansing insults the Lord who has provided this means of purification. When we transgress we sin against ourselves and our fellows, but, most seriously, we sin against God. David knew that truth, for, after his sin against Bathsheba and her murdered husband, he cried out to

---

[22] Research published in May 2001 by NetValue, an internet monitoring firm, and reported in *The Daily Telegraph*, 10 May 2001.

the Lord, 'Against you, you only, have I sinned and done what is evil in your sight.'[23]

The universality of need

This cleansing provision was available not only to the Israelites but also to *the aliens living among them* (10). The ritual's provisions testify to humanity's wider need, and, along with similar passages (9:14; 15:15–16, 29),[24] both look back and point forward. They reflect on the promise to Abraham (a key idea in Numbers) that, as the spiritual father of 'many nations', he would be the means of blessing 'all peoples on earth',[25] and anticipate the time when people the world over would respond to the good news of cleansing in Christ through the universal mission of his church.[26]

The continuity of grace

This ritual was to be *a lasting ordinance* (10, 21). It was available not merely during their wilderness travels, when death was a recurrent feature of their social landscape. God had given this visual aid a place in his law so that future generations would realize both the danger of defilement and the necessity of cleansing. This ceremonial provision foresees a time when God would make a unique, once-for-all sacrifice by which people may receive the forgiveness freely available to all who repent, turn away from their sins and acknowledge Christ as their Saviour.

Our problem is infinitely more serious that that of the polluted Israelites. They were disturbed by ceremonial impurity; we are guilty of moral corruption. They were at fault because they had touched a corpse; our offence is that we are dead, slain by sin's destructive power in our lives. Those who are 'dead in … trangressions and sins' can be made alive only by coming to the Christ who died for them and rose again.[27] The death that saved the criminal who died alongside Jesus is as effective today as on that first Good Friday.[28] Jesus' prayer for his forgiveness,[29] and for millions like him, is gloriously answered whenever a defiled person acknowledges his or her inner pollution.

[23] Ps. 51:4.   [24] Exod. 12:19, 48–49; 22:21; Lev. 24:22.
[25] Gen. 17:4; 12:3; cf. 17:6; 18:18.
[26] Matt. 28:18–20; Luke 2:32 (Is. 42:6; 49:6); 24:46–48; Acts 1:8; 9:15; 11:18; 13:38, 46–48; 14:27; 15:7–11; 28:28.
[27] Eph. 2:1, 4–5.   [28] Luke 23:39–43.   [29] Luke 23:34.

The costliness of purity

Before any Israelite had become defiled, a costly sacrifice had been offered. The animal was mature and perfect; it had never been used for ploughing, so there was not the slightest blemish on it. A greatly valued economic asset with the potential to produce calves, it could have provided generous amounts of milk, a source of continuing income. Its young life was cut off so that others would not be cut off (13, 20); it died so that unclean people (7, 8, 10, 11, 13, 14, 15, 16, 17, 19, 20, 21, 22) might be released from their isolating defilement.

The availability of cleansing

Once the animal had been slain and burnt, its ashes were preserved for times in the future when polluted Israelites would need cleansing. The ashes had only to be mixed with *fresh* (literally 'running' or unpolluted) *water* and sprinkled on the contaminated person, and he or she would be ceremonially clean. It is a vivid portrayal of the sacrifice of Christ, by whose death on the cross we may now be pardoned, with every stain of pollution entirely removed. Nothing prevents that miraculous act of cleansing but our pride, self-will, stubborn unbelief and disobedience. The Bible uses a wide range of vivid and arresting images to describe the cleansing that is ours in Christ.[30] There is no need for defiled people to continue in their sin.[31]

Its fulfilment

The red heifer's ritual imagery foreshadows Christ's achieving eternal salvation for defiled humanity. By his unique death and resurrection, those who are outside the camp, 'far away' in spiritual terms,[32] are brought within the redeemed community.

First, the heifer had to be unblemished (*without defect*, 2). Dedicated to this unique purpose, it had *never been under a yoke* (2). The spotlessly perfect Son of God came into the world solely and entirely to do God's will by procuring our salvation.

Secondly, a death in the past effects cleansing in the present. The animal was killed not simply to respond to an immediate emergency but to meet an ultimate need. This feature distinguishes it from the usual sacrificial system of the Old Testament. Although Christ died for us historically on that first Good Friday, the

[30] Ps. 51:2; Is. 44:22; Ps. 103:12; Mic. 7:19.
[31] 1 Cor. 6:9–11.   [32] Eph. 2:13, 17.

benefits of his death are as effective for us as on the day of his transforming sacrifice.

Thirdly, only undefiled people could administer the cleansing ritual. *A man who is clean* (9) collects and preserves the ashes, and later, at the moment of need, *a man who is ceremonially clean* (18) sprinkles the purifying waters on the defiled man or woman. Christ is both the cleansing sacrifice and the one who mediates its benefits to us, and he is without sin, as New Testament writers frequently affirm.[33]

Fourthly, the decontamination process involved the absorption of the impurity. The uncleanness was taken up by the one administering the cleansing process. As the Lord Jesus died on the cross he absorbed our sin into his own person, so that, as Paul expresses it movingly, 'God made him who had no sin to be sin for us, so that in him we might become the righteousness of God'.[34] Using the famous Servant Song of Isaiah,[35] Peter richly expresses the same truth: 'He himself bore our sins in his body on the tree.'[36]

Fifthly, the decontaminating procedure was costly; the unpolluted people who collected the ashes and later sprinkled the cleansing waters became unclean. The greatest cost of our Saviour's unique sacrifice was that a pure, holy and righteous Father turned his face from his sin-bearing Son, so that Jesus cried out in anguish, 'My God ... why have you forsaken me?'[37]

Finally, the red heifer had to be slain outside the camp. A sacrifice for the sin of defilement had to take place away from the holy sanctuary at the centre of the camp.[38] Jesus was taken outside the city to Calvary, the arena of death, rejected by his contemporaries and thrust beyond the confines of their religious institutions.[39] In order to effect the cleansing of their fellow Israelites, some members of the community had to be prepared to leave the safe confines of the camp and make their way beyond its boundaries to help those who, unless purified from their pollution, could not hope to come within the clean and secure community.[40]

Yet, however rich the Christological parallels within this impressive red-heifer ritual, one huge factor separates this Old Testament means of cleansing from its fulfilment in the unique sacrifice of Christ. That fulfilling sacrifice is the leading theme of the letter to the Hebrews.

It was of the greatest importance in Old Testament times for the camp to be kept clean from defilement. The pollution was real and isolating, but the cleansing available was nothing other than

[33] 2 Cor. 5:21; Heb. 4:15; 7:26; 1 Pet. 1:19; 2:22; 1 John 3:5.
[34] 2 Cor. 5:21.   [35] Is. 52:13 – 53:12.   [36] 1 Pet. 2:24.   [37] Mark 15:34.
[38] Heb. 13:11–12.   [39] Luke 23:18.   [40] Heb. 13:13.

ceremonial purification. It did not reach into what Bunyan called the 'disturbed' or 'wounded' conscience. Christ's sacrifice was not a ceremonial de-pollution exercise but an inner cleansing that washes the sinner completely clean. 'The ... ashes of a heifer sprinkled on those who are ceremonially unclean sanctify them so that they are outwardly clean. How much more, then, will the blood of Christ, who through the eternal Spirit offered himself unblemished to God, cleanse our consciences from acts that lead to death, so that we may serve the living God!'[41] This red-heifer provision anticipated something infinitely greater. The sprinkled water permitted the defiled Israelite to rejoin the camp; the shed blood of Christ enables the cleansed sinner to enter heaven.

---

[41] Heb. 9:13–14.

20:1 – 21:3
18. Coping with crises

Life is precariously unpredictable. Everything seems to be moving along smoothly when, suddenly, we are confronted with unexpected demands. One adversity follows hard on the heels of another. As Moses drew towards the close of his life's work, it seems as though everything was against him. It is hardly surprising that, in a moment of testing, he lost control and did something he deeply regretted, and with sad consequences.

First, he suffered family bereavement (20:1), then serious opposition (2), further complaints from his discontented contemporaries (3–5), intense frustration over their rebellious spirit (10), and severe disappointment at the news that neither he nor his brother would enter the promised land (12). A sensitive man, he shouldered the burden of guilt arising from the fact that not only the truculent people but he too had grieved God, and then he had to cope with the painful experience of hearing the Lord's firm 'No' to an ambition he had treasured for a lifetime.

Additionally, his people's most direct route to Canaan was blocked by a hostile nation (14–21), necessitating an exhausting detour when the Israelites naturally longed to reach their destination. Then came another bereavement in the loss of his brother, Aaron (22–29), followed by an unexpected military attack during which some of Israel's troops were captured (21:1). A succession of events such as these would have daunted the most resilient of spirits.

Israel's leader must have faced many a day with a heavy heart. These biblical characters did not belong to a make-believe world where, because they loved God, everything automatically went well for them. Their experience hardly supports the optimistic euphoria of the 'prosperity theology' people, with their assurance of health and wealth. The Bible is more realistic and more honest. When we have, as the Puritan Richard Baxter says, 'wine and vinegar in the same cup', the bleak experiences drive us to God: 'did you never see one "walking in the midst of the fiery furnace" with you?' And they encourage us to look ahead, for 'there is none of this inconstancy in heaven'.[1]

As these different events suddenly appeared on his daily agenda, there were times when Moses was confronted with danger; but, in the sovereign plan of God, even the least welcome experiences could be transformed into creative opportunities for God. The narrative invites us to consider its different personalities and contrasting scenes.

The bereaved brother (20:1, 22–29)

The chapter opens and closes with a family bereavement. Within four months (20:1; 33:38), Moses lost both his sister and his brother. Sadly, since the departure from Egypt both Miriam and Aaron had featured in discouraging events, and the Scripture makes no secret of their alarming disloyalty (12:1–16).[2] Yet, despite their mistakes, they had been his life-long partners, to say nothing of their devoted family ties. At the beginning of his life Miriam had been a protective sister, and later Aaron had proved a supportive brother. To be suddenly bereft of their help and companionship at such a crucial stage in the long journey must have been a severe loss.

Later generations looked back on this desert trio, Moses, Aaron and Miriam,[3] and gave thanks for their faithful speaking and serving during those long years in the wilderness. God's people learnt from their mistakes[4] as well as from their achievements. Aware of their weaknesses, Moses must also have been grateful for the many good things they had shared with him during those decades in the desert. Two themes may have passed through his mind when he felt his bereavement most acutely.

God's dependable promises

Although he missed the companionship of an older brother and sister, their departures were undeniable evidence of the reliability of God's word. At Kadesh Barnea the Lord had said that every member of that older generation of rebellious Israelites would die in the desert. On innumerable occasions, Moses witnessed the burial of one of those unbelieving travellers, but now the lesson had come home for the first time to his own family. Miriam had

[1] Richard Baxter, *The Saint's Everlasting Rest* (1650), I.5, II.3.
[2] Exod. 32:1–6, 19–25.   [3] Mic. 6:4.   [4] Deut. 24:9.

been among those persuaded by the grim report of the untrusting spies and, along with thousands of others, she too had died, just as the Lord had declared (14:21–23, 26–35).

Decades after the Kadesh Barnea revolt, Moses and Aaron stood before another crowd of unbelieving, ungrateful rebels, and, in a moment of intense frustration, both men lost their temper. The Lord told them that, because of their sin, they too would be kept out of the promised land. Now, Israel's high priest, Aaron, had died. God's words are pledges of his will and purpose. Aaron's sad death was yet another reminder that what the Lord says he means (23:19).

The Lord who had denied entrance to the older generation had guaranteed conquest to their children. The word that was sadly confirmed at every funeral was just as reliable as the new generation faced a better future. Believers can cope with life's threatening hardships when they know that God has made 'very great and precious promises'[5] about their comfort, resources and destiny. With such firm assurance they face the future with confidence and peace.

Heaven's assured security

When the two brothers climbed side by side on their last journey together up the slopes of Mount Hor, Moses knew that his older brother was on the threshold of death. In language reminiscent of the patriarchs, it twice says that Aaron was gathered to his people (24, 26). The words were 'an intimation of immortality',[6] deliberately recalling the passing of Abraham, Isaac and Jacob[7] into that better land for which they were destined. The Israelite understanding of the life to come was not as precise and explicit as in the New Testament, but the narrative points beyond the place of Aaron's burial to the moment of Aaron's arrival, not in the land he had hoped to see, but in the land he was meant to possess.

The hope of heaven is not an escape mechanism but the Christian realist's assurance of survival. As Jesus faced death, he described a time when his disciples would sit not in that upper room but around a better table in the eternal kingdom.[8] Such confidence contrasts sharply with today's cynical dismissal of 'pie in the sky when you die'. Jesus guaranteed his followers a secure future. He knew that, in their inevitable trials, they would need that wider perspective of his promised heaven.[9]

---

[5] 2 Pet. 1:4.   [6] Hertz, p. 212.   [7] Gen. 15:15; 25:8; 35:29; 49:29, 33.
[8] Luke 22:29–30; Matt. 8:11.
[9] Cf. the bouyant certainty of John 11:25; 14:1–3; Rom. 14:8–9; 2 Cor. 4:16 – 5:5; 1 Pet. 1:4–9; 1 John 3:2–3; Jude 24–25; Rev. 5:6–14.

175

The persistent grumblers (20:2–8)

Fresh from the burial of their sister, Moses and Aaron found themselves confronted, yet again, by hordes of angry people. Their expressed need (*no water*, 2) was natural enough and, if transmitted in prayer to a generous God, would have elicited a speedy response. The anxiety became an opportunity for renewed murmuring rather than for dependent prayer.

When Paul wrote to the Corinthians he did not want his readers 'to be ignorant of the fact' that, during these wilderness wanderings, the Lord had been abundantly generous to an ungrateful people[10] but they did not respond to his loving provision. He gives examples of the divine disappointment.[11] The narrative before us explains why 'God was not pleased with most of them',[12] and suggests some attitudes of mind that continue to displease God.

First, they opposed his servants. Instead of approaching their leaders as effective intercessors, the crowds treated them as moral scapegoats. Throughout the years, Moses and Aaron had had a bad time of it with this unhappy mob, and the grounds of their complaint now were much the same: things had been infinitely better in their idealized past. Their present diet was detestable and life's future prospects were agonizing (21:4–5). The crowd *gathered in opposition to Moses and Aaron*. Ostensibly, this unhappy congregation *quarrelled with Moses* (3) but, in reality, they were complaining against God.

Secondly, they belittled his wrath. 'God was not pleased' with Korah, Dathan and Abiram (16:31–35), and his judgment was expressed in the earthquake, fire and plague. Such men and their colleagues had 'treated the LORD with contempt' (16:30), and now these complaining people were doing exactly the same, publicly regretting that they too had not fallen under that mighty hand of God's judgment: *'If only we had died when our brothers fell dead before the LORD!'* (3). Far from being humbled and chastened by the experience of the earlier rebels, they wished it had happened to them.

We live at a time when there is scant regard for God's holiness. His name is openly misused on radio and television. Our blasphemy laws are challenged and disregarded. Stage plays, films and stand-up comedians treat sacred things with scorn. The incarnation becomes a hilarious Christmas joke; the crucifixion of God's Son a scurrilous logo on T-shirts. The holiest of things are publicly

[10] 1 Cor. 10:1–4.   [11] 1 Cor. 10:5–12.   [12] 1 Cor. 10:5.

derided. A sick world invites the judgment of a holy God. In such an alien environment, believers take pains to ensure that they do or say nothing that belittles the holiness of God, the beauty of the Christ and the purity of the Spirit.

Thirdly, they minimized his power. They blamed Moses for the exodus. Only God could have liberated them from the stranglehold of their cruel oppressors, and he had publicly demonstrated his power by judging their captors, authenticating his servants and effecting their deliverance. Denying God's sovereign initiative and saving action, these wilderness rebels say that Moses is responsible for it all: *'Why did you bring us up out of Egypt?'* (5) and *'Why did you bring the LORD's community into this desert?'* (4). What an affront to almighty God to attribute those stupendous wonders to a mere man, and one they were opposing anyway!

Fourthly, they resented his will. They contrasted *this terrible place* (5) with the fertile land they had left. There was surely irony in their grievance that there were no *grain or figs, grapevines or pomegranates* (5) in the wilderness when the last three had been carried back by the spies as evidence of Canaan's abundant fruitfulness (13:23). They could have enjoyed such choice produce and plentiful supplies of *grain* (5) if they had only responded to the passionate appeal of Caleb and Joshua (14:6–9) instead of taking up stones to kill them (14:10). They had nobody but themselves to blame. It was God's determined will to keep that unbelieving generation out of the land, not only to judge them righteously by giving them precisely what they wanted ('If only we had died … ', 14:2), but to teach an essential lesson to generations to come. Those who sow the seeds of disobedience reap a harvest of discontent.

Finally, they despised his generosity. Obsessed by what had been denied, they forgot what had been given. They frequently recalled the luxurious meals of Egypt (11:5; 16:13)[13] or visualized the attractive diet of Canaan (16:14), and saw both in stark contrast to their barren wilderness experience. Longing for what we want, we ignore what we have received. They forgot his mighty acts of deliverance. They ignored the daily evidence of his presence and the nightly assurance of his protection. They despised his unfailing gift of nourishing food, the ready supply of necessary water and restful locations where they enjoyed shelter. They marginalized his immense kindness in keeping them free from sickness and disease, even protecting their feet from discomfort and their clothing from wearing out. During those long years in the desert, they had 'not

---

[13] Exod. 16:3.

lacked anything'.[14] But they were not remotely grateful. Moses and Aaron listened to the complaints of the multitude until they could bear it no longer. They went from the company of a disgruntled people into the presence of a holy God.

The untrusting leaders (20:6–13)

Moses and Aaron hurried to the Tent of Meeting and *fell face down* in the presence of God, *and the glory of the LORD appeared to them* (6). After the continuing harassment of the crowd, that visible revelation of God's presence and affirmation of his approval must have brought immense relief to the two leaders. He told the leaders to take a staff, possibly the one Moses had used effectively throughout the pilgrimage,[15] or Aaron's staff, taken *from the LORD's presence* in the Tent of Meeting (9) and kept there for such an occasion 'as a sign to the rebellious', to 'put an end to their grumbling' against the Lord (17:10).

With the staff in his hand, Moses was to stand in front of a nearby rock and *speak* (8) to it in the presence of the grumbling people. All Moses was required to do was to be God's spokesman and do *just as he commanded him* (9). But something went terribly wrong for, although an abundant supply of water came rushing out of the rock, fully meeting the people's needs, it came at immense personal cost to the two leaders.

While *the community and their livestock drank* (11), the Lord told the two leaders that because of what had happened at that rock face, they too would not be allowed to enter the land of promise. They had both suffered unpleasant experiences in leadership, but this was the bitterest blow of all. Moses later pleaded with the Lord for a change of mind;[16] the narrative suggests why his request was not granted.

First, they disobeyed God's command. Although the shortage of water when they left Egypt was met by the Lord's order, 'Strike the rock',[17] his precise instructions on this occasion at Kadesh were not the same. Here Moses was specifically told, *'Speak to that rock before their eyes and it will pour out its water'* (8). Moses was told that by this means he would *bring water out ... for the community* (8) but, uncharacteristically, he did not do what was commanded.

At first, he *took the staff from the LORD's presence, just as he commanded him*, but, instead of speaking to the rock, he spoke to

---

[14] Deut. 2:7; cf. Exod. 13:21–22; 14:1–31; 15:26–27; 16:11; 17:1–16; Deut 8:4; Neh. 9:21.
[15] Exod. 4:2–5, 17, 20; 7:19–21; 8:5, 16; 10:12–13; 14:15–16; 17:5–6, 8.
[16] Deut. 3:23–27.   [17] Exod. 17:6.

the people. As they gathered before him, he used the occasion to address them aggressively as *rebels*, and then struck the rock twice in their presence. Had he done what he was told and spoken to the rock, the gushing water would have been a sign of the Lord's omnipotence. Only God could make a word into a waterfall.

Secondly, they misused God's gifts. Moses and Aaron were equipped by the Lord with two specific gifts: leadership and communication. Here, they misused the gift of leadership. As the Lord's servants, they were meant to be models of submissive obedience. The people expected them to do everything *just as he commanded*. In the teaching of Numbers, nothing is more important than obeying what God says, and here was Moses at the end of his life failing to do exactly what he was told. In that moment, this great and gifted leader misused his gift of leadership and did what he wanted rather than what God demanded.

They also misused the gift of communication. Both men had spoken powerfully for God throughout their lifetime, and the great things the Lord said to them are preserved for us in Scripture. That day, at the rock face, Moses used the gift of speech to harangue the people rather than to exalt the Lord. 'Instead of making the occasion a joyful manifestation of God's effortless control over nature, they had turned it into a scene of bitter denunciation.'[18] The heedless crowd deserved to be called *rebels*, but that was not what the Lord wanted them to hear that day. A visible display of his astonishing mercy was spoilt by the angry rebuke of a self-willed speaker. When God generously endows his servants with the gifts they need, they must not be used for personal satisfaction or for human applause.[19]

Thirdly, they obscured God's glory. The Lord's accusation was brief but direct: *'you did not trust in me enough to honour me as holy in the sight of the Israelites'* (12). Lack of faith would keep the older generation out of the land, and now even Moses and Aaron had failed because they *did not trust* the Lord's word. They thundered at the people with their own words, when the Lord had planned a silent demonstration of his unique power. The people's thirst was quenched, but the Lord was robbed of an opportunity for his name to be exalted as a holy, merciful and generous God.

Finally, they hindered God's people. The huge multitude had not deserved the divine compassion, but the Lord was eager to reveal it. They left the scene of miraculous power, thinking primarily of what Moses had said (*'Listen, you rebels ...'*, 10) and done (*struck the rock twice with his staff*, 11). The leaders had

[18] Moriarty, p. 93.   [19] 1 Pet. 4:11.

drawn attention to themselves rather than to the Lord. Addressing the rock face would have glorified the Lord. The people were robbed of an opportunity for adoration and praise.

Moses was a compelling communicator and, over the years, the people learnt many choice things from his exemplary life as well as from his faithful teaching. At Kadesh that day, he had no lessons to share except a tragically negative one: those who refuse to do what God says receive less than he wants to give.

The loveless neighbour (20:14–21)

The Israelites hoped to move on quickly from Kadesh, travelling through Edomite territory before proceeding towards Canaan via the Jordan. Moses sought permission from Edom's king, recognizing that such a massive contingent of pilgrims could have alarmed the Edomites. Despite Moses' repeated appeal, however, they firmly denied access to God's people, demonstrating their resistance by a display of military aggression.

Scripture's portraiture of its leading personalities is gloriously balanced. Immediately following the disappointing story of Moses' failure at the rock face, this brief travel narrative describes some of his qualities as a gifted negotiator. In earlier life, the former prince in Egypt had learnt a few things about harmonious relationships with other nations. He is a master tactician who did nothing to compromise his faith.

Moses' sensitivity is illustrated in the opening words of his message: *'This is what your brother Israel says.'*[20] Direct descendants of Esau, Jacob's twin brother, these people had family ties and the Edomites needed to be reminded of them. Their king would naturally fear an uncontrolled multitude devastating his territories, but he might grant to brothers what would be denied to foreigners.

Moses' compassion, too, is evident in the story. He is sensitive to Edom's fears but also concerned about Israel's problems. He tells Edom's king about *the hardships that have come upon* the Israelites. That word *hardships* describes the travellers' extreme weariness and exhaustion. Moses had used it[21] when he told his father-in-law how utterly 'worn out' the Israelites were by their adversities. He feels intensely the tribulations of his people and is concerned to get them to their destination as smoothly as possible.

Moses' courage is demonstrated in the rich testimony he

---

[20] Cf. Deut. 23:7.   [21] Exod. 18:8; cf. also Neh. 9:32.

expresses to people who do not share his faith. In almost credal terms, he tells them how good the Lord has been to his people, sharing their anguish (*'The Egyptians ill-treated us'*, 15), answering their prayers (*'he heard our cry'*), anticipating their needs (*'and sent an angel'*)[22] and effecting their deliverance (*'and brought us out of Egypt'*, 16). Even though he wanted to get on the right side of an unbelieving king, he was not ashamed of expressing their infinite debt to a loving God.

Moses' diplomacy was conveyed in a delicately worded message. He requested that his huge caravan of travellers might be allowed access to Edom on the condition that they would not walk over their fields, enter their vineyards or use their wells. They promised to confine themselves strictly to *the king's highway*, an ancient road between Damascus and the Gulf of Aqaba, used by traders for centuries. They assured the Edomites that, although numerous, they were a highly disciplined company who would not *turn to the right or to the left* until they had *passed through* the country.

Moses' persistence was needed, for the Edomites threatened armed resistance if God's people were so much as to set foot on their land. Moses was not easily dismissed. It was worth a renewed appeal, for he knew how much time and physical effort would be saved if only Edom's king could be persuaded to change his mind. Perhaps this ruler was genuinely troubled about the enormous quantities of precious water that might be consumed by travellers and their cattle. So Moses anticipated the problem, giving a firm guarantee that they would meet the costs of any water. But their heartless *brothers* were adamant (*'You may not pass through'*), forcefully making their point by threatening them with *a large and powerful army* (20).

Moses' faith was tested, for here was yet another huge discouragement. Edom's refusal meant that the jaded crowd must move off towards the south, marching in the opposite direction to Canaan, circumventing Edomite territory and adding many miles of exhausting travelling to their long journey. Moses must have found it hard to understand why an omnipotent God had not touched the heart and moved the will of Edom's king. We cannot always understand why our prayers are not answered in the way we hope or why the way ahead appears strewn with obstacles, but God knows the future and it is safe in sovereign hands.

Edom's heartless resistence to Israel's plea went down in history as a cruel rejection of God's people. This godless refusal of a compassionate opportunity carries its own warning; present selfishness

---

[22] Cf. Exod. 23:20.

invites future judgment (24:18–19).[23] The king's callous words ('*we will … attack you with the sword*') came home centuries later.[24]

The chosen successor (20:22–29)

Frustrated by this callous refusal, God's people began their tedious detour of Edom's lands, eventually reaching Mount Hor. With a sense of deep foreboding, Israel's multitude watched as Moses, Aaron and Eleazar began to climb the mountain. They heard later that, at the summit, Aaron's ceremonial garments were taken from the old priest and placed on the shoulders of Eleazar (26–28). The act symbolized the transference of priestly leadership from one generation to the next, exactly as the Lord had directed. It was further confirmation to the Israelite community that what the Lord planned and provided was coming to pass. The two old leaders would not enter the land, but those spiritual realities for which they had worked and prayed would certainly be perpetuated. 'God buries his workmen but continues his work.'

As Eleazar came down from the mountain, he was dressed in the garments of Israel's high priest. The waiting community knew that, although they were under different spiritual leadership, the same ideals were guaranteed. God had made provision for the continuance of his people's spiritual life by announcing that the priests' responsibilities were to be shouldered by Aaron's sons.[25]

Here was further visible evidence of the dependability of God's word and his pledge to stay with his people for ever. Israel's circumstances would change and the context of their service vary enormously over the centuries, but obedient people would hand on his truth from one generation to another. The sight of Aaron's appointed successor was further visible evidence of God's unchanging provision, sovereign purposes and continuing presence. Only Aaron had left them, not God.

The vanquished aggressors (21:1–3)

Moses' troubles were far from over. A Canaanite king became aware of the approaching Israelites and, ruthlessly determined to keep them away from his territory, attacked the travellers, taking some of them captive. It was Israel's first experience of defeat since, ignoring God's orders almost forty years earlier, they had

[23] 2 Sam. 8:11–14; 1 Kgs. 11:14–16; Is. 21:11–12; 34:5–17; Jer. 49:7–22; Ezek. 25:12–14; Joel 3:19; Obad.
[24] Amos 1:11–12.
[25] Exod. 28:4, 43; 29:4, 9, 35; 39:27; Lev. 1:7–8; 6:9; 8:1.

made an attack on southern Canaan. That was at Hormah, meaning 'destruction' (14:45). Here is the story of 'Hormah revisited'. The Lord encouraged them with the assurance that, if they obeyed him, he would reverse the fortunes of earlier failure. This historical fragment became reassuringly parabolic. A later prophet expressed it with heartening eloquence; the Lord was restoring the years the locusts had eaten.[26] Through this unexpectedly early encounter with Canaanite soldiers, God's people learnt some crucial lessons.

First, they were prayerful. There is no mention of prayer in the approach to the Edomites for a safe passage through their land. It would be wrong to infer from silence that they had not sought the Lord's will, but, whatever they had done about the king of Edom, they certainly prayed about *the Canaanite king of Arad* (1). He had taken some Israelites as prisoners of war and the community took their problem into the presence of God. Decades earlier at Hormah, the older generation had ignored God's word, doing precisely what suited them, with disastrous consequences. Now, the people were determined to act more responsibly. Distressed over their reduced ranks, they earnestly sought the Lord, and he *listened to Israel's plea* (3).

Secondly, they were resolute. They made a *vow to the* LORD that, if they were victorious against the Canaanites, they would put their captives and all their possessions under the ban; that is, they would keep nothing for themselves but express their indebtedness to the Lord by offering everything to him. It was a symbolic way of putting God first and, unlike some of their successors,[27] they were true to their word.

Thirdly, they were encouraged. This initial victory was won at the place of earlier defeat. The Lord was assuring them that, in coming days, things would be different. When the Lord *gave the Canaanites over to them* (3) it was an immense boost to their morale. This first conquest became the precursor of later triumphs (21:21–35). On the threshold of Canaan, the Lord was assuring them that, by his grace and in his power, life could be different.

Moses could not yet put all his troubles behind him. There were further sadnesses ahead, but, at this stage at least, he rejoiced in some welcome encouragements. For all his achievements, in this section of the book especially, Moses is portrayed as a very human figure with natural frailties and disappointments. Luther rejoiced that these great biblical personalities were people like us, plagued by the same faults yet sustained by the same grace.

[26] Joel 2:25.   [27] Josh. 7:1–26; 1 Sam. 15:1–23.

Moses was a great and holy prophet with whom God himself conversed and through whom he transmitted the Law to the people of Israel. However, no matter how holy he was, he was nevertheless a sinner, and was barred from entering the land of promise ... Aaron too was tainted with sin. In short, in all the saints from Adam down to our day, we detect flaws ... all the saints had ugly large blots and blemishes in their character. Peter denied Christ; Paul persecuted him. If they had not been under the great, broad heaven of grace and forgiveness, the devil would have besmirched them and us too.[28]

---

[28] Martin Luther, *Sermons on the Gospel of John,* in *Luther's Works* 22 (St Louis, MO: Concordia, 1957), pp. 120–121.

21:4–9
19. Life for a look

Following the spectacular reversal of fortunes at Hormah, one might imagine that the Israelite people would be exultantly grateful. Hormah had become the scene of triumphant conquest (21:3) rather than of ignominious failure (14:45). The defeat of Arad's king might be a prototype for future military enterprise: pray, honour God, and trust him to secure the victory. Israel's people could face the future with bouyant confidence.

Yet, compelled by harsh circumstances *to go round Edom*, the Israelites *grew impatient* (4). Within weeks of giving thanks that their lives had been spared, they were complaining again that their meals were unappetising (5). The terrain was difficult. Lawrence of Arabia described its 'hopelessness and sadness, deeper than all the open deserts we had crossed … there was something sinister, something actively evil in this snake-devoted Sirhan, proliferant of salt water, barren palms, and bushes which served neither for grazing nor for firewood'.[1]

In ancient times, the area was notorious for its poisonous snakes. During its campaign to Egypt, Esarhaddon's army had to deal with its 'two-headed serpents whose attack spelled death'.[2] Lawrence, who testified to 'a shuddering horror of all reptiles', made special mention of their presence in this region:

> … the plague of snakes which had been with us since our first entry into Sirhan, today rose to a memorable height, and became a terror … this year the valley seemed creeping with horned vipers and puff-adders, cobras and black snakes. By night movement was dangerous: and at last we found it necessary to walk with sticks, beating the bushes while we

[1] T. E. Lawrence, *Revolt in the Desert* (London: Jonathan Cape, 1927), p. 132.
[2] *ANET*, p. 292; cf. Herodotus III.109 for a hair-raising description of 'the winged serpents of Arabia'.

stepped warily through on bare feet ... they got so on our nerves that the boldest of us feared to touch the ground.[3]

Israel's experience of these lethal reptiles quickly brought them to their senses. The familiar narrative of the bronze serpent describes the Lord's healing provision for this truculent multitude. Following its graphic use by the Lord Jesus to illustrate the saving effects of his death on the cross,[4] the story was imaginatively interpreted by early Christian teachers.[5] The passage has important things to say about sin, adversity and mercy.

The gravity of sin (21:4–5)

The reference to Israel's *impatience* literally means that their 'soul was shortened',[6] a word later used to describe Samson's reaction to Delilah's wearisome nagging, when 'she prodded him day after day until he was *tired to death*'.[7] The people were irritable and fractious, depressed at having to make such a long trek round Edomite territory. Physically exhausted and emotionally stressed, they became spiritually arid. Frustrated and weary, it was not long before they began to repeat their fault-finding recital of familiar complaints. There was little that was new except that, instead of pinning the blame on their leaders, they hurled their accusations in the face of the Lord: *they spoke against God and against Moses* (5). Their anger was expressed in resentment about their preferable past, gloomy future and frugal present.

First, they were wistful about the past. Instead of rejoicing in the encouragement of recent victory, they reflected again on the infinitely superior advantages of the old days. Once more, they wished they had never left Egypt. Both God and Moses were jointly to blame for robbing them of a better life in captivity: '*Why have you brought us up out of Egypt ... ?*' (5).

It is a profane accusation: if only they could have reversed the miraculous plan of God's salvation, and returned to the oppressive regime of Egyptian slavery! Turning their backs on the Lord's mighty acts of deliverance, they wished he had not made a covenant with them at Sinai as their saviour and sovereign. It was a near blasphemous observation; it is hard to envisage the depths to which this mercurial multitude could sink.

---

[3] Lawrence, *Revolt in the Desert*, pp. 131–132.   [4] John 3:14–15.
[5] *Epistle of Barnabas* 12.6; Justin Martyr, *First Apology* 60; *Dialogue with Trypho* 94; Tertullian, *Adversus Marcion* 3.18; *On Idolatry* 5; Cyril of Jerusalem, *Catechetical Lectures* 13, 20.
[6] Riggans, p. 158.   [7] Judg. 16:16, my emphasis; cf. Zech. 11:8.

Secondly, they were fearful about the future. Unlike their predecessors, their bodies had not been strewn in the wilderness at Hormah (14:45) yet, once again, they sighed about the inevitability of death. Their only immediate prospect was a desert funeral: *'Why have you brought us ... to die in the desert?'* That this grievance is followed with a complaint about food and drink suggests that many of them may have feared starvation or dehydration. It gave sad expression to their lack of faith in a God who had met their needs across the decades.

Thirdly, they were resentful about the present. It was not only that they missed Egypt's varied diet (11:5; 20:5);[8] they despised the monotonous meals God had provided: *'There is no bread! There is no water! And we detest this miserable food!'* (5). The reliable, nutritious supply of manna was dismissed as 'contemptible' and 'worthless' (NKJV) and, once more, they grieved because they never saw 'anything but this manna' (11:6). The adjective they used to describe the manna so contemptuously is not found elsewhere in the Old Testament; coming from a root meaning 'slight' or 'trifling', it indicated really menial food.[9] They could not possibly have derided the Lord's kindness more.

A contemporary psychotherapist has spoken about the basic problems that cause people to seek help, identifying them as 'the fearsome foursome'. All four make their appearance in this narrative: resentment (*'Why have you brought us up out of Egypt?'*), fear (*'to die in the desert'*), self-absorption (*'we detest this miserable food!'*) and guilt (*'We sinned when we spoke against the LORD'*).[10] At the heart of the people's discontent was a series of conspicuous spiritual defects.

First, they did not acknowledge his power. Their deliverance from Egypt uniquely demonstrated his omnipotence and now they regretted it ever happened. How could anyone witness the astonishing miracle at the Red Sea and not believe that the Lord was on their side? Even in those days they whined that they were about to die in the desert,[11] though God had better things in store for them.

Secondly, they did not appreciate his generosity. Ever since that dramatic escape from the tyranny of their oppressors, the Lord had fed them with this heaven-sent gift. The manna had sustained Israel's people over the past four decades. Could they not thank

---

[8] Exod. 16:3.
[9] In Ugaritic it was used to describe horse fodder: Milgrom, pp. 173, 317.
[10] All four made an earlier appearance at 11:1, 4–6 (self-absorption), 11:11–15 (resentment), 12:11 (guilt) and 13:31–33 (fear).
[11] Exod 14:11–12.

187

him for its miraculous supply rather than denigrate its dietary limitations? Ingratitude has no place among believers; it is pagans who do not give thanks, not Christians.[12]

Thirdly, they did not recognize his mercy. He had fed them with manna on days when they least deserved it. It was not given to them as a reward for faithfulness; its daily supply had fallen gently during their times of strident rebellion and sick apostasy as well as in periods of grateful contentment.

Fourthly, they did not accept his sovereignty. It still irritated them that the older generation would not see the promised land, but repetitive complaining would not alter it. The Lord was keeping them out of Canaan, not in order to be vindictive, but to prepare a better community for the tough days that lay ahead. Crowds of persistent complainers would hardly make a competent invasion force. Life does not always give us exactly what we want, and for most of us there are inevitable disappointments. When we find ourselves in circumstances we are powerless to change, it hardly helps to turn life into an incessant dirge.

Finally, they did not trust his word. The desert community were more adept at itemizing their grievances than at counting their blessings. The Lord had promised to meet their needs, and it was iniquitous to forget his faithfulness, despise his care and deny his providence. They were his greatly loved children,[13] a truth treasured by their later prophets,[14] and he would not allow anything to befall them that was outside his sovereign will.

The assets of adversity (21:6–7)

Some people learn to cope with petty trials only by encountering greater ones. Wearied by their continuous complaining and godless rejection of his saving mercies, *the LORD sent venomous snakes among them; they bit the people and many Israelites died* (6). In human life, adversity is rarely a lonely visitor; it is usually accompanied by insights not always perceived in better times. Some emerge in this dramatic story.

First, friends are supportive. As soon as the people started to die from the bites of these poisonous snakes, they turned instinctively to Moses. Only hours before, they had spoken against him (5); now they could not wait to reach him. Their fellow grumblers had rebellious spirits and malicious tongues, but such friends are little help in acute distress. They hurried to a man of God who would

---

[12] Rom. 1:21. [13] Exod. 4:22; Deut. 32:6.
[14] Is. 63:16; 64:8; Jer. 3:19; 31:9; Hos. 11:1; Mal. 2:10.

listen to their troubles and identify with their grief. When difficult experiences befall us, reliable friends are an immense mercy. Israel's wise men regularly testified to the superlative worth of good friends, and urged the godly to cultivate the qualities of dependable friendship.[15] God's Son valued his friends.[16] As he approached his loneliest hours, he thanked his disciples for their genuine love and sympathetic understanding during life's intense pressures.[17]

Secondly, sin is destructive. In their voluble discontent, they hurled their accusations in the face of God and addressed his servant aggressively. Such is the egotistical preoccupation of human self-absorption. Nothing can ward off rebelliousness like unexpected trouble or something people are powerless to handle. Adversity enables the sufferer to distinguish the trivial from the crucial, the marginal from the central. The lethal bites of *venomous snakes* would be more persuasive than all the eloquence of Israel's leaders. As they lay on their beds, tossing with fever and feeling their lives ebbing away, they did not find it hard to say, '*We sinned.*'

Thirdly, prayer is crucial. They had been thundering at God with their incessant complaints, and had to be represented at his throne by someone who could approach God for them. The grossly maligned leader became the urgently needed intercessor. Adversity sifts our priorities; they were no longer interested in more refined culinary provisions. They knew that Moses was a friend of God, and pleaded earnestly for something that now mattered more than food or drink. Trouble had changed their values and reshaped their ambitions. P. T. Forsyth made the point that God's 'final purpose in all trouble' is to drive us closer to himself: 'The joiner, when he glues together two boards, keeps them tightly clamped till the cement sets ... So with calamities, depressions and disappointments that crush us into closer contact with God. The pressure on us is kept up till the soul's union with God is set.'[18] Nobody could deny that these threatened and dying Israelites were 'tightly clamped'. They urged Moses to plead with God: '*Pray that the LORD will take the snakes away from us*' (7).

Our world urgently needs informed intercessors. Millions of our contemporaries hardly ever pray for themselves. World leaders, politicians, economists, educators, planners and technologists make huge decisions, rarely considering the responsibility of prayer. Contemporary society is increasingly godless and some of those who never pray need an intercessor. Millions of children in the

---

[15] Prov. 17:17; 18:24; 27:6, 10.   [16] John 11:1–3, 5, 36; 12:1–3; 15:13–14.
[17] Luke 22:28.
[18] P. T. Forsyth, *The Soul of Prayer* (London: Charles Kelly, 1916), p. 19.

world belong to families where God's name is not honoured and they have no-one to pray for them. Eighty-five per cent of the UK's children and young people have no meaningful connection with a local church or Christian organization. Could we not take the specific name of some unprayed-for child to the place of prayer, that he or she may be brought to Christ?

The miracle of mercy (21:8–9)

The travellers were surrounded by dying people, and powerless to do anything about it. *Moses prayed for the people* (7), and God answered his prayer: *'Make a snake and put it up on a pole; anyone who is bitten can look at it and live'* (8).

This description of what the dying people were to do in their anguish portrays some crucial dimensions of the divine mercy. Recalling its interpretation by Jesus in his conversation with Nicodemus,[19] the narrative presents an Old Testament paradigm of salvation.

Uniquely provided

Nobody could possibly doubt that this miraculous act of salvation was from Israel's God, acting in mercy, power and wisdom.

First, this desert miracle was evidence of God's mercy. The healings were not effected by a metal artefact but by the Lord who had planned their deliverance. One Jewish interpreter said these wilderness pilgrims were given 'a token' of God's salvation and that 'he who turned toward it was saved, not by what he saw, but by thee, the Saviour of all'.[20] Across the centuries people have always been tempted to magnify the symbol rather than glorify the Lord and, as we shall see, Israel's later use of this bronze serpent was a grim example of such misplaced worship.

Secondly, this desert miracle was an expression of God's power. This was the last time the travellers were wistful about the greater attractions of Egypt (5). Currid believes that the Lord's use of both *pole* and *snake* emphasized the impotence of human resources. Egypt's banners, ensigns and standards were sacred objects invested with divine power, and their people 'revered the serpent for both the danger and protection it presented'.[21] Here in this scene of human weakness and impending death, the Lord was deliberately using familiar Egyptian power-symbols in 'a scene of polemical taunting ... Both the serpent and the standard were emblems of the

[19] John 3:14–15.   [20] Wisdom of Solomon 16:6–7, RSV.
[21] Currid, p. 147.

power and sovereignty of the gods of Egypt. But in Numbers 21 they actually reflect the omnipotence of Yahweh alone. Only he can protect and heal the people ... Even though many Israelites desire to return to Egypt, the Egyptian gods can do nothing for the Hebrews.'[22]

Thirdly, this desert miracle was an example of God's wisdom. The Lord chose this unusual means to convince the people that their healing came from him alone. Calvin makes the point that, at first sight, nothing would seem 'more unreasonable' than that the sight of a brazen serpent 'should extirpate the deadly poison'. But 'this apparent absurdity was far better suited to render the grace of God conspicuous' than if the Lord had chosen some other method. If God had simply removed the serpents, unbelieving Israelites would have put it all down to 'an accidental occurrence, and that the evil had vanished by natural means'. If God had solved the problem by providing something to apply to the bites, 'bearing an affinity to fit and appropriate remedies', they would have put the healing down to suitable medication, and 'the power and goodness of God would have been thrown into the shade.' In order to persuade them that they were indebted solely to the mercy and power of God, 'a mode of preservation was chosen so discordant with human reason, as to be almost a subject for laughter'.[23] When those who looked at the bronze serpent suddenly began to recover from their raging fever, nobody could doubt that the Lord alone was their healer.

Totally undeserved

Here was salvation for sinners. Victims were not healed on the basis of their religious devotion, moral achievement or spiritual excellence. They were rebels, guilty of impatience, anger, unbelief, rebellion, criticism, resentment and ingratitude (4–5). They had publicly vilified the God who had blessed them, and had flung their criticisms in the face of his servant; yet here he was, offering them a way of escape. Now, in their anguish, these disloyal people were no longer preoccupied with trivialities; they had forgotten Egypt's pleasures and the desert's inconveniences. Their present concerns were literally a matter of life and death.

The vivid story is an uncomplicated parable of God's astonishing grace. He presents his gift of salvation to undeserving rebels who have despised his gifts, spurned his mercy, rejected his word and slandered his name. The bigoted intellectual aristocrat who

[22] Ibid., p. 155.   [23] Calvin, IV, p. 155.

guarded the clothes of Stephen's murderers was incensed at the
audacity of the early Christian preachers who proclaimed the
uniqueness of Christ. Determined to put an end to their mission,
he set out to execute their leaders, imprison their followers and
silence their witness.[24] Yet, while such 'murderous threats' were on
his lips, the glorified Lord met him as he pursued his errand of
bitter hatred: 'Saul, Saul, why do you persecute me?'[25] No wonder
the apostle could write later about the unique demonstration of
divine love in the work of Christ: 'when we were God's enemies,
we were reconciled to him through the death of his Son'.[26]

In John's Gospel, Christ's teaching that precedes his bronze-
serpent illustration makes it clear that his salvation was for people
not remotely worthy. Like those contemporaries of Jesus, our
lives are spoilt by our spiritual ignorance,[27] the determined rejection of Christ,[28] social superiority,[29] gross materialism[30] and stark
unbelief,[31] but, as with those wilderness rebels, he chooses to save
those who least deserve it.[32]

Urgently necessary

Life for many was slipping away. The lethal poison was destroying
them and within hours they would die. It was not a moment for
reflection, postponement or debate. Others might have had the
time to discuss whether the visual impact of a metal object might
have therapeutic value, but it was not a topic for the dying. If they
wanted to live they must look, and must do so without a moment's
delay. The unexpected crisis caused them to reflect on life's values.
Illness can do that in any life. C. S. Lewis reminded us that 'pain
insists upon being attended to. God whispers to us in our
pleasures, speaks in our conscience, but shouts in our pains; it is his
megaphone to rouse a deaf world.' Pain 'is a terrible instrument; it
may lead to final and unrepented rebellion. But it ... removes the
veil; it plants the flag of truth within the fortress of a rebel soul.'[33]

The distraught pilgrims who looked in their sickness were not
only healed; they escaped the condemnation of unbelief. The
bronze-serpent saying has an undeniable judgment context in the
Fourth Gospel. Those who look to Christ 'shall not perish' and
will 'not [be] condemned', but 'God's wrath remains' on those
who, in determined unbelief, reject God's Son.[34]

[24] Acts 7:58; 8:1–3.   [25] Acts 9:1–4.   [26] Rom. 5:10.
[27] John 1:10, 26; 2:20–21; 3:10.   [28] John 1:11.   [29] John 1:46.
[30] John 2:13–14.   [31] John 2:18; 3:4.   [32] Rom. 5:8; 1 Tim. 1:13–16.
[33] *The Problem of Pain* (London: Geoffrey Bles, 1940), pp. 81, 83.
[34] John 3:16–19, 36.

Earnestly sought

In acute distress, the people indicated their change of heart by two things: repentance and confession of sin. Those who had the strength to do so found their way to Moses' tent, acknowledging, 'We sinned when we spoke against the LORD and against you' (7). Repentance is literally a 'change of mind'. In the light of this lethal disaster, they changed their mind about God, life, and food. God might prove to be a compassionate healer (8–9) rather than a disappointing provider (5). Life might be a privileged opportunity rather than an intolerable burden. Food might be a beneficent gift rather than an idolatrous preoccupation. Visited by trouble, they had changed their mind about their past grievances, present hardships and future prospects.

Graciously mediated

When the people repented, Moses prayed. The assaulted leader became the compassionate intercessor. 'Pray that the LORD will take the snakes away from us'. So Moses prayed for the people (7). The rebels had spoken so fiercely against God that they felt their need of a go-between. The Lord, who had grieved over the multitude's determined words of rejection, heard Moses' earnest plea for their salvation. Christians rejoice that they have a Mediator supremely greater than Moses.[35]

Divinely guaranteed

God responded to Moses' prayer by speaking. The miracle was initiated, effected and authenticated by God's unique word. The Lord provided Israel with both word and sign, a verbal and visual assurance of his saving power. They heard his dependable promise and were instructed to make this bronze snake, an outward token of his merciful deliverance. God declared that they would be healed if they looked; their part was to trust what he said. God's word of promise transformed the devastating scene. Israel's metalworkers could have made any number of copper snakes for the stricken people to grasp in their hands, and every helpless victim would have perished. That would have been mere sympathetic magic or worthless superstition, not, as in this narrative, a miraculous intervention. The visible sign encouraged their faith in the promise God had given. As Luther said,

> the serpent which Moses raised up in the desert did not make alive through its inherent character ... but the Word which was added to that brazen serpent was life-giving because God

[35] Luke 23:34; Rom. 8:34; 1 Tim. 2:5–6; Heb. 7:25.

commanded the serpent to be set up and added the Word, 'Whoever looks at it will be healed.' This Word you do not have if you form a serpent from bronze today ... the reason for healing lay ... in the command from God ... and in the promise of deliverance.[36]

Every believer's salvation depends on that saving word of God. Christians affirm the biblical truth that those who turn from their sins and put their trust in the Christ who died for them will be saved.[37] God has said it. It must be true. It can be trusted. Millions throughout the world testify today to the total reliability of that unchanging promise.

Widely available

There was no preferential treatment for anyone suffering from a potentially lethal snake-bite. Priests and Levites were in exactly the same need as those who belonged to other tribes: *'anyone who is bitten can look ... and live'* (8). When Jesus reminded Nicodemus of this familiar story, he assured him of that gloriously inclusive 'everyone'. Issues of race, gender, achievements, status and experience may well have significance in other contexts, but not in the quest for eternal salvation. This undeserved gift of eternal life is for 'whoever believes'.[38] There are no exceptions; the excluded are those determined not to look to the Christ who saves.

Personally appropriated

Anybody could look, though not everybody did. All that was required was a believing look, and healing was assured. Nothing more was necessary; nothing else would do. The simplicity would have been a deterrent to some; the gospel still is an offence to the wise. It was typical of the Lord to give these terrified people an opportunity to trust his word without straining their intellectual capacities. The youngest member of the community could do it as easily as the oldest traveller. Weak or strong, ignorant or erudite, poor or prosperous, all were alike dependent on that single look at the uplifted bronze replica of the dreaded snake.

[36] Martin Luther, 'Lectures on Genesis 1 – 5', in *Luther's Works* 1 (St Louis, MO: Concordia, 1957), p. 227.
[37] John 1:12; Acts 13:38; 1 Pet. 2:24; 1 John 1:9.
[38] John 3:16–18, 36; cf. 5:24.

Immediately effective

There was no delay between looking and living: *Then when anyone was bitten by a snake and looked at the bronze snake, he lived* (9). No other cure could produce an instant transformation. God healed them immediately so that nobody could possibly deny that he alone had effected the healing. At one moment, the lethal poison was making its way inexorably through their veins with only one predictable outcome – death. Yet faith in the Lord who had told them to look, and the willingness to do so, would counteract their infection, guarantee their healing, transform their life and change their destiny. There was only a look between inevitable death and promised life.

Those who look to Christ for salvation are saved in the moment of trusting. The Gospel that preserved this bronze-serpent story[39] also records the Saviour's promise 'that everyone who looks to the Son and believes in him shall have eternal life'.[40] At the beginning of the Fourth Gospel, John the Baptist urged his contemporaries to look to Jesus as the Lamb of God;[41] at its close, a doubter was invited to look at the pierced hands of Christ. The man who had said, 'Unless I see the nail marks', did see, and believed.[42]

The desert incident is parabolic. It invites anyone aware of sin's power and penalty to look to Christ. Sadly, across the centuries, people have frequently looked elsewhere in their spiritual need. Some have looked to their own moral achievements, while others, crippled by guilt, have looked despairingly at their sins. Many have looked to other people to help them, even good people, but helpless people for all that.

In seventeenth-century England, George Fox began by looking in the wrong place. Burdened about his sins, he sought help from the church's ministers. 'Take tobacco and sing psalms' was all that one could offer as a remedy for his guilt. Fox 'reasoned with him about the ground of despair and temptations, but he was ignorant of my condition ... Tobacco was a thing I did not love; and psalms ... I could not sing.' Worse than that, the clergyman betrayed a confidence and ridiculed his remorse: 'he told my troubles, and sorrows and griefs to his servants, so that it got among the milk lassies; which grieved me, that I should open my mind to such a one ... and this brought my trouble more upon me.'[43] Help came as Fox looked not to clerics but to Christ:

[39] John 3:14–15.   [40] John 6:40.   [41] John 1:29.   [42] John 20:24–28.
[43] George Fox, *The Journals*, ed. Nigel Smith (Harmondsworth: Penguin, 1998), p. 8.

And when all my hopes in them, and in all men was gone, so that I had nothing outwardly to help me, nor could tell what to do; Then, O then I heard a voice, which said, 'There is one, even Christ Jesus, that can speak to thy condition.' And when I heard it my heart did leap for joy. Then the Lord did let me see why there was none upon the earth that could speak to my condition, namely, that I might give him all the glory.[44]

On a bleak January morning in 1850, a guilty Essex teenager listened to an unfamiliar preacher expounding a text from Isaiah: 'Look unto me and be ye saved ... for I am God and there is none else.'[45] In that Primitive Methodist church in Colchester, the young Charles Haddon Spurgeon looked and found new life in Christ.

Jesus explained to his disciples that, like that bronze serpent in the desert, he too would be 'lifted up'. He would die a sacrificial death on the cross. If women and men looked away from their sins, self-effort and reliance on religious observances or moral achievements, they could be released from the vicious sting of sin's power and the fear of death, receiving the undeserved gift of eternal life. His 'lifting up' was a direct reference to his death by crucifixion.[46] By such a miracle of divine mercy, millions throughout human history would look and live.

Postscript

This memorable story has a sobering sequel. The greatest blessings can become the worst temptations; beautiful things can be corrupted by human sin. As Israel's pilgrims struck camp and 'moved on' (10), nobody could have imagined that one day the bronze serpent would become an idolatrous distraction. The pilgrims must have been so impressed by the miracle, and grateful for the mercy it signified, that they carried it with them into Canaan. Israel did with the bronze snake what Gideon did with the golden ephod: 'it became a snare'.[47]

About 700 years after their miraculous deliverance from those lethal bites, a different kind of poison was infecting the spiritual life of God's people. The bronze snake Moses had made became an idol, much like the sacred stones and Asherah poles of Canaanite religion. People started 'burning incense to it'. It was probably 'erected in the Temple courtyard where it could be seen and worshipped', and where 'the offerer would stare at the snake,

---

[44] Ibid., pp. 13–14.   [45] Is. 45:22, AV.   [46] John 12:32–33.
[47] Judg. 8:27.

hoping to repeat the Mosaic miracle of healing ... Moreover, since the Canaanites regarded the snake as a cultic symbol of renewed life and fertility, it may have become over time a bridge to pagan worship within the Temple itself.'[48] During a period of spiritual reformation, King Hezekiah recognized its idolatrous use and wisely ordered its destruction.[49]

It is a sad but necessary reminder that, however meaningful, outward symbols can become 'salvation substitutes', tragic denials of the reality they are intended to convey. For all their infectious enthusiasm and heroic witness, it was not long before some early Christian teachers came to rely on religious ceremonies, good works, charitable generosity or moral attainments rather than on the Christ who died for them. Troubled by the danger of unethical Christianity, some writers emphasized human responsibility at the expense of divine grace: 'By your hands you shall work for the redemption of your sins.'[50] In time of persecution, suffering and martyrdom became a guarantee of salvation: 'The sins of all these have been taken away because they suffered for the name of the Son of God.'[51] In other words, what the Christian does takes precedence over what Christ did. Such ideas issue in a doctrine of self-salvation, the sad antithesis of the biblical message of divine generosity and undeserved grace.

[48] Milgrom, p. 460.   [49] 2 Kgs. 18:4.   [50] *Epistle of Barnabas* 19.10; *Didache* 4.6.
[51] *Shepherd* of Hermas, Parable 9, 28. T. F. Torrance, *The Doctrine of Grace in the Apostolic Fathers* (Edinburgh: Oliver and Boyd, 1948), 133–141.

197

21:10–35
20. The march to Moab

This next section, the last travelogue of the book, extends to the time when the Israelites reached their strategic destination prior to crossing the Jordan, *the desert that faces Moab* (11), *the border of Moab* (13), *the valley in Moab* (20) and, finally, 'the plains of Moab ... across from Jericho' (22:1). It 'creates the impression of a determined and purposeful march toward the promised land'.[1] On their way through the Transjordan, the travellers recorded a series of changing experiences. Not all of their camping sites can be precisely located, but the purpose of the passage is more doctrinal than geographical. It offers a portrait of the Israelites' dependence on God for continuing guidance, essential resources and military success.

The passage draws on considerable geographical detail, but it is far more than a formal account of their final trek through difficult terrain.[2] One of its striking features is its subtle interplay between divine enablement and human response. In this respect, it continues a theme equally prominent in the previous narrative, where God provided the means of Israel's healing, but only for those who would respond by looking at the uplifted serpent. The Lord meets his people's needs; their part is to obey and trust him.

As they moved along from place to place, different people (all unnamed, except Moses) were given distinctive tasks. We meet travellers, pressing on with their journey (10), writers, recording important geographical and military data (14), singers, celebrating the Lord's gift of priceless water (17), diggers, even among the nobility, making the precious water accessible to the people (18), diplomats, conveying important messages to an alien nation (21), soldiers, fighting battles when there was no other way to reach

[1] Budd, p. 240.
[2] G. A. Smith, *The Historical Geography of the Holy Land* (London: Collins, 1966), pp. 377–378.

their destination (23–24), victors, rejoicing in the Lord's power over their opponents (24–26), poets (or 'ballad singers'), preserving the victories of other nations as well as their own (27–30), spies, engaging in important reconnaissance exercises to maximize their military opportunities (32), and dependent warriors (34).

By means of these deliberately selected incidents about the long journey through the Transjordan area, the narrative reflects Israel's convictions about the nature of God as omnipresent (in the guiding cloud), omniscient (identifying a hidden source of water) and omnipotent ('handing over' their enemies to them). They have already proved that he is their healer (21:4–9); here they acknowledge him as guide, provider and conqueror.

Their continuing guide (21:10–15)

The previous wilderness scene where, at God's command, 'Moses made a bronze snake and put it up on a pole' (21:9) had been the arena of both judgment and mercy. It had tragic associations for many families as they buried in the desert those who had grown 'impatient on the way' (4). Yet, despite the sadness, it was time to move on. Yesterday's mistakes must not hinder today's opportunities. The 'venomous snakes' episode marks the last of Israel's recurrent murmurings; by this time the people were more intent on anticipating their gains than on itemizing their losses. The paragraphs convey their own sense of increasing momentum. The vast multitude *moved on ... they set out ... and camped ... in the desert that faces Moab towards the sunrise. From there they moved on* (10–11).

Although the passage does not make specific reference to the guiding cloud, it was unfailingly present as the Lord had promised. Their movement from one location to the next was totally dependent on that visible sign of his presence and purpose for, as he had promised (9:15–23),[3] the Lord continued to guide his people.

Supporting the travel detail, the narrative quotes from a poetic account of military successes, citing specific locations, *the Book of the Wars of the LORD*, a literary source unknown to us apart from this isolated reference.[4] Something is clearly missing from the beginning of the quotation from the book; the phrase '... *Waheb*

---

[3] Exod. 13:21–22.

[4] Other Old Testament examples of anthologies or collections are the 'Book of Jashar' (Josh. 10:12–13), which included David's lament over the death of Saul and Jonathan (2 Sam. 1:17–27), 'the book of the annals of Solomon' (1 Kgs. 11:41), the 'records of Samuel ... Nathan ... and Gad' (1 Chr. 29:29), and 'the prophecy of Ahijah ... and ... the visions of Iddo' (2 Chr. 9:29).

in Suphah and the ravines' calls for an opening verb and subject. D. L. Christensen has suggested that the initial words referred to God's action as Israel's leader. This possible emendation of the text (14–15) can only be hypothetical, though it certainly supports one of the main themes of Numbers, that the Lord initiates his people's achievements. Christensen's translation reads:

> The LORD came in a whirlwind;
> He came to the branch wadis of the Arnon.
> He marched through the wadis;
> He marched, he turned aside to the seat of Ar,
> He leaned toward the border of Moab.

Christensen suggests that the 'picture painted here is that of the Divine Warrior poised on the edge of the promised land … He has come in the whirlwind with his hosts to the sources of the river Arnon in Transjordan. He marches through the wadis turning aside to settle affairs with Moab before marching against the Amorite kings to the north, and then across the Jordan to Gilgal and the conquest of Canaan.'[5]

Gordon Wenham agrees that this 'reinterpretation of these difficult lines produces poetry with a clear metre and an authentic ring about it'. There are passages with similar ideas of God as 'the divine warrior' elsewhere in the Old Testament, each with precise geographical references, as here.[6] This 'would make a fine opening to a poem called *The Book of the Wars of the Lord*', but, as a purely 'conjectural emendation, its validity is ultimately undemonstrable'.[7]

Their generous provider (21:16–18)

Israel's most recent complaints had largely concerned the absence of water (20:2, 5; 21:5), and as they travelled through the scorching Transjordanian terrain, the people were in desperate need of it. However, there is no record here of discontented grumbling.

It was a time for trusting. Their journey brought them into an area where their omniscient God knew that, hidden from their sight, was an underground water supply. The water was not visible but it was available.

Milgrom cites G. A. Smith, who says that in 'a northern

---

[5] D. L. Christensen, 'Num. 21:14–15 and the Book of the Wars of Yahweh', *Catholic Biblical Quarterly* 36 (1974), pp. 359–360. Milgrom (p. 177) and Budd (p. 239) favour this emendation.

[6] Deut. 33:1–2; Judg. 5:4–5; Ps. 68:7–35.   [7] Wenham (1981), pp. 159–160.

tributary of the Arnon, the Arabs dig out with their hands, pits in the gravel of the dry torrent bed in which water gathers'. 'These water pits are called *bir, biyar*, the exact equivalent of the Hebrew *be'er*, "well"', and are in 'the very neighbourhood where Israel was encamped'. This wadi 'is the only place north of the Arnon where water comes to the surface in the manner described' in this passage.[8]

There are periods in our lives when we may be severely tested and it seems as though the necessary help is simply not there. The God who has promised to meet all our needs[9] will never fail us. At such times we must renew our confidence in the Lord, who will never let us down, and patiently wait, looking expectantly for his promised resources.[10] As this vast multitude began to feel thirsty, he gave Moses the pledge of assured supplies: *'Gather the people together and I will give them water'* (16).

It was also a time for working. Although the Lord had brought them to their underground supply, the people had to dig deeply into the sand before the water began to flow. The poem's words

> *about the well that the princes dug,*
> *that the nobles of the people sank –*
> *the nobles with sceptres and staffs*

may preserve a detail about the travellers' working customs, when their tribal leaders dug the first spadefuls of sand, indicating that this was a community activity and that, in some way, all should be involved. Everybody needed water, rich and poor alike; everyone wished to be represented in an enterprise of eager cooperation with God's purposes.

It was also a time for singing.

> *'Spring up, O well!*
> *Sing about it.'*

The grateful people struck up the notes of a workman's or 'celebratory song'[11] as they dug deeply through layers of sand and rock. They sang to the hidden well, urging it to yield its priceless treasure; but in doing so they were praising the God who had brought them to the place where daily needs were abundantly supplied.

---

[8] Milgrom, p. 178, citing G. A. Smith, *The Early Poetry of Israel* (1912), p. 64.
[9] Phil. 4:19.   [10] Heb. 10:35–38; Rom. 5:3; Jas. 1:3–4, 12; 5:11; 1 Pet. 1:6–8.
[11] Ashley, p. 413. Sturdy, p. 151, says that similar songs are sung by modern bedouin.

Their invincible conqueror (21:19–35)

In addition to daily guidance and replenished resources, the people hoped for military success. On the other side of the Jordan, a whole land, now occupied by other nations, had to be possessed, so they were preparing themselves for inevitable conflict. Moreover, on the east side of the river, the hostile presence of two other nations was an immediate challenge.

Once again, as in the hidden-well story, we meet the subtle interplay between divine omnipotence and human response. Travelling north along the east of Moab, they came to the Amorite border. The Israelite travellers were not loveless aggressors. On reaching Amorite territory, they sought permission to pass through King Sihon's land, giving the assurance that they would not rob his people of essential supplies. As with their approach to the Edomites (20:16–17, 19), they promised to keep to *the king's highway*, the ancient caravan route constantly used by merchants and tradesmen. The Amorites were as stubbornly resolved to keep them out of their land as the Edomites had been. Now, however, the circumstances were different. Israel had no alternative route as at the time of the Edomite refusal. It was a moment of crisis.

The king of the Amorites *marched out into the desert against Israel* (23) but the omnipotent Lord went ahead of the Israelite soldiers and gave them victory. He had said centuries earlier that, at the right time, he would give them that Amorite territory,[12] and had never forgotten the promise. Emphasizing the remarkable nature of their military achievement, the narrative quotes from another poem (27–30), 'an old anti-Moabite taunt song',[13] written to celebrate an earlier Amorite conquest of the Moabites. On that occasion, Chemosh, the god of the Moabites,[14] had not given his worshipping subjects the victory they needed (29). By contrast, the unfailing Lord enabled his people to overcome a foe that could boast considerable military success. No wonder the king of Moab became concerned as Israel's huge numbers drew closer to his territory (22:2–3). Balak's fear was unfounded, for the Lord did not intend his people to invade Moabite territory,[15] but he did plan to give them the land of Bashan occupied by the subjects of their giant-king Og. That was the next challenge.

Although victorious over Sihon's army, the travellers had every reason to be fearful. The territory ahead was inhabited by those warriors of gigantic stature who, decades earlier, had terrified the

---

[12] Gen. 15:16.   [13] Budd, p. 247.   [14] Judg. 11:24; 1 Kgs. 11:7.
[15] Deut. 2:9.

older generation (13:28, 32–33). King Og of Bashan had enormous physical proportions. His bed was 'more than thirteen feet long and six feet wide'[16] but, though mere men might be terrorized by his massive physique, the Lord told Moses that he was no threat to an omnipotent God: *'Do not be afraid of him, for I have handed him over to you, with his whole army and his land'* (34).

Hearing of Israel's victory over their Amorite neighbours, the people of Bashan naturally prepared their best soldiers for battle. The towering figure of Og, leading *his whole army*, must have been a daunting sight to Israel's fighters. But the Lord *handed … over* the giant king to a people who had earlier called themselves diminutive grasshoppers (13:33), and *they took possession of his land* (36).

Their victory owed everything to divine sovereignty rather than to military potency. Earlier, they had been a carping and complaining horde of malcontents, tragically divided among themselves, wishing they had never left Egypt, and even anticipating a return to the scene of their previous captivity. Yet, despite such glaring imperfections, God was on their side.

Og's territory in Bashan was noted for its oak forests and rich pasture,[17] so fertile and 'suitable for livestock' (32:4) that two of the tribes later asked if they might remain there with their herds instead of crossing the Jordan with the rest. God's word was coming true before their eyes; here was land 'flowing with milk and honey'. They did not deserve his generosity, but his gifts are on the basis of divine mercy, not human merit.

Subjugating the kingdoms of Sihon and Og was the greatest possible encouragement to a people challenged by greater tests in the land beyond Jordan. It 'ranked with the Exodus as a paradigm of God's miraculous intervention on behalf of his people'.[18] Their victories east of the river went down in their history as a perpetual reminder of the Lord's omnipotence in time of human vulnerability.[19] The Lord who had given them victory on one side of the Jordan would not fail them on the other.

[16] Deut. 3:11.   [17] Amos 4:1; Is. 2:13; Ezek. 27:6.   [18] Milgrom, p. 179.
[19] Deut. 1:4; 2:24 – 3:11; 4:47–49; 29:7–8; Josh. 9:10; 12:1–6; Judg. 11:19–23; Neh. 9:22; Pss. 135:10–12; 136:19–26.

22:1 – 24:25
21. Seeing with the seer

The next three chapters of Numbers contain some of the book's finest literary material and theological teaching. We begin by recalling the graphic story of Balak and Balaam.

Its scenario

News of Israel's conquests spread quick ly throughout Moabite territory. Balak, its ruler, was distraught at the prospect of an invasion, particularly as the travellers had just conquered the Amorites, a people who had earlier subdued Moab. His disturbed mind hit on a bright idea: he would seek supernatural help rather than rely solely on military strength. Why not call in a widely acclaimed soothsayer, Balaam from Mesopotamia,[1] and pay him handsomely to put an inhibiting curse on the Israelites? Balak's soldiers could then engage in battle with a people whose prospect of military success was blighted from the start. Armed with an enticing fee, Balak's messengers went on their ten-day journey to Balaam. Though he was a pagan engaged in divinely forbidden witchcraft and necromancy, the eastern magician asked the Lord what he was

---

[1] The Tell Deir 'Allah texts suggest that Balaam may have had a considerable reputation throughout the region. Deir 'Alla is about 25 miles north of where the Israelites camped in the plain of Moab. The texts were discovered in present-day Jordan in 1967, written in black and red on lime-plaster fragments from an earthquake-shattered sanctuary wall. Although they date from about the eighth century BC, they may well preserve ancient local material. One of four columns describes Balaam (ben Beor) as 'a seer of the gods', who 'saw a vision, like an oracle of El'. See Wenham (1997), p. 85, and his bibliography, p. 90; Mark W. Chavalas and Edwin C. Hosteller, 'Epigraphic light on the OT', and Mark W. Chavalas and Murray R. Adamthwaite, 'Archeological light on the OT', in Baker and Arnold, pp. 46–47, 93–94. Davies, pp. 281–284, maintains that 'there can be no doubt that the Balaam mentioned here is the same as Balaam, son of Beor' of Num. 22 – 24.

to do about the Moabite request. Right at the beginning he was forbidden to *put a curse on those people, because they are blessed* (22:12). Balaam sent a negative reply to Moab's king.

Annoyed at the seer's refusal to help, Balak renewed his request with a more impressive delegation, promising Balaam that he would be *handsomely* rewarded if he cursed the Israelites (22:17). Balak seemed to know that money mattered to the seer. Balaam said he cannot possibly *go beyond the the command of the LORD*, even if Balak gave his entire *palace filled with silver and gold* (22:18), but suggested that the delegation might stay overnight so that he might ask the Lord again about their request. God told the seer that he could return with the delegation but must do only what the Lord would tell him. The next morning, Balaam *saddled his donkey and went with the princes of Moab. But God was very angry when he went* (22:21–22).

It was not the most comfortable of journeys either for the animal or for its passenger. On three occasions an angel blocked their path. Each time, the donkey, aware of this divine messenger brandishing a sword, kept turning aside, and during one encounter Balaam's foot was badly crushed against a wall. Not knowing why the animal was being so extraordinarily stubborn, Balaam struck her with his staff. Annoyed by this unjustified beating, the donkey suddenly provided a unique contribution to the story by making a strident vocal protest. Astonished to be in the company of a talking donkey, Balaam suddenly saw the angel for himself and promptly realized why his normally compliant animal had been so difficult. The angel told him that the awkward donkey had saved his life, and but for her repeated refusal to go ahead God's messenger would have killed him.

The angel said that God was willing for Balaam to go to Moab, but he must speak only the words the Lord would give him. The delegation returned to Moab with the seer, who was possibly cheered at the prospect that he might still earn some extra cash. Bewildered by the delay, King Balak gave Balaam a frosty reception: *'Did I not send you an urgent summons? Why didn't you come to me? Am I really not able to reward you?'* (22:37). The king took Balaam to the mountain of *Bamoth Baal* (so named because of its association with pagan worship) and prepared costly sacrifices as the seer instructed. Balaam asked the king to wait beside the seven altars he had erected while *he went off to a barren height* (23:3) to receive God's word.

A series of messages was then given to Balaam, totally contrary to what the king desired. Israel was persistently blessed, not cursed. Desperate for an immobilizing curse, Balak kept on repeating the futile process, making fresh offerings and still hoping for a divine change of mind. In the end, the king returned home, angry and frustrated. He had not received the word he wanted but, by means of these messages, the Israelites were given the encouragement they needed on the threshold of the Canaanite invasion.

Before interpreting the message of these three chapters, we ought to reflect on their literary quality. It may help us to understand their dramatic impact on the Hebrew mind across the centuries and why they influenced New Testament teaching as well as Old.[2]

Its artistry

Throughout the ancient Middle East, storytelling was a superlative art and, under the inspiration of God's Spirit, the Israelites were gifted raconteurs. Devoted parents accurately recounted stories such as these in their families.[3] One can imagine excited Hebrew children at bedtime: 'Tell us about the day the donkey talked.' Yet, memorable as these narratives are, they are more than entertaining tales. They are part of uniquely revealed Scripture and infinitely more important than mere ancestral memories.

Stories have acquired fresh value in this postmodern generation. People's interest is rarely captured by abstract concepts or precisely defined ideas; they enjoy hearing about living situations, specific experiences and actual events. 'Narrative theology' has come into its own, and a range of new terms and definitions has emerged to explain and refine the art of discerning the message of these gripping stories. As unique, inspired, authoritative Scripture, the Balaam narrative continues to speak with fresh relevance to every succeeding generation. In Stephen's dramatic exposition of Old Testament Scripture he described these stories about Moses and his contemporaries as 'living words to pass on to us',[4] that is, not solely to the spiritually resistant Sanhedrin, but to us in twenty-first-century society. The story of the talking donkey and its bewildered owner is a narrative preserved for us, women and men at the beginning of a new millennium, who, like those Israelite pilgrims, pursue our journey into an uncertain future.

This 'masterpiece of ancient Israelite narrative art'[5] has something to say to communicators of God's word in the twenty-

---

[2] Deut. 4:3; 23:4–5; Josh. 13:22; 24:9–10; Judg. 11:25; Neh. 13:2; Ps. 106:28–29; Hos. 9:10; Mic. 6:5; 2 Pet. 2:15; Jude 11; Rev. 2:14.
[3] Deut. 6:6–7.   [4] Acts 7:38, my emphasis.   [5] Noth, p. 178.

first century. The encounter of an anxious pagan king and a materialistic soothsayer is told in excellent prose and memorable poetry, with several exchanges of specific, repeated words and motifs, all designed to capture and maintain the interest of the hearer. These include the categories of 'seeing' and 'speaking'; it all starts because King Balak *saw all that Israel had done to the Amorites* (22:2). The king saw a danger and sought a seer.

Throughout the ancient world, men like Balaam earned their living as fortune-tellers or soothsayers; their trade was to 'see' into the future of people who paid handsomely for a favourable message. But this Mesopotamian seer could not see the angel of the Lord obstructing his path. The perceptive donkey, by contrast, could see the angel plainly enough. Moreover, the mercenary speaker, well rewarded for saying the right things, could not speak what he was paid to say; yet the donkey was not dumb. The animal became daringly eloquent as she saw the Lord's angel standing before her with a drawn sword.

Other elements of quality storytelling are found in this intriguing narrative. The element of surprise is important in a good story. Here is a famous Babylonian soothsayer, widely renowned for guaranteed success (22:6), who cannot oblige one of the best-paying customers in the entire region (22:7, 16–17, 37). Here is an animal that literally will not take her troubles lying down (22:27); this donkey knows how to speak up for herself. We cannot imagine what is going to happen next.

The element of humour is not far from the surface. A famous seer could not see what was obvious to a donkey, and a professional speaker could not deliver the goods. When he did speak he could say only what angered his wealthy customer. The eloquent messenger was silenced, but the silent donkey talked.

Notice also the storyteller's use of irony, heightened by the skilful juxtaposition of identical phrases. The angry seer addressed his animal (*'If I had a sword in my hand, I would kill you right now'*, 22:29), knowing that she could not answer back – but she does. The harmless donkey's only offence had been the saving of Balaam's life from *the angel ... with a drawn sword in his hand* (22:23). The donkey became a blessing to an instrument of cursing. Balaam would have become the animal's executioner though she had been his saviour.

The element of repetition is put to excellent use in the narrative. The words *these three times* reappear in the story: on the lips of the donkey (22:28), the angel (22:32–33) and the king (24:10). Three times Balaam is reminded of the considerable material benefits of his sinister work (22:17, 37; 24:11), and the frustrated

Balak finds himself in three unproductive encounters with the helpless seer (22:39–23:3; 23:13–15, 27–29).

The element of mystery pervades the story. The narrative does not merely entertain the itching ear; it teases the enquiring mind. We are not always certain about what is going on. When Balaam received the Moabite delegation, he told them to wait overnight until he could *bring back the answer the* LORD *gives* (22:8). Whatever Balaam's religious allegiance may have been, he was not a believer in Israel's God, yet he was used by the Lord. What are we to make of that?

Israel's God first told the pagan seer that he must not go with Balak's messengers (22:12). Later, he was permitted to go (22:20), but God was angry when he did so (22:22). Did God change his mind? Is it possible here that our omniscient God became angry because he alone knew *why* Balaam was going (greedily, still hoping for a handsome fee), *how* he was going (deceptively, leading Balak to imagine there might yet be a curse), and *where* he was going, to *Bamoth Baal*, a hilltop shrine dedicated to Baal worship – pleasing Moab's king but insulting Israel's Lord?

Again, it might be inferred from the narrative that in earlier attempts to discern the divine message Balaam may have resorted to pagan sorcery (24:1), but at the third encounter *the Spirit of God came upon him* (24:2). Could the Holy Spirit use the voice of a godless sorcerer who earnt his living by doing something expressly forbidden by God?[6] Intriguing puzzles hold the attention of the hearer. Later features in the story may unravel these mysteries, so we listen all the more carefully.

The use of imagery is fascinating. Familiar word-pictures convey great spiritual realities. The ox and the lion assume greater prominence in the ensuing story than any donkey. Balak was disturbed because thousands of Israelite travellers might plunder his limited resources, *as an ox licks up the grass of the field* (22:4). Those are the words that Balaam first heard from the terrified king and, in the Lord's message, the seer was clearly told that pagans had every reason to fear Israel's God. Taking up the ox imagery, the Lord twice described his empowered people as having *the strength of a wild ox* (23:22; 24:8). On the threshold of a demanding invasion they are reminded of their miraculous exodus. It was God who *brought them out of Egypt* (23:22); that was the source of this wild ox's strength. Past victories inspire future confidence.

The animal imagery continued as the people heard not only of a domesticated donkey and an empowered ox but also of a

---

[6] Exod. 22:18; Lev. 19:26, 31; 20:27; Deut.18:11.

victorious lion. In the power of the Lord's invincible might, the people would *rise like a lioness* and *rouse themselves like a lion* (23:24). And again, *Like a lion*, well fed after it has overcome its victim, *they crouch and lie down*, and *like a lioness – who dares to rouse them?* (24:9). Balak had every reason to be afraid. If God was against him, the invaders would not gently *lick up everything around ... as an ox* (22:4); they would be more like a ferocious lion, who will *not rest till he devours his prey and drinks the blood of his victims* (23:24). The graphic imagery is unforgettable, but they were truths more for Israel's ears than for Balak's.

Its characters

We turn now to look at the characters in the drama; each of them has important things to say to us in the modern world.

The terror-stricken king

Balak *was filled with dread* (22:3); literally, 'a sickening dread came over him' whenever he thought about the approaching multitude, and he told his senior counsellors of his anxiety (4). Many of our contemporaries can sympathize with him. Fear is one of the recurrent hazards of our time. Like so much anxiety, his worst fears were groundless. God had told Moses not to 'harass the Moabites ... you are to pass by the region of Moab'.[7] The great Victorian preacher Charles Haddon Spurgeon used to say that 'anxiety does nothing to rob tomorrow of its sorrows; it only robs today of its strength'. We have something to learn from Balak – so much anxiety is wasted emotional energy and unnecessary mental torture. We need to recall what Jesus said about the tyranny of worry.[8]

The manipulated seer

The seer thought he might make a small fortune by telling Balak things he wanted to hear. The king would gladly have surrendered part of his wealth to banish his fears, retain his possessions, secure his country and protect his people. Balaam vainly imagined he was able to do anything he liked, but he had not begun to reckon with a sovereign God. His pagan notions about those pseudo-deities he usually had dealings with concentrated on the most appropriate offerings to make to them, the right way to placate or humour them and the best places to stand in order to obtain their favours

[7] Deut. 2:9, 18.   [8] Matt. 6:25–34.

and meet the client's requirements. Given the right treatment, such gods could easily be flattered, controlled or subdued. But Israel's God could not be bought or cajoled into doing anything that mere humans might want or not want. He had declared plans for his people, and neither a fearful king nor a greedy soothsayer could thwart them. Balaam was a voice God was determined to use, nothing more, and he could do little to prevent it. We have something to learn from Balaam. We must not arrogantly assume that, given appropriate spiritual formulas, correct prayer-language or sufficient intensity in our belief mechanisms, God can be persuaded to do something contrary to his wise purposes.

The astonished donkey

The animal had never spoken before and would never do so again. She too was an instrument in the hand of God. It was the Lord who *opened* both the dumb *donkey's mouth* (22:28) and the blind seer's *eyes* (22:31). By means of this brilliant story, the Lord presented his people with an encouraging message and some great doctrinal truths. A series of fine theological propositions, however lofty and inspiring, might decay in the dust, but the story of an eloquent donkey would endure for ever. She plays a role in a greater drama than anything the most ambitious donkey might begin to imagine. When God wants to announce great themes, influence multitudes, change lives and shape destinies, he will use whoever and whatever he wishes – a pagan king, a greedy sooth-sayer, even a voiceless donkey. This compelling narrative is not about what human beings plan but what God achieves. In the unfolding of his will he can use anything or anybody to achieve his righteous ends.

Throughout Scripture we are repeatedly confronted with frail instruments who are used to further the purposes of God: a mercenary patriarch who deceives his brother,[9] an innocent youth unjustly confined in an Egyptian dungeon,[10] a quick-tempered refugee guilty of manslaughter,[11] an obscure leader fighting a battle single-handed with only an ox-goad as his weapon,[12] a terrified tribesman hiding his meagre supply of corn from the invader.[13] When God makes his mind up to do something he can use anything – ox-goads, a pagan soldier's dream, trumpets, jars, torches, even donkeys – to further his wise designs. This donkey is our teacher; nobody should be discouraged because of meagre equipment. Over the centuries, the Lord has taken special delight

[9] Gen. 27:1–41.   [10] Gen. 39:1–23.   [11] Exod. 2:11–15.   [12] Judg. 3:31.
[13] Judg. 6:11–12; 7:8–21.

in choosing and using the world's nobodies to do his will, to further his work and to convey his message, 'so that no-one may boast before him'.[14]

The theological message of this story is of infinitely greater importance than the attractive vehicle by which it is conveyed, and to these great truths we now turn.

Its message

Encouraged by earlier victories, the Israelite travellers had reached the Moabite plain. Their promised destination was in full view as they pitched their tents *along the Jordan across from Jericho* (22:1). The prospect of crossing that river was daunting to any but the most courageous; nobody knew what perils might lie ahead. We are all amateurs in tomorrow. The older generation must have often recalled the depressing pessimism of those ten spies – alien territory, unforeseen dangers, walled cities, massive occupants. Now, another collection of 'grasshoppers' was here, about to invade giant country (13:32–33). What was needed was an unforgettable word from the Lord, assuring them that the Balaks and Balaams of this world were under the sovereign control of God: *The LORD put a message in Balaam's mouth* (23:5, cf. 16). He 'blesses the insiders through the outsider'.[15] God's word through the soothsayer became a message of rich assurance to the apprehensive pilgrims. The 'Balaam oracles' focus on five biblical themes.

God's privileged people (23:1–12)

In the context of threatened cursing they were reminded of promised blessing. This first oracle's language, graphic word-pictures and leading ideas deliberately echoed the great patriarchal stories in Genesis about the blessing of Abraham and his family. Like themselves, Abraham was on pagan territory when God told him to embark on a journey into the land now confronting the travellers. He too was a pilgrim, with limited physical resources, but the Lord promised this elderly, childless man that from his eventual family would emerge a 'great nation'. The travellers were unaware of the threat of intimidating curses, but God was renewing the Abrahamic promise of undeniable blessing, and using familiar words and phrases to do so. The patriarch had been firmly assured: 'I will bless those who bless you, and whoever curses you I will curse.'[16]

---

[14] 1 Cor. 1:29.   [15] Fretheim, p. 111.   [16] Gen. 12:2–3.

Ignorant of their rich history, the pagan seer could not possibly have realized that his vocabulary and metaphors would take the Israelites back to their spiritual roots. The soothsayer imagined he was privately addressing Balak; in reality, he was publicly encouraging Israel. God's first message through Balaam reiterated God's first promise to Abraham. It was a twofold promise of both people and land. At the time it was given, Abraham and Sarah had neither. They were a childless couple with nothing other than a divine promise, but that was enough.

Now, on the threshold of Canaan, one part of the promise had been gloriously fulfilled. Here they were, a people whose numerical strength directly fulfilled the patriarchal promise: 'Look up at the heavens and count the stars – if indeed you can count them … So shall your offspring be.'[17] When Balaam's message became known in the camp, the promises to Abraham would come rushing back into their minds: 'The whole land of Canaan … I will give as an everlasting possession to you and your descendants after you; and I will be their God.'[18] 'I will surely bless you and make your descendants as numerous as the stars of the sky and as the sand on the seashore. Your descendants will take possession of the cities of their enemies.'[19]

Far from being the object of cursing, God's people would become the instrument of blessing: 'and through your offspring all nations on earth will be blessed'.[20] The Israelite people had heard these patriarchal promises from their earliest days, and now, through Balaam's message, they were confronting the travellers with renewed assurance. The seer's first oracle identified Israel's unassailable security, distinctive identity, unique heritage and ultimate destiny.

First, Balaam recognized their unassailable security (23:7–8). The soothsayer makes no secret of his impotence. How could he possibly *curse those whom God has not cursed* or begin to *denounce those whom the* LORD *has not denounced*? A distinctive blessing was pronounced on the Israelite people, in which the Lord promised to 'keep' or protect them (6:24).[21] Those who had received Aaron's blessing were safe from Balaam's cursing. Their confidence was in the one who put words of blessing into the mouth both of Israel's devout priest and of Balak's mercenary sorcerer.

The promise to Abraham had made it clear that anyone cursing them would find their condemning words recoiling back on themselves: 'whoever curses you I will curse'.[22] Balaam's occult powers

---

[17] Gen. 15:5. [18] Gen. 17:8. [19] Gen. 22:17. [20] Gen. 22:18.
[21] Pss. 91:3–13; 121:5–7. [22] Gen. 12:3.

were highly dangerous, but the seer was powerless to damage people God was determined to bless. In the days ahead, as they entered a new land and an alien culture, no harm could befall them through its wizards and witches, seers and soothsayers, magicians and necromancers. The Lord was supreme over all such hostile powers, and his sovereign will could not be frustrated. He would protect their homes and conquer their enemies, guarding them from both visible dangers and invisible powers. It was Balaam who was cursed, not the Israelites; within a short time the destructive schemer met his death under the judging hand of a righteous God (31:8, 15).

Secondly, Balaam emphasized their distinctive identity (23:9). From *the rocky peaks* the soothsayer identified that huge encampment of pilgrims as a *people who live apart and do not consider themselves one of the nations.* At the beginning of their journey, Moses had distinguished the Israelites 'from all the other people on the face of the earth',[23] a people set 'apart from the nations, to be [his] own'.[24] The pagan soothsayer reminded God's people of their uniqueness. The Lord had created the world and its nations, and all were under his sovereign control. He was not simply Israel's God, a national or tribal deity with no concern for those who lived beyond her boundaries. As Abraham discovered, the 'Judge of all the earth'[25] was concerned about Sodom's immorality as well as Israel's destiny. Abraham was also told of Israel's unrivalled status in the purposes of God, not to encourage self-aggrandizement, but that through her instrumentality other nations might be enriched: 'all peoples on earth will be blessed through you'.[26] They were an elect nation, separated to him, a people who would take his distinctive message to the ends of the earth.

Thirdly, Balaam identified their unique heritage (23:9–10a). The oracle's geographical location is significant. Balaam went to the *rocky peaks* of a neighbouring mountain, where at least some of the Israelite multitude might be clearly seen. Soothsayers considered it advantageous to be on a high place with an unrestricted view of the people to be cursed, or where the flight of birds might suggest the right message for their anxious customer. Those towering *peaks* and *heights* (9) of Balaam's message reminded the alert Israelite of the old patriarch's climb to an elevated place in Canaan from where, centuries earlier, he had looked in each direction to the land of promise: 'All the land that you see I will give to you and your offspring for ever.'[27] Now, the predicted offspring had arrived on the verge of the promised land.

[23] Exod. 33:16.   [24] Lev. 20:26, cf. 24.   [25] Gen. 18:25.   [26] Gen. 12:3.
[27] Gen. 13:15.

The seer testified to his inability to number such a vast crowd of people: 'Who can count the dust of Jacob or number the fourth part of Israel?' (10). The God who had miraculously multiplied their numbers would surely fulfil the other part of his promise by bringing this huge multitude into the land of his choice. Even the language used by Balaam recalls the earlier message to Abraham: 'I will make your offspring like the dust of the earth, so that if anyone could count the dust, then your offspring could be counted.'[28] Now, centuries later, Balaam was quoting the precise words God spoke to the patriarch: 'Who can count the dust ...?' For military purposes, the men alone had been counted in the census, but nobody could begin to estimate even a part of their total numbers.

What confidence was inspired by that little phrase count the dust! Across the centuries, innumerable grains of desert sand had become their inspiring visual aid. Balaam's message was unforgettably appealing because those patriarchal promises were on the lips of a pagan orator who could scarcely have known anything about God's encounter with Abraham. They could not fail to be reminded of the unfailing faithfulness of a God who was determined to work out his sovereign plan for his people.

Finally, Balaam coveted their ultimate destiny (10b). The seer's pronouncement merges into a personal desire: 'Let me die the death of the righteous, and may my end be like theirs!' (10). On the lips of such a money-conscious sorcerer, the wish to die the death of the righteous might be nothing other than the hope that, with advancing years, he might accumulate goods, property and security; but the second part of the parallelism, may my end be like theirs, suggests that he may have had something more in mind than earthly benefits. Though veiled, his longing may even point to the blessings of a life beyond.

Balaam's forlorn hope that he might share the death of the righteous may preserve echoes of the patriarchal story. Abraham and his godly contemporaries were frequently identified as 'righteous' or 'upright'.[29] At the close of a purposeful life, the patriarch 'died at a good old age ... full of years; and he was gathered to his people'.[30] Unlike godless Balaam, Abraham had honoured God and passed to his appointed destiny. There was a world of difference between Balaam's life and that of the patriarch. The seventeenth-century minister Philip Henry used to say that 'all who would go to heaven when they die, must begin their heaven while they live'.[31] Balaam's

---

[28] Gen. 13:16.   [29] Gen. 15:6; 18:19, 23–33.   [30] Gen. 25:8.

[31] Memoirs of the Life, Character and Writings of the Rev. Matthew Henry, ed. J. B. Williams (1828; Edinburgh: Banner of Truth, 1974), p. 212, where Matthew Henry recalls his father's saying about heaven.

sentimental request was not granted. A ruthless opponent of God's people and purposes, he died the death of the wicked (31:8, 16).

The message of this first oracle would eventually encourage the Israelites, for whom it was primarily intended, but it was disastrous news as far as Balak was concerned. Drawing again on the language of blessing and cursing so characteristic of those patriarchal promises, the Moabite king protested to Balaam, 'I brought you to curse my enemies, but you have done nothing but bless them!' (11). The seer insisted that he could speak only 'what the LORD puts in my mouth'. Rejecting what he had heard, Balak believed it was worth another try. King and seer found another mountain and a different view, but identical sacrifices. Balak waited patiently, hoping for a better response. The second oracle expounds two great themes, both strikingly relevant for a people about to enter a new land: God's dependable word (23:18–20) and invincible presence (23:21–26).

God's dependable word (23:18–20)

The waiting king hoped for a message different from the one he had just heard. Perhaps Balaam had persuaded Israel's God to change his mind. 'Arise, Balak, and listen; hear me, son of Zippor' (18). The king was riveted to the spot: 'Stand up, Balak, and pay attention.' He waited for news of the immobilizing curse, but the seer emerged with a rich doctrine of God.[32] Israel's enemy expounded Israel's faith. The opening section of the second oracle announces that in God's word believers will discover truths to receive (18–19a), promises to trust (19b) and commands to obey (20).

In God's word, first, there are truths to receive (18–19a). Before they entered the promised land, the Israelites needed to be reminded of the nature and attributes of God. This uniquely inspired portraiture was of vital importance, for they would soon encounter people with other religious allegiances. They served gods that could be persuaded to grant the wishes of the worshipper. Israel's God demanded subservience to his will and could not be coaxed into meeting vacillating human desires.

The word describes God's unique nature: God is not a man. Moab's king could not treat Israel's God as though he were a slightly larger version of himself. He is totally and completely

---

[32] See R. B. Allen, 'The theology of the Balaam oracles', in J. S. Feinberg and P. D. Feinberg (eds.), Tradition and Testament: Essays in Honor of C. L. Feinberg (Chicago, IL: Moody, 1981), pp. 79–119.

different from the creatures he has made. He is eternal, perfect, holy, righteous, loving, good, generous and unchanging – a God to be worshipped.

The word defines God's moral character. He will not *lie*. In order to achieve their ambitions, both king and seer were prepared to trade in untruths; but Israel's God was not like that. If he spoke to his people they could rely on its veracity. There is nothing remotely false or deceptive about such a perfectly righteous God; he can be trusted.

The word declares God's unchanging purpose. He will not *change his mind*. This truth of God's immutability announced by this pagan seer was handed down across the decades and through the centuries. Samuel used almost identical words when dealing with the tragedy of Israel's first king: 'He who is the Glory of Israel does not lie or change his mind; for he is not a man, that he should change his mind.'[33] God was not like the prevaricating pseudo-deities with whom Balaam had dealings. He had made a pledge to Abraham,[34] and that promise of people and land would never be revoked.

The word affirms God's unlimited power. The Lord does not merely announce great truths; what he says he does. *'Does he speak and then not act?'* (19). Twice in these oracles (23:22; 24:8), Balaam told Balak that God had brought his enslaved people out of Egypt. At the burning bush, he had told Moses that he was going to be their deliverer, and he was. He keeps his word and displays his might because his character is at stake. When the elderly Abraham climbed Mount Moriah with his young son, demonstrating beyond doubt his unswerving obedience to the divine decree, God took a vow: 'I swear by myself ... I will surely bless you.'[35] He would never go back on that declared 'I will'.

In God's word, Israel was also given promises to trust (19b). The subjugated seer hurled his question in the face of the frustrated king: *'Does he promise and not fulfil?'* God had repeatedly said he would bless his people with this twin gift of numerical strength and geographical security. These reliable promises reverberate throughout the Pentateuch, cheering each successive generation with their staggering guarantee. The unbelievable must be true because God has said it. F. B. Meyer used to say that it was not so much that Abraham believed the promise; he trusted the Promiser.

The Bible is packed with promises;[36] they are ours to trust and appropriate. They are not limited in relevance and appeal to the

---

[33] 1 Sam. 15:29.   [34] Gen. 13:14–17; Heb. 6:13–18.   [35] Gen. 22:16–17.
[36] 2 Pet. 1:4; 2 Cor. 7:1.

biblical characters who first received them, but are for all who trust the Promiser and gratefully accept what he generously gives: continuing forgiveness,[37] eternal life,[38] superlative peace,[39] renewed strength,[40] constant guidance,[41] sufficient grace[42] and a destiny in heaven.[43]

In God's word, finally, Israel was also given commands to obey (20): *'I have received a command to bless; he has blessed, and I cannot change it.'* Balaam could not possibly hear God say one thing and then choose to do something else. It was entirely different from the machinations and manipulations that were part of the seer's usual stock-in-trade. If a pagan soothsayer came up with an unacceptable message, he might try another tactic to procure a change of mind and get a different response, or even visit another god for a better result. This was not the way the Israelite people were to think of God. He meant what he said (so they were to believe his promises) and they must do what he said (they were to obey his commands).

This second oracle develops the theme of the Lord's total reliability. He had not addressed them from the remote distance of a heavenly court. He was alongside them as they contemplated their journey into an unexplored future.

God's invincible presence (23:21–24)

Throughout history, believing people have rejoiced in the certainty of God's presence with them. In their chequered experiences and uncertain travels, the patriarchs were deeply aware of it.[44] In the lavish prosperity of an Egyptian household and the grim adversity of the local prison,[45] Joseph depended on it. Moses undertook the hazards of leadership in the wilderness community because he was repeatedly sustained by it.[46] Now, in the plains of Moab, Balaam's oracle reminded these travellers of the Lord's presence in their camp and on their journey. In a series of graphic images, this reliable (19) word assured them that he would always be with them.

Their guardian was with them. *'No misfortune is seen in Jacob, no misery observed in Israel'* (21). Balak desperately wanted the Mesopotamian magician to *see* something destructively evil in the pilgrims' pathway, but their sovereign Lord was with them to

---

[37] 1 John 1:7–9.   [38] John 3:16.   [39] John 14:27; 16:33; Phil. 4:7.   [40] Is. 40:31.
[41] Pss. 48:14; 73:24; Is. 48:17.   [42] John 1:16; 2 Cor. 12:9; James 4:6.
[43] John 11:25; 14:1–3; 2 Cor. 4:16 – 5:5.
[44] Gen. 21:22; 26:28; 28:15; 31:3, 5, 42.   [45] Gen. 39:2–3, 20–21, 23.
[46] Exod. 3:12; 33:14; Deut. 4:37.

ensure that no disaster or *misfortune* ('*āwen*), *misery* ('*āmāl*), 'evil'[47] or 'calamity'[48] would come their way, whatever a soothsayer might wish. God alone could see clearly into Israel's future and he was determined to bless them with success in Canaan. He would guard his people from threatening disasters on the other side of the Jordan.

That word translated *misfortune* ('*āwen*) may also be rendered 'iniquity',[49] which may suggest a different interpretation: 'He has discovered no iniquity in Jacob' (NEB), referring to Israel's ideal status in God's sight, a pure and righteous people. Was Balaam saying that as the Lord looked at his people, he saw them not as under a curse but as the holy community he wanted them to be? Perhaps it was a challenge to the Lord's people to live up to God's declared ideal; those who value his presence will reflect his holiness.[50] However, given this book's context of Israel's repeated disobedience and failure, its message may be that Israel was to be free 'not from moral blemishes but from material disasters'.[51]

Their king was with them. '*The LORD their God is with them, the shout of the King is among them*' (21). Once again, Balaam's message encouraged Israel as it recalled the great events of Israel's past. In their song of thanksgiving,[52] the newly released captives from Egypt had shared the assurance of God's kingship. It was a truth reiterated throughout their history,[53] especially in times of crisis.[54] This conviction about the Lord's sovereign rule was of immense encouragement to the early Christian communities during times of fierce persecution.[55] Political treaties or covenants made in the ancient Near East were executed and ratified by kings, and it is 'as Israel's sovereign that the Lord made a covenant with her and gave her the law. But he was no distant emperor: he lived and reigned among them.'[56]

Their conqueror was with them. The *shout of the King* vividly depicts a ruler's armies returning from battle, celebrating an outstanding victory. The camp rings with the excited acclaim of the triumphant soldiers revelling in the good news of their success. Christian believers rejoice that, though the conflict is often fierce, and the hardships daunting, *the shout of the King is among them*;

[47] As in Job 4:8; 11:11; Ps. 36:4.   [48] As in Job 18:12.
[49] As in Mic. 2:1.   [50] Hab. 1:13.   [51] Davies, p. 262.
[52] Exod. 15:18.   [53] Pss. 9:7; 10:16.   [54] Is. 6:1, 5; Ezek. 1:26–28; Dan. 7:9.
[55] Rev. 4:2, 9–10; 11:15; 19:6.
[56] Wenham (1981), p. 175, who also observes that the tabernacle 'was set up to be a portable palace, with the ark as God's throne'. Israel's camp 'was organized on the model of the Egyptian army with the companies encamped in square formation around the royal tent at the centre'.

they are 'more than conquerors' through the Lord who loves them.[57]

Their redeemer was with them. The victorious acclaim has the perspective of history about it. God's people could point to precise and verifiable events when God had acted redeemingly for them. At the close of Israel's journey, a pagan seer testified to the miracle of its beginning: *God brought them out of Egypt*. A God who, in the face of persistent opposition from a mighty nation, could effect the release of such a vast multitude of enslaved captives can do anything for those who trust him.

Their enabler was with them. Empowered by him, *'they have the strength of a wild ox'* (22). Balak's fear that the Israelites would 'lick up everything around' them 'as an ox licks up the grass of the field' (22:4) would be more than realized in the experience of Israel's enemies. Far from gently grazing as domesticated cattle, they would be like the dangerously strong wild ox,[58] or even worse, *like a lioness*, or a ferocious lion *that does not rest till he devours his prey* (24) – vivid imagery repeated in the following oracle (24:9).

Their protector was with them. The message assured the Israelite people that, with God as their defender, *no sorcery* could be effective *against Jacob*, and *no divination against Israel* (23). Under the sovereign protection of an omnipotent God, they could not be harmed by soothsayers. 'Balaam speaks here from his frightful experience. He has no means in his bag of tricks to withstand the blessing of Israel.'[59]

This reflection on the Lord's continuing care gave way to exultant testimony: *'See what God has done!'* (23). Balaam had been used yet again to declare a divine blessing rather than to pronounce a demonic curse. Balak was nearly out of his mind in anger: *'Neither curse them at all nor bless them at all!'* (25). The seer again confessed his total inability to do or say anything other than whatever the Lord said.

Intent on cursing the approaching Israelites, Balak believed it was worth one more try. Perhaps a changed site and another lavish collection of offerings might influence Israel's God. But how could this pagan king possibly imagine that a different geographical location and a further collection of sacrificial animals could persuade God to alter his character (19a), change his mind (19b), fail his people (19c) break his promise (19d) and withdraw his blessing (20)? Yet Balak was determined to have a third attempt at this supernatural manipulation exercise, and Balaam was willing to

[57] Rom. 8:37.   [58] Deut. 33:17; Job 39:9–12; Ps.22:21.   [59] Allen, p. 902.

go along with it. Rather than tell the king that, on the basis of what Israel's unchanging God had already declared, it was a waste of time and money, he gave the king fresh orders about the necessary sacrifices (27–30). Was the seer, in his mercenary preoccupation and continuing unbelief, unable to see for himself the truths he had communicated so persuasively? Eloquent tongues are not always matched by believing hearts.

God's abundant provision (24:1–9)

In this third message Israel was presented with a magnificent word portrait of their immediate future as God intended it, and, in the following oracle (24:15–17), with their ultimate future when God's chosen Messiah would emerge as their leader and victor.

As Balaam was about to speak again, he found himself overwhelmed by the divine presence, and abandoned the paraphernalia of sorcery he had used earlier. The seer *looked out and saw* rows of Israelite tents, *encamped tribe by tribe* surrounding the tabernacle. *The Spirit of God came upon him* with another message for Moab's frustrated king:

> 'The oracle of Balaam son of Beor,
>   the oracle of one whose eye sees clearly,
>   the oracle of one who hears the words of God,
>   who sees a vision from the Almighty,
>   who falls prostrate, and whose eyes are opened ...'

His message is a model of excellent communication skills. First, it addresses the need. As the travellers looked across the Jordan they must have wondered what plans God had in store for them once they crossed the river. Would they have sufficient food and shelter for their families? How would the present occupants of the land be vanquished? After forty years of precarious desert wandering, did their future offer any kind of permanent security? Balaam's message is a graphic description of God's generous abundance, reminding his people how privileged they are: *'How beautiful are your tents, O Jacob, your dwelling-places, O Israel!'* (5).

Secondly, it pleases the ear. Carefully chosen words are superb vehicles for the transmission of life's most important message. Here is magnificent poetry, making excellent use of the familiar structure of Hebrew parallelism whereby identical, related or contrasting ideas are presented on successive lines: *tents/dwelling-places* (5), *valleys/gardens* (6a), *aloes/cedars* (6b), *water/seed* (7a), *king/kingdom* (7b), *devour/break* (8b), *lion/lioness* (9), *bless/curse*

(9b). The poetry is an excellent memory aid, ensuring that these great truths are not quickly forgotten.

Thirdly, it attracts the eye. The message is brilliantly illustrated. The graphic portraiture of this third oracle employs different types of highly visual imagery, impressing the hearer with its message of the Lord's bounteous sufficiency. A domestic illustration (*tents/ dwelling-places*, 5) is followed by the geographical (*valleys/ gardens*, 6a) and the horticultual (*aloes/cedars*, 6b). Priceless mineral assets (*water*, 6b–7a) are matched by physical increase (*seed*, 7b), when the imagery changes to regal (*king/kingdom*, 7c), historical (*brought … out of Egypt*, 8a), military (*devour/break*), and animal (*ox, lion, lioness*, 8a, 9a).

Finally, it informs the mind. The vivid imagery is an effective literary device, conveying important doctrinal ideas and spiritual principles to the hearer. God would meet his people's needs by providing life's necessary resources: they would enjoy tribal harmony (*beautiful … tents* and secure *dwelling-places*, 5); geographical advantages (*valleys … spread out … gardens beside a river*, 6); agricultural fertility (*aloes planted by the LORD … cedars beside the waters*, 6) and mineral assets (note the repetition, *beside a river … beside the waters … Water will flow … abundant water*, 6–7). A predictable supply of water is the greatest of all blessings in such a climate. The reference to *buckets* probably describes its conveyance from rivers or wells by water-carriers who would irrigate their crops). They would experience numerical strength (*seed* may echo the Abrahamic promise, reminding them again of the assurance given to the patriarch concerning their predicted growth)[60] and national security (*Their king will be greater than Agag*, 7, may predict a forthcoming victory[61] or *Agag* may have been 'a common name among the Amalekite kings [like the names Abimelech in Philistia and Ben-Hadad in Syria]').[62] God's people would also know spiritual confidence (they are reminded that the God who *brought them out of Egypt*, 8, cf. 23:22, would effect their conquest of Canaan) and military success (*They devour hostile nations … with their arrows they pierce them*, 8). Just as the truculent Egyptians were devoured by the waters of the Red Sea, and the Canaanite king of Arad (21:1–3) and Sihon and Og (21:21–35) were overcome by Israel's armies, so would Israel's enemies be destroyed in the inevitable conflicts that lay ahead.

---

[60] Gen. 13:16; 15:5; 17:2–7; 22:17–18.   [61] 1 Sam. 15:8.

[62] Allen, p. 906. See Exod. 17:8–13 for the Amalekites' first attack on Israel after leaving Egypt, and again at the time of the old generation's ignominious defeat (14:45).

The message is a timely reminder that those who inherit his blessings (23:20), trust his word (23:19) and enjoy his presence (23:21) will never lack his provision. The oracle is brought to a dramatic conclusion when, ignorant of its source, the pagan seer repeats the promise made to the patriarchs: *'May those who bless you be blessed and those who curse you be cursed!'* (9).[63] They were the words King Balak, also unknowingly, had used in flattery to describe the soothsayer's reputation (22:6). They had proved true in the unexpected oracles the king had received; those whom Balaam had repeatedly blessed would enjoy that blessing, and the intended curse would fall on the soothsayer's head (31:8, 16).

On hearing this third message, the angry Balak was furious (10–11) and *struck his hands together* in derision and contempt.[64] He ordered Balaam to return home, emphasizing the fortune he had forfeited (*'I said I would reward you handsomely'*, 11) by his refusal to curse the Israelite multitude. Balaam repeated his total inability *to go beyond the command of the LORD* (13). In due course, he would return to his native country, but he surprised the frustrated king with the promise of a final message. This closing oracle was both unsolicited and unwelcome, warning Balak of *what this people will do to your people in days to come* (14).

God's sovereign purposes (24:15–25)

Enlightened by the Spirit, the seer viewed horizons far beyond Jordan and Canaan. Looking along the corridors of time, he discerned the features of one who would appear on the national (17a) and international (17b–24) scene, changing the course of history: *'I see him, but not now; I behold him, but not near'* (17). The message lit a flame of hope in the life of the Israelite people that was treasured by millions: their Messiah would come. The prediction gained further prophetic insights across the centuries, was passed on to the church and, with new dimensions of understanding, reached perfect fulfilment in the coming of Christ. Its message of hope has several dimensions in this concluding oracle.

First, it is a future hope. Inevitably, at that time, Israel's gaze was focused on the conquest of Canaan. Balaam's concluding message transferred their thinking from the present to the future, from the immediate to the ultimate. No worthwhile community can live merely for today. It needs noble ambitions to lure it on to better things. However good the circumstances may appear, there

---

[63] Gen. 12:3; 27:29.   [64] Job 27:23; Lam. 2:15.

must always be something infinitely better on the horizon. The Swiss theologian Emil Brunner wrote his exposition of Christian hope after losing two sons in their early twenties, when a theological concept became for him 'a burning issue of personal life'. Through hope, 'what is merely future and potential is made vividly present and actual to us'. Hope 'is the positive, as anxiety is the negative, mode of awaiting the future'. What 'oxygen is for the lungs, such is hope for the meaning of human life ... take hope away and humanity is constricted through lack of breath'.[65] We cannot survive without it.

The Israelite travellers naturally had their minds set on the horizons of conquest, but this message pointed them forward to greater and better ideals. That 'not now' dimension was vital for them and for us. All too easily, we become absorbed by the claims of the immediate, but everyone must face the challenge of the ultimate. The apostle Paul reminded the first-century churches not to become so engrossed with the preoccupations of the present that they forget the reality of that which was to come. When life for him was both difficult and dangerous, those certainties saved him from losing heart.[66]

Secondly, it is a secure hope. There was no reason for uncertainty. The note of definiteness rings through the oracle and no Israelite could possibly be left in the slightest doubt of God's declared intention to fulfil his purposes. Notice the repeated *will*: *'A star will come ... a sceptre will rise ... He will crush ... Edom will be conquered ... Israel will grow strong. A ruler will come out of Jacob ... Amalek ... will come to ruin at last ... you Kenites will be destroyed ... Ships will come ... they will subdue ... but they too will come to ruin'* (17–24). God's determined 'I will' is as clear here as in his original promise to Abraham, 'I will bless you.'[67] As surely as that promise of Israel's origin, nature and purpose had been fulfilled, so would this clear promise about her destiny.

Thirdly, it is a regal hope. It is focused not in a nation's conquests but in a leader's character. A king would come: *'A star will come out of Jacob; a sceptre will rise out of Israel'* (17); *'A ruler will come out of Jacob'* (19). Throughout the ancient world the *star* symbolized royalty, and the *sceptre* was a recognized image of regal status.[68] Israel could anticipate not only settlement in the land but a prosperous nation under the rule of a good, reliable and mighty king.

---

[65] Emil Brunner, *Eternal Hope*, trans. Harold Knight (London: Lutterworth, 1954), pp. 219, 7.
[66] 2 Cor. 4:16 – 5:10.   [67] Gen. 12:2.   [68] Ps. 45:6; Amos 1:5, 8.

Initially, the Israelite people naturally saw this prophecy fulfilled (300 years after their settlement in Canaan) in the coming of David, their ideal king. David became a fine leader, effective in conquering many of Israel's enemies, as depicted in the closing verses of the oracle.[69] But Israel's teachers soon came to see greater significance in this prophecy than the foretelling of the Davidic monarchy. It pointed forward to the coming of Israel's Messiah, and the earliest rabbis used the verses to focus attention on their messianic hope,[70] a view shared by the famous Dead Sea Scroll community at Qumran.[71] Early Christian expositors naturally believed that they referred to the coming of God's Son, the 'bright Morning Star'.[72] This final prediction by Balaam may relate 'to the royal triumphs in the period of the early monarchy', but the precise victories described here 'prefigure the greater conquests of Christ at his first and second advents'.[73]

Fourthly, it is a victorious hope. The final oracle describes a time when this promised king would vanquish Israel's menacing enemies in the surrounding nations. It is a feature of later prophecy to group together a series of messages (or 'taunt songs' as they are sometimes described) that depict the inevitable judgment of other nations, particularly those who have arrogantly assumed dominance because of their earlier military accomplishments.[74] Their teaching is extremely important in the biblical tradition, testifying to God's sovereignty over the nations. He is not a mere territorial deity, like Chemosh of Moab, interested solely in the welfare of those who acknowledge him. He is the God of all the earth[75] and all the nations are under his controlling hand. Such a message would have been of immense comfort to the Israelite travellers about to cross over into a land already inhabited by worshippers of other gods.

Finally, it is a unique hope. The conquests Israel would enjoy would not be due to their superior numbers, military skills or political diplomacy. Their victories would become a testimony to the power of Israel's God: *'who can live when God does this?'* (23).

Great world empires rose, boasted and disappeared. Over a period of 400 years, those Israelite slaves in Egypt had dared to hope that, because of what God could do for them, their day

---

[69] 2 Sam. 8:2, 13–14.   [70] Milgrom, p. 207.

[71] J. M. Allegro, 'Further messianic references in Qumran literature', *Journal of Biblical Literature* 75 (1956), pp. 183–184.

[72] Rev. 22:16. Justin Martyr, *First Apology* 32; *Dialogue with Trypho* 106.

[73] Wenham (1981), p. 179.

[74] Is. 13–21; 23; Jer. 46:1 – 51:58; Ezek. 25–32; Amos 1:1 – 2:3; Obad.

[75] Gen. 18:25; 1 Kgs. 22:19; Dan. 7:9; Rev. 4:2.

of deliverance would come.[76] Once they settled in the land, marauding nations like Midianites terrorized the people, but unlikely heroes like the fearful Gideon could testify to what God had done in routing their enemies.[77] Later, when the arrogant Philistines held Israel in their iron grip, a blind and chained Israelite prisoner in Gaza was used to bring them to their knees. Samson's contemporaries could only marvel at what God had done.[78] During Saul's precarious kingship those troublesome Philistines were put to flight by what God did to their physically massive leader, using a mere boy to defeat a man who had harassed armies. As that young shepherd reached for his sling, the sound of his triumphant yell astonished the enemy as it rang through the valley: 'it is not by sword or spear that the LORD saves; for the battle is the LORD's, and he will give all of you into our hands.'[79] At the close of that victorious encounter David was only too ready to testify to what God had done.

The same could be said of menacing Moabites (17b), proud Edomites (18), arrogant Amalekites (20), invincible Kenites (21), cruel Assyrians (22), boasting Babylonians, prosperous Persians, powerful Greeks and triumphant Romans. Like the taunt songs of the later prophets, the closing lines of Balaam's oracles gave voice to one of Scripture's cardinal truths – God is sovereign. He is not simply in control of Israel's destiny; the whole world is in his hands.

Teaching of this kind is scarcely popular in a postmodern culture like our own. Instead of looking to a sovereign God and a saving Christ for help, our contemporaries are encouraged to achieve their own goals, utilize their own resources and fulfil their own dreams. Patterns of self-salvation are more acceptable than theologies of hope: 'Attain your own potential, without reference to external moral standards, religious traditions or social norms. Believe in self-empowerment.' The idea of looking to Christ for immediate or ultimate salvation is considered outdated, irrelevant, even distasteful. This rejection of biblical teaching is not confined to sceptics of Christianity. The message of hope that a *star will come* has been treasured across the centuries by millions of Jewish people, but among some of their successors in the postmodern scene, 'doctrines connected with the coming of the Messiah ... have seemed totally implausible. With the exception of strictly Orthodox Jews and the Hasidim, most Jews have ceased to adhere to these traditional convictions.'[80]

---

[76] Exod. 15:3–13.   [77] Judg. 7:22.   [78] Judg. 16:28–30.   [79] 1 Sam. 17:47.
[80] D. Cohn-Sherbok, *The Jewish Messiah* (Edinburgh: T. and T. Clark, 1997), p. 171.

A contemporary (and probably not representative) Jewish scholar argues that they 'should free themselves from the absolutes of the past', because 'these ancient doctrines can be superseded by a new vision of Jewish life which is human-centred in orientation'. Biblical authority is dismissed, for it is no longer 'plausible to assert that any religious outlook is categorically true'. Jews 'should recognize that their Scriptures are simply one record among many others', not 'as possessing truth for all humankind'. They should now 'rely on themselves to shape their own destiny'. 'Instead of looking to a heavenly form of redemption, the Jewish community must now rely on itself for its own survival and the redemption of the world.'[81]

Contrary to all such popular forms of self-salvation, biblically convinced Christians declare that in Jesus, the unique Son of God, the Messiah has come, to effect for humankind the salvation we cannot possibly achieve for ourselves. They are also persuaded that one day he will come back to this world as its only redeemer, Lord and king. Christians anticipate with incomparable gratitude this promised return of Christ, their *star*, their *sceptre* and their *ruler* (17, 19).

Before leaving these truths communicated through Balaam, we remind ourselves that, at the time, Moses, his colleagues and compatriots knew nothing of these potentially perilous events on the mountaintops surrounding their camp. Balaam's occult powers directly challenged the divine purpose to bless his people. At the time, Israel was ignorant of the hidden danger from which God graciously guarded them. The reassuring certainties conveyed by this unlikely preacher came to their notice, passed on perhaps by Balak's princes (22:13, 15, 21) or Balaam's servants (22:22), who were party to these unusual dealings, and were preserved for God's people by the Spirit who inspired them. But this story of Israel's unusual blessing has a tragic sequel. Balaam probably told the Moabites that, 'though he could not curse the Israelites, he knew a way whereby the Israelites would curse themselves'.[82] To that disastrous event we now turn.

---

[81] Ibid., pp. 183–184, 188, 197.   [82] Hertz, p. 263.

25:1–18
22. A tragic sequel

'Balaam got up and returned home' (24:25), but before he did
so the seer showed his true colours, presenting Balak with a
different strategy for the decimation of Israel's armies. What
was not possible by sorcery might be achieved by idolatry.
Balaam suggested that some Moabite women (possibly Baal-shrine
prostitutes)[1] might visit Israel's encampment, inviting the men to
one of their orgiastic religious celebrations. After a lifetime on a
severely restricted diet, some of Israel's soldiers were ready for a
good meal and the accompanying revelry. Balak took Balaam's
advice (31:16). Participation in the Moabite food festival meant
sharing in the veneration of their gods. Tragedy followed as these
compliant Israelite men *joined in worshipping the Baal of Peor* (3).
We shall look at those involved in the story of Israel's fall.

The ruthless enemy

Behind Israel's idolatrous defection was an opponent more sinister
than Balak, one who is always at work to defile and damage God's
people – the devil. Throughout the wilderness journey he had used
every possible device to create disruption and devastation in the
Israelite camp: discontent (11:1–6), damaged relationships within a
leading family (12:1), jealousy (12:2), fear (14:31), rebellion (14:4,
10), disobedience (14:40–45), rivalry (16:1–3), disloyalty (16:41 –
17:5), quarrelling (20:3–5) and irreverence (21:4–5). At the Moabite
border he had failed hopelessly with his pernicious strategy of
sorcery, but now he was ready with a different device: the allure-
ment of sexual immorality. When the devil fails at one enterprise,
he quickly makes use of another. Peter described the destructive

---

[1] *Zānâ* ('commit sexual immorality', 'play the harlot', RSV) is the word used to
describe common prostitution.

enemy as 'a roaring lion', constantly on the prowl, looking for 'someone to devour'.[2] He found many a 'someone' in Israel's camp on the day the Moabite women came to invite the men to their local party. Christians need to be alert to devilish dangers.[3]

The mercurial men

The last thing we read about Israel's men was their exuberant rejoicing in what God had done in giving them victory over kings Sihon and Og (21:25, 35). Ability to conquer in one realm of life does not guarantee security in others. These soldiers had the strength to fight menacing external enemies but lacked the power to overcome their inward foes. The passage identifies three enemies to which they speedily capitulated.

The first was immorality. In Israel's social environment, few of those men would be unmarried. They knew only too well that *to indulge in sexual immorality* (1) was to violate the commandments.[4] Unless the Moabite women were unmarried cult prostitutes (a distinct possibility), they also were married, so the Israelite men had coveted other men's wives and committed adultery with them, breaking their own marriage vows as well as defiling those of other people. Broken marriage relationships are not confined to the ancient world. Infidelity is sadly characeristic of our time. Sex has become one of the most exalted idols of our age and the Bible is not short of warnings about its destructive powers.

Throughout the biblical story and since, the misuse of sexual appetite has ruined many a promising person, wrought havoc in families and destroyed wider communities. Sodom's sin of deviant sexual behaviour was 'so grievous' to the Lord that the city had to be destroyed.[5] Improper sexual relationships led to serious trouble between Jacob's sons and the Shechemite people.[6] Manipulated by uncontrollable sexual appetites, people can live double lives, like one of Jacob's sons, Judah, who ordered the execution of a woman guilty of prostitution, only a few months after he had paid his price to sleep with her.[7]

Sexual enticement failed to destroy young Joseph[8] but did immense harm to Samson[9] and David,[10] and millions since have drifted into moral bankruptcy by misusing a physical gift God intended for married couples. The early Christian people knew from the start that it could destroy their churches, so their inspired

[2] 1 Pet. 5:8. [3] 2 Cor. 2:11. [4] Exod. 20:14. [5] Gen. 18:20–21; 19:1–29.
[6] Gen. 34. [7] Gen. 38:1–26. [8] Gen. 39:6–12.
[9] Judg. 14:1–3; 16:1, 4. [10] 2 Sam. 11:1–27.

teachers warned of its dangers and deliberately set high standards of Christian behaviour in a world where sexual immorality was rife. When the young church debated the tensions between Jewish and Gentile Christians, they maintained that whatever distinctive practices might or might not be encouraged, sexual purity was to be a hallmark of every genuine believer, whatever their ethnic background.[11] When Paul instructed the believers at Corinth about exemplary Christian behaviour, he used this specific incident in Numbers 25 as a warning not to 'commit sexual immorality, as some of them did'.[12] Some of that church's members were all too aware of its perils.[13]

Idolatry was the next enemy. The scheming Moabite women deliberately invited those persuadable men *to the sacrifices of their gods*, and they *bowed down before these gods*. Here again, they disregarded the commandments. They knew them by heart and heard them from the lips of devout parents as well as faithful Levite teachers; but it is one thing to know the Scripture and quite another to obey it. Ezekiel made it clear that this act of idolatry at Baal Peor was not an isolated event; he exposed the frequency of the wilderness community's idolatrous practices. They had been plainly told that they must not acknowledge any god but the Lord, nor must they participate in the adoration of idols: 'You shall not bow down to them or worship them.'[14] Yet those very words, *bowed down before these gods*, describe the tragic defection of these Israelite men.

Ours is an idolatrous age. We must not limit our perception of idolatry to the statuettes of pagan culture. In a sinful world, all manner of things, innocent or sinister, have idolatrous potential. Anything is an idol if it comes between us and God. Luther said that everyone 'who falls away from the knowledge of Christ necessarily rushes into idolatry'.[15] In contemporary society, people idolize homes, jobs, possessions, sexuality, relationships, food, drink, entertainment. All these things, harmless or appropriate in their proper setting, become controlling powers that displace God in human thinking. Christians today need to heed the closing warning in John's first letter: 'Dear children, keep yourselves from idols.'[16] When Paul reminded the Corinthians of this incident of idolatrous immorality with the Moabites, he summed it all up with a similar warning: 'Therefore, my dear friends, flee from idolatry.'[17]

---

[11] Acts 15:20, 29. [12] 1 Cor. 10:8. [13] 1 Cor. 6:9–11, 18–20.

[14] Exod. 20:3–4; cf. Ezek. 20:15–18, 23–24.

[15] 'Lectures on Galatians', in *Luther's Works* 26 (St Louis, MO: Concordia, 1963), p. 397.

[16] 1 John 5:21. [17] 1 Cor. 10:14.

These apostolic exhortations are as relevant at the beginning of this new century as they were in the first.

The third enemy does not appear in such a stark and ugly guise as the earlier two, and its part in the episode is easily missed. These men were initially lured into the Moabite camp by the prospect of sitting at a well-laden Moabite table. After years on a restricted diet, the gastronomical appeal of a local Moabite feast was too great a temptation for many of them. It was when they were well fed and had also consumed plenty of strong wine that, like their forefathers at the golden-calf débâcle, 'they sat down to eat and drink and got up to indulge in revelry'.[18]

Many of our contemporaries with healthy appetites might object to accusations of gluttony, but far too many people waste food, buy more than they can possibly eat, or consume too much alcohol, when millions of their global neighbours go hungry every day. There is something scandalous about extravagant luxury in a world where multitudes are seriously deprived of life's basic necessities.

The aggrieved Lord

While these sordid events took place in the Moabite camp, *the LORD's anger burned against them* (3). The Israelite men had offended his holiness, ignored his word, dishonoured his name, marred his testimony and incurred his wrath. Moses was told to act in judgment towards the leaders whose clansmen had participated in this outrage, presumably because they had not used their influence to restrain them. Those who had *joined in worshipping the Baal of Peor* (5) were to be executed. The offence was such a public act of apostasy that it could not possibly be overlooked. Along with the golden-calf incident, with which it has many parallels,[19] it went down in Israelite history as one of their worst acts of idolatrous behaviour, an ugly stain impossible to obliterate from their corporate memory.[20]

The brazen offenders

On hearing of the offenders' transgression and the Lord's wrath, the people gathered around *the entrance to the Tent of Meeting* and wept bitterly. While they were engaged in an act of public remorse, Zimri, one of the Israelite men, brought a Moabite woman into the camp, so defiling its purity, and took her to his family tent in order to have intercourse with her (6).

[18] Exod. 32:6.   [19] Wenham (1981), pp. 184–185.   [20] Ps. 106:28–31; Hos. 9:10.

Twice in the narrative we are told that this woman, Cozbi, was a person of some standing among the Moabite people. She came from the family of *a tribal chief* (15), and was *the daughter of a Midianite leader* (17). Is it possible that Zimri, himself the son of an Israelite clan leader (14), entertained the prospect of union with a prosperous Moabite family, despite the divine prohibition of such relationships?[21]

Totally ignoring the people's grief and the moral leadership of Moses, Zimri acted defiantly, breaking the commandments in the presence of Israel's congregation. If the sin of the many was offensive to the community, the brazen immorality of the Simeonite man was an act of provocative insolence impossible to tolerate. To have done so would have been offensive to God and the worst possible example to Israel's youth. One man in the company was determined to do something to restore the Lord's honour among those people who continued to reverence him.

The zealous priest

In the Baal-Peor narrative two characters are portrayed in stark contrast; both are in positions of considerable social influence. One was the son of a leading Simeonite family, the other the grandson of Aaron. One illustrates blatant insubordination, the other unconditional obedience. The Israelite travellers were within sight of the promised land; they were on the threshold of religious and moral danger. The worship of Baal was not confined to the region of Peor. Hilltop shrines littered the Canaanite countryside; each was the scene of corrupt and pornographic fertility ceremonies that included immoral rites, cult prostitution and child sacrifice. Confronted with such sinister temptation, would Israel have the moral weakness of Zimri or the spiritual commitment of Phinehas?

There was little temptation to engage in debased fertility rites in the middle of a vast, inhospitable desert; but now, about to enter an agricultural milieu, they must not minimize the seriousness of sin. To compromise with evil, as they had just done, was to incur God's wrath. Facing a morally precarious future, they needed a visual example of what it meant to obey him. At this tragic moment in their history, Aaron's grandson became Israel's role model, obedient to God's word, zealous for God's honour and committed to God's service.

---

[21] Exod. 34:15–16.

Phinehas was obedient to God's word

Practices such as those at Baal-Peor were totally forbidden. The Israelites were told to destroy such altars[22] and break down their pornographic Asherah poles. Compromise would prove a disastrous 'snare'.[23] Before they left Sinai, the Israelites had been warned that alien religious rituals would confront them with spiritual and moral danger. Following the golden-calf episode, they had been told about what would happen if they entered into close relations with people with other religious allegiances. It anticipated the Baal-Peor tragedy with a frighteningly identical scenario: 'for when they prostitute themselves [zānâ, the same word used to describe the Baal-Peor apostasy, Num. 25:1] to their gods and sacrifice to them, they will invite you and you will eat their sacrifices'.[24]

Phinehas knew that Zimri's parading of that Midianite woman at the moment when the congregation was grieving about Israel's sin was a public rejection of God's will for his people. The notoriously corrupt example must be countered by a good one. As one of Israel's teachers, the priest knew that the penalty for such idolatrous and immoral practice was death, and he acted swiftly as the community's judge.[25] Here was one man ready to do God's will, however unpopular. By his swift action *the plague against the Israelites was stopped* (8). It was certainly time for someone to take action, for, when Phinehas *took a spear in his hand* (7), those whose lives had been claimed by the plague had already risen to 24,000 (9).

Phinehas was zealous for God's honour

The priest's intervention saved the lives of thousands. Here was a man willing to put God first, whatever the cost. It was not only that specific commandments had been broken; the honour of God's name was at stake. If the sin had been overlooked, what would those Moabites have thought about Israel's exclusive spiritual allegiance and their high moral standards for both individuals and communities? They might have imagined that people could worship Israel's God and behave as corruptly as they liked. What a testimony that would have been to the surrounding nations!

The public honour of God's name was even more important for the Israelites than it was among their Canaanite neighbours. The Lord said Phinehas was *'as zealous as I am for my honour among*

---

[22] Exod. 23:24; Lev. 26:1.   [23] Exod. 34:12–14, 17.
[24] Exod. 34:15–16.   [25] Exod. 22:20; cf. Deut. 13:6–11.

them' (11). God was to be exalted and adored within their community; not ignored, disgraced and despised as he was both by the offensive practices at Baal-Peor and by the adulterous behaviour of the couple back in the Israelite camp. Phinehas personified the priestly ideal: 'he revered me and stood in awe of my name'.[26] The honour of God's name is a crucial priority for the contemporary believer, living as we do in a society that has scant regard for spiritual values and moral purity.

Phinehas was committed to God's service

Every community needs exemplary leaders and moral guardians. It was the responsibility of the Aaronic priesthood and their Levite colleagues to uphold spiritual standards in an age when the divine will was constantly challenged by alien cultures. As the Israelites camped at their last staging-post at Shittim (33:49), here was visible evidence that, however degraded the moral environment, there were still those determined to walk with God in uprightness and to turn others away from sin.[27] Phinehas represented a new generation, people ready to commit themselves to the Lord, his worship, word and work. It was the divine intention that in every generation there would always be those who shared the zeal of Eleazar's son.

The ruinous incident at Shittim testified to the wilderness community about the nature of God's holiness (he cannot tolerate sin), mercy (his appointed priest *made atonement for the Israelites* so that *he did not put an end to them*, 13, 11) and justice. Zimri, Cozbi and their immoral accomplices did not escape the divine judgment. Neither did the depraved Moabite and Midianite hordes who, by enticing the Lord's people, 'followed Balaam's advice and were the means of turning the Israelites away from the LORD' (31:16). They too came under the judgment of a just and righteous God (16–18; 31:1–24). Anticipating a different life in a new environment, the severely chastised Israelites were taught that trifling with sin has lethal consequences.

[26] Mal. 2:5. [27] Mal. 2:6.

PART 5. PRESSING ON
(26:1 – 36:13)

26:1–65
23. Facing a different future

After the plague the LORD *said to Moses and Eleazar, son of Aaron the priest, 'Take a census of the whole Israelite community'* (1–2). It was time to start again. With the exception of Moses, Caleb and Joshua, everybody counted at the beginning of the journey (1:1 – 4:49) had perished in the desert. The list of tribes, clans and families that opens this final main section of the book has been preserved for a purpose; four specific issues are raised by these ancient records.

Their military context

The names of those enrolled in this second census follow precise instructions about the Midianites who, on Balaam's advice, had 'deceived' the Israelites (25:16–18; 31:16) and were the cause of widespread death in the camp. All the men *twenty years old or more who* were *able to serve in the army of Israel* were to be enlisted as the community's soldiers, preparing themselves for conflict not only with Midian's forces in the Transjordan region (31:1–24) but also on a more widespread scale when they entered Canaan. After such huge losses in the Baal-Peor apostasy, Israel's leaders needed to know exactly how many able-bodied men they could count on in the inevitable conflicts of the future.

Homer's famous mythology presents us with a graphic description of life's challenges in terms of a journey (the *Odyssey*) and a battle (the *Iliad*). The journey is prominent in Numbers, the conflict in Joshua. In New Testament teaching, the two images of journey and warfare are used to describe the Christian life; the believer is both pilgrim and soldier.

The warfare theme is given repeated emphasis in the first census at the beginning of the book (1:3, 20, 22, 24, 26, 28, 30, 32, 34, 36, 38, 40, 42, 45; cf. 10:9); there are no victories without effort. No portraiture of the Christian life is realistic and biblical if it denies this element of conflict and costliness. Paul, who was often in the presence of Roman soldiers,[1] made frequent use of military imagery to convey the responsibility, discipline and cost of the Christian life.[2]

In the New Testament teaching about Christian warfare, three aspects are specially prominent: the severity of the conflict,[3] the reliability of the resources[4] and the guarantee of victory.[5] The same three themes inspired the best of Israel's men as they prepared for conflict on the other side of the Jordan. Anticipating their strenuous encounter with Canaanite soldiers, they had to know that they could count on men who were *able to serve in the army of Israel* (2). The context of this second census reminds the modern reader that in the course of the believer's journey there are many battles. We must not be numbered among those who, daunted by hardship, 'shrink back'[6] like the old unbelieving generation (14:3–4), but among those who press on, steadily pursuing the victory.

Their geographical purpose

It was important to know the precise numbers in each tribe so that freshly conquered territory could be wisely and justly divided among the vast community. Following the repeated funerals of the past forty years, the figures varied from tribe to tribe. A comparison of the first and second lists shows that some, like Judah, Issachar and Zebulun (1:27, cf. 26:22; 1:29, cf. 26:25; 1:31, cf. 26:27) had more men than when their parents left Egypt; others fewer (1:21, cf. 26:7; 1:25, cf. 26:18): in Simeon's case, drastically so (1:23; 26:14). It was vital to know the exact numbers for the purposes of equitable land distribution: *'The land is to be allotted to them as an inheritance based on the number of names'* (52).

Like two structural pillars, the first and second census lists 'provide the key' to the book's 'unifying theme'.[7] Each introduces a main section, the old generation and the new. In this second part of the book, the pilgrim community was undergirded with renewed assurance that, despite the sins and failures of their parents, the new generation would enter the land God had promised to give them. This promise was confirmed and visualized by three events.

First, the census itself is a promise that this huge desert community, whose large numbers testify to the fulfilment of half of the

[1] Phil. 1:13; Col. 4:18; Philem. 9, 23.   [2] 1 Tim. 1:18; 6:12; 2 Tim. 4:7.
[3] Rom. 8:35–37.   [4] Rev. 2:7, 11, 17, 26, 28; 3:5, 12, 21; 12:10–11.
[5] Rom. 7:24–25; 8:37; Rev. 7:13–17.   [6] Heb. 10:36–39.
[7] Olson (1985), pp. 83–124.

Abrahamic promise ('to your offspring'), would witness the realization of its second half – 'will I give this land'.[8] The numbers were counted to ensure that each tribe would receive enough land on the other side of the Jordan river. Secondly, in the next chapter, the five daughters of a member of Manasseh's tribe would seek Moses' advice about land allocation for their family (27:1–11). Legal issues such as land rights must be determined, even though possession of Canaan is still a military ambition, not a physical reality. The third event (27:12–23) concerns the appointment of Moses' successor. Israel's present leader would not enter the new land, but he knew that his contemporaries would. At that time, a new leader would 'lead them out' in battle and 'bring them in' (27:17), back to their homes in safety at the conclusion of each military campaign.

The act of numbering the travellers confirmed their faith, clarified their ambitions and focused their priorities. They were people with a future. As they gathered their statistics, the Lord was identifying his tenants for the new land. Technically, they would never be landowners, only privileged tenants; for God was the owner.[9] That is why he was entitled to displace its previous occupants. He had permitted the Canaanites to use it for hundreds of years, but they had seriously defiled it[10] with their socially damaging, morally perverse and spiritually corrupt practices. Now, he proposed to remove them from their tenancy and hand the land over to his own people, on the clear understanding that they acknowledged it as his and not theirs.[11]

Their ethical warnings

This second census list is more than a repetitive recital of tribes, clans, families and individuals. As different names are introduced, it is as though they would have jogged the corporate memory, exposing the community's greatest dangers during recent and more distant history. The warnings were as relevant to Israel's future as they had been in her recent and distant past. There are five such references, each worthy of reflection.

First, the list is introduced by recording the divine command to Moses following the appalling *plague* (1) that robbed Israel of 24,000 potential soldiers. The Baal-Peor apostasy went down in the community's annals as a tragic illustration of their persistent

---

[8] Gen. 12:7.   [9] Lev. 25:23.
[10] Gen. 15:16; Lev. 18:24–28; Deut. 9:4; 12:30–31; 18:9–12.
[11] A fact publicly affirmed in their Jubilee celebrations, Lev. 25:23; see C. J. H. Wright, *God's People in God's Land* (Carlisle: Paternoster, 1990), pp. 10–23.

rebellion. It paralleled the equally serious golden-calf episode that preceded their journey from Sinai. Sadly, within sight of the end, they had grieved God yet again by their idolatry and immorality.

The second reference comes in the record of Reuben's tribe, possibly listed first out of deference to his position as Jacob's first-born son, though, centuries earlier, he had forfeited that privilege through sin, having slept with Bilhah, his father's concubine.[12] The editor of the second census list draws the reader's attention to two later members of that tribe, *Dathan and Abiram* (9), who created havoc in the camp by their jealous revolt against Moses (16:1–35). That rebellious enterprise threatened the unity of the Israelite travellers and undermined the distinctive leadership roles assigned by God to Moses and Aaron. Anything grieves God if it disrupts the harmony of his people. The compiler of the second census list took the opportunity of this Dathan and Abiram reference to inform every reader that the offenders were judged by the Lord: *And they served as a warning sign* (10).

The third ethical reference pre-dates the wilderness journey by several centuries. It belongs to the patriarchal period and concerns the two sons of Judah, *Er and Onan*, who *died in Canaan* (19). Scripture's searing testimony to Er, Judah's privileged firstborn, is simply that he was 'wicked in the LORD's sight'.[13] We do not know the precise nature of his offensive behaviour, but the stark reference in the patriarchal narrative is a jolt to every sensitive reader's conscience. What we are in the world's sight is of marginal importance: social status, position, wealth, privilege, all perish in the dust. What we are in God's sight[14] is of crucial and eternal significance.[15] When Er insisted on living in a manner abhorent to God, his creator and sustainer, 'the LORD put him to death'.[16]

The sin of Er's younger brother, Onan, is more specific. Under the traditional terms of Levirate marriage, a brother was required to provide a childless sister-in-law with a male heir, but Onan repeatedly refused to make this possible,[17] an offence which, out of concern for the childless wife, grieved God. He too died.

In providing this brief reference from patriarchal history, the second census list not only tells us that Er and Onan *died in Canaan* but invites recollection of how they died – under the hand of God's severe judgment. It was a salutary warning to people who, like sinful Er, might live wickedly in Canaan or, like selfish Onan, become indifferent to the needs of others.

The fourth reference concerns the Levites, who, as at the first

[12] Gen. 35:42; 49:4.   [13] Gen. 38:7.
[14] Heb. 4:13; Ps. 33:13–15; Prov. 5:21; Jer. 16:17; 23:24; Dan. 2:22.
[15] Gen. 16:13.   [16] Gen. 38:7.   [17] Gen. 38:8–10; 46:12.

census, were again listed separately (57–60; cf. 3:1–20). Aaron is important in these narratives as the original leader of Israel's priesthood, and it is natural, therefore, for the compiler of the census to make a special note of his male children, those who would assist and eventually succeed him. Early in their priestly ministry his first two sons, Nadab and Abihu *died when they made an offering before the* LORD *with unauthorised fire* (61), a serious incident also recorded in the first census (3:2–4).

The detail is repeated in this second list to remind Israel's people that life must be lived according to God's rules. He had clearly indicated how and by whom incense offerings should be presented, and the fact that these two were the high priest's sons did not give them liberty to ignore God's word.

Finally, at the conclusion of the second census (63–65), the reader is reminded that the names listed are totally different from those recorded by Moses and Aaron prior to their departure from Sinai. Aaron, along with thousands of his contemporaries, had died in the desert. Moses himself had but a short time to live. Once he had supervised the Midianite campaign (31:1–54), sorted out what might have been a disastrous eventuality about land preferences (32:1–42) and preached his final message to the people (the substance of Deuteronomy), he too, like his elder brother and sister (20:1, 24), would be 'gathered to his people'. (27:13).[18]

The second list was a sober reminder of all those who had perished in the desert, and unnecessarily so. From among the original multitude who had left Egypt forty years earlier, only Caleb and Joshua would enter the new land. They were excellent role models among the new generation, visibly demonstrating the necessity of wholehearted (cf. 14:24; 32:11–12) trust in God's word and obedience to his will.

Their theological importance

The list is no mere collection of near-forgotten names, a recital of irrelevant tribal ancestry. Once again, these records preserve some important aspects of the biblical doctrine of God.

God is reliable

The fact that these lists follow the tribal pattern encourages the alert reader to recall the blessings pronounced by Jacob on his sons.[19] God repeatedly promised the patriarchs that one day their

---

[18] Deut. 34:5–8.   [19] Gen. 49:1–28.

progeny would enter the land, and here they were, numbering a greater multititude than Abraham, Isaac or Jacob could possibly have imagined. Although over 600,000 men of the old generation had perished in the desert, 'God marvellously brought to pass' that almost 'the same number of persons should still remain'. People 'must be blind four times over who do not behold in this bright mirror God's wonderful providence ... and his steadfastness in keeping his promises'.[20]

God is just

God makes his promises, but his children must not imagine that they are thereby free to behave exactly as they wish. They can forget their privileges and reject their blessings as the unbelieving generation did at Kadesh Barnea. They spurned the passionate appeal of Caleb (13:30; 14:6–9), resolved to appoint a new leader (14:4), wished they had never been redeemed from Egyptian tyranny (14:2), planned to return to captivity (14:4) and offended God (14:11–12). He vowed that such a disobedient and ungrateful community was fit for the destiny it sighed for: 'If only we had died in ... this desert!' (14:2, 28–29, 32–35). In their sick rebellion they had 'banded together' against God (14:35). Those who deliberately, consistently and unashamedly oppose God will do so at immense personal deprivation. Jesus, Stephen and Paul each warned their contemporaries of such dangers.[21]

God is generous

This crowd of travellers were about to leave their final staging-post (33:49) in the plains of Moab, and would do so in numbers only slightly less in size than the multitude that left Egypt. Over the past four decades the new generation had buried their unbelieving parents, but there had been no serious decline in their numbers. One of the differences between the first and second census lists is that in the second the names of clans and their various families are added (e.g. 5–7), a feature not included in the first numbering (e.g. 1:20–21). It is as though the compilers wanted to place on record the indebtedness of the new generation to a God who did not exterminate them along with their disobedient parents; once more, he had been true to his promise that their children would be protected and preserved (14:31) throughout their desert journey.

[20] Calvin, IV, p. 251.
[21] Matt. 23:13–29; Luke 19:41–44; John 9:39–41; Acts 7:51–53; 13:42–51; 23:12–35; 28:17–29; Rom. 2:5–11; 10:21.

The parents had failed miserably, but here was conspicuous proof of the Lord's generosity. In this case, the sins of the fathers had not fallen upon their children. The shepherds of the forty desert years (14:33) were about to become the soldiers of the conquest and the farmers of the future. Those who pursue God's will prove his goodness to those who put him first.

God is sovereign

One practical purpose of the census was to organize the fair distribution of land: *'To a larger group give a larger inheritance, and to a smaller group a smaller one'* (54). Distribution according to size was wise and simple enough, but what about precise locations? Once they had conquered the occupants of the land, a greater problem lay on the administrative horizon: how would they determine the specific areas to which they would be allocated?

Each inheritance was *to be distributed by lot among the larger and smaller groups* (56). The problem was thus solved by leaving the precise choice to the Lord himself. It was his land, not theirs, and he would decide which parts of the newly conquered territory should be allocated to a particular tribe. As sovereign Lord, he was not only the land's owner, but the people's Lord. As an omniscient God, he knew what was in the best interests of each tribe, and by the familiar means of lots he would indicate which part of the country most suited their temperament, skills and gifts.[22]

God is merciful

The list provides further evidence of God's undeserved grace. Dathan and Abiram had played a prominent part in a hostile attack on Moses and Aaron (16:1–3). They had conspired with Korah, a Levite who appears to have coveted the more prominent status of the Aaronic priesthood. Like his accomplices, Korah came under the hand of God's severe judgment (16:4–35) but Korah's sons were not to blame for their father's role in the threatening revolt, nor were they made to pay for his rebellious initiative. *The line of Korah, however, did not die out* (11). The Korahite clan was to continue as Levite assistants despite the fact that one of their ancestors had brought disgrace upon their wider family; his crimes were not to be the cause of their deprivation.

Centuries after that wilderness revolt, two Israelite prophets

---

[22] Prov. 16:33, the lots being used in the presence of God (Josh. 18:8–10) and accompanied by prayer (1 Sam. 14:41).

communicated God's word concerning the Babylonian exile. Like this younger generation in the wilderness, the exiles might have feared that they would suffer because of parental disobedience. The message of both Jeremiah and Ezekiel assured them that, despite the familiar proverb about divine retribution, ('The fathers have eaten sour grapes, and the children's teeth are set on edge'),[23] they would not be punished because of the apostasy and immorality of earlier generations: 'The soul who sins is the one who will die',[24] not the innocent child or guiltless successor.

The names of Korah's sons were found in the titles of uplifting and challenging psalms.[25] The 'fathers' defiled the wilderness tabernacle; the 'children' enriched the adoration in Jerusalem's temple. One of Korah's progeny declared his priority: 'I would rather be a doorkeeper in the house of my God than dwell in the tents of the wicked.' He had shunned the rebellious self-seeking of his notorious ancestor, believing that 'favour and honour' are bestowed by God, not greedily coveted by human beings, as Korah did. As they crossed into Canaan, Korah's sons proved that 'no good thing does he withhold from those whose walk is blameless'.[26] Those who follow their steps share their testimony.

---

[23] Jer. 31:29. [24] Ezek. 18:4, 20. [25] Pss. 42; 44 – 49; 84 – 85; 87.
[26] Ps. 84:10–11.

27:1–11
24. Human rights and divine commands

The new generation's census estimated their military strength and determined their land requirements. Unusually, its compilers recorded one family without sons (26:33). Five women in Manasseh's tribe knew that in the eventual distribution of territory nothing whatever would come their way. In Israel, the family inheritance passed from father to son; daughters had no legal right to land on the death of their father. In normal circumstances, a daughter would receive a generous dowry from her father when she married. From that point on she was her husband's responsibility; the father had done all that was legally necessary by way of financial provision. This 'patrilineal' inheritance tradition ensured that land did not pass outside the family. But what happened if an Israelite father like Zelophehad died without sons? The narrative serves to reiterate five important themes which, in various forms, recur throughout the book.

Trust the Lord's word

The possession of the new land was yet to take place, but Zelophehad's daughters had no doubt about a successful invasion. The women's request was made to Moses publicly at *the entrance to the Tent of Meeting ... before Moses, Eleazar the priest, the leaders and the whole assembly* (2). By this means the whole community was not only confronted with the daughters' appeal but encouraged by their staunch faith. After the long years in the wilderness, land possession was no longer a distant prospect but an imminent event. Their father had *died in the desert* (3), but his daughters belonged to the new generation (14:3, 31–33).

Year by year, these children had patiently waited for the

fulfilment of God's word, learning to accept the promises their parents had rejected. As Zelophehad's daughters made their public request, the rest of the multitude realized that here, at least, were five women who genuinely believed that God would fulfil the promise he had made forty years earlier (14:31). Though contrary to long-accepted custom, these daughters were petitioning for land rights. Their appeal was a further encouragement to the waiting pilgrims. God would be true to his word. 'They had not yet entered the land nor were their enemies conquered', but they made their appeal 'as if the tranquil possession of their rights were to be accorded to them that very day'.[1]

Heed the Lord's warnings

These women vividly recalled Korah's disastrous revolt and were at pains to dissociate their father from any part in it. Although he had been buried in the desert, a sad testimony to his place among the old generation, he had not been *among Korah's followers, who banded together against the* LORD (3). He had *died for his own sin,* suffering the penalty of thousands of others for obstinate unbelief at Kadesh Barnea.

As at the recent census (26:8–10), the community that gathered to hear Zelophehad's daughters was again reminded of the seriousness of sin. The grim events of the past were recalled, not to increase their corporate guilt, but to intensify their personal resolve. In his revolt against Moses, Korah, the 'insolent' Levite, had been joined by 250 Israelite men, 'well-known community leaders who had been appointed members of the council' (16:2). Zelophehad was probably a respected leader in Manasseh, the kind of person who might well have belonged to such a council. But, as his daughters were quick to point out, he had not been among those who objected to the distinctive leadership roles of Moses and Aaron.

These women probably knew the importance of dissociating their father from Korah's disruptive action. Not only were serious offenders like Korah executed, but, as with innocent Naboth,[2] 'their property was confiscated as well'.[3] After Kadesh Barnea, their father had been a loyal member of the community; unlike Korah, he had not added the sin of sedition to that of unbelief.

---

[1] Calvin, IV, p. 256. [2] 1 Kgs. 21:1–19; cf. Dan. 3:29.
[3] Wenham (1981), p. 193; J. Weingreen, 'The case of the daughters of Zelophehad', *Vetus Testamentum* 16 (1966), pp. 518–522.

Seek the Lord's help

Grieved that their *father's name* might *disappear from his clan because he had no son* (4), the women sought help from a higher source (1b–2). The women did not know what to do, but they knew where to go.

As Moses heard their petition, he appreciated the reasonableness and urgency of their request, but could not say what was appropriate in their case. Ever since the people had left Sinai, he had served as Israel's judge in legal matters. Colleagues had legislated on simple issues, but he dealt with the difficult cases,[4] and this concern about women's land rights was certainly not straightforward.

The women had sought the Lord's help, and Moses did exactly the same; how else could he know the right answer to such an important enquiry? He 'was not ashamed to confess his ignorance, until he had been instructed by the mouth of God'.[5] Good spiritual leaders acknowledge a greater authority, so Moses went into the presence of God to discern the Lord's mind on the issue. A clear decision, one way or the other, would naturally affect other women in similar circumstances.

Moses *brought their case before the LORD*. This was not an isolated experience for Israel's leader. Three times in the book we are told that, uncertain of the way ahead, he entered the place of dependent prayer (9:8; 15:34–35; 27:5).

Discern the Lord's will

In an intensely patriarchal society, the plea of these women ran counter to Israel's culture; it might have been summarily dismissed. Appeal to the people's history and legal traditions would have caused their legitimate request to fall on deaf ears. It was not simply that Zelophehad's daughters were appealing against accepted precedent. God's people were about to move into a new land where trade and commerce would bring them into frequent contact with people of other nationalities. They would soon discover, if they did not know it already, that among those differing cultures it was widely accepted that land and property could pass to an unmarried daughter when there was no surviving son. Milgrom observes that 'the concession made by the Bible to Zelophehad's daughters had been anticipated in Mesopotamia by a millennium'.[6]

---

[4] Exod. 18:13–16, 22.   [5] Calvin, IV, p. 257.
[6] Milgrom, p. 482; cf. also *ANET*, p. 220; Z. Ben-Barak, 'Inheritance by

If Israel's values had been solely decided by contemporary norms, Zelophehad's daughters hardly needed Moses' help. However, God's people had been taught that legal practice, commercial conduct, community standards and personal behaviour must be determined by the divine will. It was wrong simply to accommodate to the conventions and standards of the surrounding world.[7]

It was important, therefore, not only on account of precedent, but because of contemporary culture, to seek God's mind on this important issue. In this case, the Lord believed that the normal practice of their neighbours was good and just, but it was vital for Moses to seek his mind. In most other instances, it would be morally and spiritually disastrous to allow contemporary culture to shape their thinking and to determine their behaviour.

Obey the Lord's command

The Lord confirmed that the request of these five Israelite women is perfectly appropriate: *'You must certainly give ... their father's inheritance over to them'* (7). Moreover, it is not only the daughters' rights that were determined, but also the correct order of inheritance should there be neither daughters nor sons. In such a case, the family possessions should go to the owner's brothers, or *the nearest relative in his clan* (11). Firm instructions would ensure justice for people who might otherwise be deprived, and minimize the disputes that would sometimes arise concerning the property of a deceased family member. The fact that the concerns voiced by Zelophehad's daughters emerge again as the book closes (36:1–13) illustrates their importance in the life of the community. Issues of domestic harmony, legal justice and human rights are part of God's compassionate provision for his people. What he had declared as his will on this matter was to be not only recorded in their ancient documents but observed in their continuing life: *'This is to be a legal requirement for the Israelites, as the* LORD *commanded Moses'* (11). The people who listened to the request of these women and waited until Moses had discerned the divine will

---

daughters', *Journal of Semitic Studies* 25/1 (1980), pp. 22–33; J. Paradise, 'A daughter and her father's property at Nuzi', *Journal of Cuneiform Studies* 32/4 (1980), pp. 189–207; G. R. Driver and J. C. Miles, *The Babylonian Laws* 1 (Oxford: Clarendon, 1956), p. 335, where it 'may be inferred from certain passages in the Laws themselves and from various documents that daughters did in fact sometimes share the paternal estate with their brothers'.

[7] Exod. 34:11–16; Deut. 7:1–6; Rom. 12:1–2; 1 Pet. 1:14–16.

received another reminder of a familiar instruction: what God says must be done.

Zelophehad's daughters wanted to know God's will about a specific matter concerning their future. Life often confronts us with occasions for important decision-making, and it is not always easy to know what we are meant to do. Seeking guidance is a crucial dimension of mature Christian experience, and this narrative illustrates four helpful principles.

First, these women recognized their need of help beyond themselves. Our postmodern culture encourages self-determinative living; it insists that one should not recognize authorities of any kind that clash with self-interest. Contrary to this egocentric preoccupation, believers want their lives to be directed and controlled by a wise and loving God who has plans and purposes for them.[8]

Secondly, Zelophehad's daughters brought their need to a godly leader. Their particular concern about their inheritance could not be determined by themselves, but Moses was a reliable person in Israel whose help they could seek. When we are uncertain of the way ahead, a conversation with a prayerful friend can add fresh dimensions to our thinking. Other people sometimes identify perspectives that may not have occurred to us.

Thirdly, prayer was the most important component in this guidance-seeking exercise. Moses did not merely give his best mind to it; he talked with God about it.[9] God's Word has many promises of help for those who desire to know his will when making important decisions.[10]

Fourthly, the request of these women was an exercise in patience. They had to wait while *Moses brought their case before the* LORD (5), and we do not know how long it was before they were given a reply. We are to 'wait patiently'[11] for the unfolding of God's will and not imagine we can receive guidance immediately on demand. The Lord may deliberately withhold his response because we need to give more thought to all the issues before us. In his time, we shall know what we are meant to do, for just *as the* LORD *commanded Moses* (11) so he will direct us too.

---

[8] Jer. 29:11.   [9] Exod. 33:11.
[10] Pss. 25:4–5; 48:14; 73:24; Prov. 3:5–6; Is. 58:11.
[11] Pss. 25:14; 37:5, 7; 40:1; 130:5; Is. 30:18.

27:12–23
25. Leadership lifestyle

The story of how Joshua became Moses' successor was important to God's people, for, in addition to its appearance here, it is recorded on three further occasions.[1] It is natural that it should feature after the new generation's census. Gifted and outstanding leader though he was, Moses was to die in the desert, guilty of disobedience and unbelief, like the rest of the old generation. The obedient and trusting Joshua represents the new generation destined for the land of promise. In describing both the departing old leader and the emerging new one, this narrative expounds the ideal characteristics of every leader, old or young.

The leader's priority

The narrative is punctuated with the dialogue of dependence: *Then the LORD said to Moses* (12); *Moses said to the LORD* (15); *So the LORD said to Moses* (18); *Moses did as the LORD commanded him* (22); *Then he … commissioned him, as the LORD instructed through Moses* (23).

Nothing is more important in Christian leadership than the leader's personal walk with God. Yet, in the pressures of busy lives, this essential feature is easily marginalized. Moses always gave it high priority. Prior to the construction of the tabernacle, a 'tent of meeting' was pitched at the outskirts of the camp so that he could go there for fellowship with God.[2] During such times, leaders acknowledge their need, confess their sins, receive their instructions, discern their message, refine their ambitions and extend their horizons.

---

[1] Deut. 3:21–29; 31:1–9; 34:1–12.   [2] Exod. 33:7–11.

The leader's confidence

As Moses communed with God, he received a message about the divine plan for his future: *'Go up this mountain ... and see the land I have given the Israelites ...'* (12). A mere glimpse seems a tantalizing offer when the man longed to set foot in the new land, but we need to know something of Israelite land rights to appreciate what 'seeing' the new country really meant.

In Hebrew legal practice, the act of 'viewing' land played an important part in their formal processes of purchase. The 'legal transfer of property took place when the purchaser looked it over'.[3] Earlier, Abraham was told to 'look' out at the land the Lord promised to give to his successors.[4] For the patriarch, to 'see' the country was to receive assurance of certain possession. In Christ's parable about the great banquet, a prospective land-purchaser excuses himself from attending the meal because he has to view land he has purchased.[5] We hastily dismiss his excuse as facile; who would dream of buying unseen land? The man was in fact saying that he was required to attend the formal viewing of the land, an act by which this newly purchased property would be legally transferred to his ownership.

Christian leaders are not always followed or respected; there are times when the people with whom they invest their best years of service may disappoint them or let them down. Every leader needs the biblical reminder that God always fulfils the promises he has made, as Balaam's message had confirmed (23:19). When Joshua came to the close of his life's work, he testified to his fellow Israelites that 'not one of all the good promises the LORD your God gave you has failed. Every promise has been fulfilled.'[6] That is the leader's fortifying assurance. As Moses looked out on the extended territory from the heights of Nebo, the Lord was giving him the legal assurance of impending possession.

The leader's destiny

'After you have seen it, you too will be gathered to your people, as your brother Aaron was' (13). The promise that the old leader would soon join his spiritual ancestors is one of the earliest

[3] A. Phillips, *Deuteronomy*, Cambridge Bible Commentary (Cambridge: Cambridge University Press, 1973), p. 30; David Daube, *Studies in Biblical Law* (Cambridge: Cambridge University Press, 1947), pp. 28–35.
[4] Gen. 13:14–15. [5] Luke 14:18.
[6] Josh. 23:14; cf. 1 Kgs. 8:20, 24, 56; 2 Chr. 6:10, 15; Neh. 9:8b; Ps. 77:8b; Jer. 29:10; 33:14.

(though veiled) insights into the biblical doctrine of heaven. Old Testament references to the life to come are limited and partial; they await the clear definitions that could best be revealed by the Lord Jesus, who would open heaven to all believers.[7] However undeveloped the reference is, it makes two undeniable affirmations; believers have an assured future and anticipate a corporate heritage.

First, Moses was promised an assured future. He will be 'gathered to his people'; there is nothing tentative about it. The phrasing of such a promise would not be appropriate if Moses was merely to disappear in the dust, a forgotten figure of ancient history with no future in God's purposes. Instead, Moses would enter God's heaven; and, as visible confirmation of that assured destiny, he appeared centuries later as a recognizable person on another mountain top in the land he had longed to enter. At the mount of transfiguration,[8] Moses' ambition ('Let me go over and see the good land beyond the Jordan')[9] was fulfilled after all.

Secondly, Moses could anticipate a corporate heritage. As a distinct individual he would be gathered with other people who had known and loved God across the centuries. He would meet his *brother Aaron* (13; 20:24) and a vast multitude of committed believers. Among the myriads of God's *people* (13) was Elijah, with whom he appeared on the mount of transfiguration. In this saying, and in the later identification of these two great representatives of the law and the prophets, there is at least a hint that God's assured future will involve clearly recognizable individuals, united for ever with the whole redeemed people of God. Balaam had longed that when death came, his life's end might be like that of the righteous (23:10), a forlorn hope for the pagan seer but a guaranteed prospect for Israel's devoted leader.

All leaders need wider horizons in their work for God. Everything we do for him needs to be set within the firm context of eternity. Life is longer than our years. Christ urged his followers to remember their destiny,[10] and, as the apostles exercised their ministry in the difficult times Jesus had predicted, it was with unshakeable confidence in an infinitely better future life.[11]

The leader's responsibility

The old leader knows only too well why he had been numbered with the old generation: *for when the community rebelled at the waters in the Desert of Zin*, he and Aaron had disobeyed the

---

[7] John 11:25; 14:1–3.   [8] Luke 9:30.   [9] Deut. 3:25.   [10] Luke 12:35; 21:5–38.
[11] Rom. 14:7–12; 2 Cor. 4:16 – 5:10; 1 Thess. 4:13 – 5:11; Heb. 13:14; Jas. 5:7–9; 1 Pet. 5:4; 2 Pet. 3:1–18; 1 John 3:2–3; Jude 17–21.

Lord's command, *to honour God as holy before their eyes* (14). Along with his brother, Moses had not followed his instructions carefully and, in a moment of evident frustration, had become as guilty as every other member of the old generation (20:12). When God gives his orders he does not make exceptions for favoured leaders. The same high standard required of others is expected of them. God's refusal to let Moses enter the land was a perpetual warning to successive generations. If a godly man like Moses could not escape the consequences of disobedience, neither could they.

Every leader has a primary responsibility to know, explain and maintain high biblical standards for everyday life, and the Lord must be honoured as holy in every aspect of our behaviour. We cannot preach one ideal for others and be content with something less for ourselves. In his famous handbook for pastors, Gregory the Great maintained that the Christian leader is 'like a physician to a sick person', and how can a doctor hope to 'heal the afflicted while he carries a sore on his own face'?[12]

The leader's compassion

Despite evident mistakes, the old leader did not lack fine qualities. He loved God's people intensely and was anxious about the future leadership of that vast and vulnerable community. Moses earnestly sought God for his successor: *'May the LORD ... appoint a man over this community ... who will lead them out and bring them in'* (16–17). Without strong, reliable leadership this huge and diverse crowd could wander, *like sheep without a shepherd* (17). Though painfully disappointed that he would not enter the land, he was deeply concerned about those who would. They had grumbled against him, marginalized his importance, rejected his leadership and disobeyed his orders, but he still loved them. How compassionate of Moses to share with God his natural anxiety about their future! In Christian leadership, love matters most. The finest skills, the richest experience and the best resources are of minimal worth if leaders do not love their people.

The leader's encouragement

In his plea that Israel might be provided with his successor, Moses addressed the Lord as *the God of the spirits of all mankind* (15), a description used in an earlier prayer (16:22). Reflecting on the experience of his long life, the old leader had confidence in an

---

[12] Gregory the Great, *Pastoral Care* I.9, Ancient Christian Writers 11 (London: Longmans Green, 1950), p. 38.

omniscient, sovereign and caring Creator who knew every individual Israelite, desired only the best for their future and was uniquely able to select the best possible leader. The 'source of the breath of all flesh'[13] was aware of the right person to lead this community in such crucial days of transition. He knew their opponents as well, and knew a quality person who could lead Israel against them. A medieval Jewish paraphrase of Moses' prayer expresses it perfectly: 'You are acquainted with the spirit of every individual and should appoint a man who will know how to deal with each one of them in accordance with his own temperament.'[14] It is immensely reassuring to leaders to know that their lives are in the hands of such a God. The most minute detail does not escape his notice;[15] nobody can stray beyond the boundaries of his sovereign control.

The leader's assignment

Moses' prayer for the right successor combines the leadership qualities of strength and love in two images that merit reflection: the first military, the second pastoral.

The leader's responsibility *to go out and come in before them* may refer primarily to his successor's role in conquest, the commander taking his soldiers out to battle. Strong and resilient, he would be at their head in expeditions, knowing the best way to mobilize his troops effectively as he led them out, and concerned not only about military strategy but about his soldiers' well-being. Valuing their lives, and the welfare of their families, he would need to act responsibly so that at the end of hazardous encounters he could safely *bring them in*, back to base. Such leadership demands resources of courageous strength, exactly what the Lord required of Joshua as the Israelites were about to cross the Jordan.[16] The Lord knew that such an exacting military assignment was beyond Moses' strength. He had been a fine wilderness leader; a man with different gifts was necessary if Israel was to conquer Canaan.

Good leaders combine strength with love. The second image is pastoral. The Lord's people needed a compassionate shepherd as well as a fearless commander. Moses had exercised such a ministry during their wilderness journey,[17] and Israel needed another man of shepherd-like commitment. The imagery of *sheep without a shepherd* (17) is used in Scripture to describe those who 'have no master', a vulnerable community,[18] people in need of loving care.

[13] Milgrom, p. 234. [14] *Num. Rabba* 21:15, quoted in Milgrom, pp. 234, 325.
[15] Heb. 4:13–16. [16] Josh. 1:6–9. [17] Ps. 77:20; Is. 63:11.
[18] 1 Kgs. 22:17; Ezek. 34:5; Matt. 9:36.

There would be difficult days ahead for Moses' successor. His equipment would need to include compassion for the flock as well as courage for the fight.

These twin qualities need to be finely balanced; some leaders have an abundance of one but are deficient in the other. God himself models the ideal combination: 'you, O God, are strong, and ... you, O LORD, are loving'.[19]

The leader's resources

When the Lord chose Moses' successor, he did not provide an identical replica of the old leader. The new project required someone with different gifts. Joshua, Moses' dependable partner of the last forty years, had already proved himself an able assistant. The Lord told Moses that Joshua was *a man in whom is the spirit* (18). The expression may well refer to those spiritual qualities evident in his earlier role as military commander,[20] reliable colleague,[21] prayerful companion,[22] loyal protector (11:28), exemplary representative (13:2, 8, 16) and passionate communicator (14:6–9). Now, Joshua was confronted with a totally different challenge, the conquest of Canaan and Israel's settlement in their new environment. New skills would be required, and *the God of the spirits of all mankind* (16) had the exact person.

Joshua could rely on fresh resources for different tasks. Years earlier, Moses had given this young man Hoshea a new name, Joshua (13:16), a testimony to the truth that in the Lord God alone is 'salvation'. In earlier life young Joshua had witnessed a wide range of different situations in which the Lord had saved his people – from slavery, drowning, thirst, hunger, and military onslaught.[23] In their new situation, the Lord would continue to deliver Joshua and his people if they became fearful or when they were confronted by natural barriers and fortified cities.[24]

The Holy *Spirit* (18, NIV margin) would provide the new leader with the necessary equipment for challenging tasks. Those who respond to God's call are always guaranteed adequate resources. As a public confirmation of this Spirit-endued assignment, Moses was to lay his hand on his successor, commissioning him for his new ministry. The imposition of hands was a visible token of the transference of blessing[25] from one to another (8:10).

---

[19] Pss. 62:11–12; cf. 59:9, 17.   [20] Exod. 17:8–16.   [21] Exod. 24:13; 32:17.
[22] Exod. 33:11.
[23] Exod. 12:1–36; 14:10 – 15:5; 15:22–27; 17:1–7; 16:1–16; 17:8–16.
[24] Josh. 1:9; 3:1–17; 5:13–15; 6:1–27; 8:1–29.   [25] Gen. 48:14.

The Lord provided the resources for the task, but Moses was also commanded, *'Give him some of your authority'* (20). The retiring leader had to be willing to hand over some of those responsibilities that he had carried for the past forty years. Old leaders have sometimes been less than enthusiastic about handing over the Lord's work to younger successors. Moses was a man of fine spiritual stature to hand over the reins so lovingly.

The leader's dependence

Joshua was *to stand before Eleazar the priest, who will obtain decisions for him by enquiring of the Urim before the LORD* (21). He was not to make his own decisions but was to look to two interrelated sources of help.

First, he needed the partnership of others. Joshua would succeed Moses, as Eleazar had succeeded Aaron (20:22–29). As Joshua faced these heavy new responsibilities, Eleazar was at his side as a colleague, advisor and friend. Joshua was to *stand before* the high priest, an expression indicating attentive submission and readiness for service.[26] Good leaders are not self-opinionated autocrats; they acknowledge their partnership in a shared ministry.

Secondly, he needed the guidance of God. Eleazar was not allowed to be a despotic or dictatorial colleague. He was to seek God's mind *by enquiring of the Urim*. Joshua was to *stand before Eleazar*, and Eleazar was to stand *before the LORD*. Neither was free to pursue his own will. The Urim and Thummim were probably two flat stones, coloured differently on each side and kept in a pocket in the high priest's breastplate.[27] They were used by the high priest to cast lots in order to determine what God's mind might be on issues requiring a decision. It is the Holy Spirit's work to encourage, strengthen and preserve our mutual co-operation and to lead us into a clear awareness of God's will.[28]

The leader's obedience

In this crucial matter of discovering his successor, the old leader made sure that he did exactly what the Lord had told him to do; he and Eleazar commissioned Israel's new leader just *as the LORD instructed* (23). The book's leading introductory theme of total obedience (1:19, 54; 2:34; 3:51; 4:37, 41, 45, 49) is repeated here as the ministry of Moses gradually drew to its close. Those who reflected on this succession narrative would not miss its dramatic

[26] Jer. 23:22a; Luke 1:19.   [27] Exod. 28:30; Lev. 8:8; 1 Sam. 28:6; Ezra 2:63.
[28] Eph. 4:3; Rom. 8:14.

contrast between what took place at the waters of Meribah (*'you disobeyed my command'*, 14) and what happened here at the appointment of Joshua, when *Moses did as the LORD commanded* (22).

These Old Testament stories convey a salutary warning. The fact that we may have endeavoured to live at our best so far is no guarantee that it will always be so. Some gifted servants of God have yielded to serious temptation in later life. Like Moses at Meribah, they have failed to honour the Lord as holy in the sight of others, and have brought pain to themselves, damage to others and grief to God. Tragically, Moses became guilty of the same sins of disobedience and rebellion that he had earlier exposed in God's people. It is easier to identify sin in the lives of others than to detect it in our own. Paul warned his converts of the lurking danger: 'So, if you think you are standing firm, be careful that you don't fall!'[29] When Joshua assumed his new responsibilities, he was repeatedly urged to make obedience to God the highest priority both for himself and for his people.[30] Nothing is more important.

---

[29] 1 Cor. 10:12; cf. 9:24–27; Rom. 11:17–22.   [30] Josh. 1:7, 16–18; 5:13–15.

28:1 – 29:40
26. Variations on a majestic theme

These two chapters (28 – 29) describe Israel's offerings and feasts over a one-year period. These sacrifices could be offered only after the people had settled in Canaan, since they required the produce of livestock farming and agriculture impossible in the arid desert. The annual festivals could not be celebrated in the manner required until the people had become a settled community. God's instructions about Israel's worship thus conveyed a renewed assurance that they would cross the Jordan as he has promised.

The two chapters present us with a priest's calendar, describing the community's worship pattern in its daily (28:1–8), weekly (28:9–10), monthly (28:11–15) and annual (28:16 – 29:40) celebrations. Similar lists are found earlier in Numbers (15:1–16) and elsewhere in Scripture.[1] This particular calendar concentrates on the responsibilities of the priests in the correct ordering of the sacrificial system, whereas the list in Leviticus deals more with the worshipper's obligations. Joshua had just been reminded of the important role to be played in the community's spiritual life by the high priest, Eleazar (27:21), and his colleagues. There now follows a description of their duties and privileges each day of the year. Celebratory adoration pervades these chapters.

Israel's pattern of worship was essentially a two-way transmission. The sacrifices were 'dramatized prayers', expressing the deepest human longings, and 'dramatized divine promises or warnings', vividly communicating the Lord's mind to his people about everyday life.[2] The striking visual aids described here are variations on the majestic theme of the Lord's unchanging nature and attributes.

---

[1] Exod. 29:38–42; Lev. 1 – 7, 23; Ezek. 45:18 – 46:15.   [2] Wenham (1981), p. 29.

God is worthy of our best

Worship is the joyous acknowledgment of God's worth. This calendar of Israelite devotion begins with God's command to his people: *'See that you present to me at the appointed time the food for my offerings made by fire'* (28:2). The regulations governing this sacrifice in Leviticus 1 repeatedly insist that it is to be burnt in its entirety. Other sacrifices, though expressing Israel's adoration, were divided by the priest: part was offered to the Lord, some was distributed to the priests and their families and some, at times, was shared by the offerer in a celebratory meal. However, in the burnt offering that heads this list, 'the priest is to burn all of it on the altar'.[3] Nothing was kept back for either priestly or personal use. It symbolized the truth that the Lord deserves the best we can give him.

The same truth is also depicted here by the high quality of everything offered. The lambs were to be physically perfect, *without defect* (3, 9) and the bulls likewise (11, 19). Their sacrifices must be totally unblemished (28:31; 29:2, 8, 13, 17, 20, 23, 26, 29, 32, 36). Similarly, for their daily cereal offering they must use the best *fine flour* (28:5, 9, 12, 13, 20, 28; 29:3, 9, 14) or 'choice flour' of the 'finest grade',[4] best-quality flour that had been finely ground and not hastily prepared. Similarly, the *oil from pressed olives* (5) means 'pure oil' that had been 'pressed in a mortar'.[5] The tabernacle's lampstand[6] and these daily cereal offerings[7] required this high-value 'clear oil of pressed olives'. These daily offerings visually portrayed the truth that, such was the greatness and generosity of God, nothing but the best was good enough for him.

Sadly, God's people have not always offered their best. In the years after the exile, Malachi spoke fearlessly against both priests and people who had the audacity to present crippled and diseased animals; such offerings were acts of contempt rather than tokens of gratitude. God wished they would leave their altar fires unlit; he had no intention of accepting such objectionable sacrifices.[8]

God gives what he promises

The gifts required in the daily presentation of these cereal offerings could not have been presented during Israel's wilderness journeys. The arid desert terrain, the precarious climate and their frequent migrations militated against regular harvesting, and, naturally, such

---

[3] Lev. 1:9, 13.   [4] Milgrom, p. 119.   [5] Ibid., p. 239.   [6] Exod. 27:20; Lev. 24:2.
[7] Exod. 29:38–40.   [8] Mal. 1:6–10.

sacrifices were not required of them in those circumstances. Now, they were about to enter a land 'flowing with milk and honey'; before long the manna would cease to fall around their camp and they would be eating choice produce in a better country.[9] In the literary structure of this book, earlier regulations about cereal offerings (15:1–21) appeared immediately after Israel's refusal to enter Canaan. It encouraged the young, at least, to believe that one day they would be able to present such choice gifts to God. Now, the new generation were within sight of that promised country and their pattern of worship included the presentation of gifts from a rich and fertile land. This calendar is a further testimony to the reliability of God's promises. They would enter a land of abundant fruitfulness. Not only is God worthy of our best; far more importantly, he keeps his word and always gives the best to his people.

God is pleased by our obedience

A familiar priestly phrase echoes throughout these chapters. Israel's offerings would be *an aroma pleasing* to the Lord (28:2, 6, 8, 13, 24, 27; 29:2, 6, 8, 13, 36). God would be pleased not by their pungent odour but by his children's obedience to his commands. Once those sacrifices ceased to express love and obedience, they became offensive to him. The Lord hated the incessant noise of trampling feet as religious but loveless people crowded the temple in eighth-century BC Jerusalem. Isaiah inveighed against their meticulously performed rituals; they were objectionable, not merely useless. Through Isaiah, the Lord told such people he 'took no pleasure' in even the best of their well-fattened animals.[10] Far from such 'meaningless' sacrifices being *an aroma pleasing to the* LORD, they were a despicable 'gift of nothing'.[11]

In our postmodern culture, submission to God's plan for human life is hardly a popular concept. People are encouraged to do whatever gives them immediate, maximum pleasure. They must not be diverted from their own desires by religious traditions, moral conventions or social norms. 'If it feels good, do it' is the contemporary behaviour motto. Such egocentric thinking runs counter to God's pattern for human life, perfectly exemplified in Christ, who surrendered himself completely to the perfect will of God.[12] At no point did he cherish the slightest desire to please himself. He came to this world specifically to pursue the Father's purpose for

---

[9] Josh. 5:11–12.   [10] Is. 1:11–13.
[11] J. A. Motyer, *The Prophecy of Isaiah* (Leicester: IVP, 1993), p. 47.
[12] Luke 22:42; John 4:34; 5:30b; 6:38.

his life.[13] The highest Christian ambition is to follow his steps,[14] not heedlessly to tread our own.

God pardons our sins

Though we may cherish lofty ideals, we do not always reach them; but the awareness of our failure drives us to God. Israel's pattern of worship recognized our need of forgiveness. Throughout the calendar there are repeated references to pardon, cleansing and restoration to fellowship with God. There was provision for a *sin offering* (28:15) *to make atonement* (28:22) for the offender. During Israel's festivals the sacrifices offered would *make atonement* (28:22, 30; 29:5) for their sins. The Day of Atonement was the special annual occasion when every Israelite was assured of complete forgiveness through the *sin offering for atonement* (29:11). That day provided every guilty member of the community with a striking visual aid as their sin was transferred to a male goat, 'for the sin offering for the people'. Its blood was sprinkled on the atonement cover in the Tabernacle's Most Holy Place, so that 'the uncleanness and rebellion of the Israelites' could be completely forgiven, 'whatever their sins have been'.[15]

The Day of Atonement's striking visual impact was maintained as a live goat was then brought to the Tent of Meeting. The high priest placed both his hands on its head, confessing 'all the wickedness and rebellion of the Israelites – all their sins', and putting them 'on the goat's head'. Then the live goat was sent away into a solitary place in the distant desert, typifying the removal of the people's transgressions,[16] so that the Lord would 'remember their sins no more'.[17]

No-one can pretend that they have not sinned, and nobody can escape sin's consequences. The sin offerings and festivals, and especially the annual Day of Atonement, were frequent reminders of Israel's moral vulnerability. Time and again, they grieved God by their grumblings, rebellion and blatant disobedience. Even the best of them failed to obey every aspect of God's law (20:1–13). Both the famous and the anonymous had to be assured that, however far they had wandered from God, there was a way back to the divine presence. For the Christian, the death of Christ on his cross is the only perfect sacrifice for sin. It was offered once for all, and, unlike the sacrifices described in this calendar, had no need of repetition.[18]

---

[13] Rom. 15:3; 2 Cor. 8:9; Phil 2:5–11; Heb. 10:5–7; Ps. 40:6–8.　　[14] 1 Pet. 2:21.
[15] Lev. 16:15–16.　　[16] Lev. 16:20–22.　　[17] Jer. 31:34.　　[18] Heb. 10:1–18.

Throughout the centuries God's people valued these visible reminders, identifying their sins, exposing their guilt and pointing clearly to its remedy. These visual presentations ensured that God's people did not become casual about their sin or indifferent to its effects.

Before we can hope to offer anything to the Lord we need first to receive the priceless gift that no amount of money, service, duty or moral attainment can ever buy – the full and free forgiveness that is ours only in Christ.

God plans for our leisure

The calendar describes the offerings to be presented on the Sabbath (28:9–10) in addition to those required on a day-to-day basis. Israel's worship pattern gave special prominence to this weekly occasion for worship, necessary rest from the pressures of everday work, and essential family time. Even their animals would benefit. During the Israelites' harrowing experience of slavery in Egypt,[19] God's people were made to work without regular times for essential relaxation and physical renewal. Israelites were never to subject their employees to similar misery; every manservant and maidservant was released from his or her customary duties on that day. The local aliens, travellers or visitors from other countries and cultures, unaware of Israel's social customs, soon discovered that this day was different.

In the contemporary world, Sunday is no longer special. People who would not choose to work are frequently required to do so. God's compassionate provision of regular physical rest is ignored, to the detriment of personal health and family life. The Lord knows that such relentless pressure is not good for us. People ignore 'the Maker's instructions'[20] at their peril. The fact that another account of the Decalogue[21] presents the Sabbath's weekly pattern within the context of creation suggests that a day of rest is not simply an obligation for believers but of immense benefit for everyone.

[19] Deut. 5:15.
[20] Eileen Bebbington, *The Maker's Instructions: Six Bible Study Outlines on the Ten Commandments* (Swindon: Bible Society, 1986), and J. John, *Ten* (Eastbourne: Kingsway, 2000), pp. 185–213.
[21] Exod. 20:11.

God acts powerfully for us in love

After the calendar has outlined the offerings to be presented daily, weekly and monthly, it turns to a description of the great annual festivals of the Israelite people, beginning with Passover (28:16–25). This celebration recalled the community's deliverance from the Egyptian aggressor. For 400 years they had longed for freedom, but hopes of salvation were beyond their best dreams.

God planned that his people should commemorate the events of their spectacular salvation annually, deliberately recalling the night of their unique escape. The annual Passover became a reminder of past salvation and a symbol of perpetual deliverance. Throughout their history, Israel remained a vulnerable minority, threatened by nations whose military power dwarfed their own. Egyptians, Midianites, Philistines, Assyrians, Babylonians, Persians, Greeks, Romans – the grim catalogue of successive oppressors spans the centuries.

Passover declared not only God's power but also his justice. For four centuries those Israelite people had been cruelly abused by their Egyptian slave-drivers, but this annual festival announced that the Lord rescues minorities, the downtrodden and oppressed of each succeeding generation. Throughout history, the exodus event has spoken powerfully to people beyond Israel suffering under tyrannous regimes. In many parts of our world, freedom is denied, restricted or held only precariously. Passover was an annual reminder that God acts in justice towards the oppressed. Evangelicals acknowledge the necessity of keeping such issues constantly on their agenda. One of the twenty-one succinct affirmations of the Manila Manifesto issued at the 1989 International Congress on World Evangelization ('Lausanne II') declares: 'We affirm that the proclamation of God's kingdom of justice and peace demands the denunciation of all injustice and oppression, both personal and structural; we will not shrink from this prophetic witness.'[22]

God generously supplies our needs

The festivals of Weeks, Trumpets and Tabernacles (or Booths) were additional periods of rest as well as of corporate thanksgiving, each providing a further opportunity to reflect on God's generosity in feeding, guiding and protecting his people. As with the weekly

---

[22] J. D. Douglas (ed.) *Proclaim Christ until he Comes* (Minneapolis, MN: World Wide Publications, 1990), p. 26.

Sabbath and the annual Passover and Day of Atonement, the Israelites were commanded not to engage in any form of regular work at these times. Israel's annual holidays were occasions when families could be united, and friends and neighbours could join together to celebrate God's goodness.

The feast of Weeks or *the day of firstfruits* (28:26) marked the beginning of the wheat harvest and the end of the barley harvest. It is also called the 'Feast of Harvest',[23] and was later known as Pentecost because it was held *fifty* (*pentēkonta* in Greek) days after the Feast of Unleavened Bread (Passover). The Lord had given the people choice agricultural produce and they expressed their gratitude by offering the earliest and best, the *new grain* (28:26), to God.[24]

More space is devoted in this calendar to the Feast of Tabernacles (29:12–39) than to the other festivals. It was a further opportunity to celebrate the Lord's bounteous liberality. The Weeks festival was mainly agricultural, while Tabernacles was primarily historical in focus. God's people spent the days of this special holiday living in temporary 'Booths' (an alternative name for the festival) like the old generation during their forty years of travel. God had lovingly cared for them, providing manna, water, guidance (the pillar of cloud by day) and protection (the pillar of fire by night), all necessary if they were to arrive in the promised land. The Tabernacles festival[25] was an annual reminder that God never denies his children immeasurably abundant provision.

This calendar was a token to the travelling community that they were about to enter a period of rich agricultural prosperity. Lavish gifts of animals, cereals, olives and fruit could be presented only by people who had received supplies exceeding their highest expectations. The devoted offerings of the Israelite community were visual variations on the theme of God's incomparable grace.

[23] Lev. 23:15–16; Exod. 23:16.   [24] Exod. 23:19; 34:26.
[25] Lev. 23:33–43; Deut. 16:13–15; Neh. 8:13–18.

30:1 – 31:54
27. Keeping promises and identifying dangers

Keeping promises (30:1–16)

The previous section closed with the detail that, in describing their pattern of worship, 'Moses told the Israelites all that the LORD commanded him' (29:40). As this new chapter unfolds we hear the old leader again as he transmits instruction ('*This is what the LORD commands*', 1) about vows and oaths. The theme, which emerges on several occasions in the book (6:1–21; 15:3, 8; 21:1–3), follows naturally after a passage about their obligatory offerings, for 'vows were usually sealed with a sacrifice; and, when the prayer was answered, another sacrifice would be offered'.[1]

Over the centuries, vows became part of Israel's religious culture. Individuals making a fervent request in prayer[2] might add to their petition a vow that, if the prayer was answered, they would fulfil a specific promise, as Hannah did when she gave birth to her long-awaited child.[3]

These regulations begin by affirming that any male Israelite who made *a vow to the LORD or takes an oath to bind himself by a pledge* must do what he had promised (2). Likewise, a woman without parental or marital ties (*a widow or divorced*, 9) had nobody to check or question her vow, so it too had to be honoured. An unmarried woman, however, was required to inform her father of any vows she had made. If he raised no objection or received her information in silence, she was free to fulfil her vow. If he objected, she was no longer under any spiritual obligation concerning her pledge: *the LORD will release her because her father has forbidden her* (3–5).

If a single woman made a vow prior to marriage, she was

---

[1] Wenham, p. 206; cf. 15:3; Lev. 7:16; 22:17–18; 23:38; Ps. 50:14.
[2] Gen. 28:20–22.   [3] 1 Sam. 1:11, 24.

obliged to inform her husband of it when she married. Once again, if he did not object, *the vows or the pledges by which she bound herself* would *stand*. If her husband raised an objection when he heard of the vow, he would nullify *the vow ... by which she* had bound *herself* and she would be released from her obligation (6–8).

If a married woman made a vow or took an oath, she was required to inform her husband about it. Like the father, the husband was similarly obliged to state his objection at once if her vows were to be nullified. If he delayed registering his unhappiness concerning the vows until *some time after he* heard *about them, then he* was *responsible for her guilt* should he insist that she was not to keep the vows (10–15).

These regulations concern *relationships between a man and his wife, and between a father and his young daughter still living in the house* (16). They need to be understood in the light of marital harmony and family solidarity, and Israel's acute sense of corporate responsibility. They direct attention to four important biblical themes.

The Lord's honour

Vows and oaths must not be made carelessly and hastily. The theme was developed in Moses' final message to the community before they crossed the Jordan.[4] The later story of Jepthah's vow illustrates the seriousness with which these convictions were held: 'you have given your word to the LORD. Do to me just as you promised.'[5] The same theme is found in a number of psalms;[6] the Lord Jesus also emphasized the importance of dependable promises and truthful speech.[7]

The individual's integrity

Scripture has several things to say about the danger of making rash promises in threatening situations, only to abandon them when the trouble blows over.[8] Those who make promises to God but do not honour them offend him by the sin of careless speech and their betrayal of trust. We rely on the dependability of God's word (23:19); he ought to be able to trust ours. This conviction lies behind the regulations here concerning vows and oaths, addressing, as they do, the danger of the *rash promise* (30:6) as well as those made thoughtfully and seriously in God's presence. These basic

---

[4] Deut. 23:21–23.   [5] Judg. 11:33–39.
[6] Pss. 22:25; 50:14; 61:5, 8; 66:13–14; 76:11; 116:14.
[7] Matt. 5:33, 37; cf. Jas. 5:12.   [8] Prov. 20:25; Eccles. 5:2, 4–7.

rules about speech emphasize how necessary it is for us to say only what is true, helpful and reliable.

The family's protection

God's people put a high value on harmonious family life. Parents were to be honoured and their views and feelings respected.[9] Nothing must undermine or threaten the bond between parent and child, husband and wife. In these domestic contexts, partners had to consider others when making promises to God; it was not appropriate for a person to make a vow or to take an oath that might have serious ramifications for other members of the family. In such matters, anything said by a daughter or wife by way of a vow, oath or pledge had to be submitted to the scrutiny of the father or husband. By this means it was quickly ascertained whether the promise endangered the harmony of a happy marriage or adversely affected other members of the family unit.

For example, vows concerning money or property might be made by a well-meaning person acting thoughtlessly or impulsively. Such promises were subject to the scrutiny of the father or husband morally responsible for the welfare of the entire family. The Lord regarded the family as the most important social unit in the community and insisted on preserving its peace and unanimity. In times like ours, when family life is seriously threatened, we do well to discuss ambitions and plans with our partners and not act unilaterally, thereby ignoring the adverse effect our decisions might possibly have on others. Communication problems are often at the root of strained or severed relationships. Many a marriage has broken down because one partner has acted as though the other did not exist.

The woman's rights

In our culture, we may find ourselves challenging traditions like these, which naturally reflect the customs of a patriarchal society.

We note that, while regarding the father or husband as head of the household,[10] these rules also went some way to protect the woman from the domineering parent or partner. If no objection was raised to her vow when it was first voiced, then the male head of the family had lost his opportunity to annul it. If he did so, he would become guilty before the Lord. The father or husband who was irritated by the promise made by his daughter or wife could

[9] Exod. 20:12; Deut. 5:16; Eph. 6:1–4; Col. 3:20–21.
[10] Eph. 5:22–31; Col. 3:20–21.

not turn round after a few days and say that he had now decided to oppose the vow. The 'immediate-response principle' protects the woman against an overbearing male. She too had her rights in relationships, and the Lord insisted that they be respected.

Before leaving this section, it might be helpful for us to ask whether the Israelite practice of making vows has anything to say to us about our own commitment to the Lord. It has been said that if we are always sacrificially forgoing something and specifically undertaking something for the Lord, it helps to keep our dedication fresh.

Identifying dangers (31:1–54)

This next chapter describes an attack on local Midianites, *to carry out the LORD's vengeance on them* (3). At the grim apostasy at Shittim they had treated Israel 'as enemies when they deceived [them] in the affair of Peor' (25:18). Moses recruited a thousand men from each of the twelve tribes to go out to fight *along with Phinehas son of Eleazar, the priest, who took with him articles from the sanctuary and the trumpets for signalling* (6). The soldiers killed the Midianite men (but not the women), returning with captives and booty. On reaching the outskirts of the camp, they encountered an angry Moses. He pointed out that in the Baal-Peor tragedy it was the women who were the immoral participants. The captains were ordered to execute all the women (except the virgins) and the boys.

The troops who had killed anyone or touched a corpse were required to remain outside the camp for a full week to purify themselves before re-entering the community. Clear instructions were then given concerning the purification of the booty, which was to be counted and divided, not merely among the troops but also among those who had stayed behind in Israel's camp. Part of the plunder was to be allocated to the Lord's servants and work. When these items had been counted, the soldiers realized that they had not lost a single man in battle; and as an expression of gratitude and *to make atonement* for themselves (50) they offered sacrifices to the Lord.

In our different culture, the passage raises numerous ethical problems. In our tragically divided world, we are rightly horrified at vicious and escalating acts of 'ethnic cleansing' and widespread genocide. On most continents there is alarming evidence of bitterness and aggression as global neighbours, even fellow nationals, fail to live harmoniously together. Some of this racial, tribal or sectarian bitterness is reflected in a people's social culture and often reaches far back into distant history. The country's children are infected by hatred imbibed from their earliest days. There seems no limit to the bitterness and physical cruelty perpetually spawned in such grim circumstances. Nearly a million Tutsis were murdered by their Hutu enemies in East Africa. Now that the Tutsis are back in power, it is estimated that 130,000 Hutu suspects are in prison, and that, at the present rate of dealing with them, the judicial process would take a couple of centuries.

Two things are important, therefore, as we attempt an exposition of this narrative. First, rather than begin with an adverse judgment, we must patiently try to understand exactly what lies behind these events and then seek to interpret the passage to discern what we may learn from it. For all its stark, uncompromising action, this passage of Old Testament Scripture must, like all others, contain some message of warning, rebuke and encouragement.[11] Our part is to understand precisely what it is saying to us in the early twenty-first century. Harsh as they read, these events were initiated by the Lord. It might be profitable, therefore, to focus on the narrative's concept of God's nature, attributes, values and provisions. We shall see that the passage echoes a series of ideas that appear throughout the book. They were truths of immediate relevance as the Lord's people stood on the threshold of their new land, and they are equally important for us as we too face an uncertain future.

God's word obeyed

The LORD said to Moses, 'Take vengeance on the Midianites for the Israelites ...' So Moses said to the people, 'Arm some of your men ... to carry out the LORD's vengeance on them ...' (1–3).

The instruction to attack the Midianites (2) repeated an order given immediately after the tragedy at Shittim, 'as a result of Peor' (25:16–18). Moses' men were doing precisely what they had earlier been commanded to do. Moreover, the Lord here reminded his servant that he was about to be *gathered to* his *people* (2), language that recalls Moses' earlier failure to do exactly what the Lord had said (27:12–14; cf. 20:12–13, 22–24). Uncharacteristically, in those unguarded moments at 'the waters of Meribah', Moses had behaved like the disobedient and unbelieving old generation. Now, surrounded by the new generation, the old leader was at pains to do everything the Lord required.

[11] 1 Cor. 10:6, 11; 2 Tim. 3:16; Rom. 15:4.

God's justice expressed

Deliberate transgression invites tragic consequences. The extermination of these Midianites was an act of divine judgment upon an idolatrous and immoral people who had done their utmost to corrupt Israel's faith. King Balak had been unsuccessful in destroying God's people by employing a renowned sorcerer, so, on Balaam's advice (16), he had infiltrated Israel's ranks with idolatrous and immoral women who would introduce them to Baalism's pornographic rituals and sexual practices.

Phinehas became the messenger of God's judgment (25:6–15), and although at the time all the other offending Midianites had escaped punishment, such disastrous evil could not be overlooked. Israel's soldiers were the instruments of God's wrath towards the many as Phinehas had been to the offensive couple. Those troops were among the first to fulfil the promise made to Abraham: 'your descendants will come back here, for the sin of the Amorites has not reached its full measure'.[12] These Caananite and Transjordanian Baal-worshippers had practised this debased fertility religion for decades, and many thousands of people had been corrupted by their obscene practices. Sexual prostitution became part of their religious scene, and it is likely that those Moabite women who enticed the Israelites to their camp were professionally engaged in such licentious activity. Here, as God judged these Midianites by means of this surprise Israelite attack, it was the beginning of a more extensive condemnation of these debased Canaanite practices. The unchecked sins of the Amorites and their Baal-worshipping partners had now reached its full measure.

God is not partial in his judgment. He does not have high standards[13] for one set of offenders while turning a blind eye to others. The Israelite men who had openly engaged in these pernicious acts suffered the death penalty (25:8–9), and now those Moabites and Midianites who had introduced them to such immoral rituals would also experience God's wrath. Under Israelite law, adultery was punishable by death.[14] The Israelites involved in the Baal-Peor defection were guilty not only of marital infidelity but of spiritual adultery as well. They had forsaken their uniquely faithful divine Husband and gone after other lovers.[15]

God is just, righteous and holy, and cannot tolerate sin. There are no exceptions. Even the devoted old leader had to suffer a

[12] Gen. 15:16.   [13] Deut. 10:17; Acts 10:34–35.   [14] Lev. 20:10.
[15] Is. 54:5; Jer. 3:12–14; 31:32.

measure of punishment because of his unbelief, disobedience and rebellion at Meribah, and was to die on the wrong side of Jordan (20:12; 27:12–14).

God's promises fulfilled

Recruiting the troops for this brief Midianite campaign, Moses was to ensure that no more than 1,000 men came from each of the twelve tribes. A striking force of 12,000 men would be hopelessly outnumbered, but Moses did exactly as he was told. The victory was to testify to God's unwavering faithfulness, not to Israel's military skill. On leaving Egypt, God had promised that he would send his angel ahead of them, routing the armies of their oppressors. 'I will be an enemy to your enemies ... Do not bow down before their gods ... or follow their practices ... I will ... throw into confusion every nation you encounter.'[16]

When those 12,000 men left for the Midianite encampment, their confidence was not in the size of their army but in the power of God. The slender troops returned victorious, boasting not in their numerical strength, physical prowess or military tactics but in the abundant generosity of a God who, fulfilling his promise, had met their weakness with his incomparable strength.[17]

The apostle Paul knew that in spiritual warfare, the 'weapons we fight with ... have divine power to demolish strongholds'.[18] Every Christian has a personal battle-zone of some kind.[19] Holiness of life cannot be achieved solely by human effort; neither can it be attained without it. Some element of conflict plays a vital part in the sanctification of every Christian but, essentially, all the resources are guaranteed in Christ.

God's people protected

Moses' anger at the partial obedience of the returning soldiers may surprise us. His army had spared those perverted Midianite women responsible for the Baal-Peor apostasy. The order to execute these offenders and their male children sounds harsh until we remember that more was at stake than sparing the lives of some offending women. These were the people who had caused the death of 24,000 Israelites who came under the judging hand of a holy God. Their depraved enticements caused those weak-willed men to break the covenant agreement found in the Ten Commandments. They became wilful idolaters, offending their 'jealous' God.[20] Most of

---

[16] Exod. 23:22–24, 27.   [17] 2 Cor. 12:9.   [18] 2 Cor. 10:4.
[19] 2 Tim. 2:3; 1 Tim. 6:12; cf. 2 Tim. 4:7.   [20] Exod. 20:3–6.

those Israelite men were married, yet they committed adultery in the Midianites' tents and perhaps at their religious shrines.[21] They coveted sexual relations with immoral women[22] and paid dearly for it.

The extermination of the offenders, and of the children who would perpetuate such debased religious practices, was an act of judgment on them but a demonstration of mercy to Israel. It guarded the Lord's people against serious pitfalls in coming days. Drastic measures were necessary to forestall potential disaster. In the next chapter we shall read that, after the conquest of Canaan, two and a half tribes were to return, by agreement, to that Transjordan area. Unless removed, these same Midianite men and women would have been able to renew their attempt to destroy Israel by immorality. Their pornographic shrines would have been within easy reach of the newly settled Israelites, presenting the young generation with fresh temptations. East of the Jordan, the Midianite danger would have been a recurrent peril unless something radical was done about it before crossing into Canaan.

The Lord knew that, once these Israelite travellers settled in their new land, Baalism would become a religious and moral hazard. So, before he left them, Moses gave them the Lord's command; on arriving in Canaan they were to destroy all the 'carved images' of the Baal worshippers, and to 'demolish all their high places'. If, instead of driving them out, they had fraternized with the people of the new land, they would have debased their faith, compromised their integrity, dishonoured their God and degraded themselves. God has no favourites. If the Israelites failed in this matter, then, God said, 'I will do to you what I plan to do to them' (33:50–56) Their holy God was not vindictive towards Israel's enemies; he was jealous for Israel's purity. If they jeopardized that, they too would be judged.

God's holiness acknowledged

Recalling the book's earlier teaching (5:2; 19:1–22), the victorious soldiers who had *killed anyone or touched anyone who was killed* were ordered to *stay outside the camp seven days* (19).

Contact with a corpse was regarded as a defiling encounter, inappropriate for those who served the living God. Ceremonially unclean victors would contaminate 'holy' people inside the camp, so they could return to their tents only after spending a week

[21] Exod. 20:14.   [22] Exod. 20:17.

outside the community, at the end of which they would be *purified with the water of cleansing.*

The spoil also had to be purified, either by fire or by water. The soldiers returned from the conflict with the customary booty, but the cleansing of all clothing, wooden items, utensils and jewellery brought from the enemy camp was an urgent necessity. Nothing must pollute the community. In New Testament times, Paul urged the Corinthian believers to ensure that their lives were not damaged by the moral corruption of their notoriously evil environment. Close relationships with unbelievers (in marriage, for example) could do irreparable harm to their faith. Quoting a group of relevant Old Testament passages[23], the apostle urged his readers to purify themselves 'from everything that contaminates body and spirit, perfecting holiness out of reverence for God'.[24]

In a postmodern society like our own, with its highly subjective values and moral relativism, it is easy for Christians to become absorbed in a spiritually alien culture. Believers have the privilege of witnessing to the power of the indwelling Christ by adopting a counter-cultural lifestyle, not allowing the world around them to squeeze them into its own mould.[25] Postmodernism's 'Do exactly what pleases you' mentality has no appeal for those whose primary motivation is to honour God, please Christ, obey the Spirit and help others.[26]

God's compassion illustrated

Once the booty was ceremonially purified by *the water of cleansing* (23), the spoils were divided, one half to be shared by *the soldiers who took part in the battle*, the other among *the community* (26–27). The 12,000 Israelite soldiers rightly received a larger proportion when the total amount was shared between them, the other half being evenly distributed throughout the rest of the people. God recognized that some people in that camp may have been willing to go to battle but, given their deliberately small army, were denied the opportunity. Others were too old or too weak to fight, yet they had material needs just as much as anybody else. Widows and orphans were the Lord's special concern,[27] and he particularly wanted them to benefit from these resources.

The principle of the generous distribution of plunder is contrary to traditional practice among ancient near-eastern peoples.[28] In the

---

[23] 2 Cor. 6:14–18, quoting Lev. 26:11–12; Is. 52:11; 2 Sam. 7:14–15.
[24] 2 Cor. 7:1.   [25] See J.B Phillips' paraphrase of Rom. 12:1–2.
[26] Matt. 6:33; 2 Tim. 2:4; 2 Cor. 5:9; Rom. 8:5; 15:2; 1 Cor. 10:24.
[27] Exod. 22:22; Deut. 10:18; 24:17, 19, 21; 26:12.   [28] Harrison, p. 388.

neighbouring nations, everything a soldier gained as plunder became his own property, and he was not required to part with any of it, except whatever he thought appropriate to offer as a gift to his god.

After the allocation of plunder, both halves were then to *set apart as tribute for the* LORD a proportion of what they received (28). The hazardous service of the troops was further recognized in that they were required to pay a smaller proportion to the Lord's work; more was required of those who had not been sent to the fight.

The fact that everybody benefited materially from the conflict testifies to the Lord's concern for all his people, not just for those in frontline activity. The principle shaped Israel's later practice on the distribution of plunder in warfare.[29]

God's servants maintained

When the booty had been distributed throughout the camp, everybody realized that a proportion of each share must be given *to Eleazar the priest as the* LORD'*s part* (29). The soldier's offerings, *one out of every five hundred, whether persons, cattle, donkeys, sheep or goats* (28), were allocated for the support of Israel's priests. Those who had not been part of the fighting force gave one fiftieth to maintain the ministry of the Levites, who were *responsible for the care of the* LORD'*s tabernacle* (30). A larger proportion was expected of the non-combatants because there were considerably more Levites to support than priests.

Precise numbers of all the captives and animals were carefully listed. The Lord wanted such detail to be recorded as a testimony to his unfailing kindness to his people. Their response was to bring these gifts to the Lord for his continuing work. As the long journey was nearing its end, the new generation gave generously, as their parents had done before it began (7:1–88). Scripture preserves inspiring passages that describe and encourage the generous giving of God's people across the centuries.[30] We are their privileged successors.

God's mercies declared

When Israel's commanding officers counted the returning troops, they discovered that not one single man had been lost in the conflict. It was a token of God's unique power and the

---

[30] Gen. 14:18–20; Exod. 35:4–29; 36:2–7; Deut. 26:1–11; Ezra 2:68–69; Mal. 3:8–12; Acts 4:32–35; 1 Cor. 16:1–2; 2 Cor. 8:1–15; 9:6–15; Phil. 4:10–19; 1 Tim. 5:17–18.

trustworthiness of the promises he had made about going before them to vanquish their enemies. Their Lord could save by many soldiers or by relatively few.[31] The senior men in the army wanted to acknowledge their indebtedness to the Lord publicly: *'So we have brought as an offering to the LORD the gold articles each of us acquired'* (50).

They not only offered the best (*gold*) they had received; they also wanted *to make atonement* for themselves *before the LORD* (50). Although the Lord had sent them to the battle, their involvement had brought them into contact with death and, feeling unclean (even disturbed) by the conflict, they longed that their gifts might *make atonement* for them. The soldiers had returned with some sense of guilt. Their eyes had looked upon scenes that might later trouble a sensitive conscience. Possibly the physical act of counting the returning soldiers (49) was a form of census activity that defiled them. The language of Exodus 30:11–16 is echoed here; used in 'the service of the Tent of Meeting', those gifts of gold became *a memorial for the Israelites before the LORD* (54).[32]

The Hebrew word used in this narrative about gifts *to make atonement* (*kipper*) is derived from a word (*kōper*) meaning 'ransom price'. A *kōper* was the sum a condemned offender might be permitted to pay in order to escape the death penalty.[33] 'It allowed a guilty person to be punished with a lesser penalty than he deserved.'[34]

These army officers were declaring their gratitude to God that the lives of 12,000 Israelite soldiers had been spared. More than enough tears had been shed in Israel because of the Baal-Peor apostasy (25:5), without the anguish of further widespread bereavement. In bringing their gifts of gold, the army's leaders publicly testified to the undeserved generosity of a merciful God.

Personal testimony no longer has the role it once did in the life of evangelical churches. The early Methodist people rejoiced in every opportunity to speak in their band and class meetings about what the Lord had done for them personally. Occasions when believers express their recent experience of God's grace, guidance and providence can strengthen the most timid speaker, enrich the hearers and magnify the Lord.[35] Up-to-date testimony is the dependent Christian's *memorial ... before the LORD*, one of the great treasures of the church.

---

[31] 1 Sam. 14:6.   [32] Cf. Exod. 30:16.   [33] Exod. 21:30.

[34] G. J. Wenham, *Leviticus*, New International Commentary on the Old Testament (London: Hodder and Stoughton, 1979), pp. 28, 60.

[35] Ps. 66:16.

God's uniqueness confirmed

This encounter with the Midianites was the last military engagement in Moses' life. It must have been a rich inspiration to those Israelite soldiers to know that the old leader was there in the camp, confident that, because God had sent them, they would return as victors. Moses knew that, although it was his last battle, it was certainly not theirs. Moses' final conflict confirmed God's sovereignty over the nations and his supremacy over the meaningless idols of paganism, the religious nonentities of Israel's new neighbours.

In such a culture, 'battles were regarded as waged between national gods, whose people did the actual fighting. If a nation was defeated it was because the national deity was angry with his people.'[36] The ninth-century Moabite Stone records that Israel's victory over them was due solely to the displeasure of the Moabite god Chemosh.[37] Though Moses' destiny was to climb the mountain rather than cross the river, it must have been an immense relief to the old leader to witness the conquest of the Midianites by such a relatively small army. If God's people could defeat those who had earlier lured them into apostasy, then, given the same divine resources, anything was possible. It demonstrated beyond doubt that, despite their appalling mistakes, arrogant disobedience, repeated grumbling and occasional defection over the past forty years, Israel's Lord was still on their side.

Lessons for today

Before leaving this narrative we reflect on some significant issues that emerge from it.

First, there are ethical dimensions to this narrative which the contemporary reader may find jarring. We may well understand some chapters and verses better in the future than we can at the moment. The Puritan minister John Robinson was right to insist that 'the Lord has yet more light and truth to break forth from his Word'. Further reading, quiet reflection, other people's views and the perspective of later experience may provide us with fresh insights into stories and sayings that puzzle us. Writing about things at present beyond our grasp, Richard Baxter said, 'Had all these

[36] Harrison, pp. 381–382.
[37] *ANET*, p. 320: 'Omri, king of Israel, he humbled Moab ... for Chemosh was angry at his land.' For bibliography of the Moabite Stone, see *NBD*, pp. 835–836.

been needful, to us they had been revealed'.[38] A time is coming when we shall know everything,[39] but that day has not yet arrived, and the trusting experience may be a necessary factor deepening our faith.

Calvin maintained that, 'when God's judgments surpass our understanding, we should, in sober humility, give glory to his secret, and to us incomprehensible, wisdom'. People who 'seek to know more than is fitting, elevate themselves too high'.[40] We need to trust that God knows best and always acts entirely for his people's good.

Secondly, God hates sin. The Baal-Peor treachery went down in Israel's history as the worst possible example of spiritual adultery and degrading immorality. The immediate death of the Israelite offenders and the later punishment of the perpetrators convinced every Israelite of God's holy judgment on the adamantly disobedient and persistently disloyal. It is a theme that cannot be dismissed as an outdated feature of Israel's bygone faith. We do no credit to the New Testament if we marginalize its uncompromising teaching about judgment. It is expressed as forcefully in the message of Jesus[41] as in the later writings of the apostles and their colleagues.[42]

Thirdly, syncretism is perilous. The idolaters at Shittim imagined that they could retain some notional allegiance to the Lord while worshipping Baal at the same time. The Canaanite fertility god might well procure additional benefits; a wider geographical spectrum might invite a broader religious loyalty. Nothing could have been further from the truth. The death of the Israelite adulterers and the victory over the Midianites were visible proof that the followers of other gods were not only prone to disappointment but doomed to destruction.

In a pluralistic society, Christians remain convinced that other religions, ancient or modern, are misguided distortions of the truth, not optional alternatives to a biblical faith. Such conviction runs counter to our postmodern culture with its consumerist approach to world religions. All are considered as equally valid, and any assertion of the exclusive claims of Christ is dismissed as objectionable intolerance. One contemporary rabbi maintains that his

---

[38] Richard Baxter, *Dying Thoughts*, in *Practical Works* 18, ed. W. Orme (London: James Duncan, 1830), p. 259.

[39] 1 Cor. 13:12.   [40] Calvin, IV, p. 264.

[41] Matt. 5:21–22, 30; 7:1–2, 21–23; 8:12; 10:15, 24–28, 32–33; 11:20–24; 12:36–37; 13:40–43, 49–50; 16:27; 18:8–9; 25:31–46; R. V. G. Tasker, *The Biblical Doctrine of the Wrath of God* (London: Tyndale, 1951), pp. 26–37. This valuable lecture has recently been reprinted in *Themelios* 26/2 and 26/3 (Spring and Summer 2001).

[42] 1 Cor. 3:12–15; 2 Cor. 5:10; 2 Thess. 1:4–10; 1 Tim. 5:24; Heb. 9:27; Jas. 5:1–6; 1 Pet. 4:17; Rev. 22:12.

Jewish faith 'should be seen as only one among many ways in which human beings have attempted to make sense of the Ultimate'. The 'varied truth-claims of the world's faiths must be regarded as human icons ... Neither Jew, Muslim, Christian, Hindu nor Buddhist has any justification for believing that his own tradition embodies the uniquely true and superior religious path – instead the adherents of all the world's faiths must recognize the inevitable human subjectivity of religious conceptualization.'[43] Contemporary pluralistic theology dismisses both the authority of Scripture and the uniqueness of Christ's person and work. With a dogmatism he would consider unacceptable in others, John Hick asserts that 'the idea that Jesus proclaimed himself as God incarnate and the sole point of saving contact between God and man is without historical foundation, and represents a doctrine developed by the church. We should therefore not infer, from the Christian experience of redemption through Christ, that salvation cannot be experienced in any other way.'[44] While wishing always to be compassionate and understanding towards people of other faiths, disciples of Jesus remain convinced of his deity and the distinctive apostolic claim that 'there is no other name ... by which we must be saved'.[45]

Fourthly, we should leave vengeance to God. This narrative about the destruction of the Midianites is descriptive, not prescriptive. It relates how Israel acted, under divine instruction, at a specific moment of time and for a particular purpose. It does not provide *carte blanche* approval for acts of reprisal or retaliation, or for the exercise of personal vendettas. King Saul had been ferociously cruel to David and, given the right opportunity, the fugitive had abundant reason to get his own back; but he persistently refused to do so. He believed that the rectification of injustice is best undertaken by the Lord: 'May the LORD judge between you and me. And may the LORD avenge the wrongs you have done to me, but my hand will not touch you.' After sparing Saul's life, David reminded the pursuing king of an old saying, 'From evildoers come evil deeds.'[46] Saul might have insisted on doing such things, but David had no desire to be numbered among vindictive people. At the end of his life, David confessed his faith in 'the God who avenges me' by showing 'unfailing kindness' even in dark days.[47]

---

[43] D. Cohn-Sherbok, *Modern Judaism* (London: Macmillan, 1996), pp. 221, 246, 248.
[44] J. Hick, *God and the Universe of Faiths* (London: Macmillan, 1988), p. 145.
[45] Acts 4:12; cf. John 6:38–51.
[46] 1 Sam. 24:13.   [47] 2 Sam. 22:48, 51; cf. Pss. 94:1; 149:7.

The same truth was on the lips of the great prophets when they thought of the cruelties inflicted on God's people by surrounding nations. God had no intention of overlooking such heartless evil.[48] The apostle Paul urged his readers not to seek revenge but to 'leave room for God's wrath'. Quoting Moses, he urged them to leave such matters in the hands of a just and righteous God: '"It is mine to avenge: I will repay," says the Lord.'[49]

Finally, we should make the pursuit of holiness a renewed priority. The Midianite hazard could not be ignored. Those immoral idolaters could have stolen back into Israel's towns and villages once the two and a half tribes had settled back in the highly fertile Transjordan region. The potential danger had to be removed. The narrative is almost parabolic. It depicts a radical lifestyle that identifies weak spots and potential dangers, and distances us from them. We need to deal ruthlessly with anything that obscures our vision of God, veils the beauty of Christ, challenges the truth of Scripture, silences the voice of the Spirit, marginalizes the needs of others and exalts ourselves.

We all have vulnerable areas. Jesus used stark imagery when describing the cure. The sexually lustful had better remove the wandering eye; the greedy hand must be amputated. Eternal issues are at stake. There is no room for compromise. However costly, Jesus knew it was better to 'lose one part of your body than for your whole body to go into hell'.[50] Paul described the same painful process as 'putting to death the misdeeds of the body' in the power of the indwelling Spirit.[51] It is a costly yet fruitful process. A swift Midianite conflict was infinitely preferable to a compromised faith that, across godless years, would gradually disappear.

[48] Is. 34:8; Jer. 46:10; Ezek. 25:14, 17. [49] Rom. 12:19, quoting Deut. 32:35.
[50] Matt. 5:27–30.   [51] Cf. Rom. 8:13.

32:1–42
28. Alternative destinies

The English novelist Graham Greene was sometimes asked whether the characters in his novels were modelled on people in real life. Greene replied that they certainly were, though in most cases he had shaped for those individuals 'alternative destinies'. Where the real-life characters suffered severe hardship, in his novels he gave their story a brighter outcome. Others who had little to disturb their egocentric round of pleasure and prosperity experience adversity in his fiction, and become more sympathetic towards others.[1]

Here in Numbers 32 is an account of the Israelite people suddenly confronted with an alternative destiny. It is a dramatic story of potential failure – threatened (1–5), exposed (6–15) and averted (16–42).

Failure threatened (32:1–5)

As the Israelites looked across the river to their appointed destination, they encountered a crisis that threatened the success of the forthcoming invasion. The tribes of Reuben and Gad, blessed with *very large herds and flocks*, specially appreciated the highly fertile east Jordan area that had been recently taken, and began to shape for themselves an alternative destiny. What point was there in exposing themselves to the physical dangers of the conquest when the land the other side of the river was not as good as where they were now camping? Could their two tribes make the Transjordan area their own by remaining exactly where they were, in a prosperous region with unimaginable agricultural potential, surrounded by their families and livestock? The remaining ten

---

[1] Graham Greene, *Ways of Escape: Autobiographical Reflections of a Novelist* (London: The Bodley Head, 1980), p. 84.

tribes could then be free to allocate the land in Canaan among themselves once it had been conquered. Their proposal was forthright and definite: 'Do not make us cross the Jordan' (5).

The request plunged the Israelites into crisis. On the surface, their suggestion seemed harmless enough. Why should one sixth of the people expose themselves and their families to risk when there was perfectly good land precisely where they were living? If people were to be killed in the conquest, what was the point of thrusting even more Israelites into danger? But these two tribes were putting their desires above the welfare of the entire community.

The narrative is rich in teaching value. It exposes those sins of omission that can be just as damaging in our lives as the more obvious sins of commission. Moses puts his finger on their potential sin: 'If you fail to do this, you will be sinning against the Lord; and you may be sure that your sin will find you out' (23).

We can grieve the Lord by what we fail to do as well as by what we do. James puts it bluntly in his practical letter: 'Anyone, then, who knows the good he ought to do and doesn't do it, sins.'[2] In one of his parables, Jesus tells the story of a 'servant who knows his master's will' but fails to do it, incurring severe punishment.[3] Sins of omission are starkly exposed in that triple collection of parables in Matthew 25 where the characters are judged for the sin of doing nothing. The foolish virgins did not take oil for the lamps. The servant did not put his talent to use. The inactive 'goats' did not feed the hungry, provide drink for the thirsty, shelter the homeless, care for the sick or show compassion to the prisoners. They grieved the Lord by what they failed to do.[4]

Moses must have been specially frustrated by this appeal to stay east of the Jordan when he himself would have given anything to have crossed that river. Here was a man who had been forbidden to enter the promised land, having to hear an appeal from people who did not want to enter it. There is much to learn from Moses' analysis of and response to the Gadites' and Reubenites' request.

Failure exposed (32:6–15)

The two tribes needed to look carefully at the implications of their request. By not crossing the Jordan with the whole community they would be grieving God, discouraging others and harming themselves.

With considerable pastoral artistry and communication skills, Moses exposes this potential failure. He confronts the two tribes

---

[2] Jas. 4:17.   [3] Luke 12:47.   [4] Matt. 25:3, 24–30, 41–46.

with the implications and consequences of a wrong decision. The issues he raises are not confined to this specific problem of potential tribal disharmony in the remote ancient world. These arresting narratives are Scripture's warnings 'to keep us from setting our hearts on evil things as they did'.[5] They are failures to which we are equally exposed in the twenty-first century.

Failure to conquer selfishness (32:5)

That their recently conquered land was highly *suitable for livestock* (1) was beyond doubt. Over 600 metres above sea level, the terrain was extensive, well watered and exceptionally fertile. But in making this proposal, these two tribes were thinking only of themselves. Moses could not conceal his anger at their self-regarding request: *'Shall your countrymen go to war while you sit here?'* (6).

The Reubenites may have been 'claiming their rights' as the direct successors of Jacob's eldest son. The firstborn in Israel had distinct privileges and, although these had been forfeited because of Reuben's sin,[6] they may have hoped that family privilege would give them the right to choose the best for themselves. For many people, self-interest is the primary determinative feature in life's choices. Oswald Chambers used to define sin as 'my right to myself'. Christians have other priorities; their thinking is determined and controlled by God's right to themselves.

Selfishness is a recurrent danger in a postmodern society. Millions of our neighbours are urged to pursue courses of action that actively foster self-gratification as a primary goal in life. Nothing could be more contrary to the biblical presentation of the Christian ideal. Christ had no desire to please himself, and he is every believer's perfect model. Their dominant ambition is to glorify God and to serve others.[7] Anything that actively encourages us to magnify self is suspect.

Failure to encourage others (32:7)

'Why do you discourage the Israelites from going over into the land the LORD has given them?' (7) If the invasion of Canaan was to succeed, everyone would have to put their fellow *countrymen* (6) before themselves. If those two tribes dropped out, the remainder would cross the Jordan weakened by the serious depletion of their numbers. The apostle Paul told the Corinthians that one of the

---

[5] 1 Cor. 10:6.   [6] Gen. 35:22; 49:4.
[7] Rom. 15:2–3; Mark 10:45; Luke 22:25–27; John 13:13–17; 2 Cor. 8:9; Phil. 2:7.

reasons God's Son went to the cross was to slay that innate selfishness that blights the story of every promising life. Jesus died that 'those who live should no longer live for themselves but for him who died for them and was raised again'.[8]

Moses deliberately contrasted their preferred destiny and opulent ease (*'you sit here'*) with the deprivations of the rest who would *go to war* (6). The depleted tribes would be in serious danger of losing heart, just as the community did forty years earlier when they stood on the threshold of the promised land.

When making major decisions in life, Christians think not only of the benefits that might come to them but of the effect their choices might have upon others. In an age of strident individualism, such an outlook is hardly likely to be popular, but the believer's living is shaped by a Christian counter-culture. When, after a long and tiring day's work, Jesus entered with his disciples into a restful home, they looked around for someone to perform the slave's work. When Christ had washed the feet of all of them, was there one among them who would kneel to do the same for their Lord? Or were they so stunned by his matchless humility that nobody stirred? With his slave's work done, Jesus said that he had left them an example, 'that you should do as I have done for you'.[9] He was underlining by example and by speech the crucial necessity of putting the needs of others before our own.[10]

Failure to learn from yesterday's mistakes (32:8–11)

'This is what your fathers did when I sent them from Kadesh Barnea to look over the land ... they discouraged the Israelites from entering the land the LORD had given them' (8–9). That grim experience went down in Israel's history as a tragic example of disobedience, rebellion and unbelief,[11] and here was a new generation with a plan that exactly repeated the blunders of the old. The language Moses used deliberately recalls the story of the old generation's rebellion at the Canaanite border forty years earlier.[12]

The old leader urged these tribes to learn from their history how to avoid sinning afresh in the same way. Similarly, the apostle Paul told the Corinthian believers that these events from Israel's past ought to be regarded by us as stark warnings to keep us from sin.[13] The narratives of Scripture are a rich storehouse of truth. We can learn from the errors of people in biblical times. One of Scripture's

[8] 2 Cor. 5:15. [9] John 13:3–15. [10] Phil. 2:3–4; Rom. 12:10; 1 Cor. 10:24, 33.
[11] Ps. 95:8–11. [12] Wenham (1981) p. 213, n. 1. [13] 1 Cor. 10:6–11.

ways of guarding us from sin is by the forthright manner in which it describes the hazards and pitfalls in the lives of its best characters. We are meant to learn from their mistakes; they have been recorded 'to teach us'.[14]

These tribes of Reuben and Gad had lived through that tragic experience when the fearful and unbelieving community rebelled in the desert; they had buried their parents in the wilderness, and yet here they were, about to make an identical mistake. Exactly like their forebears forty years earlier, they were saying they did not wish to enter the land. They were being challenged about something that had become part of their own life history. Each of us has much to learn from our past lives – the wrong decisions, the unbelieving actions, the distorted thinking, those unhelpful things we may have said and done. If we have asked the Lord for forgiveness, such sins have been gloriously forgiven. Only immature Christians think they have nothing to learn from past mistakes. Moses appealed to these two tribes not to rerun the Kadesh Barnea calamity.

Failure to follow the example of God's best people (32:12)

The two tribes were about to copy their disobedient parents rather than heed the radiant example of Caleb and Joshua. Moses' direct warning repeated familiar language to contrast the unbelieving majority decision of the old generation (*'they have not followed me wholeheartedly'*) with the zealous commitment of the trusting minority, Caleb and Joshua: *'they followed the LORD wholeheartedly'* (11–12).

What an excellent thing it is when believers have good spiritual mentors, people with high spiritual standards and convinced biblical ideals! Just as there are characters and events in Scripture to warn us, so there is a huge number of biblical personalities whose example inspires us. They made mistakes, of course, but we can be lured on to better things by the story of their surrender, heroism, prayerfulness, sacrifice and trust.

There can be no better example than that of the Lord Jesus. Peter told his churches that, in times of persecution and intense hardship, they must recall the way Jesus lived, served, prayed and died.[15] In times when it was costly to be Christian, the first readers of the letter to the Hebrews were also urged to remember the great characters of Israel's faith, the famous[16] and the anonymous,[17] a 'great cloud of witnesses'[18] to the love, grace and power of God in

[14] Rom. 15:4.   [15] 1 Pet. 2:21.   [16] Heb. 11:4–32.   [17] Heb. 11:33–38.
[18] Heb. 12:1.

human life. In the strength given to them, they accomplished great things[19] and, in the same power, others endured ghastly things.[20] With an active faith, some changed the situations in which they found themselves; others with a passive faith could not possibly change their conditions (persecution, imprisonment, opposition, hardship, suffering), but could suffer such things heroically as a testimony to God's unfailing grace. Those persecuted Christians were also reminded of the radiant example of their own 'leaders, who spoke the word of God' to them, so that they might ponder 'the outcome of their way of life and imitate their faith'.[21] The persuasive power of a rich example is immensely important in Hebrews – the example of Old Testament saints,[22] New Testament believers,[23] church leaders[24] and, most important of all, the unchanging Christ, who is 'the same yesterday and today and for ever'.[25]

In addition to these biblical personalities, there is the rich testimony of God's people across the centuries. Christian biography is an abundant source of inspiration, encouragement and challenge. The story of some great Christian has caused many a believer to change direction in life. Their influence transcends denominational barriers. David Brainerd, an eighteenth-century Presbyterian missionary to the Delaware Indians, died in his thirtieth year; but, across successive decades, countless people were transformed by the example of his sacrificial life and prayerfulness. Jonathan Edwards, whose daughter was to have married Brainerd, published Brainerd's journal, which spoke directly to later generations of believers, leading them to new levels of spiritual commitment and missionary service. John Wesley urged his Methodist colleagues to read the pioneer missionary's life: 'Find preachers of David Brainerd's spirit and nothing can stand before them.'[26] Equally inspired by the journal, William Carey encouraged his Baptist mission group in India to read it together three times each year: 'Let us often look at Brainerd in the woods of America, pouring out his very soul before God.'[27] One of Carey's contemporaries in India, the young Anglican Henry Martyn, said of Brainerd, 'I long to be like him' and to 'be swallowed up in a desire to glorify God'.[28] Jim Elliot, martyred by Auca Indians in 1956, wrote

[19] Heb. 11:33–35a.   [20] Heb. 11:35b–38.   [21] Heb. 13:7.   [22] Heb. 11:4–39.
[23] Heb. 10:32–39.   [24] Heb. 13:7.   [25] Heb. 13:8; cf. 3:1–6; 4:14–16.
[26] The Journal of Rev. John Wesley 5, ed. N. Curnock (London: Epworth, 1938), p. 226 (8 August 1767).
[27] S. P. Carey, William Carey (London: Hodder and Stoughton, 1923), p. 249.
[28] Constance E. Padwick, Henry Martyn, Confessor of the Faith (London: SCM, 1922), p. 89.

in his own diary of Brainerd's influence in stirring him to secret and passionate prayer.[29] One exemplary life reaches countless others.

Failure to discern God's estimate of their sin (32:14)

As soon as Moses had reminded these tribal leaders of the enormity of their parents' sins ('*The LORD's anger burned against Israel*', 13), he turned in a flash from the past to the present, from the old generation to the new: '*And here you are, a brood of sinners, standing in the place of your fathers and making the LORD even more angry with Israel*' (14).

Rarely do we see ourselves as we really are. As these tribes approached Moses with their selfish request, they did not for a moment consider that, in God's sight, they were *a brood of sinners*, a scornful term found nowhere else in the Old Testament. They thought of themselves as a group of astute farmers making the best of their agricultural prospects, or devoted husbands securing the well-being of their vulnerable wives, or protective fathers desiring the best for their dependent children, or alert opportunists grasping a chance that might never return; but in God's eyes they were nothing other than *a brood of sinners*. Obsessed with their own interests, their sole ambition was to make themselves happy, wealthy and secure. They did not think for a moment that by their selfishness they were making the Lord *even more angry* than he had been at Kadesh Barnea.

In every situation in life we need to reflect not on what satisfies us, or on what meets with the approval of others, but on what pleases God. They were on the brink of incurring the Lord's anger, and this, doubtless, played a great part in causing them to pull back. One of the many reasons we need to make time for the regular, systematic and reflective reading of God's Word is that Scripture presents us with a realistic view of ourselves. The Bible encourages us but does not flatter us. It exposes our faults, challenges our apathy, identifies our weaknesses and corrects our mistakes. It makes us face our own frailties and, in the light of its teaching, seek the Lord for the cleansing of the past, the power to live differently and a greater sensitivity to sin's damaging effects in human life.

[29] Elisabeth Elliot, *The Journals of Jim Elliot* (London: Pickering and Inglis, 1979), pp. 143–144, 166, 172–173.

Failure to pursue the Lord's will (32:15)

The two tribes vainly imagined that all they were asking was that they might be excused the journey to Canaan, nothing else. Moses knew that more was at stake than a request for non-compliance with a prearranged plan. God's purpose was that his people should cross that river and enter their new land. So often in life, people become so preoccupied with their own dreams and ambitions that they are blind to the implications and possible consequences of their decisions. Moses saw it all with vivid and shattering clarity. For these two tribes to stay east of Jordan at that time would be spiritually disastrous. They would not merely be turning away from following the Israelites; they would be turning away from following the Lord. The Kadesh Barnea experience was about to be repeated: *'he will again leave all this people in the desert'* (15).

Failure to realize when the enemy is at work

These tribes had not considered the consequences of their proposed action. To them, the request seemed innocent enough, but the devil was using their selfish interests in a further attempt to bring Israel to renewed *destruction*, and they would be the cause of it (15).

Israel's adversary, the enemy of souls, had done his utmost to frustrate God's purposes in bringing his people to the border of their new land. He had caused them to be pursued by an irate Egyptian army[30] and had fostered a deep discontent when they met with natural adversities.[31] Internally, he had caused them to be angry with God's appointed leader[32] and, externally, had exposed them to the attack of fierce, marauding invaders.[33] He had lured them into demoralizing idolatry[34] so that they not only broke the covenant agreement[35] but ascribed their miraculous deliverance to the work of a handmade god. He had encouraged them to complain about their hardships (11:1) and to be discontented with the provision of daily nutritious food (11:4–9). He had created serious division within their appointed leadership (12:1–2; 16:1–4) and blinded the people to the reliability of God's promises (13:30; 14:7–9). He had made the travellers impatient so that they opposed their leader and 'spoke against God' (21:4–5). The enemy had tried to destroy them by witchcraft and sorcery (22:1–7), and had brought disaster in the camp by the hideous sins of sexual immorality and blatant idolatry (25:1–15).

---

[30] Exod. 14:5–12. [31] Exod. 16:1–3. [32] Exod. 17:3–4. [33] Exod. 17:8.
[34] Exod. 32:1–6. [35] Exod. 20:1–4.

Now, the enemy embarked on a new tactic. What could not be achieved by other means might now be accomplished by tribal defection, disloyalty and disunity. The two tribes had little idea that what they conceived as an expedient plan was nothing other than an enemy device. Another reason to study God's Word and to listen attentively to its faithful and applied exposition is that it prepares us for the enemy's subtle onslaughts.

Failure averted (32:16–42)

This story, unlike others in Numbers, has a happy outcome. The leaders of Reuben and Gad paid careful attention to the forthright things Moses said, and came back to the old leader with a better proposition. The two tribes acknowledged the truth of what Moses had shared in his eloquent and persuasive preaching. The four steps in their radical change of outlook are as relevant in our Christian lives as in the experience of these travellers over 3,000 years ago.

Repentance

They had a radical change of mind; that is the meaning of the word 'repentance' (Greek *metanoia*) in the New Testament. Instead of lingering behind they went right to the front of the Lord's army as they crossed the river. The tribes of Reuben and Gad formed the advance guard. The passage describing the invasion says that the 'men of Reuben, Gad and the half-tribe of Manasseh crossed over, armed, in front of the Israelites, as Moses had directed them'.[36] These two tribes changed their mind about themselves, the Lord, others and life.

First, they changed their mind about themselves. Listening to Moses, they realized how true was his exposure of their selfishness. They agreed that they had acted as *a brood of sinners* (14), whose self-centred ambitions would seriously affect others, damage themselves and grieve God. Under the influence of Moses' message, they saw themselves as they really were.

Secondly, they changed their mind about the Lord. They vainly imagined that he was not interested in the minor details of the invasion plan, and that they were free to do more or less whatever they wished. Moses' response to their request convinced them that, far from pleasing the Lord, they were displeasing him. They could anger him as much by their self-regarding proposals as their parents had done by their unbelieving rebellion.

[36] Josh. 4:12.

Thirdly, they changed their mind about others. In planning this selfish alternative, they had disregarded the needs of the other ten tribes, who would be seriously impoverished by their defection. They realized that the needs of the community ought to take precedence over the wishes of the individual.

Finally, they changed their mind about life. Moses' words, accusing them of sitting idle (6), had stung them. Canaan was not going to be conquered by indolent people. Israel's immediate need called for dedicated partners and willing soldiers. There was time enough in the future for ambitious agricultural projects, but first a home across the river for the majority of Israel's people had yet to be conquered.

Obedience

Their change of mind was immediately expressed in a declaration of loyal service: *'we are ready to arm ourselves and go ahead of the Israelites until we have brought them to their place'* (17). By volunteering to be in the first rank of the troops, they were exposing themselves to the fierce brunt of the enemy attack. Their affirmations of obedience resound throughout the narrative: *'We your servants will do as our lord commands'* (25); *'your servants, every man armed for battle, will cross over to fight before the LORD, just as our lord says'* (27); *'Your servants will do what the LORD has said'* (31).

Obedience is the key to mature and effective Christian living. When, in the closing moments of his life, Moses pronounced his blessing on these tribes, he commended one of them with words that find an echo in the life of every obedient believer. The people of Gad had 'carried out the LORD's righteous will'[37] rather than their own selfish desires.

In the matter of obedience, as in all else, the Lord Jesus is our perfect model. He 'learned obedience from what he suffered',[38] which means that at every stage in his life he yielded himself afresh to God's will and purpose, and remained constantly and totally obedient to everything that was required of him. His incarnation was motivated by obedience[39] and his baptism was prompted by obedience.[40] His priorities were controlled by obedience, as in the wilderness temptations when he submitted himself afresh to the teaching of Scripture, the will of God and the conquest of evil.[41] His love for God was demonstrated by obedience: 'I do exactly what my Father has commanded me'.[42] His destiny was

---

[37] Deut. 33:21. [38] Heb. 5:8. [39] Heb. 10:5–7. [40] Matt. 3:14–15.
[41] Matt. 4:1–11. [42] John 14:31.

determined by obedience; nothing was allowed to deflect him from its course, not even the love of well-meaning but misguided friends.[43] His surrender was characterized by obedience, as he knelt in a secluded garden and repeatedly prayed, '... not as I will, but as you will ... may your will be done'.[44]

Surrender

The obedience the two tribes offered was not dutiful or grudging. They gave themselves fully in service to the Lord: *'We will not return to our homes until every Israelite has received his inheritance'* (18). It was an act of immediate, total and unqualified commitment.

Trust

The two tribes requested that, before moving on, they might be allowed to *build pens* on the east of Jordan for their *livestock and cities* to house their *women and children* (16). While they were away in Canaan, fighting battles for the whole community, their *wives and children* would *live in fortified cities, for protection from the inhabitants of the land* (17). Moses permitted them to do so, agreeing that once Canaan had been conquered they would be free to return to their newly built homes in the Transjordan region.

It was an act of courageous faith. Other tribesmen would have their wives and children alongside them as they settled in various parts of the new land. If the two and a half tribes wanted to return to the east Jordan area, they would have to trust God to 'keep' (6:24) their families safe while they were fighting on the other side of the river.

Often in life, when we make commitments involving obedience and surrender, we have to trust God for the outcome. We cannot know how it will all work out, but if we pursue the Lord's righteous will, then, in his providential care, he will ensure that we do not suffer. The story of the 1924 Olympic athlete, Eric Liddell, is known to our generation through the widely acclaimed film *Chariots of Fire*. His experience encourages anyone responding to Christ in obedience and surrender. Liddell had refused to run on a Sunday in the heats for the 100 metres, a decision that might have cost him success as a prospective winner; but he took to heart a message scribbled in a note to him: 'Those who honour me I will honour',[45] and the Lord did so. Transferring to the 400 metres, Liddell won the race and set a new record.

[43] Mark 8:31–33.　　[44] Matt. 26:39, 42.　　[45] 1 Sam. 2:30, AV.

The closing verses (34–42) provide historical and geographical detail about the settlement of the two tribes. They identify the *fortified cities* and *pens for their flocks* built by the tribesmen of Gad (34–36) and Reuben (37–38) as well as the half tribe of Manasseh (39–42), to which Zelophehad's daughters belonged (27:1–11; 36:1–12).

An intriguing postcript says that some of the old cities conquered in the east Jordan region were given new names (38). It was not appropriate for committed Israelite people to live in towns such as *Nebo* and *Baal Meon*, dedicated to pagan deities. These people who settled on the east side of the river wanted to make a fresh start by living in communities that removed all traces of paganism. They acknowledged the Lord's goodness in giving them a new land. By his undeserved grace, Christians have been given a new name and an infinitely better life; 'the old has gone, the new has come!'[46]

---

[46] 2 Cor. 5:17; cf. Rev. 2:17; Acts 11:26.

33:1–56
29. Recollections and resolutions

Moses' next assignment was to provide a written account of Israel's wilderness journey, listing forty-two places where they had camped.[1] In third-century Alexandria, Origen knew of critics who questioned this chapter's value. The celebrated teacher maintained that 'we cannot say of the Holy Spirit's writings that there is anything useless or unnecessary in them ... We ought rather to ... turn the eyes of our mind to him who ordered this to be written and to ask of him their meaning.'[2]

The list is 'a litany of the Lord's deliverance'[3] rather than a mere geographical itinerary. Far from simply recording camping places on a tedious journey, it testified to biblical truths for a new generation in their onward journey. Gratitude for the past inspired confidence for the future.

Recollections of the past (33:1–49)

At the LORD's *command Moses recorded the stages in their journey* (2). Many of the new generation were children and young people when their parents camped at these locations, and remembered only too well some miraculous events that took place at the various campsites. As elsewhere in this book, the geographical and historical detail serves a theological purpose, presenting a rich doctrine of God.

---

[1] It is not a complete account, as certain places referred to in the book are not included in the itinerary (Taberah, 11:3; Mattanah, Nahaliel and Bamoth, 21:19, for example), while it mentions other places not referred to elsewhere (33:13, 19–29). For helpful discussions of the travel itinerary, see Wenham (1981), pp. 216–230; G. I. Davies, *The Way of the Wilderness* (Cambridge: Cambridge University Press, 1979), and Currid, pp. 121–141.

[2] Origen, p. 247.   [3] Allen, p. 984.

A God who secures victories

The Israelites set out from Rameses on the fifteenth day of the first month, the day after the Passover. They marched out boldly in full view of all the Egyptians, who were burying all their firstborn, whom the LORD had struck down among them; for the LORD had brought judgment on their gods (3–4).

The start of the journey was the greatest miracle of all. It was an enterprise impossible to achieve by merely human means and methods; unarmed slaves were no match for Egypt's well-trained soldiers. As an eloquent testimony to the uniqueness of their rescue, the Decalogue, that brilliant summary of the covenant agreement, began with God's reminder of this unique redemption: 'I am the LORD your God, who brought you out of Egypt, out of the land of slavery.'[4]

This reference to God's initiative in releasing his people testifies to his dependable word (*the Passover*, the final 'plague' on Egypt's firstborn, exactly as he had promised),[5] invincible power (*They marched out boldly in full view of all the Egyptians, who were burying all their firstborn*) and incomparable nature (*for the LORD had brought judgment on their gods*). The new generation's soldiers would need these reminders that if they were to be successful in their next military enterprise, they must acknowledge God's uniqueness, trust his promises and receive his strength.

A God who meets emergencies

They left Pi Hahiroth and passed through the sea into the desert (8). When they had pitched their tents 'by the sea, directly opposite Baal Zephon',[6] the terrified Israelites looked up and saw on the horizon a huge Egyptian army, determined to return all of them to their slave camps. It marked the first occasion of grumbling against Moses: 'Was it because there were no graves in Egypt that you brought us to the desert to die?'[7] They were trapped, a swiftly pursuing army behind them in their 'best chariots'[8] and a huge expanse of water in front of them. With no human means of escape, Moses assured his distressed people, 'The LORD will fight for you',[9] as he did, opening a miraculous corridor through the sea.

The new generation's soldiers were certain to meet obstacles in

---

[4] Exod. 20:2. [5] Exod. 12:12–13 [6] Exod. 14:1–2, 9. [7] Exod. 14:11–12.
[8] Exod. 14:7. [9] Exod. 14:14.

their invasion of Canaan. Joshua and Caleb remembered that there were well-fortified cities with impregnable walls and physically colossal inhabitants; but a God who can lead his people safely through an impassable sea barrier would overcome all their difficulties in unfamiliar territory.

A God who provides necessities

... and when they had travelled for three days in the Desert of Etham, they camped at Marah.
They left Marah and went to Elim, where there were twelve springs and seventy palm trees, and they camped there ...
They left Alush and camped at Rephidim, where there was no water for the people to drink (8–9, 14).

The three-day journey that followed their deliverance through the sea was a time of testing. The recollection of places like Marah, where (until God intervened) the water was undrinkable,[10] and *Elim*, where twelve springs bubbled with good water, and *Rephidim*, where water burst out of the rock, brought the new generation fresh assurance that, whatever problems lay ahead, the Lord would be with them and meet their needs in critical times.

Moreover, *Rephidim* was a reminder that God provides not only natural resources such as water, but physical strength as well. The Lord had slain the Egyptian pursuers, but they were soon facing the Amalekite marauders.[11] Once again, the Lord provided everything necessary. Through Moses' prayer on the top of the hill, Joshua and his men were victorious at its foot. As Israel's fighters glanced to the hilltop, they knew that the uplifted hands of Moses and his partners were raised for their deliverance. The Lord would hear and answer such dependent intercession.

The stories recalled by some of the places in this itinerary were vivid reminders of the necessity, power and effectiveness of prayer. In several crises the people had grumbled to Moses and he had 'cried out to the LORD'.[12] His prayers for the people brought a swift response from the God who had promised to supply everything necessary for the journey.

A God who judges iniquities

Several locations recalled Israel's transgressions. In addition to those occasions when the people grumbled against Moses, there

[10] Exod. 15:25 [11] Exod. 17:8–13. [12] Exod. 15:24–25; 17:4.

were times, as at *Kibroth Hattaavah* (16), when they angered the Lord by their discontent (11:1–34), and as at Kadesh (36), where they doubted his word, opposed his servants and rejected his will (13:31–14:38). At *Abel Shittim* (49) they worshipped Moabite and Midianite gods and indulged in sexual orgies with pagan women (25:1–15). In each of these instances, the sins of the offenders could not be overlooked.

Even their godly leaders came under God's judgment. *At the* LORD's *command Aaron ... went up Mount Hor, where he died* (38). Their high priest had grieved the Lord more than once (12:10–12; 20:12). His offence at Hazeroth (12:16) was forgiven, but his sin at Meribah, along with Moses, had serious consequences. The two leaders would not enter the new land (20:12, 24). More, not less, is expected of people entrusted with spiritual responsibility. It was a salutary reminder to the new generation of the holiness and righteousness of God. Even spiritual exemplars like Moses and Aaron could not escape sin's consequences.

It would be a mistake for the new generation to face the future ignorant of, or indifferent to, the power and effect of human sin. Some of these place names issued strong warning signals to those who were about to enter Canaan. The new land would confront them with fierce temptations; they must not imagine that they could compromise with evil.

Resolutions for the future (33:50–56)

The Lord had commanded Moses to write (2); now he ordered him to speak (50–51). The recollection of the past should inspire confidence, issue warnings and encourage trust for the days ahead. Moses' message contained a radical command, a loving provision and a necessary warning.

A radical command (33:51–52)

The written record took account of the enormity of Israel's sins in the desert, but there were greater dangers ahead. The Canaanite deities they had worshipped at Shittim had revered shrines in the new land. Recognizing sin for what it is, they must *drive out all the inhabitants of the land* (52). There was no room for syncretistic worship whereby they could acknowledge their unique Lord and also pay their respects to idols. All *their carved images* and *cast idols* must be destroyed, and the invaders must *demolish all their high places* with their pornographic Asherah poles. Baalism was a fertility cult, maintaining that worship of its god would guarantee

292

an abundant harvest. To procure such benefits its worshippers used shrine prostitutes and indulged in degrading sexual practices at these *high places*. But the Israelite people had entered into a covenant with their God, and a prohibition of adultery[13] was part of the Decalogue's covenant agreement.

The worship of Baal was not only erroneous but offensive to Israel's holy God. Its corrupting influence would have a destructive effect on God's people unless they had the will to deal drastically with those immoral shrines as soon as they conquered the land. In addition to its offensive sexual connotations, Baalism included the practice of child sacrifice, yet another breach of the commandments: 'You shall not murder.'[14] Preaching to the community before they crossed the river, Moses warned them about Canaan's 'detestable ways'.[15] Their rituals were physically brutal as well as morally depraved, and the Israelite invaders were to root out such barbaric practices. In order to accomplish this punitive destruction, the Israelites were assured that 'the LORD your God will drive out those nations before you'.[16]

The Christian believer has something to learn from this divine command. There can be little progress in holiness without a radical rejection of sin. Jesus made that clear in his teaching[17] and the New Testament writers applied his message to life in their morally damaging first-century world.[18] Ours is an even more depraved society; the call to holiness is a divine imperative, not an optional invitation.

A loving provision (33:53–54)

The negative command about the eradication of evil is followed by a positive one concerning the distribution of the newly conquered land (53–54). Although the land was God's gift (53), without clear instructions the allocation of tribal territory might provoke serious disharmony and rivalry. It was a unique experience for these nomads to possess their own land, and some guidance had to be given regarding equitable distribution.

The familiar use of lots (26:52–56) would eliminate competition for preferred geographical areas: *Whatever falls to them by lot will be theirs* (54). Major decisions of this kind were best placed beyond the sphere of human debate.[19] People must keep within their ancestral tribes and not wander wherever their inclinations

[13] Exod. 20:14.   [14] Exod. 20:13.   [15] Deut. 18:9–12.   [16] Deut. 18:12.
[17] Mark 9:43–47.
[18] Rom. 12:2; 2 Cor. 7:1; Eph. 4:1; 4:17 – 5:15; 1 Pet. 1:14–17; 1 John 2:15–17.
[19] Josh. 14:1–5; Prov. 16:33; 18:18.

might take them. The tribes, clans and families varied in size, so that while a precise region might be determined by lots, the allocated areas must be commensurate in size with the numbers involved. When the Lord made plans for their settlement in Canaan, he did everything possible to minimize tribal rivalry, clan disputes and family quarrels concerning where the people were to live.

A necessary warning (33:55–56)

Moses conveyed the Lord's dual warning to the people: first, about the harassment of the Canaanites if they were not eliminated, and, secondly, the judgment of the Lord if Israel proved disobedient in the matter.

The Lord's message to the potential invaders sounded the note of sober realism. They were a heedless people and, on the issue of removing the pernicious Canaanites, he anticipated the likelihood of non-compliance: *'But if you do not drive out the inhabitants of the land, those you allow to remain will become barbs in your eyes and thorns in your sides. They will give you trouble ...'* (55). The subsequent story shows that the warning fell largely on deaf ears. At the close of his life, Joshua was still pleading with his contemporaries to do what the Lord had commanded: 'Do not associate with these nations that remain among you; do not invoke the names of their gods ... they will become snares and traps for you, whips on your backs and thorns in your eyes ... throw away the foreign gods that are among you and yield your hearts to the LORD, the God of Israel.'[20]

The problem blighted the spiritual life of God's people across the centuries, right up to their enforced exile to Babylon.[21] At that time, this crucial warning came to tragic fruition. In order to rid them of offensive idolatry and syncretistic worship, the Lord did to his people what he had planned for the Canaanites: he expelled them from the land. From bitter experience, his people learnt that God keeps his word, both in benevolent promise and threatened judgment.

---

[20] Josh. 23:7, 13; 24:23.
[21] Judg. 1:27–2:3; 2:10–19; 3:5–6; 1 Kgs. 11:1–10; 16:29–33; 2 Kgs. 14:4; 16.3–4; 17:1–23; 21:1–16; Jer. 19:5; Ezek. 7:20–22; Amos 5:26–27.

34:1 – 36:13
30. Generous provision

'I have given you the land' (33:53). Throughout the book, in narratives, sayings and laws (13:2; 14:8, 16, 23, 30; 15:2, 18; 27:12; 32:7, 9, 11), God repeatedly confirmed his promised gift The words *'When you enter ... the land that will be allotted to you'* (34:2) sound that same note of renewed assurance. The Lord went ahead of his people, meeting a variety of essential needs. The closing chapters describe his geographical, spiritual, legal and tribal provision.

Geographical provision (34:1–29)

Once they crossed over from the east Jordan area, the Israelite travellers would take possession of Canaan, a land that belongs to the Lord (33:53). He had decided to put it into the care of better tenants,[1] who needed to know their precise geographical frontiers so that they would not encroach on territory that God had not given them. They were not to be aggressive expansionists, building an empire. God is the 'Judge [or Ruler] of all the earth' and intended to 'do right' for other nations as well as for Israel.[2] He defined the southern (3–5), western (6), northern (7–9) and eastern (10–12) boundaries of Israel's new country, and indicated that their new home would have three distinctive features.

It would have extensive territory (34:1–12)

For most of their history, only part of this region was occupied by the Israelites. With the exception of times of economic prosperity and military strength during the reigns of David and Solomon,

[1] Gen. 15:16.
[2] Gen. 18:25; cf. Judg. 11:27; Ps. 60:6–8; Is. 40:22–24; Amos 2:1; 9:7.

God's people did not inherit the whole of the region. The western frontier, for example, was the Mediterranean Sea; and during the early centuries of the occupation the coastal strip was the home of the perpetually harassing Philistines, with frequent raids by Israel's western neighbours.[3] The invading community did not 'drive out all the inhabitants of the land' (33:52) as they were commanded, to their great cost. God has immeasurably more to give us than we can possibly imagine. There is more grace than we have yet known, more power than we have yet utilized, more love than we have yet received.[4] The frontiers of God's spiritual resources extend far beyond anything we might envisage.

It would be justly allocated (34:13–29)

The Lord told his people how the land was to be distributed. Eleazar the priest, their spiritual leader, and Joshua, their military commander, were to *appoint one leader from each tribe to help assign the land* (18). Given the quarrelsome rivalry that had sometimes marred the wilderness journey, every possibility of controversy, disharmony and friction must be minimized. Ten tribal leaders were to share with the community leaders in the fair division of tribal territories, according to the plan from the Lord laid down by Moses (33:54). Only ten men were required, as *two and a half tribes* were to return to the east Jordan area once the invasion had been successfully completed (13–15).

It was natural that a trusted member of the old generation, Caleb, should be one of this land allocation team. A man who had 'followed the LORD wholeheartedly' (32:12) would put God first rather than succumb to selfish interests or tribal pressure. Apart from Caleb, these ten men (19–29) appear nowhere else in the book. They were chosen by God for this specific purpose, and were going to do it to the best of their powers. Their responsibilities must have taken months of thorough work for, once the lots had been cast for the specific tribal region, delicate continuing negotiations ensured that the larger clans had more space than the smaller ones and that families within the clans were fairly accommodated.

In the work of Christ, every believer has a specific opportunity to serve the Lord in one capacity or another. He helps us to discern what our gift may be, provides the strength, wisdom and grace to do that work well, and deserves all the glory for anything that is achieved.[5] These tribal leaders were reliable people who

---

[3] Josh. 13:2–3; Judg. 3:2–4; 1 Sam. 4:1–11; 13:16 – 14:46; Is. 9:8–12.
[4] Jas. 4:6; Eph. 3:20; 3:19. [5] 1 Pet. 4:10–11.

would complete their unique assignment to the best of their powers, for the blessing of others and to the glory of God. Our work for Christ demands nothing less.

It would have exemplary leaders

This list of men responsible for the assignment of territory has a special feature in common with a similar list with which the book opened. The first chapter records the tribal leaders entrusted with the first census (1:2–15); many of their names included God's name, conveying a spiritual message to the community.

Theophoric ('God-bearing') names are also found in this list. Many of these new-generation tribal leaders may have left Egypt as children or teenagers. They must have been under the age of twenty at the time of the Kadesh Barnea rebellion or they would have died in the desert. Some were born in the wilderness, but their parents had given them names that testify to great doctrinal realities: *Shemuel* ('heard of God'), *Elidad* ('God loves'), *Hanniel* ('grace of God'), *Kemuel* ('God establishes'), *Elizaphan* ('God protects'), *Paltiel* ('deliverance is God') and *Pedahel* ('God ransoms'). The fact that the Lord himself chose these particular men (16, 29) suggests that these tribal leaders were true to their names. As believers, we too have a theophoric name, 'Christian'.[6] To bear this name is an undeserved privilege and a huge responsibility.

Spiritual provision (35:1–8)

As we have seen in the case of the leaders' theophoric names, the closing section of Numbers occasionally returns to features that characterized the book's opening chapters. The responsibilities of the Levites were an important theme as the Israelites began the desert journey (1:47–54; 3:5 – 4:49; 8:5–26), and now, at its close, the community was given precise instructions about the towns where the Levites would live after the settlement. They were not to be given a specific section of the new land (18:24) like the other tribes, because their supportive pastoral ministry was to be exerted wherever the Israelite people settled. The Levites were to be allocated forty-eight towns (35:6–7) with *pasture-lands around the towns* (4) *for their cattle, flocks and all their other livestock* (3). Precise measurements were given so that nobody could complain that they had encroached on other people's territory. Their

---

[6] Acts 11:26.

pasture-lands were to extend on the four sides of their towns. Two important features are noticeable here.

The Lord's practical concern for his servants

God laid it down that these spiritual leaders must be given secure homes and a reasonable livelihood. He expects his people to see that those who have been called to his work have appropriate provision for themselves and their families. The New Testament makes such obligations very clear in its teaching to the young churches. Christians at Philippi made sure that Paul's needs were generously supplied[7] and the apostle taught all his churches to take their financial responsibilities seriously.

The Lord's spiritual concern for his people

Along with the priests, these Levites were the Lord's representatives in the community. It was important, therefore, that every Israelite should be within reach of a Levite counsellor and helper: *'The towns you give the Levites ... are to be given in proportion to the inheritance of each tribe: Take many towns from a tribe that has many, but few from one that has few'* (8).

The Lord's concern that spiritual help should be accessible to all challenges our indifference to contemporary evangelism and missionary outreach. About 20% of the world's population have yet to hear of Christ. In the last quarter of the twentieth century it was estimated that there were at least 12,000 unreached people groups (as defined by subculture and dialect) who were without any knowledge of the saving gospel.[8] No Christian 'Levite' lives within easy reach of their towns and villages.

Legal provision (35:9–34)

Six of these forty-eight Levites' towns were also designated as *cities of refuge, to which a person who has killed someone may flee* (6). The Lord knows that wherever people live closely together there will be mutual hurt, disputes, disagreements, personal vendettas, even violence and aggression. The covenant agreement prohibited murder;[9] the shedding of blood would pollute the land (33), and their new country must not be defiled (34). God was going to

---

[7] Phil. 4:14–16.

[8] J. D. Douglas (ed.), *Proclaim Christ until he Comes* (Minneapolis, MN: World Wide Publications, 1990), pp. 345, 55.

[9] Exod. 20:13.

manifest his presence there, and described their territory as '*the land where you live and where I dwell*' (34). His people were to live harmoniously together, and the priests and Levites would serve as their counsellors and advisors.[10] Aggressiveness and brutality could spread through an entire community and, before long, a vulnerable people could be torn apart by civil war, particularly in that ancient near-eastern culture, where blood feuds were common. If a person was killed, either accidentally or intentionally, tribal, clan and family rivalries could plunge an entire community into chaotic disorder. Clear legal guidelines were given by Israel's compassionate and righteous God.

Accidental death

In his compassion for the innocent offender, the Lord provided six *cities of refuge*, three on each side of the Jordan (13–14).[11] These were locations, with Levites in residence, *to which a person who has killed someone accidentally may flee. They will be places of refuge from the avenger, so that a person accused of murder may not die before he stands trial before the assembly* (11–12). This provision was not only for the Israelites but for *aliens and any other people living among them* (15). Any person, whatever their ethnic background, who had accidentally caused the death of someone else must be protected from an angry avenger determined to kill the offender, whether the latter meant to harm the victim or not.

These asylum towns must be easily accessible within a given region, with good road links from other parts of the area. If the distance was too great for the fleeing offender to cover, an avenger might easily 'overtake him ... and kill him even though he is not deserving of death, since he did it to his neighbour without malice aforethought'.[12] Once the Israelites settled in the land, Joshua received precise instructions as to what the innocent offender was to do on arrival at one of these cities of refuge. He was to 'state his case at the gate before the elders of that city', who were to 'give him a place to live with them' until 'he has stood trial before the assembly' gathered in that locality.[13]

The community was given examples of possible accidents that could lead to the death of a fellow Israelite at the hands of someone *who did not intend to harm* the person who was killed (22–23), and Moses' later teaching provides the further example of a fatal forestry accident.[14] If, on weighing all the facts, the local

[10] Mal. 2:6–7. [11] Deut. 4:41–43; 19:1–13; Josh. 20:7–9. [12] Deut. 19:3, 6.
[13] Josh. 20:4, 6. [14] Deut. 19:5.

assembly of elders and judges confirmed that it was not an intentional killing, the person responsible could live a securely protected life within the *city of refuge*. He was not allowed to leave the city; this restriction of his liberty was an appropriate reminder of the sanctity of human life. It was a small price to pay for his safety when, however innocently, his action had led to the termination of a human life and caused immense grief to a fellow Israelite's family. Even then, the offender did not necessarily have to stay in the city for the rest of his life, for on *the death of the high priest* (25, 28, 32) it would be safe to leave the city without fear of reprisal.

There has been considerable discussion why the high priest's death plays a part in these legal provisions. In God's mercy and sovereignty, it may indicate, for the offender, the commencement of a new era. In the ancient world, the death of a king was sometimes marked by the release of prisoners.[15] In Egypt, for example, a pharaoh's death could guarantee the remission of capital crimes. The death of one such pharaoh provided Moses with an opportunity to return from Midian without fear of punishment for his manslaughter offence forty years earlier.[16] In Israel's case, the high priest's death had a similar effect in the life of the community.

Compulsory residence in the city would protect the offender, but neither this nor the payment of money (32) could atone for the death. That could be achieved only by the offering of another life; the high priest's death may have been regarded as a substitute for the death of the person killed accidentally.

Intended killing

Serious conflicts could lead to bitterness, brutality and violence. Israel's Lord was a God of righteousness and justice as well as of compassion. The cities of refuge offered no protection for the determined murderer. He had ignored the covenant obligation not to take human life, and so must lose his own. Supporting these provisions for the capital punishment of murderers, there are precise regulations, vital for the proper enforcement of justice within the community.

First, when anyone was accused of murder, it was essential for at least two witnesses to testify concerning the crime: *no-one is to be put to death on the testimony of only one witness* (30).

Secondly, the accused person was compelled to face the consequences of this extremely serious sin by the surrender of his own

[15] Noth, p. 255.   [16] Exod. 2:11–15, 23.

life. God is the giver of life and he alone may take it.[17] No offender was to be excused the death penalty simply by making a monetary payment as compensation to the deceased person's nearest relative or family (31). The same rule prohibiting the substitution of financial settlement applied to the person guilty of unintentional manslaughter (32). Both murder and manslaughter 'incur blood guilt and pollute the land and both require atonement: murder by the execution of the murderer and manslaughter by the natural demise of the high priest'.[18]

Thirdly, the murdered person's kinsman was to be the avenger of blood, and he alone must carry out the execution (16–21). A provision of this kind prevented the interference of vindictive members of a community who might hastily take matters into their own hands, perhaps killing an accused but innocent person wrongfully.

Fourthly, such offences were an affront to God's character. To rob a person of life grieved the Creator, and deliberately polluted the land the Lord had given. The wilful murderer was a thief (robbing God of a fellow human being's life) and a desecrator (defiling the land the Lord had given). The Lord insisted on the highest possible standards because he was going to manifest his presence among them in the new land: *'for I, the LORD, dwell among the Israelites'* (34).

Eight themes emerge in these legal regulations concerning manslaughter and murder (9–34).

1. The sanctity of human life. Life was humankind's most precious gift and to rob someone of it was the most serious crime possible. Likewise, everything must be done to prevent further loss of life through the perils of a blood feud.

2. The necessity of impartial justice. The main purpose of these six cities of refuge (11) was to ensure that the Israelite people had time to question witnesses, gather evidence and consider all the issues involved concerning the death of a man or woman, and to prevent the wrongful accusation of anyone within the life of the community.

3. The element of corporate responsibility. The accused person must stand *trial before the assembly* (12). The case must be brought before a properly constituted gathering of unbiased people, possibly from outside the immediate locality where the offence took place. In debatable cases *the assembly must judge* between the person accused and *the avenger of blood* (24).

4. The equality of humankind (15). If a foreigner, displaced

---

[17] Gen. 2:7; Job 1:21.   [18] Wenham (1981), p. 238.

person, slave or refugee became implicated in a case involving the loss of life, that person could be assured of a just hearing; the same law applied to everyone, whether Israelite, alien or anybody else.

5. The place of substitutionary atonement (25). The tragic extinction of human life could be expiated only by the death of a substitute, not by the offer of mere money.

6. The importance of reliable evidence (30). Nobody considered guilty of murder could lose his life simply because a community member brought an accusation against him. A vindictive person might even set someone up, killing a third party so that the murder might be pinned on his enemy, leading to the death of an innocent person – merely on the flimsy evidence of one man.

7. The reality of God's judgment. *Atonement cannot be made for the land on which blood has been shed, except by the blood of the one who shed it* (33). The divine judge had passed sentence, and would not be placated by the payment of ransom money.

8. The presence of divine holiness (34). All transgression is sin against the God who dwells in the land. David cried out in his guilt: 'Against you, you only, have I sinned and done what is evil in your sight.'[19]

Before leaving this section, we need to reflect on its relevance in our very different historical, cultural and social context. It raises the controversial question of capital punishment, an issue on which many thoughtful Christians disagree. With the authority of this Scripture and parallel verses, many believers hold that, based on the principle of retributive justice,[20] the death penalty still stands. Other Christians are equally convinced that, although this law was God's word for his people, it was not his last word on the subject. The Mosaic law also ordered the execution of Sabbath-breakers, adulterers, idolaters and blasphemers. Are they also to be executed today? On this issue, some Christians will argue that this Old Testament law ought to be retained. Others will claim that it has been superseded by wider biblical teaching concerning divine mercy, the teaching of Jesus, the ministry of the Holy Spirit (helping us to compare any passage of Scripture with others), the exercise of human conscience, and the danger of serious miscarriage of justice whereby an innocent person may be robbed of life and later shown by new evidence to have been innocent.

Although Christians may disagree on the subject, we are united in our concern regarding other forms of 'murder' within modern society, such as abortion, suicide and euthanasia.

It is said that, as far as the preservation of human life is con-

---

[19] Ps. 51:4.   [20] Exod. 21:12–14; Deut. 19:11–13.

cerned, the pregnant woman's womb is the most dangerous place in the modern world. In 1998, there were an estimated 44,000 conceptions to women under eighteen in England and Wales, a 2% increase from 43,000 the previous year. Just over 40% of these conceptions led to a legal abortion.[21]

Suicide is self-murder. God alone creates life, and must be the only one to take it. Any distressed person who feels he or she has little reason to live deserves maximum support, and loving counsel should include a sensitive warning that God's Word firmly prohibits self-murder. The Giver of life has promised to sustain us, however difficult our days. He lives with us (34), and will see that, in the darkest circumstances, we receive life's necessary resources. To terminate life wilfully is to wound the God who created it.

Campaigners for voluntary euthanasia are doing everything possible in the contemporary scene to promote the freedom of individuals to take their own lives, and they facilitate that act by providing information on the best means of doing so. Those who vigorously promote voluntary euthanasia argue that to oppose it is to rob the individual of a basic human right. But God's rights are at stake here, not human rights. Human life is not ours to take. Breath is his gift to us, and he is the only one with the authority and right to bring human life to an end.

Tribal provision (36:1–13)

Following the successful appeal made by Zelophehad's daughters (27:1–11), a specific query had arisen concerning the ownership of land on the marriage of such daughters.

The matter arose among the tribe of Manasseh, half of which would eventually return to the fertile area east of the Jordan (32:33). The future ownership of land[22] was not, therefore, a theoretical issue about unknown territory yet to be possessed on the other side of the Jordan. It concerned highly valuable land where they were now camping, land the tribe did not want to lose just because a woman from one of those tribes married a man from another tribe. For on her marriage, land ownership would pass to her husband, thus reducing the tribal possession. If, in similar circumstances, other daughters did the same, it could seriously harm tribal unity and deplete their resources, 'placing islands of non-Manassite holdings in the midst of their tribals lands, as well as reducing the amount of land in the Manassite inheritance (3)'.[23]

---

[21] 'Conceptions in England and Wales, 1998', *Population Trends*, Spring 2000 (London: The Stationery Office), pp. 86–104, Table B.
[22] Josh. 17:3–6; 22:1–9. [23] Ashley, p. 659.

The land provisions of the Jubilee year (4) would not help in such a situation. In that fiftieth year, land that had been bought had to be returned to its original owner or his descendant. This compassionate measure protected families deprived of land through financial hardship due to serious illness and inability to work, or the death of the main breadwinner. Jubilee emphasized that all land belonged to the Lord[24] and he wished it to revert to the family originally entrusted with it, so that they were not permanently dispossessed. The Jubilee law was of no help in the issue raised by these leaders, however, because it referred only to purchased, not inherited, land. These leaders sought the Lord's mind through Moses and his colleagues.

The Lord commanded that daughters who had inherited land must marry within their own tribe: *No inheritance may pass from tribe to tribe* (9). This continuation of the story of Zelophehad's daughters may at first appear mundane as a literary conclusion to the book, but it illustrates some of its most prominent themes.

The unity of the people

From the beginning of the journey, everything possible was done to eliminate tribal rivalry. Since their beginnings in Jacob's family, each tribe had different characteristics, qualities, resources and areas of vulnerability. These were highlighted in Jacob's patriarchal blessing of his children[25] as he spoke about what would happen to his sons 'in days to come'. The theme is further developed in Moses' blessing of these distinctive tribes before he took leave of them.[26]

When this vast company of people was on the move, there were occasions when their unity might have been threatened. Such times of friction and discord are carefully recorded in this honest account of Israel's disappointing journey (13:30–33; 14:1–10; 16:1–50; 21:4–9) as warnings from one generation to the next.

One interesting feature about the new generation is that they were not quarrelsome, as the old generation certainly was. Zelophehad's daughters did not lead a rebellion regarding land rights; they came for help to the Tent of Meeting (27:2), and did so in the presence of the united community. When the Reubenites and Gadites wanted to settle down on the east of the Jordan, they approached Moses rather than stage a revolt (32:1–5). When the leaders of Manasseh were troubled about the potential loss of tribal territory, they shared their problem with their leader so that he could discover the divine will.

[24] Lev. 25:23.   [25] Gen. 49:1–28.   [26] Deut. 33:6–25.

During past decades, Christians of many denominations have engaged in considerable debate and practical experiment to promote church unity. One rejoices whenever the Lord's people come closer to each other, and undertake activities together that enrich their fellowship and demonstrate to the unbelieving world their oneness in the things that matter most. However, true biblical unity cannot be achieved merely by ecumenical dialogue. Unity is God's gift to his people whenever, like these desert pilgrims, they acknowledge the primary authority of God's Word.

The care of the family

Land ownership was a major family concern: *The family heads of the clan of Gilead ... came and spoke before ... the heads of the Israelite families* (1).

The family was Israel's key social unit, ordained by God. Genesis begins with the story of history's first family and its tragic jealousy.[27] It continues with the story of other families, their potential,[28] problems[29] and preservation,[30] and traces the development of and disruption to the life of patriarchal families in the story of Abraham, Isaac, Jacob and Joseph.

The family is a privileged and vulnerable social unit. Early legislation in Numbers deals with the distressing theme of unfaithfulness in marriage, and the jealousy of a suspicious husband accusing an innocent wife of infidelity (5:11–31). In later narrative, even Moses' family is not free from disharmony and rivalry. His elder brother and sister were offended by his marital relationship, and it was only as the criticized leader pleaded with God that the situation was healed (12:1–16). Moses' wider family circle was also disrupted by envy and bitterness. Korah was Moses' cousin (16:1; 3:19) and, once again, it was the intercession of a family member that brought healing as Aaron 'made atonement' for the plague-ridden community (16:1–50).

The book emphasizes that even such an admirable concern as care for the family can become inordinate. The Israelite travellers refused to enter Canaan because they put anxiety for their families before the will of God (14:3). The children they were eager to protect entered the land (14:31), while their disobedient parents were buried in the desert. Even the best things in life can become idols if they come between us and the Lord's will. Jesus warned his disciples that faithfulness to him would sometimes provoke tensions, even persecution, within a family.[31]

[27] Gen. 4:1–16.   [28] Gen. 4:17–22, 26; 5:24.   [29] Gen. 4:23–24; 6:1–7; 9:18–29.
[30] Gen. 6:8 – 9:17.   [31] Matt. 10:21, 34–39.

The stewardship of the land

It was not possessiveness or greed that caused the Manassite family heads to approach Moses about the ownership of tribal land once a daughter married. Their particular territory had been allocated by the Lord, and, as responsible stewards, they must preserve the gift God had entrusted to them. They would not be personally deprived if a non-Manassite husband came to live next door. It was a commendable concern for the whole tribal family that led them to express their misgivings to Moses.

Stewardship is a central biblical theme. It is particularly significant in Numbers, the opening chapters of which deal with the stewardship of service (the priests and Levites, 3:1 – 4:49; 8:5–26; 18:1–7), of time (offering a specific period to God as a Nazirite, 6:1–21), of possessions, as the whole congregation exercised when they brought gifts for the worship of God and support of his servants (7:1–88; 15:1–21; 18:8–32), and of our bodies, keeping them pure (symbolized in 5:1–4; 19:1–22) and not contaminated by degrading practices, as in the corruption of Baal-Peor (25:1–15).

As believers, we belong to God and our bodies are to be used to his glory. Moreover, as Creator he has also appointed us as stewards in his world. The 'land' has been entrusted to our care. Global warming is but one issue of major concern in the contemporary ecology debate. Over a thousand scientists on the Intergovernmental Panel on Climate Change predict that the average surface temperature is set to rise by between 1 and 3.5°C by the end of this century. Rainfall will diminish in many parts of our global village, including some that provide huge quantities of cereal crops for other parts of the world. The warming of the oceans will affect sea levels, with serious flooding in low-lying areas such as the Ganges delta in Bangladesh, Egypt's Nile delta and many small islands in the Pacific and Indian Oceans. The stewardship of the earth's resources ought to be of special concern to God's people, so that we not only seek governmental measures to control the consumption of fossil fuels but do everything possible to reduce our own use of energy. The created world is not our personal property to use as we desire or to plunder for our own satisfaction, all at the expense of the next generation.

The dependence of the leader

These leaders knew that if they approached Moses regarding their concerns, he would seek to discern the Lord's mind about the issues they raised. Although Numbers deals with many practical issues in the life of God's travelling people, it is a testimony not simply to the necessity of good organization but to the primacy of dependent prayer (7:89; 10:35; 11:10–11, 21–23; 12:13; 14:13–19; 16:15, 22; 20:6; 21:7; 27:5, 15–17).

In their better moments, the Israelite people encouraged Moses to enter God's presence to receive his word, and promised that, hearing it, they would obey[32] – which brings us to our final point.

The obedience of the reader

The book's closing sentence directs the reader's attention to one of its central themes: obedience to God's word. These Manassite leaders recognized that, in the earlier order regarding the distribution of tribal land, Moses spoke exactly as he had been *commanded* (2a). He had shared the Lord's word about the land rights of Zelophehad's daughters, having been *ordered* to do so (2b). That word *command* recurs throughout this closing chapter (2, 5, 6, 13), and its final sentence not only addresses the subject of tribal-land regulations but reflects on the teaching of the entire book: *These are the commands and regulations the LORD gave through Moses to the Israelites* (13). As the old leader shared these particular words with the new generation, they were camping *on the plains of Moab by the Jordan across from Jericho*. That concluding phrase, repeated throughout these closing chapters (22:1; 26:3, 63; 33:48, 50; 35:1, 36:13), conveys far more than a geographical location. It is a daring and reliant testimony.

The *plains of Moab* had been effectively conquered. The ground beneath their feet was already theirs through the power of a God who works miracles. But two problems remained for an invading army: a deep river[33] and an impregnable city. *Jordan* and *Jericho* were formidable obstacles to occupation. How could anybody possibly convey this huge contingent of nomadic people across that fast-flowing river, and how could an untrained army capture a well-fortified (13:28) city like Jericho?[34] The secret was in total obedience. Neither barrier was to be overcome by intellectual skills, geographical proficiency, crowd manipulation, army intelligence or military strategy. Two doctrinal factors prompted their obedience: God's presence and God's power.

God's presence was a guaranteed reality. After camping by that obstructive river for three days, the community's officers announced the Lord's instructions. Bearing the ark, the priests were to enter the river, ahead of the people: 'This is how you will know

---

[32] Exod. 19:7–8.   [33] Josh. 3:15.   [34] Josh. 2:1; 6:1.

that the living God is among you.' Even though at that season 'the Jordan is in flood all during harvest', its waters 'stopped flowing' and 'piled up in a heap', just as the terrifying waters of the Red Sea had done for the old generation.[35]

God's power too was an undeniable certainty. Outside Jericho, the new generation's leader would meet 'the commander of the army of the LORD', symbolically prepared for battle 'with a drawn sword in his hand'. Falling 'face down to the ground in reverence', Joshua addressed the invincible conqueror with words that should be on our lips whenever we open God's Word: 'What message does my Lord have for his servant?'[36]

With Jericho's impregnable walls in the background, the courageous soldier was commanded to remove his shoes: 'Take off your sandals, for the place where you are standing is holy.'[37] The precise words recall exactly what was said to the old generation's leader over forty years earlier as he stood before a flaming bush in the desert of Midian.[38] Here was a visible reminder to Joshua of the truth of God's reliable word: 'As I was with Moses, so I will be with you.'[39] A barefoot soldier would be highly vulnerable, but, if the divine commander's first battle order was for the leader to remove his sandals, then that must be done. 'And Joshua did so.'[40]

The simple command to acknowledge God's holiness, recall God's power and obey God's word was the essential prelude to divine instructions about the capture of Jericho.[41] Such orders would strain any soldier's obedience to the limit. They sounded more like suggestions for an ecclesiastical procession than a strategy for a military encounter. But Joshua 'did so', and the city was taken.

With the aid of this brief geographical detail, *Moab ... Jordan ... Jericho*, the conclusion of Numbers offers fresh hope and renewed confidence, a new land and a better future. In God's time, we too may cross a river and, by grace alone, enter a city.[42]

---

[35] Josh. 3:7, 10, 15–16.   [36] Josh. 5:13–15.   [37] Josh. 5:15.   [38] Exod. 3:5.
[39] Josh. 1:5.   [40] Josh. 5:15.   [41] Josh. 6:2–5.
[42] Heb. 13:14; Rev. 21:2, 10; 22:1–3.

Other titles in The Bible Speaks Today series

New Testament

The Message of the Sermon on the Mount (Matthew 5 – 7)
Christian counter-culture
John Stott

The Message of Matthew
The kingdom of heaven
Michael Green

The Message of Mark
The mystery of faith
Donald English

The Message of Luke
The Saviour of the world
Michael Wilcock

The Message of John
Here is your King!
Bruce Milne

The Message of Acts
To the ends of the earth
John Stott

The Message of Romans
God's good news for the world
John Stott

The Message of 1 Corinthians
Life in the local church
David Prior

The Message of 2 Corinthians
Power in weakness
Paul Barnett

The Message of Galatians
Only one way
John Stott

The Message of Ephesians
God's new society
John Stott

The Message of Philippians
Jesus our Joy
Alec Motyer

The Message of Colossians and Philemon
Fullness and freedom
Dick Lucas

The Message of Thessalonians
Preparing for the coming King
John Stott

The Message of 1 Timothy and Titus
The life of the local church
John Stott

The Message of 2 Timothy
Guard the gospel
John Stott

The Message of Hebrews
Christ above all
Raymond Brown

The Message of James
The tests of faith
Alec Motyer

The Message of 1 Peter
The way of the cross
Edmund Clowney

The Message of 2 Peter and Jude
The promise of his coming
Dick Lucas and Christopher Green

The Message of John's Letters
Living in the love of God
David Jackman

The Message of Revelation
I saw heaven opened
Michael Wilcock

Bible Themes

The Message of the Living God
His glory, his people, his world
Peter Lewis

The Message of the Resurrection
Christ is risen!
Paul Beasley-Murray

The Message of the Cross
Wisdom unsearchable, love indestructible
Derek Tidball

The Message of Salvation
By God's grace, for God's glory
Philip Graham Ryken